African American Lives

The Struggle for Freedom

Volume II

Clayborne Carson
Stanford University

Emma J. Lapsansky-Werner
Haverford College

Gary B. Nash
University of California, Los Angeles

New York San Francisco Boston
London Toronto Sydney Tokyo Singapore Madrid
Mexico City Munich Paris Cape Town Hong Kong Montreal

Publisher: Priscilla McGeehon
Senior Development Editor: Dawn Groundwater
Executive Marketing Manager: Sue Westmoreland
Media and Supplements Editor: Kristi Olson
Production Manager: Charles Annis
Project Coordination, Text Design, and Electronic Page Makeup: Electronic Publishing Services Inc., NYC
Cover Design Manager: Wendy Ann Fredericks
Cover Designer: Kay Petronio
Cover Photos: *top left:* returning African American soldier reunites with family in postwar Seattle. Louise Carson collection; *bottom left:* Selma March, Alabama, 1965, © Bruce Davidson/Magnum Photos; *right:* John W. Moseley, Majorette at National Elks Convention, 1945, the Charles L. Blockson Afro-American Collection, Temple University
Photo Researcher: Photosearch, Inc.
Manufacturing Buyer: Roy Pickering
Printer and Binder: Quebecor World Taunton
Cover Printer: Phoenix Color Corp.

For permission to use copyrighted material, grateful acknowledgment is made to the copyright holders throughout this book, which is hereby made part of this copyright page.

Library of Congress Cataloging-in-Publication Data
Carson, Clayborne, 1944–
African American lives : the struggle for freedom / Clayborne Carson, Emma Lapsanksy-Werner, Gary Nash.
p. cm.
Includes bibliographical references and index.
ISBN 0-321-02586-5 (hardcover)—ISBN 0-201-79487-X (pbk. : v. 1)—ISBN 0-201-79489-6 (pbk. : v. 2)
1. African Americans—History. I. Lapsanksy-Werner, Emma. II. Nash, Gary B. III. Title.
E185.C356 2005
973'.0496073—dc22

200411882

Please visit our website at http://www.ablongman.com.

ISBN 0-321-02586-5 (Single Volume Edition)

ISBN 0-201-79487-X (Volume I)

ISBN 0-201-79489-6 (Volume II)

1 2 3 4 5 6 7 8 9 10—QWT—07 06 05 04

Brief Contents

Detailed Contents

CHAPTER 13

"Colored" Becomes "Negro" in the Progressive Era 320

CHAPTER 14

The Making of a "New Negro": World War I to the Great Depression 346

CHAPTER 15

The New Politics of the Great Depression 374

First Person Documents

Preface

> Those who profess to favor freedom and yet depreciate agitation, are people who want crops without ploughing the ground; they want rain without thunder and lightning; they want the ocean without the roar of its many waters. The struggle may be a moral one, or it may be a physical one, or it may be both. But it must be a struggle. Power concedes nothing without a demand; it never has and it never will.
>
> —*Frederick Douglass*

African American Lives: The Struggle for Freedom is designed to help students in the survey course gain an understanding of that struggle. It introduces the concepts, milestones, and significant figures of African American history. Inasmuch as that history is grounded in struggle—in the consistent and insistent call to the United States to make good on constitutional promises made to all its citizens—this book is also an American history text. Hence, the milestones of mainstream American history, economy, politics, arts and letters are interwoven in its pages.

But *African American Lives: The Struggle for Freedom* seeks to do something more. It engages the reader in viewing history through the lens of many biographies and through the perspectives of people who lived those struggles to ensure, in the words of Langston Hughes' famous poem, that "America Will Be." This unique biographical approach to African American history positions African American lives at the center of the narrative and as the basis of analysis.

BIOGRAPHICAL APPROACH

African American Lives:The Struggle for Freedom tells the stories of the lives of both the illustrious (abolitionist Martin Delany) and the ordinary (planter Isaiah Montgomery), the public and the private perspectives of those who shaped the African American story. Some individuals are famous for their specific contributions; other individuals are representative of a larger idea, a concept of a people who have inhabited the American continent for more than half a millennium.

Throughout the book we examine the struggles of African Americans to define their own identities, the development of nationalist ideas and rhetoric, Americans' struggle with the concept of race, and the growth of the politics of race from the Republican Party to the Rainbow Coalition. Wherever possible, we enliven and give authenticity to the story through the words of contemporary participants. With all that, we keep the story concise, fast-paced, and compelling.

Within these pages, we try to capture the essence of the African American experience. The book presents African American voices; it sees history through African American eyes. The events and the themes around which these lives were organized are defined so as to impose order on the often disorderly past and to interpret that past as modern historical research has revealed it. The biographical approach both guides the story and animates the history. In each chapter, individual African Americans are the pivot points that provide a window on the historical changes of their generation. Life stories capture the rush of events that envelop individuals and illuminate the momentous decisions that, collectively, frame the American past and present.

While humanizing history, the biographical approach has another important advantage: It is an antidote to the poisonous notion of historical inevitability. Too often, expressions such as *the sweep of history, the transit of civilization, manifest destiny,* and *the march of progress* plant the idea that history is inexorable, unalterable, and foreordained—beyond the capacity of men and women to change. That idea has been used to justify a winner's history—an approach that diminishes the full humanness of those who were captured and traded as slaves. Books with a winner's history approach also work to absolve those who traded in slaves and profited from their labor. To promote the understanding that no individual is forever trapped within iron circumstances beyond his or her ability to alter, we ground every chapter in the experience of *people* rather than *forces*.

The interwoven human stories in this textbook demonstrate that in every age, in every part of the country, at every level of society, African Americans refused to allow history to crush them. Instead, they were shakers and shapers of their own world insofar as this was possible. Whether in the small space of plantation quarters or Harlem walkups, or criss-crossing a nation, or calling for the unity of Africans dispossessed and dispersed around the globe, African Americans have shaped their world even as they contested and transformed their subordinate roles in American society. That often they did not succeed in their plans or could not fully realize their hopes does not diminish their strivings. It does not alter the fact that for many, nothing was passively accepted; everything was contested or negotiated. The struggle for dignity and respect is part of the human condition. It has been no different for a dispossessed African American minority determined to transcend the contempt of their fellow Americans.

Just as African American lives are inarguably part of the long process by which Americans have strived to achieve the promise of the national motto *E pluribus unum*—from the many, one—so too *African American Lives:The Struggle for Freedom* is not a story set in stone. It is the product of our constantly changing understandings of the past, new insights about historical possibilities, and new historical research. In that ongoing effort, African American history has achieved breadth and depth in recent decades, indeed has become one of the most vibrant components of American history, reshaping the way we understand everything from the American economy to innovations in science, politics, and the arts. Drawing on the last half-century of recast historical narrative, *African American Lives: The Struggle for Freedom* crafts a new synthesis that not only enriches our understanding of the black experience in America but alters our conception of American history in the whole.

COVERAGE AND ORGANIZATION

In *African American Lives: The Struggle for Freedom,* the distinctive people and events of American history are all here: the Europeans' first encounter with new people and a new environment, the American Revolution and its shaping of humanitarian ideals, the War of 1812, the Missouri Compromise, sectional conflicts, wars from the Civil War through this century's war against terrorism, cultural trends from the resistance poetry of revolutionary-era Phillis Wheatley through modern-day hip hop.

African American Lives: The Struggle for Freedom comprises twenty-one chapters. Chapters 1–7 explore the period up to 1830, when most Africans in North America were enslaved. The book begins, as all human history begins, in Africa with ancient history and the rise of empires in West and Central Africa during the period American and western historians think of as the Middle Ages. European contact and the growth of the slave trade are followed by an analysis of the new conditions of slavery in the Americas. To understand how Africans were not all enslaved in the same ways and in the same conditions, the chapters treat the formation of notions about race and how they figured in the descent into slavery in different zones of European settlement—French, Dutch, and Spanish as well as English—in the Americas. The galvanizing effect of the American Revolution and the decades thereafter during which free black people in the North and in the South built families, founded churches, forged friendships and communities, and struggled for autonomy and dignity are central themes.

Chapters 8–14 examine pivotal junctures in African American history that parallel the American focus on reform and nationality. The 1830s marked the first years when the majority of black Americans were not forced immigrants but rather born on American soil. Echoing the religious reawakening that undergirded both abolitionism and a vigorous defense of slavery, slave and free African Americans alike claimed their voice in an international antebellum debate about the future of American democracy. Then, through a long and merciless Civil War, the end of slavery, and the South's attempt to recreate the essence of slavery, black Americans persisted in holding forth, before white Americans and the world, the guarantees of equality and citizenship built into the new constitutional amendments. The post–Civil War dispersal of newly freed African Americans to every corner of North America shows how, in the face of a still-hostile white America that abandoned Reconstruction, black people built families, communities, and viable economic lives; established churches, mutual aid and literary societies, and businesses; and launched schools and publishing ventures as they sought to transform themselves from slaves to soldiers and citizens and to wrest equality and justice from white America.

Chapters 15–21 address African American life in modern America. We devote attention to the increasing diversity of African Americans and how—during world wars, the Great Depression, and other momentous national and international transformations—they struggled for full participation in a society still marred by racist attitudes and practices. Throughout twentieth-century scientific, technological, and economic changes, one theme permeates African American strategies for securing justice and equal opportunity: the ongoing struggle for a positive sense of identity amidst racism and destructive racial stereotypes. Whether in fighting the nation's wars; helping build the modern economy; adding to the explosion of cultural creativity through innovations in music, art, film, dance, and literature; or emerging on the political stage at the local, state, and national level, African Americans in the last century are portrayed as the principal innovators of the nation's most important liberation movement.

SPECIAL FEATURES AND PEDAGOGY

Complementing the multitude of stories connecting African American lives and American history, this book has several features we consider essential elements of a braided analytic narrative.

- *First Persons:* Each chapter contains several primary documents called "First Person" that bring authentic firsthand accounts from the past to the page. These written and spoken words help us comprehend, as no modern paraphraser can do, how African Americans such as Olaudah Equiano, Mary Ann Shadd Cary, and Pauli Murray understood their world and sought to transform it. A headnote puts each primary document in context. Many documents end with a reference to the book's companion website (www.ablongman.com/carson/documents), encouraging students to view a longer version of the document online.
- *Timelines:* Timelines help students fix the most significant developments in African American history as they are framed in the larger, more familiar American story. These are positioned at the beginning of each chapter directly following an opening vignette.
- *Chapter-opening Vignettes:* Focusing on personal stories such as the rebelliousness of Venture Smith or the wartime experience of First Lieutenant Thomas Edward Jones, these vignettes draw students into the chapter period and herald the chapter's events and themes.
- *Conclusions:* A summary of the main ideas and events of each chapter, and a look ahead to the next, can be found in the Conclusion.
- *Further Reading:* At the end of each chapter are suggestions for further reading. Here we provide a sampling, rather than an exhaustive list, of fresh histories as well as classics, engaging autobiographies and historical novels students can explore for primary sources, visual material, historical essays, and personal interpretations.
- *Visual History:* Each chapter includes a complement of graphic materials and illustrations—maps, charts, photographs, lithographs, and paintings—that provide a visual window on the past. These visual materials are intended to unfold an additional dimension of the narrative, reinforcing the student's sense of seeing history as participants saw it. To sharpen complex or subtle concepts, tables efficiently convey a sequence of events or milestones—for example, judicial decisions, legislative acts, and protest movement flashpoints.

SUPPLEMENTS

For Qualified College Adopters

Instructor's Manual

ISBN 0-321-10852-3

Written by Jane Dabel, California State University–Long Beach, and Ann Grogg. This resource contains learning objectives, significant themes, chapter outlines, enrichment ideas, and further resources for each chapter.

Test Bank

ISBN 0-321-10854-X

Written by Beverly Bunch-Lyons of Virginia Polytechnic Institute and State University. The test bank contains multiple-choice, true/false, and essay questions for each chapter. Multiple-choice and true/false questions are referenced by topic and text page number.

TestGen-EQ Computerized Testing System

ISBN 0-321-10733-0

This flexible, easy-to-master computerized test bank on a dual-platform CD includes all the test items in the printed test bank. The software allows instructors to select specific questions, edit existing questions, and add their own items to create exams. Tests can be printed in several fonts and formats and can include figures, such as graphs and tables.

Supplements Central

http://ablongman.com/suppscentral

A helpful website where instructors can download supplements for this text including the *Instructor's Manual, Test Bank,* and the *TestGen-EQ.* Instructors will need to request a password from their sales representative to gain access.

For Students

Sources of the African-American Past, Second Edition

ISBN 0-673-99202-0

Edited by Roy Finkenbine of the University of Detroit at Mercy, this collection of primary sources covers themes in the African American experience from the West African background to the present. Balanced between political and social history, the documents offer a vivid snapshot of the lives of African Americans in different historical periods. The collection includes documents representing women and different regions of the United States. Just $2.00 when bundled with *African American Lives: The Struggle for Freedom*.

Companion Website

www.ablongman.com/carson

Students will find summaries, practice test questions, and flashcards for every chapter at this site. Longer versions of the First Person documents are also available for reference and further study.

Student Resources CD-ROM

Available free to qualified college adopters if requested when bundled with the book, this CD-ROM contains dozens of documents, images, maps, and video clips from African American history.

Research Navigator Guide

ISBN 0-205-40838-9

This guidebook includes exercises and tips on how to use the Internet. It also includes an access code for Research Navigator™—the easiest way for students to start a research assignment or research paper. Research Navigator™ is composed of three exclusive databases of credible and reliable source material, including EBSCO's ContentSelect™ Academic Journal Database, New York Times Search by Subject Archive, and "Best of the Web" Link Library. This comprehensive site also includes a detailed help section.

Penguin Books

The partnership between Penguin-Putnam USA and Longman Publishers offers your students a discount on many titles when bundled with any Longman survey text. Available titles include *Narrative of the Life of Frederick Douglass* by Frederick Douglass; *Why We Can't Wait* by Martin Luther King Jr.; *Beloved* by Toni Morrison; and *Uncle Tom's Cabin* by Harriet Beecher Stowe.

ACKNOWLEDGMENTS

We gratefully acknowledge the many colleagues who took the time to review our manuscript. Their useful comments and keen insights have made this a stronger book. Thank you:

Leslie Alexander, *Ohio State University*
Kwame Alford, *Texas Tech University*
Julius A. Amin, *University of Dayton*
Melissa Anyiwo, *University of Tennessee at Chattanooga*
Joseph Appiah, *J. S. Reynolds Community College*
Felix L. Armfield, *State University of New York, Buffalo*
Charles Pete Banner-Haley, *Colgate University*
Abel A. Bartley, *University of Akron*
Donald Scott Barton, *East Central University*
James M. Beeby, *West Virginia Wesleyan College*
Diane L. Beers, *Holyoke Community College*
Nemata Blyden, *George Washington University*
Robert Bonner, *Amherst College*
Ronald E. Brown, *Westchester Community College*
Kimn Carlton-Smith, *Ferris State University, Long Beach*
Stephanie Cole, *University of Texas, Arlington*
Jane E. Dabel, *California State University, Long Beach*
Bruce J. Dierenfield, *Canisius College*
A. G. Dunston, *Eastern Kentucky University*
Patience Essah, *Auburn University*
Melvin Lee Felton Jr., *James Sprunt Community College*
Paul S. George, *Miami-Dade College*
Brian Gordon, *St. Louis Community College*
Lenworth Gunther, *Essex County College*
Laura Graves, *South Plains College*
Olivia B. Green, *Miles College*
Kevin Joseph Hales, *Parkland College*
Carmen V. Harris, *University of South Carolina at Spartanburg*
James Harrison, *Portland Community College, Cascade*
Sharon A. Roger Hepburn, *Radford University*
Ranford B. Hopkins, *Moorpark College*
Carol Sue Humphrey, *Oklahoma Baptist University*
Creed Hyatt, *Lehigh Carbon Community College*
Eric R. Jackson, *Northern Kentucky University*
W. Sherman Jackson, *Miami-Ohio University*
Randal M. Jelks, *Calvin College*
Cherisse R. Jones, *Arkansas State University*
Theodore Kallman, *San Joaquin Delta College*
Maghan Keita, *Villanova University*
Ben Keppel, *University of Oklahoma*
Daniel Kilbride, *John Carroll University*
Lisa King, *Morgan State University*
William M. King, *University of Colorado*
Alec Kirby, *University of Wisconsin at Stout*

Anne Klejment, *University of St. Thomas*
Alan Lamm, *Mount Olive College*
Linda Rochell Lane, *Benedict College*
Howard Lindsey, *DePaul University*
Arletha D. Livingston, *Georgia State University*
Elizabeth MacGonagle, *University of Kansas*
Kenneth Mason, *Santa Monica College*
David McBride, *Pennsylvania State University*
Larry McGruder, *Abraham Baldwin College*
Karen K. Miller, *Boston College*
Jacqueline M. Moore, *Austin College*
Sheila H. Moore, *Hinds Community College*
Earl F. Mulderink, *Southern Utah University*
Cassandra Newby-Alexander, *Norfolk State University*
Julius F. Nimmons Jr., *University of the District of Columbia*
Phillip Oguagha, *Medgar Evers College, City University of New York*
Anthony Parent, *Wake Forest University*
John B. Reid, *Truckee Meadows Community College*
Tara Ross, *Onondaga Community College*
Jerrold W. Roy, *Hampton University*
Paul Siff, *Sacred Heart University*
Bradley Skelcher, *Delaware State University*
Dorothy A. Smith-Akubue, *Lynchburg College*
Melissa Soto-Schwartz, *Cuyahoga Community College*
Darlene Spitzer-Antezana, *Bowie State University*
Donald Spivey, *University of Miami*
Marian Strobel, *Furman University*
Michael David Tegeder, *Santa Fe Community College*
Linda D. Tomlinson, *Clark Atlanta University*
William L. Van Deburg, *University of Wisconsin*
Cheryl R. Vinson, *Miles College*
Melissa Walker, *Converse College*
Irma Watkins-Owen, *Fordham University*
Vernon J. Williams Jr., *Purdue University*
Leslie Wilson, *Montclair State University*
Keith A. Winsell, *Talladega College*
Marilyn Leonard Yancy, *Virginia Union University*

The authors would like to thank the staff of Special Collections at Haverford College and the Crisis Publishing Co., Inc., the publisher of the magazine of the National Association for the Advancement of Colored People, for the use of material published in the November 1935 and June 1938 issues of *Crisis*. The project also owes a monumental debt of gratitude to Ann Grogg. Ann was by turns editor, counselor, circuit rider, diplomat, and loyal friend. Her broad and subtle knowledge of history and of those who teach and learn it were crucial to our progress. So too was her deft editing without altering the authors' voices or meaning. We are grateful to our Longman editor, Dawn Groundwater, for sticking with us and never losing sight of the book's vision and goals.

Clay Carson offers particular thanks to Damani Rivers and Caitrin McKiernan of the King Papers Project at Stanford University for their exceptional research assistance. Susan A. Carson also helped with editing the manuscript. Tenisha Armstrong, Miya Woolfalk, and other King Project staff members and student researchers offered useful comments on the manuscript at various stages of its development. Emma Lapsansky-Werner extends a special thank you to student research assistant James Chappel and her ever-patient husband, Dickson Werner. Gary Nash thanks research assistants Grace Lu and Marian Olivas for good cheer in carrying out many tasks.

All three authors wish to thank three history editors at Longman who supported this book and facilitated its completion: Bruce Borland, Jay O'Callaghan, and Ashley Dodge.

African American Lives

The Struggle for Freedom

CHAPTER 11

Upland Cotton, rendered in oil by genre painter Winslow Homer in 1879, captures the lingering power of the slave South's tragic story—cotton, race, back-breaking labor.

Post–Civil War Reconstruction: A New National Era

Emanuel Fortune Testifies Before Congress

"They always spoke very bitterly against it," said Florida Republican Emanuel Fortune, describing his white neighbors' reaction to the idea of black people voting. Those neighbors told Fortune, "The damned Republican party has put niggers to rule us, and we will not suffer it." Fortune was testifying before a congressional committee assigned to investigate Ku Klux Klan threats and violence against black southerners. After the Civil War, when anger in many southern white communities erupted in violence, some white southerners targeted black men like Fortune who organized voters or ran for office. "I got information that I would be missing some day and no one would know where I was, on account of my being a leading man in politics," Fortune recalled.

Emanuel Fortune's story typified the experience of black political leaders who emerged in the postwar period. Relatively young—Fortune was thirty-nine in 1871—these leaders were new to politics. Just a few years earlier, they had been outsiders—many of them slaves. Now they had a political voice. Fortune, for example, had participated in the 1868 constitutional convention that qualified Florida—which had been part of the Confederacy during the war—to reenter the Union by guaranteeing black suffrage and ratifying the Fourteenth Amendment. That amendment defined citizens as anyone born in the United States and guaranteed them the right to vote, to use the courts, to own property, and to be protected by all the citizens' rights outlined in the Constitution. The fact that a black man could run for office and get elected by a black constituency demonstrated those new rights. But the threats Fortune received also highlighted the risks run by southern black men who dared to claim seats at the political table. He described Jackson County, Florida, in 1869 as being in "such a state of lawlessness that my life was in danger at all times."

CHAPTER OUTLINE

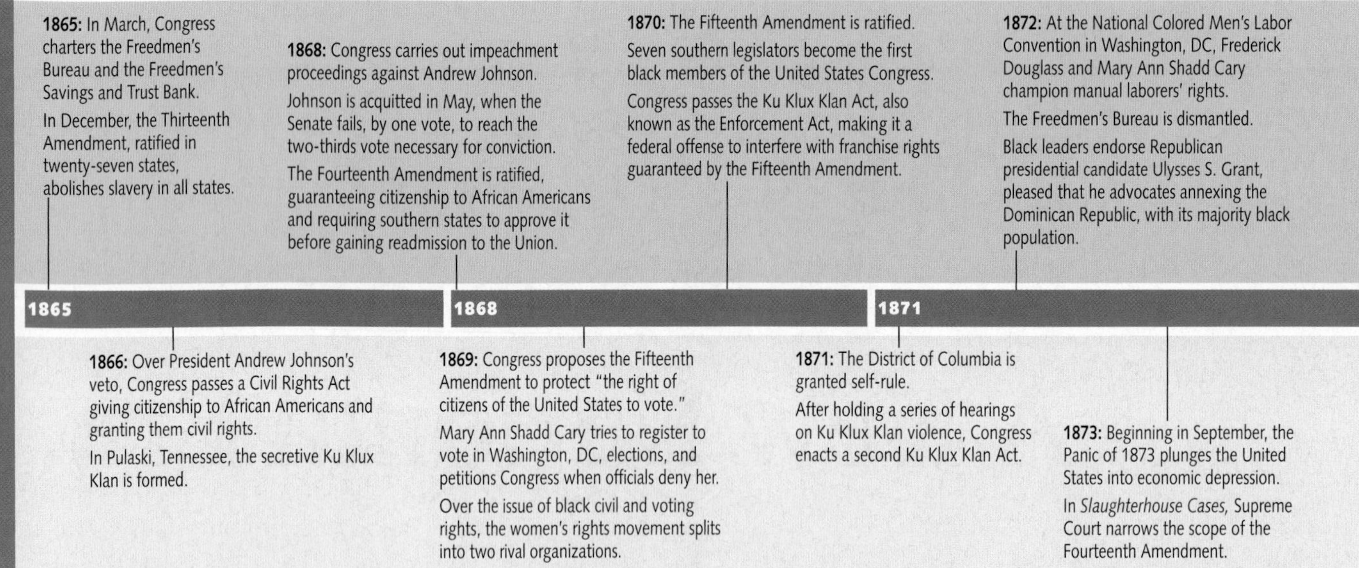

Fortune was prepared to fight back. Reputedly "a remarkably fine shot [who] practiced target shooting regularly," he was remembered by friends as a "dead shot, and he *would* shoot." He fortified his home to provide cover from an attack. Under his bedroom floor, he dug a pit from which he could open fire on intruders. Though violent threats prompted Fortune to move his family from isolated rural Jackson County to the relative safety of a black neighborhood in the city of Jacksonville, Florida, in 1870, he never relinquished his political commitment. Over the next ten years, he served as city marshal, Republican national convention delegate, county commissioner, clerk of the city market, and state congressman.

Fortune's testimony before Congress reveals the realities of the postwar South. White southerners complained bitterly about what they called "black rule" as African Americans took positions as sheriffs, justices of the peace, county clerks, and school superintendents. Yet throughout the South, only a few dozen black Americans occupied positions of real authority. Relatively few black candidates ran for office, and many black voters, intimidated by threats or actual violence in the open southern polls, where each person's vote was public knowledge, supported white politicians. Those African Americans who did run for office encountered white resentment and often threats.

With the South's return to the Union after the Civil War, race relations in that embattled region took political center stage. For the first dozen years after the Confederacy's surrender—a period that became known as Reconstruction—the federal government sent troops and agents to help restore order to the battered South and aid slaves' transition to freedom. Federal and private agencies opened schools, distributed food and medicine, and intervened in legal disputes between freed people and their white neighbors. In what many northerners considered a new national era, the federal government aimed to heal the war-torn South and to make it more like the North, physically, economically, socially and politically. While repairing fields, roads, and homes was a top priority, many northerners hoped the South would soon have new railroads, factories, banks, and wage laborers as well.

Reconstruction also extended to the national level, as black men were elected to Congress and Republican presidents appointed African Americans to positions of authority. During this era, black leaders made access to the polls their highest priority, believing African Americans could vote into office leaders who supported their goals, such as farm ownership and jobs that would allow them to move away from livelihoods that depended on white landowners. They also wanted education for their children, as literacy would, in turn,

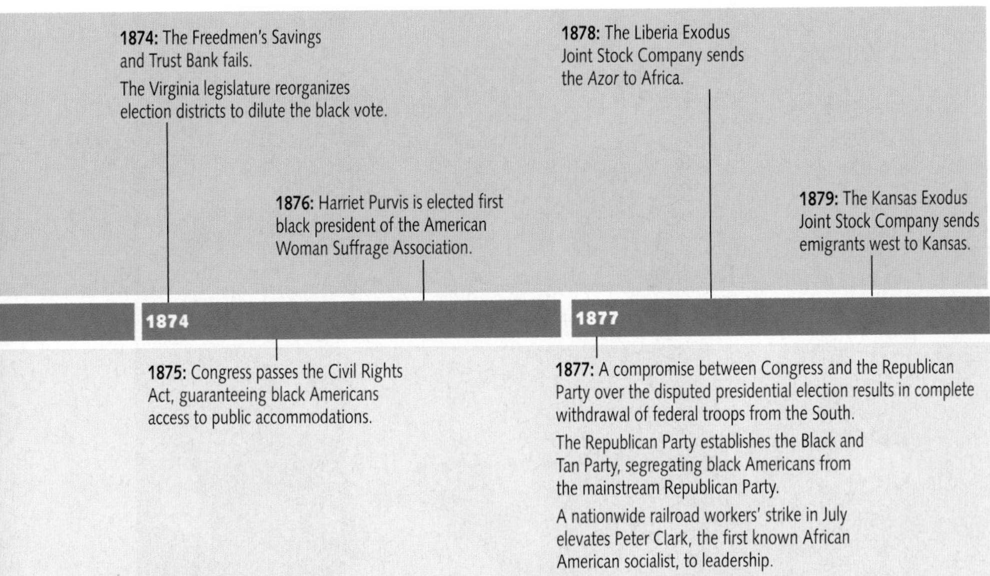

provide opportunities for entrepreneurship and political power to lift people out of poverty.

Meanwhile, most northern and southern white Americans hoped to "reconstruct" a system that tied black Americans to menial roles. A few white Americans envisioned former bondspeople becoming successful landowners or entrepreneurs, although certainly not equal members of society. Though slavery had been outlawed, persuasion, local statutes, intimidation, and widespread prejudice kept black people tied to agricultural and service jobs in both South and North.

As we saw in Chapter 10, resentful southern planters also began instituting laws—Black Codes—to keep black people subservient. These laws they backed up with violence, threats, or economic reprisals, such as dismissing black farm workers who tried to vote or encouraged others to do so. The presence of the federal Freedmen's Bureau in the South, which aimed to help former slaves become full citizens, infuriated many white southerners. Many of these planters hoped to reconstruct the old agricultural system in which wealthy white men made the laws, leaving both white and black poor people powerless.

But black Americans had sweeping ambitions: strengthening their communities economically, reassembling their families, and protecting themselves from violence and intimidation. All of these goals hinged on acquiring and protecting political rights, navigating the shifting and sometimes treacherous tides of southern and federal politics. Washington, DC—seat of the national government—symbolized the complexities of the new era. From across the nation, black Americans seeking employment and federal protection streamed into the capital city.

But federal sympathy toward freedmen and freedwomen waned after a decade of Reconstruction efforts, and federal promises went unfulfilled. Discouraged by slow progress, some black Americans again directed their hopes elsewhere—to African or western frontiers.

POSTWAR RECONSTRUCTION

On February 25, 1870, an ambitious, urbane southerner arrived in Washington, DC, with a mission: to ensure that the federal government treated black people as full citizens. That southerner was Hiram Revels—African Methodist Episcopal Church (AME) minister, former Union recruitment officer, and advocate of improving education for black people. The first black American to be elected to Congress, Revels soon discovered how fervently white congressmen resented his presence. His public service career—beginning before the Civil War and continuing until his death in 1901—reveals much about how emancipation transformed black people and about the complexities of Reconstruction.

Radical Reconstruction

Revels found Congress dominated by a coalition of northern representatives known as Radical Republicans. These politicians aimed to protect and promote the interests of black southerners and to punish white southerners for the Civil War. Simultaneously, Congress clashed with the president over how to define and protect black rights. Though the war had ended, racial tensions between the North and South continued to simmer. The Radical Republicans constituted the majority in Congress when southern seats were vacant dur-

Hiram Revels helped recruit the first black Civil War regiments in Maryland and Missouri. After his U.S. Senate service, he returned to Mississippi and became president of Alcorn, a Reconstruction-era black college. This photo of Revels with his wife and five daughters was taken in about 1870.

ing the war. By the end of 1865, many southern states had ratified the Thirteenth Amendment and rejoined the Union—just in time to elect congressmen to reclaim their prewar seats. Because black men could not yet vote, the same southern white aristocrats who had ruled in Congress before the war simply returned to their former posts.

But Radical Republicans still held the majority. Led by Pennsylvania representative Thaddeus Stevens and Massachusetts senator Charles Sumner (who returned to the Senate in 1860), they asserted the right of Congress to refuse seats to southern congressmen who had not yet sworn Union allegiance. Next they strategized on how to get southern black candidates seated in Congress in order to drive southern white men from the legislature. Through the last half of the decade, Radical Republicans pounded the South with new policies. In early 1867, Congress passed three new Reconstruction acts. The first ruling divided the South into five military districts, sending federal troops to maintain order and protect freed people. The second required the former Confederate states to hold conventions to draft constitutions that guaranteed black male suffrage. The third act stipulated that former Confederate states could send congressmen to Washington, DC, only after state legislatures had ratified the Fourteenth Amendment. This amendment, ratified in 1868, was the most important product of the Reconstruction era. It affirmed black people's citizenship, removing every trace of ambiguity left from the Supreme Court's decision in the *Dred Scott* case of 1857. It also denied former slaveowners' claims that they should receive compensation for their lost "property." Emanuel Fortune, a delegate to Florida's constitutional convention, helped his state pass these provisions. Hoping to stir northern support for punishing southerners, Congress also established a Joint Committee on Reconstruction to gather information about southern anti-black violence.

Presidential Reconstruction

Black people across the nation hoped the Fourteenth Amendment would secure them a place in their nation's economic, political, and social life. However, a milder form of Reconstruction proposed by President Lincoln and favored by his successor, Andrew Johnson, enabled the white South to resist. Hoping to heal sectional bitterness, Lincoln and some northerners favored a less punitive way for the South to reenter the Union. The South, they contended, did not possess the authority to leave the United States. Hence, southern states had always remained in the Union, and thus technically did not need to rejoin.

When Lincoln was assassinated in April 1865, the presidency fell to Vice President Andrew Johnson. A former Democratic senator from Tennessee, Johnson also favored a lenient Reconstruction policy. Reversing Congress's Confiscation Act of 1862, which had allowed the federal government to seize Confederates' property without compensating them for it, Johnson offered to pardon and to restore the property of former Confederates who took an oath of allegiance to the Constitution. He also promised to restore their confiscated land. Finally, he acknowledged North Carolina's new government, which had been reconstructed with a new constitution following the Republican guidelines that provided black men with the vote. Johnson also encouraged the other Confederate states to quickly reestablish state governments.

Thus, black rights became the focal point as Johnson battled with Congress over which branch of government would wield power in the postwar era. President Johnson vetoed Congress's Civil Rights Act of 1866, which offered limited legal rights to African Americans. He also vetoed a congressional vote to renew the Freedmen's Bureau. But Radical Republicans gathered enough votes to override Johnson's veto and pass both bills. The new president still opposed the Fourteenth Amendment because he felt it violated southern states' rights to control their citizenship. During the 1866 midterm campaign, he urged the southern states not to ratify it. His opposition only deepened the rift between the White House and Congress.

Tension between Johnson and Congress reached a climax when the president tried to remove Secretary of War Edwin Stanton, who oversaw the military occupation of the unreconstructed southern states. Johnson was incensed that Stanton encouraged military officers stationed in the South to ignore communications from the president. Seeking to undermine Johnson's authority, Congress passed the Tenure of Office Act. The ruling blocked Johnson from firing Stanton and guaranteed tenure of office to anyone appointed with the Senate's approval. Johnson responded by placing strict controls on military commanders in the South and renewing efforts to dismiss Stanton and other government officials sympathetic to congressional Reconstruction. Republicans promptly called for the president's impeachment on the grounds that he had violated several recent congressional edicts meant to prevent him from removing military or cabinet appointees without congressional approval. A three-month impeachment trial failed to remove Johnson, however, because the two-thirds majority required in the Senate fell one vote short. Once more, the contest for power between the South and branches of the federal government—ostensibly about black issues—only diverted federal attention from black people's needs.

The Fifteenth Amendment

The Fourteenth Amendment should have secured black freedom everywhere, but even as Congress enacted policies ensuring southern black men the franchise, northern black men with political ambitions had to head south to fulfill them. In a bitter irony, southern black men, so recently liberated from slavery, had more opportunities for political leadership than did black northerners. The *New York Tribune* put the matter bluntly: "They who desire the Right of Suffrage for Blacks of the South oppose the extension of the same right to Blacks of the North."

> "They who desire the Right of Suffrage for Blacks of the South oppose the extension of the same right to Blacks of the North."
> —The *New York Tribune*

This pattern of exclusion appeared in numerous northern states. In 1867, white voters in Kansas and Ohio banned African Americans from the polls by referendum. The following year, white voters in Michigan promptly rejected a new Radical Republican constitution that included black suffrage. In Connecticut, New York, and Minnesota, when put to popular vote, black suffrage was defeated. Only in Iowa could Republicans procure black enfranchisement. To protest political exclusion, Equal Rights Leagues arose in the North. Consisting of alliances between black leaders and white former abolitionists, these organizations advocated for full political equality.

By the 1868 elections, northern voters had enough of the tug-of-war in Washington. They elected moderate Republicans intent on distancing themselves from the Radicals' platform, which focused not just on full civil rights for African Americans but also on women's suffrage and the rights of labor unions. Instead of expending energies in power struggles, the moderates supported the new president: military hero Ulysses S. Grant. With conservative governments victorious in Virginia by 1869 and in North Carolina and Georgia by 1871, aggressively pro-black Reconstruction all but vanished.

Now that Republican congressmen faced a conservative southern contingent, even moderate Republicans—most of whom had rejected a black suffrage amendment—began to see that northern black voters might help them win close congressional contests. So in February 1869, moderate Republicans proposed the Fifteenth Amendment, prohibiting federal and state governments from limiting the franchise because of "race, color, or previous condition of servitude." Former Confederate states wishing to return to the Union had to ratify the new amendment. Mississippi was among the first to comply. Upon its readmission, black voters sent state senator Hiram Revels to Washington to finish out the Senate term vacated by Jefferson Davis in 1861. As a black Pittsburgh teacher commented, "The Republican party had done the Negro good [in passing the Fifteenth Amendment], but they were doing themselves good at the same time." When Revels took his congressional seat, he was as much a symbol as a politician. To black Americans and Radical Republicans, he embodied victory in the battle for full black enfranchisement. (Indeed, the Fifteenth Amendment was ratified in March 1870, just as Revels took office.) His presence symbolized the South's defeat. To moderate Republicans, he represented a concession to Radical Republican schemes—one that would preserve Republican congressional dominance.

Black Suffrage and Women's Suffrage

The passage of the Fourteenth and Fifteenth amendments exposed the fragility of the northern white and black reformer alliance. With Emancipation, war's end, and the Thirteenth Amendment, many white abolitionists were

This popular portrait of the seven black congressmen, from spring of 1873, includes several who were ending their term and several just arriving. Missing is Pinckney Benton Stewart Pinchback, elected to the Senate from Louisiana in 1872.

satisfied that black rights would come in due course. While continuing to lobby for black rights, they diverted some of their energies to promoting full citizenship for women. This connection between black rights and women's rights had been marked as early as Frederick Douglass's attendance at the 1848 Women's Rights Convention at Seneca Falls, New York. Douglass and Elizabeth Cady Stanton had long been friends, as Douglass backed Stanton's claim that "the power to choose rulers and make laws was the right by which all others could be secured."

During the war, Stanton had circulated petitions supporting the Thirteenth Amendment outlawing slavery. With ratification of the amendment, she expected antislavery leaders like Wendell Phillips to support her women's agenda in return. At issue for her was the word *male* in the Fourteenth Amendment. Previously, women had assumed they were citizens. The new amendment, which specified voters as "male inhabitants," underscored women's exclusion from the political process. Furious, Stanton refused to support the Fourteenth and Fifteenth Amendments. "My question," she challenged Phillips, "is do you believe the African race is composed entirely of males?" Stanton's friendship with Douglass also soured, as Douglass argued that the right to vote was more crucial for black men than for women. "The government of this country loves women," he contended, "but the Negro is loathed." Douglass feared a bill including enfranchisement of women could not pass, even in a Radical Republican Congress.

> "The government of this country loves women, but the Negro is loathed."
> —*Frederick Douglass*

The question of whether women had as much right to vote as freedmen found few sympathizers, even among Radical Republicans. The majority of reformers adopted a "black men first" strategy. By opposing the Fourteenth and later the Fifteenth amendments, Stanton found herself

■ TABLE 11.1 The Federal Power Struggle 1865–1877

Black newspapers recognized that often white Americans' interest in Reconstruction involved a power struggle among the three branches of government rather than the best interests of black people or the South. African American concerns frequently faded into the background. Below are some of the battles that took place during the Reconstruction years.

Date	*Congress*	*Presidency*	*Supreme Court*
1865	Establishes Freedmen's Bureau	Andrew Johnson grants "amnesty and pardon" to most Confederates, restoring confiscated land, and exiling thousands of black farmers from their land	
1866	Passes Thirteenth Amendment, abolishing slavery in all states and territories; ratified by 27 states Expands Freedmen's Bureau authority and over Johnson's veto empowers it to try civil cases for freedmen Over Johnson's veto, passes three Civil Rights Acts, including one that vacates 1857 *Dred Scott* decision and granting citizenship to black Americans Passes Fourteenth Amendment, guaranteeing citizenship and requiring Confederate states' approval; ratified in 1868	Johnson vetoes two-year extension for Freedmen's Bureau Johnson vetoes Civil Rights Acts	In *Ex Parte Milligan*, rules that neither the president nor Congress has legal power to allow other agencies to try civilian cases, except in theater of war
1867		Enforces provisions of Civil Rights Acts	In *Cummings* v. *Missouri*, rules that government may not require voters to take oaths of past loyalty
1868	Passes Tenure of Office Act, forbidding president to remove Secretary of War Edwin Stanton Impeaches Johnson; conviction fails by one vote	Removes military officers from duty, including Secretary of War Edwin Stanton	Agrees to hear a southern state's case regarding the constitutionality of Reconstruction Acts Outlaws Maryland's race-based apprentice system
1869	Passes Fifteenth Amendment guaranteeing suffrage, requiring Confederate states to ratify; ratified in 1870		Upholds congressional authority to shape Reconstruction In *Texas* v. *White*, rules that Confederate officials had never left Union, since secession was illegal
1870–71	Passes Ku Klux Klan Acts Moderate Republicans refuse to seat black Louisiana Senator P. B. S. Pinchback		
1872	Passes Amnesty Act Dismantles Freedmen's Bureau		
1873			In *Slaughterhouse Cases*, rules that only the rights of federal citizenship are protected under Fourteenth Amendment; other rights at state discretion
1875	Passes Civil Rights Act guaranteeing freedmen access to public accommodations		
1877	Compromise installs Rutherford B. Hayes as president; federal troops withdrawn from South		

■ TABLE 11.2 The Black Men Who Went to Congress in 1870

Most African American congressmen were young, ambitious, and outspoken. All represented the South, though some were born in the North. Some brought prestigious educational credentials; others brought a wisdom born of life experience. Here is a look at the first seven black men who were elected to Congress. Most went on to fruitful careers following their terms in Congress.

Name/State/ Age in 1870	*Background*	*Prior experience*	*Service in Congress*	*Post-Congress experience*
Blanche K. Bruce (1841–1898) Mississippi 29 years old	Born slave in Virginia to master and slave woman	Studied at Oberlin College; Mississippi tax assessor, superintendent of education, alderman, sheriff	Senate, 1875–1881. Supported seating of P. B. S. Pinchback, Mississippi River flood control and port development, citizenship for Chinese and Native Americans, dissolving all-black regiments	1881–1893: Register of the Treasury and DC Recorder of Deeds; trustee of Howard University
Richard H. Cain (1825–1887) South Carolina 45 years old	Born free in western Virginia to black mother, Cherokee father	Studied at Wilberforce College; delegate to SC state constitutional convention; served in SC state senate	House of Representatives 1873–1874; 1877–79. Opposed Amnesty Act; supported woman suffrage, education, and land	1878: Encouraged South Carolinians to support Liberia exodus
Robert DeLarge (1842–1874) South Carolina 28 years old	Born free in Virginia	SC constitutional convention (1868) and state legislature	House of Representatives, 1871–1873. Removed from office 2 months before his term expired because white opponent won contested election. Supported Amnesty Act, black land ownership	Magistrate in Charleston
Robert Brown Elliott (1842–1884) South Carolina 28 years old	Born in South Carolina to free black parents	Passed SC bar in 1867; editor of black Republican newspaper, the *South Carolina Leader;* SC constitutional convention; assistant adjutant-general of SC	House of Representatives, 1871–1875. Supported suppression of Ku Klux Klan, protection of black vote	Lawyer in New Orleans, Louisiana
Jefferson Long (1836–1900) Georgia 34 years old	Born a slave in Georgia to slave mother and white father	Tailor	House of Representatives, 1871–1873. Supported Ku Klux Klan Acts, opposed amnesty for ex-Confederates	Tailoring business suffered because of his continued organizing for Republican Party
John Roy Lynch (1847–1939) Mississippi 23 years old	Louisiana slave, freed when Union army seized Natchez, 1863	Elected justice of the peace; Mississippi legislature speaker of the house	House of Representatives, 1872–1876. Supported civil rights legislation	Delegate to four national Republican conventions; appointed by President Benjamin Harrison to be auditor of the U.S. Treasury for the Navy Department
Pinckney Benton Stewart Pinchback (1837–1921) Louisiana 33 years old	Born free to Georgia planter and an emancipated slave	Louisiana state senator; lieutenant governor; acting governor	Senate: elected in 1872, but never allowed to assume office. Advocated education, women's suffrage	U.S. Customs inspector; cotton planter; owner of Mississippi riverboat company; admitted to Louisiana bar in 1886; helped found Southern Normal School

cut deals that brought black cadets to West Point and the Naval Academy.

Maneuvering through Washington's corridors of power, black politicians understood that their constituents were vulnerable and their own positions fragile. They sought issues on which they could negotiate with white allies without trading away too many black political gains. The balancing act demanded constant attention and vigilance.

Some outspoken black congressmen refused to compromise or negotiate. "In my state, since emancipation there have been over five hundred loyal men shot down by the disloyal men there, and not one of those men who took part in committing those outrages has ever been brought to justice," said Congressman Jefferson Long of Georgia. "Those disloyal people still hate this Government, [and] when loyal men dare to carry the 'stars and stripes' through our streets, they are turned out of employment. When we take the men who commit these outrages before judges and juries, we find that these courts and juries remain in the hands of the very Ku Klux themselves."

Uncompromising black congressmen like Long found it difficult to push their agenda. Too few in number and too new to politics, they struggled to represent their constituents' concerns. Sometimes simply being heard was all they could hope for. For example, Long voted against the Amnesty Act, knowing this would further isolate him in a Congress bent on reconciliation. Richard Cain, a representative from South Carolina, also voted no. "I want to see a change in this country," said Cain, a northern-born minister whose calling had taken him South to fight for black justice. "Instead of colored people being always penniless, I want to see them coming in with their mule teams and ox teams, with their corn and potatoes to exchange for silks and satins. I want to see children coming to enjoy life as it ought to be enjoyed." Cain doubted that reinstating political rights to Confederates would help realize this vision. Several other black congressmen also voted no on amnesty. Even red-inked letters from the Ku Klux Klan warning of "doom sealed in blood" could not deter these men from speaking out—knowing their arguments fell on deaf ears.

Young black congressmen sought counsel from seasoned political activists like Frederick Douglass. The esteemed black leader befriended them, often hosting them at his home. Yet even Douglass misread the political realities of Reconstruction. In the 1872 presidential race, Douglass supported Republican President Ulysses S. Grant's bid for reelection. True, Grant had demonstrated only lukewarm support for black rights, but he represented the political party that had freed slaves, and he had opposed President Andrew Johnson. Grant suggested annexing the Dominican Republic—which had a large black population and was adjacent to the black Caribbean island republic of Haiti—to provide a haven where African Americans could escape white oppression while maintaining U.S. citizenship. Douglass believed in Grant's goodwill.

Douglass did not question Grant's motives, but others—notably Douglass's abolitionist friend Senator Charles Sumner, who chaired the Senate Foreign Relations Committee—suspected that annexation was a scheme to enrich white land speculators. Douglass continued to support the president, even when Grant refused to invite black representatives to the White House dinner where legislators were to discuss annexation. The black leader counted on the president's good intentions and hoped Grant would reward him with a federal appointment. With support from the black voters Douglass helped deliver, Grant won reelection—but neither annexation of the Dominican Republic nor a federal appointment for Douglass materialized. Black people now had another reminder that their vote wielded little influence unless they could enlist support from powerful white allies.

Local Politics in the South

"When we opened the school a party of armed men came to my house, seized me, carried me out and threw me in Thompson's Creek after they had belabored me with the muzzles of their revolvers . . . [saying] they 'did not want . . . any damned nigger school in that town and were not going to have it,'" Texas state senator George Ruby recalled while testifying about obstacles facing southern black politicians at the state and local levels. Some of these challenges centered on crafting effective political strategies and alliances; others involved ensuring constituents' safety in a hostile environment. Whatever forms the difficulties took, local black politicians had few southern white allies. In the South, local politics and politicians saw little intercession by white Radical Republicans on behalf of black concerns. Even the presence of federal troops could not deter threats such as those Ruby endured for merely opening a school.

Ruby quickly learned the Texas political terrain. Born in New York and educated in New England, he had lived for a while in Haiti but returned to the United States to work for the Freedmen's Bureau. Assigned to build schools in Texas, he also represented Galveston County at the Texas constitutional convention in 1868. This experience gained him the visibility to be elected to the state senate in 1869.

One of only two black state senators in Texas, Ruby had a constituency mainly of black voters and the minority of white politicians who were bent on securing federal assistance for rebuilding the state's infrastructure, refurbishing the Galveston port, and establishing an educational system benefiting poor Texans of all races.

Like Revels and other black leaders at the national level, Ruby used compromise and negotiation. He supported white Texans as well as black for patronage positions, and he tolerated the new state laws segregating public travel, parks, and even Republican political events. In return, he hoped to gain white support for laws that would restrain the Klan, give citizenship and the franchise to Native Americans (who would presumably increase the Republican party rolls), and promote schools and other services to improve the lives of freed people. He also hoped to contain the growing institution of Black Codes, those state or local laws restricting African Americans' employment choices, land ownership, free mobility, and other opportunities.

Ruby's strategy reflected his understanding of southern political realities. In the postwar era, southern politics took one of three forms: the political middle—which consisted of the vast majority of white southerners, the political right, and the radical left. The political middle, or "moderates," included many entrepreneurs and professionals as well as farmers. Many in this group had concluded even before the war that the South needed to modernize—to diversify their region's economy, develop technology and industry, and avail themselves of federal subsidies for geological surveys, railroads, factories, and ports. Moderate white southerners were not particularly interested in economic advancement for African Americans, but they envisioned black laborers as part of the new South, working in factories as well as in fields. They welcomed alliances with black leaders whom they felt could help persuade black communities to meet moderate white people's goals. As long as leaders like Ruby stayed "in their place"—that is, deferential to white people—white moderates supported black education and voting rights.

South Carolina planter Wade Hampton exemplified white moderates. Hampton believed black and white southerner leaders should unite in rebuilding the South. "Does not that glorious southern sun above us shine alike for both of us?" he asked. But Hampton and other moderates made no overtures toward social integration, viewing class and racial divisions as natural for society.

Black leaders like George Ruby cultivated political connections with white moderates like Wade Hampton among his constituency. With such alliances, he could build support for black people to obtain broader access to education and jobs in agriculture or factories. This was better than joblessness or the specter of black southerners migrating to the North in large numbers in search of jobs—a situation neither white southerners nor white northerners wanted.

Martin Delany also advocated black-white alliances. Filling in as editor for South Carolina's *Missionary Record,* Delany developed a blueprint for black-white cooperation. He felt certain that "the black man and the white man must work together . . . [to] bring about the redemption of the state and prosperity and happiness for the whole people." At the same time, he shuddered at the ever-increasing threats from such groups as the Ku Klux Klan, the Knights of the White Camellias, and the White Leagues. "The black men of this state are dependent on the whites, just as the whites are dependent on them," he wrote in 1873. Thus, he advised black southerners to relinquish "hatred and resentment" and to show themselves as "polite, pleasant, agreeable, ever ready and obliging."

> "The black man and the white man must work together."—*Martin Delany*

Persuaded by Hampton's argument that "when all our troubles and trials are over, [black and white southerners] will sleep in that same soil in which we first drew breath," Delany supported Hampton's successful bid for governor of South Carolina in 1876.

At the political right stood what some might call radical reactionaries, a small but significant group of white southerners. These included dislocated plantation owners who had lost their economic system, and a few struggling white farmers who had an emotional investment in the South's old way of life, which had given even poor white people a higher status than black people. Their anger at the ravages of war prevented them from embracing any part of a new order that enabled African Americans to progress beyond a servile role. Intent on reviving the prewar agricultural economy, radical reactionaries needed laborers to work the land, and they wanted freed slaves to do the job. They had little interest in modernizing the South and were the ones who most often instigated violence against black people. Black politicians did their best to avoid them.

The South's radical left—the third political group—argued that poor black people had more in common with poor white people than with wealthy black ones. That is, class was more important than race in working to achieve goals. Their view of a postwar South included interracial politics based on unity among poor people regardless of race. Their

Madison Hemings Recalls His Family History

Madison Hemings's story, published in 1873, reinforced white southerner's fears about interracial relations. In this interview, the sixty-eight-year-old Hemings describes a family with a biracial background. Born in Virginia, Hemings identified himself both as a black American and as the son of United States president Thomas Jefferson. Jefferson's white descendants denied this relationship until DNA testing in 1999 confirmed the story.

[After the death of his wife, Thomas Jefferson] left for France, taking his eldest daughter with him. . . . My mother accompanied her as her body servant. During that time my mother became Mr. Jefferson's concubine. . . . He promised her . . . that her children should be freed at the age of twenty-one years. . . . She gave birth to four [children] and Jefferson was the father of all of them. Their names were Beverly, Harriet, Madison (myself) and Eston. We all became free . . . [and] all married and have raised families.

Beverly left Monticello and went to Washington as a white man. He married a white woman in Maryland, and their only child, a daughter, was not known by the white folks to have any colored blood coursing through her veins. Beverly's wife's family were people in good circumstances.

Harriet married a white man in good standing in Washington City, whose name I could give, but will not, for prudential reasons. She raised a family of children, and so far as I know they were never suspected of being tainted with African blood in the community where she lived or lives. I have not heard from her for ten years, and do not know whether she is dead or alive. She thought it to her interest, on going to Washington, to assume the role of a white woman. . . .

Eston married a colored woman in Virginia, and moved from there to Ohio. . . .

I married Mary McCoy. Her grandmother was a slave, and lived with her master, Stephen Hughes, near Charlottesville, as his wife. She was manumitted by him, which made her children free. Mary McCoy's mother was his daughter.

—from The Pike County [Ohio] Republican, *March 13, 1873.*

To view a longer version of this document, please go to *www.ablongman.com/carson/documents*.

concerns included universal education, more equitable land policies, better contracts for renters, and politicians who advocated the rights of the poor. Some of their beliefs were based on socialism, a political philosophy for establishing a government that distributed wealth equally among all its members. This philosophy, which defined economic circumstance as more important than race or ethnicity, gained favor with many of the world's poor people in the late nineteenth century. Many black sharecroppers and laborers indeed understood they had more in common with poor white farmers than with wealthy black planters who benefited from the same exploitative sharecropping and tenant systems used by white planters.

As steel and mining industries began to bring about the hoped-for modernizing of southern cities like Birmingham, Alabama, and Atlanta, Georgia, a black laborers' movement gathered momentum in the South, taking some of its energy from alliances with white radicals. A small but vocal minority of southern white labor organizers embraced black radicals like Lucy Parsons, (an early organizer of Texas's Socialist Workingmen's Party, which advocated interracial labor unions), and Peter Clark of Cincinnati, Ohio, who traveled through the North and the South urging industrial workers to put class unity above racial division. Parsons, who was married to a white Texas socialist, exemplified much of what conservative white southerners feared: miscegenation, or sexual liaison between black and white people. Though such "race-mixing" was common under slavery, white planters feared that in post-slavery times, mixed-race people would feel entitled to the privileges of white Americans.

Only the most optimistic of black Americans joined the socialist ranks. Most soon recognized that white socialists had little power to effect real change. However, the idea of political parties that subordinated racial differences to class loyalty remained alive for decades. In the 1890s, when the Populist Party emerged to put many of these concerns on the national agenda, poor black southerners counted among its strongest supporters.

White Backlash

Even outside the South, white Americans found many ways to keep black people "in their place." Immediately after Congress introduced the Thirteenth Amendment abolishing slavery, white-on-black violence intensified in the North. The same night President Abraham Lincoln was assassinated, an Ohio mob torched the main building of the black Wilberforce University. The blaze destroyed all of Martin Delany's correspondence, manuscripts, and African art collections. "The hand that placed the torch," wrote Delany, was "leagued in sentiment with the same dastardly villains who struck down the greatest Chief Magistrate [Lincoln] of the present age."

Indeed, that hand had a broad span. In Philadelphia and San Francisco, in the late 1860s, white trolley riders forcibly repelled black ones when they tried to board the public transit system. In Rochester, New York, in the winter of 1867, Frederick Douglass's son-in-law, who operated a taxi pulled by what observers described as "a handsome span of greys [horses]," was so badly menaced by other drivers that he quit the trade. That same winter, in the Freedmen's Bureau offices in Washington, DC, General Oliver O. Howard had to threaten to fire his white clerks to get them to accept black coworkers.

In the South, members of the Ku Klux Klan, cloaked in white hoods, galloped on horseback to the homes of black political leaders and their supporters who tried to vote, or those who had become economically comfortable, or supposedly did not show due deference to whites. The attackers often dragged black people out of their homes and whipped or tortured them. Sometimes they killed them, mutilated them, set them on fire, or hanged them from trees—a practice that became known as *lynching*.

Between 1868 and 1876, while an estimated 20,000 black people were murdered by the Ku Klux Klan, southern officials looked the other way. Many of the victims had played an active role in local politics. One Alabama woman said the Klan had murdered her husband because "he just would hold up his head and say he was a strong Radical." Klan members meted out countless other brutal beatings to people who, like Ruby, did nothing more radical than build a school or exude confidence. Another woman reported that the "Ku Klux came to my house and took us out and whipped us, and then said 'don't lets hear any big talk from you, and don't sass any white ladies.'" Yet another woman received "forty licks with a hickory and [was] kicked in the head and hit with a pistol" to ensure that she would not "sauce [be impertinent to] white women."

The Klan's tactics helped overturn Republican Party control in Georgia in 1870, as terrified black voters stayed away from the polls. The following year, Mississippi Klansmen burned dozens of black churches and schools, torturing and killing the ministers and teachers. Still, many black southerners followed the lead of the Alabaman who said, "The Republican party freed me, and I will die on top of it. I vote every time. I will stick with the Republican party and die in it."

> "The Republican party freed me, and I will die on top of it."—*Alabama black man*

Klansmen did not limit their assaults to black people. They also harassed and murdered the few poor or idealistic southern white citizens who supported socialist groups and advocated racial equality. One white South Carolina Republican reported being "thrashed" by the Ku Klux Klan because he agreed to have polls situated at his residence,

After Emanuel Fortune's death in 1903, his son, journalist Timothy Thomas Fortune, reported, "It was natural [for him] to take the leadership in any independent movement of Negroes."

where he welcomed black Republicans and refused entrance to two Democratic voters.

The Enforcement Acts

The Fifteenth Amendment gave all black American men the right to vote—but securing that right in practical terms presented an entirely separate challenge. Affirming the federal commitment to the Fourteenth and Fifteenth Amendments, Congress passed two Enforcement Acts in 1870 and 1871—also known as the Klan Acts, because they were an effort to protect black voters from Ku Klux Klan violence. Both acts defined interference with a person's right to vote as a federal offense punishable by fine or imprisonment. In the summer of 1871, responding to Freedmen's Bureau reports of continued attacks against black southerners, Congress collected testimony from Emanuel Fortune, Robert Meacham, and hundreds of others to learn whether southern voters indeed were still unable to express their political views safely. The hearings produced thirteen volumes of testimony. In one dramatic account, a black Arkansas Republican organizer told of relying on sentinels, coded signals, and the use of religious rhetoric to convince white passersby that a political rally was "only a nigger prayer meeting."

The Enforcement Acts did little to stop violence against black people. In Louisville, Kentucky, white people mobbed and pummeled black residents who exercised their recently court-won right to ride the trolley cars. In Colfax, Louisiana, long-simmering racial hatred led local black men to arm themselves and patrol the town to protect their families from attack by white people. In a confrontation on Easter Sunday, 1873, between the black militia and the white sheriff and a posse of white men he had pulled together, the two groups exchanged fire. The battle ended with more than a dozen white men killed or wounded and two dozen black men injured. About three dozen black men were arrested and executed without a trial. Frederick Douglass's *New National Era* reported that in the wake of the incident, the local White League, bringing in guns and cannons from neighboring states, randomly shot, stabbed, and beat black citizens. They intended, they said, to set an example for "every parish in the State [so] we shall begin to have some quiet and niggers will know their place."

Racial violence broke out in the North as well. In Philadelphia, the federal government sent in a company of marines to protect black voters in the 1870 national election. The following year, when the government failed to provide such protection, a white mob murdered Octavius Catto at his Philadelphia polling place. Catto's leadership in the Pennsylvania Equal Rights League had made him a target. Having served as a major in the Union army, Catto was a beloved school principal after the war. One of his friends lamented, "The Ku Klux of the South are not by any means the lower classes of society. The same may be said of the Ku Klux of the North. Both are industriously engaged in trying to break us down." Black Americans had witnessed yet another instance of their government's inability to protect them.

The Freedmen's Bank

If reconstructing the nation politically posed daunting challenges, establishing a firm economic foundation for African Americans proved even more difficult. In 1865, Congress chartered a new bank: the Freedmen's Savings and Trust Company. It offered black people the opportunity for leadership and to save money and it made loans to help purchase land and farm equipment.

In 1870, the *New National Era* gave glowing reports of the bank's progress. Though Congress did not assume responsibility for monitoring the bank's operations, thousands of black depositors in Washington, Baltimore, New York, Louisville, and dozens of other cities trusted the bank as they painstakingly saved for businesses, farms, equipment, and homes. Year by year, coin by coin, they accumulated nest eggs they hoped would give them financial autonomy.

But the bank soon fell on hard times. In its first years, several well-known white bankers—along with Freedmen's Bureau director Oliver Howard and a national board of four dozen trustees—oversaw operations. They upheld the congressional mandate of investing depositors' money in government securities. But in 1870, during a postwar building boom and railroad expansion, Congress amended the bank's charter, enabling the managers to invest deposits in real estate and railroads. In the next few years, several white members of the bank's board secretly made unsuccessful speculative loans in these industries. By the time the results of these investments became known, the men who managed them had resigned, leaving a core of mostly black trustees to repair the damage. As one black trustee put it, "We trustees—meeting but once a month, and then only hearing statements—could really know nothing about the affairs of the bank."

Desperate to maintain black people's confidence in the bank, the trustees called on the well-respected Frederick Douglass to replace the white bank president. Douglass did so, even investing $10,000 of his own money. Yet he could not prevent the trustees from approving more bad loans. Failing to persuade Congress to salvage the bank, Douglass presided over its closing in July 1874.

As the savings of thousands of African Americans evaporated, some blamed the bank's failure on Douglass, leaving his reputation seriously tarnished. Discouraged that Congress had offered no assistance, numerous African

A woman of strong opinions, Mary Ann Shadd Cary caught the attention of outspoken white women, including fellow Washington lawyer Belva Lockwood. Throwing her energies into Lockwood's 1872 presidential campaign, Cary hoped to show her support not only for black rights but also for women's leadership.

ual trades rather than in intellectual or political leadership roles. In succeeding years, many black leaders shared her concern for the fate of the average worker.

Cary's concerns about the lack of economic opportunities for African Americans deepened when she saw the widespread poverty in the nation's capital. More than three-quarters of Washington's black families lived in alleys next to large houses where they served as laundresses, porters, handymen, and domestic servants. In the crowded alleys near the Capitol and along the Potomac River lived those who worked in government service. Many of these black households, teeming with family members and boarders, experienced living conditions as bleak as those under slavery. Malnutrition, poor health, violence, and alcoholism plagued them. Fish from local rivers and lakes and vegetables from urban gardens helped ward off starvation, but some black people resorted to prostitution and petty theft in order to survive. Others returned home to the familiar rural South. As black historian John Hope Franklin observed, "It was one thing to provide temporary relief for freedmen, and another to guide them along the road to economic stability and independence."

Despite these difficulties, many freed people managed to build vibrant communities in the capital city. The streets of Washington's poor black neighborhoods rang with the shouts of children playing games, adults performing music, and residents regaling each other with stories.

But there was typically a large gap between black political leaders, who were often economically well off, at least comparatively, and newly freed black people, who were mainly of the working class. Some black leaders—both social advocates and politicians—lost touch with the needs of ordinary black people. While they took seriously their role as advocates for racial and economic justice, their own lives came to include second homes at summer resorts, international travel, and interracial marriages. Many seemed to forget the impact of slavery on the present generation. Cary was one leader who never forgot; she dedicated herself to working for economic stability and independence for the poor.

Political Patronage and Politics

In 1871, Congress established a local government for the District of Columbia consisting of a governor and eleven commissioners appointed by the president, and a twenty-two-member board of delegates, elected by popular vote, with the power to make local laws. Though the District had no voice in Congress or in national politics, as the states did, respected black leaders—including Frederick Douglass and AME bishop James A. Handy—were elected to the board of delegates and hence had a say in local politics. The new structure, which replaced the haphazard and inefficient older structure whereby the District was governed under several conflicting jurisdictions, was seen by many northern leaders as an improvement over the old charter that had expired in 1870.

Though African Americans were in a minority in this interracial governing group, the restructured District government signaled a friendly attitude toward black residents, and dozens of loyal black Republican supporters were rewarded with political patronage positions in such agencies as the Board of Health and the Recorder of Deeds office, Patent Office, Treasury Department, Post Office, public schools, and municipal utilities. Hundreds more found employment in the new district as government clerks and service workers. Local ordinances outlawed racial segregation in public services, and operators of hotels, restaurants, concert halls, and theaters paid fines and saw their licenses suspended if they breached these laws. The Civil Rights Act of 1875, though soon to be overturned by the Supreme Court, reinforced open access to public accommodations.

Steady cash wages—a first for most black people—allowed for middle-class lifestyles for some and elevated others to elite status. Black service workers were sometimes able to save money and buy property of their own. A government employee's income allowed Frederick Douglass to leave his urban brick rowhouse and move to Cedar Hill, an estate in nearby Anacostia. Even as she railed against segregated schools, Mary Ann Shadd Cary served as the principal at the

American Missionary Association's Lincoln School—a position that placed her among the 3 percent of Washington's black workers who held a professional job. These political and social developments mirrored a phenomenon unfolding across the nation. In staggering numbers, African Americans left the countryside, relocating to urban areas where some made economic progress and began participating in local politics. They headed for Detroit and Cincinnati, for New York, Philadelphia and Pittsburgh. Black communities flourished in Baltimore, Maryland; Charleston, South Carolina; Galveston, Texas; Jacksonville, Florida; and Richmond, Virginia.

Many cities had enough black residents to support a black press. Ambitious—if sometimes short-lived—black newspapers proliferated. Across the river from Washington, DC, Alexandria, Virginia, had the *People's Advocate*. Harrisburg, Pennsylvania, boasted the *National Progress*. At the end of the 1870s, in Evansville, Indiana, Edwin Horn was publishing *Our Age*. All of these publications kept their eyes on Washington, where they began noticing a troubling development: the waning of federal protection for African Americans. In succeeding decades, Washington remained an important destination for many black Americans, but the experience of these later arrivals differed markedly from that of Reconstruction-era black Washingtonians.

THE END OF RECONSTRUCTION

Radical Reconstruction brought important gains to black southerners: schools, varied economic possibilities, and the franchise. Efforts to diversify the economy and increase access to the polls, leadership experience, and the reuniting of many families separated by slavery also improved black lives. In 1867, in New Orleans, African Americans won the right to ride the public trolley cars. Through protests and negotiations, they persuaded the car companies to admit "our citizens into all the cars, without any distinction as to color." In many southern states, Radical Republican governments passed laws granting black people access to soda fountains, opera houses, railroads, and steamboats. In 1875, Congress sought to certify these gains with a Civil Rights Act banning discrimination in public places throughout the country. But the act constituted the last piece of civil rights legislation to make its way through Congress until 1957.

Waning Federal Sympathy

Even as civil rights legislation was passed, many reformers pulled back from the enormous effort required to remake a former slave society. The same 1870 elections that brought black congressmen to power also swept away the Republican majority in the House of Representatives. With the crumbling of Republican power in the early 1870s, African American progress began to disintegrate as well. In the South, from which federal troops were gradually withdrawn, black political organizations withered away. In 1869, Mississippi had 87,000 registered black voters; eleven years later, it had just half that number. Southern Radical Republican governments in southern states gave way to conservative white Democratic ones. White southerners called these developments "redemption." A black Louisianan saw it differently in 1877: "The whole South—every state in the South—had got into the hands of the very men that held us slaves."

> "The whole South—every state in the South—had got into the hands of the very men that held us slaves." —*Black Louisianan*

The Supreme Court joined the retreat from black causes by limiting the scope of the Fourteenth Amendment. In the *Slaughterhouse Cases* (1873), the Court drew a distinction between citizenship of the United States and citizenship of a state. It asserted that the amendment applied only to the former; states had the right to define citizenship and its accompanying rights for their residents. In 1883, the Supreme Court heard several cases in the course of which it voted to overturn the 1875 Civil Rights Act. In making their decisions, the justices distinguished between political rights—guaranteed by the Constitution—and social rights—pertaining to segregation in public places, for example—which it felt involved citizens' private lives. The Court declared the federal government had no authority over social rights. The stage was now set for the so-called Jim Crow laws, which limited the rights of African Americans for the next seventy-five years.

The Compromise of 1877

The 1876 presidential contest gave Republicans in Congress a final small victory. In an election so close that it fell to the House of Representatives to adjudicate disputed electoral votes, Republicans and Democrats worked out an agreement that became known as the Compromise of 1877.

In the Compromise, southern congressmen agreed to concede the presidency to Republican can-

Simon Smith Laments the End of Hope

With the 1876 presidential election, black southerners saw their political power evaporate. Returning home to Columbia, South Carolina, Simon P. Smith, a recent graduate of Howard University, wrote to a northern friend.

I visited the state senate and house and the Democrats were very jubilant; but Republicans were in despondency. I talked with two colored representatives . . . and two colored senators. . . . They are all without hope. They all think that the colored man is done in this state. Colored men who had influence here once have no more today than I have. The Rebels are making colored men do common work for $.25 per day. How can they live! Labor is worth nothing and provision higher than anywhere else. I know not what our people will do here now.

—*from American Missionary Association Archives.*

To view a longer version of this document, please go to *www.ablongman.com/carson/documents*.

didate Rutherford B. Hayes, while Republicans agreed to make concessions to white southerners, allowing them to control local elections and to make local ordinances controlling such issues as black employment contracts and racial separation. The few remaining federal troops were withdrawn from the South, federal intervention in southern state affairs ceased, and the U.S. government agreed to appoint at least one southerner to the president's cabinet. Across the South, state governments now lay firmly in the hands of the white "redeemers," who regained local power to deny true citizenship privileges—such as the vote—to thousands of African Americans. The national Republican Party distanced itself from black interests, establishing segregated "Black and Tan" parties in an increasingly segregated South. For white Americans, the era of Reconstruction had ended.

AFRICAN AMERICANS ON THE MOVE

"I made the outside box [for Julia Haven] and her coffin, in Smith County, Tennessee. And another young colored lady . . . they committed an outrage on her and then shot her, and I helped to make her coffin." In the spring of 1880, seventy-year-old Benjamin "Pap" Singleton used these two examples of women who had been raped and killed to help a Senate committee understand why black people were fleeing the South. The investigation had been launched in response to claims by both Democrats and Republicans that the opposing political party was conspiring to provoke black people to leave the South. Republicans accused Democrats of wanting to gain control of the South by expelling black voters; Democrats insisted that Republicans sought to spread their influence outside the South. Singleton knew better: Black people were fleeing the South to avoid rape, murder, and mutilation.

Ho for Kansas!

Brethren, Friends, & Fellow Citizens:

I feel thankful to inform you that the

REAL ESTATE

AND

Homestead Association,

Will Leave Here the

15th of April, 1878,

In pursuit of Homes in the Southwestern Lands of America, at Transportation Rates, cheaper than ever was known before.

For full information inquire of

Benj. Singleton, better known as old Pap,

NO. 5 NORTH FRONT STREET.

Beware of Speculators and Adventurers, as it is a dangerous thing to fall in their hands.

Nashville, Tenn., March 18, 1878.

One of the many posters calling on southern blacks to leave for Kansas.

■ Recruiters for the new black settlements took posters such as this one to local meetings across both North and South.

The Exodusters

Benjamin Singleton, a former Tennessee slave who had escaped via the Underground Railroad through Detroit into Canada, returned to his home state after the war. Like many black Americans, Singleton soon took advantage of the 1862 Homestead Act, which offered 160 acres of government land free to anyone who would live on the property, improve it, and pay a small registration fee. With other black Tennesseeans, he started the Edgfield Real Estate and Homestead Association to establish a new black settlement in Kansas. Several families who had visited Kansas, he said, "brought back favorable reports. . . . Three or four hundred . . . went into Southern Kansas . . . and formed a colony there, and bought about a thousand acres of ground." Comparing their projects to the exodus of the biblical Hebrews from Egyptian bondage, the thousands of black Americans who went west with groups such as the Kansas Exodus Joint Stock Company in the late 1870s called themselves *Exodusters*.

The town of Nicodemus in Graham County, Kansas, on the Solomon River typifies these new African American frontier communities. By 1880, 700 black settlers had emigrated to Nicodemus, but many emigrants encountered stiff resistance even as they left home. To retain the South's cheap labor force, white southerners tried to sabotage the planned black exodus. Singleton told Congress how armed white men, positioned along the shore, blocked the Mississippi River to black travelers. They sometimes grabbed the would-be pioneers and hacked off their hands. "Now see if you can go to Kansas and work," they said. White sheriffs arrested black travelers for breach of contract (if they were contracted to a planter) or for vagrancy (if they were not). Despite these tactics, black people continued to head west. Between 1870 and 1880, the African American population in Kansas doubled to more than 40,000.

At first white Kansans welcomed the Exodusters. Eager to increase the population of farmers and defend themselves from Native Americans who resisted the white influx, some Kansas communities raised money to help black newcomers pay land fees. But many black homesteaders, with few tools or work animals, found independent farming tough going. Discouraged, many Exodusters ended up in Topeka, where they hunted for work. But this city was also home to displaced white southerners also looking for employment. Racial intimidation and lynchings became so common that the Republican mayor of Topeka, once sympathetic to African Americans, suggested the money raised for black relief might better go to returning black refugees to the South—especially agitators "who were always talking politics."

> "We don't want to leave the South, and just as soon as we have confidence in the South I am going to persuade every man to go back." —*Benjamin Singleton*

Some black leaders like Frederick Douglass urged black families to stay in the South. Only with large numbers, they contended, could black voters exert power and influence. But Douglass wrote from the relative safety and comfort of Washington. It was people like Singleton who experienced the southern predicament firsthand: "We don't want to leave the South," he wrote in 1881, "and just as soon as we have confidence in the South I am going to . . . persuade every man to go back, because that is the best country; . . . we love that country . . . but [by leaving] we are going to learn the South a lesson."

The Western Frontier

Beyond Kansas, numerous African Americans found adventure and fortune in Nebraska, Colorado, North Dakota, and along the Pacific coast. Closed out of northern and southern

■ Finishing a term as a forager (raider) for the Confederate army, Isom Dart was among the cowboys who drifted west. Joining a group of cattle thieves, he was arrested in Texas, Colorado, and Wyoming. Legend has it that he was never imprisoned.

John E. Bruce Promotes Africa

Black journalist John E. Bruce was among those who envisioned Africa as a "homeland." Before a Philadelphia audience in 1877, he argued that Africa offered black Americans freedom from racial prejudice.

I shall endeavor to show tonight why the colored American should emigrate to Africa. First, because Africa is his fatherland; secondly, because before the war, in the South he was a slave, and in the North, a victim of prejudice and ostracism; and thirdly, because, since the close of the war, although he has been freed by emancipation and invested with enfranchisement, he is only nominally free; and lastly, because he is still a victim of prejudice, and practically proscribed socially, religiously, politically, educationally, and in the various industrial pursuits.

. . . The colored American should emigrate to Africa . . . because he . . . cannot enter a hotel and obtain accommodations without paying a double price, should he be successful in entering at all. If he go to the church of God in this Christian land, he is thrust into the gallery.

. . . Africa is a country rich in its productions, offering untold treasures to the adventurer who would go there. It has a peculiar claim upon the colored American.

—*excerpted from the* Christian Recorder, *November 1, 1877.*

To view a longer version of this document, please go to *www.ablongman.com/carson/documents*.

economy and politics, many black families headed for these new frontiers. Nancy Lewis told how she and her husband, a Civil War veteran, established their Nebraska farm in the 1870s. By 1880, they counted among 2,000 black Nebraskans. Virginia-born Barney Ford, a one-time barber and ship's steward, journeyed to Denver and by 1874 had opened a prosperous hotel. Two of Frederick Douglass's sons were also among Denver's thousand African Americans. Colorful cowboy Nat Love was among several hundred African Americans in North Dakota. His prowess in an 1876 rodeo in Deadwood City gained him the nickname "Deadwood Dick." Love's autobiography, *The Life & Adventures of Nat Love, Better Known in the Cattle Country As Deadwood Dick* (1876), promoted the escapades of black cowboys. But when the book was later published as one of many mass-market stories of the West, mention of Love's African heritage was omitted.

Some black Americans got as far west as California. By 1880, as many as 6,000 reached the coastal state. Several hundred settled in each of the other western states and territories. These pioneers included cowboys, shopkeepers, prospectors, service workers such as barbers, laundresses, and domestic servants, and farmers. A few, like Biddy Mason, found California a rewarding home. Dragged across the Rocky Mountains in the 1850s when her Mormon owner joined the gold rush, Mason remained in California after the courts declared her free. Purchasing property, she ran a successful boarding-house and grocery store, donated some of her profits to black schools, and helped establish the West's first AME church.

To Africa

Driven by the same hope and frustration that motivated western migration, other black Americans looked east to Africa. In the postwar years, Martin Delany revived his dream of claiming a black nationality there. "We have no chance to rise from beggars," Delany argued. "Men own the capital that we work who believe that my race have no more right to any of the profits of their labor than one of their mules." Richard Cain, a disillusioned ex-congressman, echoed Delany's despair: "There are thousands who are willing and ready to leave South Carolina, Georgia, Florida, and North Carolina. . . . The colored people of the South are tired of the constant struggle for life and liberty and prefer going where [there are] no obstacles . . . to . . . their liberty." Partnering with AME minister Henry McNeal Turner, Delany recruited settlers for Liberia. Turner had been born free in South Carolina in 1834, studied in the North, and served as pastor for a Washington, DC, church before the Civil War. After a stint as an army chaplain, he stayed in Georgia, working for the Republican Party and the AME church. By 1877, he shared Delany's dismay at the federal government's abandonment of black southerners.

In the spring of 1878, thousands of black Americans watched the launching of the *Azor* from Charleston's wharf.

Led by Delany and Turner, and with support from Cain, the Liberian Exodus Joint Stock Company had raised more than $6,000 to purchase the ship, which now carried roughly 200 settlers to Africa. Other black families invested thousands more. But expenses exceeded the company's limited capital, and the Exodus company soon lay in financial shambles. After delivering its first settlers, the company collapsed without establishing a permanent community. Though the Liberian Exodus Company represented yet another failed dream, the image of an African homecoming remained in the black imagination. Future generations would try again.

CONCLUSION

Emanuel Fortune's testimony in 1871 before the congressional committee investigating the Ku Klux Klan revealed the violence underlying post–Civil War southern politics. The politics of this war-torn region was no longer merely a regional concern of southerners and a few abolitionist northerners. The challenges facing African Americans now dominated the national agenda.

The federal government had outlawed slavery, extended equal rights to all citizens, and mandated that all black men could vote, but the law had little to do with reality. Though Hiram Revels and other black men represented southern states in Congress, white supremacist groups such as the Ku Klux Klan used threats, torture, and murder to scare southern black would-be voters away from the polls. Still, many black politicians sought common ground to negotiate compromises with southern white politicians. Sometimes they urged their black followers to accommodate some aspect of racial oppression in return for economic gains or political representation. At the far margin of the political spectrum, radicals tried to bridge the gap between the wealthy and the disaffected. They offered hope of a society that transcended divisions of race and class. All these strategies aimed to enable black people to move toward economic and social equality.

By 1877, African Americans seemed destined to be shunted aside again. With the Compromise of 1877, the federal government completed its withdrawal from helping freed slaves gain political rights and economic security. In the postwar era, black politicians had gained seats in Congress and in state legislatures. But with the end of Reconstruction, black politicians began leaving Washington and returning to the South to manage their personal lives and fortunes and to try to forge working relationships with white neighbors. Most white people in the North and the South expected black Americans to stay in the South, resigning themselves to menial jobs, limited political power, and continued deference to white people. Indeed, in the coming decades, southern black laborers seemed doomed to jobs that ensured only subordination and debt, and black leaders understood these as the limitations within which they must operate.

Though Washington, DC, the federal capital, continued to attract black people seeking jobs and a strong black community, the American frontier and Africa lured others who dreamed of better opportunities and fresh ideas. By 1879, with the passing of many antebellum black leaders, the black cause desperately needed new energy and direction. The ratification of the Thirteenth, Fourteenth, and Fifteenth amendments had promised African Americans access to political participation. Now, with Black Codes, poverty, and violence circumscribing those promises, black Americans needed new leaders.

FURTHER READING

Bullock, Penelope L. *The Afro-American Periodical Press, 1838–1909* (Baton Rouge: Louisiana State University Press, 1981).

Butchart, Ronald. *Northern Schools, Southern Blacks, and Reconstruction: Freedmen's Education, 1862–1875* (Westport, CT: Greenwood, 1980).

Cimbala, Paul, and Randall Miller. *The Freedmen's Bureau and Reconstruction: Reconsiderations* (New York: Fordham University Press, 1999).

Cox, Thomas. *Blacks in Topeka, Kansas, 1865–1915* (Baton Rouge: Louisiana State University Press, 1982).

Dann, Martin. *The Black Press, 1827–1890: The Quest for National Identity* (New York: Putnam, 1971).

Foner, Eric. *Reconstruction: America's Unfinished Revolution, 1863–1877* (New York: Harper and Row, 1989).

Gutman, Herbert. *The Black Family in Slavery and Freedom, 1750–1925* (New York: Pantheon, 1976).

Hahn, Steven. *A Nation Under Our Feet: Black Political Struggles in the Rural South, From Slavery to the Great Migration.* (Cambridge, MA: Harvard Press, 2003).

Jaynes, Gerald. *Branches Without Roots: Genesis of the Black Working Class in the American South, 1682–1882* (New York: Oxford University Press, 1986).

McPherson, James. *Battle Cry of Freedom: The Civil War Era* (New York: Oxford University Press, 1988).

Rhodes, Jane. *Mary Ann Shadd Cary: The Black Press and Protest in the Nineteenth Century* (Bloomington: University of Indiana Press, 1998).

Saville, Julie. *The Work of Reconstruction: From Slave to Wage Labor in South Carolina, 1860–1870* (Cambridge: Cambridge University Press, 1996).

Sears, Richard. *A Utopian Experiment in Kentucky: Integration and Social Equality at Berea, 1866–1904* (Westport, CT: Greenwood, 1996).

Wilson, Kirt H. *The Reconstructin Desegregaton Debate: The Politics of Equality and the Rhetoric of Place, 1870–1875.* (E. Lansing: Michigan State University Press, 2002).

CHAPTER 12

Despite his own convictions that black people were inferior to white people, artist Frederic Remington was caught up in the romance of the Tenth Cavalry. In *The Alert*, painted in 1888, he depicts one of the many mounted patrols in the Old West carried out by African Americans.

The Post-Reconstruction Era

Booker T. Washington Teaches Black Self-Sufficiency

"My life had its beginning in the midst of the most miserable, desolate, and discouraging surroundings," recalled Booker T. Washington in 1901, when he had earned worldwide renown as an expert on educating the poor. His work opened doors and shaped destinies for hundreds of black and white Americans.

Like millions of post–Civil War southern black people, Washington began his life in poverty. As a child, he worked in a coal mine, toiling in wretched conditions. But as a teenager, his life took a turn that helped him rise above his "discouraging surroundings." Hearing about Hampton Normal and Agricultural Institute in Virginia, a new school for freed slaves, Washington made his way there in 1872. Passing a practical entrance exam—which required him to sweep the floor of a shed—he convinced the white school head, Samuel Chapman Armstrong, that he deserved a scholarship.

Working as a janitor to help pay his way, Washington soon learned Armstrong's recipe for ex-slaves' success in modern America: manual labor education along with training in hygiene, thrift, and deference to white Americans. After Washington graduated from Hampton in 1875, Armstrong asked him to return to teach a group of Native American students. The young teacher viewed his Indian students the same way many white Americans did: "Few people had any confidence in the ability of the Indians to receive education and to profit by it." Washington was part of what he described as an "experiment being tried for the first time by General [Samuel Chapman] Armstrong, of educating Indians at Hampton." Could he help Armstrong prove that education could "civilize" Indians as well as African Americans?

CHAPTER OUTLINE

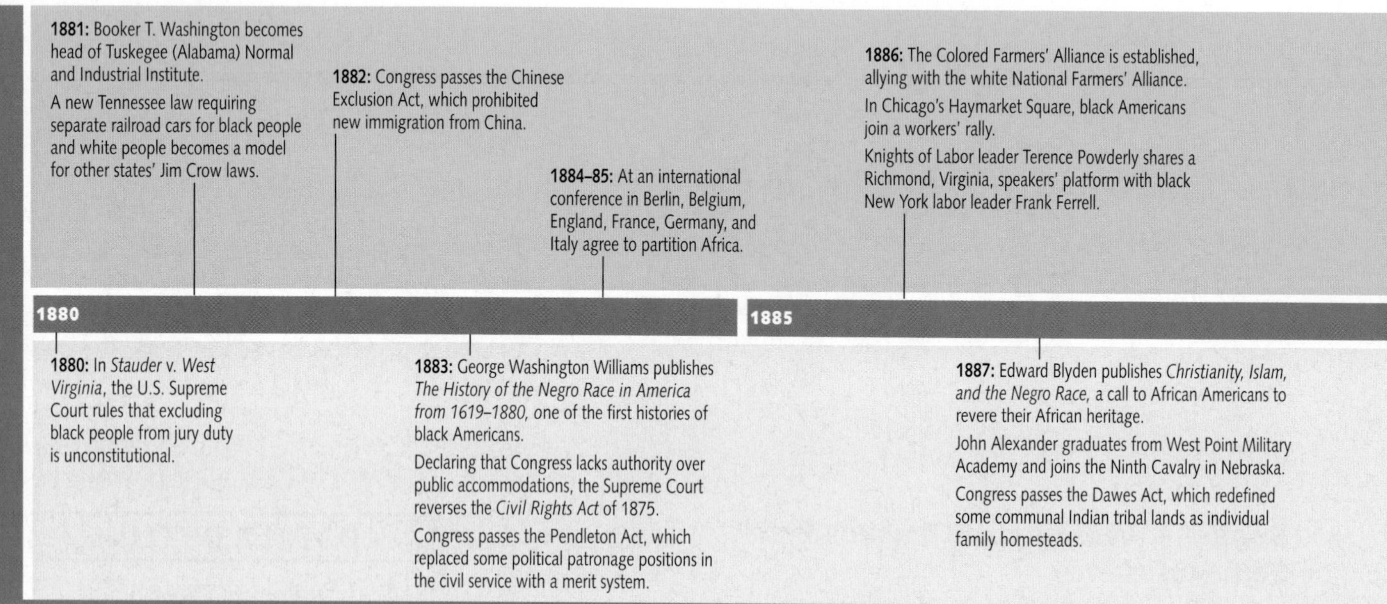

Washington discovered that his Indian students learned well. "I found that in the matter of learning trades and in mastering academic studies there was little difference between the coloured and Indian students." Watching the willingness of black students to assist the Indians taught Washington how educational programs might foster not only intellectual growth but also social responsibility. Years later, he wrote, "I have often wondered if there was a white institution . . . whose students would have welcomed . . . companions of another race in the cordial way that these black students at Hampton welcomed the red ones. How often I have wanted to say to white students that they lift themselves up in proportion as they help to lift others." Throughout his career, Washington frequently evoked images of lifting and climbing, of improving one's own life while helping others to succeed.

Washington expanded Armstrong's educational formula into a broad philosophy of black self-sufficiency that inspired many African Americans in their own rise from slavery. By 1881, with Armstrong's help Washington became head of Tuskegee Agricultural and Mechanical Institute, an Alabama school modeled after Hampton.

Washington used his own life story as an example of how the powerless could rise. His combination of perseverance, skill, and luck made his climb from poverty to power as remarkable as that of contemporary white industrialists like Andrew Carnegie and John D. Rockefeller. Such stories taught a simple but profound lesson: Acquiring a valued skill and working hard could lead to economic success. This lesson made practical sense to many black Americans.

During the harsh decades during and after Reconstruction, Booker T. Washington was an exception. Most black southerners did not gain a secure foothold in just one generation after slavery. Only about one in three African Americans had access to any schooling at all, and only one in a thousand could attend college. During the years Washington attended Hampton and established Tuskegee, millions of black southerners had no homes and suffered from hunger, illness, and humiliation. In 1877, when the federal government officially relinquished its military control over the South, the era known as Reconstruction ended. The South came back under the control of former slaveowners who continued to envision black people only as their servants. Most black southerners eked out an existence by farming someone else's land.

During the post-Reconstruction era, most white southerners sought to reinstate an economic system much like slavery—with laws and violence to back it up. In trying to build a "New South" of industry and factories, white and black Americans alike found it difficult to break away from the old farming economy.

Meanwhile, while white intellectuals developed pseudoscientific theories that white people were superior to dark-skinned peoples, African Americans sought educational

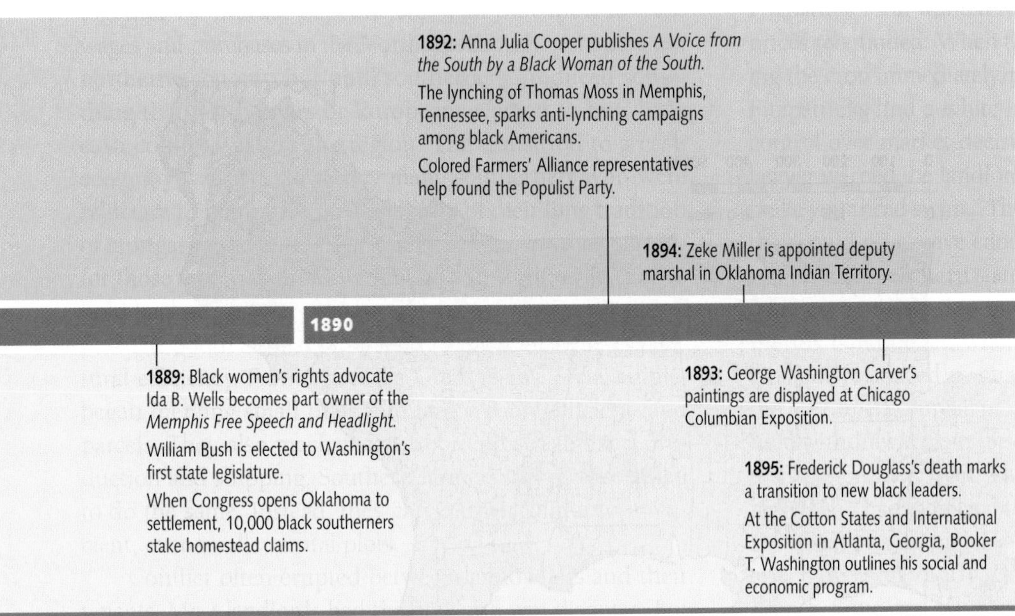

opportunities to convince the world they were morally and intellectually equal to white Americans. Education, therefore, became the centerpiece of African American strategies for progress. Many black leaders set out to train teachers or became educators themselves. Some African Americans sought social and economic opportunities in the nation's cities. A few fortunate ones received federal appointments in Washington, DC. Others settled in all-black towns to escape white domination. In an age of industrialization, some black people found allies in white workers who believed class unity was more important than racial disunity. Unions helped black workers garner a fair wage; farming alliances helped protect farmers from exploitation. Other black people again looked to the western frontier and Africa to make a new life and escape the growing violence of the late-nineteenth-century South.

REBUILDING THE SOUTH

"Many are sick and in bad condition generally," Mississippi planter Isaiah Montgomery wrote in 1879. He was describing workers who had run away because their farming contracts on Montgomery's land had trapped them in debt. Montgomery sympathized with his tenant farmers, but he himself was trapped by the same system and was in constant danger of losing his farm. He had to tighten his belt, as demand for southern cotton declined when Europeans found suppliers in other parts of the world. Isaiah Montgomery was one of the few black southerners who owned a large plantation, but his African American tenants fared no better than those who worked for white landowners. Although he dreamed of an independent black economy, Montgomery's plight and that of his workers typified the South's economic situation in the decades following the Civil War. Three-quarters of the nation's four million black citizens lived in southern states. Most farmed or sharecropped someone else's land. By 1880, a series of droughts and epidemics across the South further undermined an economy ravaged by war.

Montgomery's situation highlighted the desperation of many African Americans in their arduous rise from slavery. Even black southerners who managed to save money and obtain land found themselves in desperate straits. Many people with fewer resources sank into poverty. In ever-growing numbers, the families who worked Montgomery's land left him. Some headed for black settlements in Kansas; others simply drifted aimlessly. With each departure, Montgomery lost more of the means to make an income from his land. He also lost his investment in the seeds and provisions he had purchased for his workers, expecting to be repaid when crops were harvested.

Farm Labor and Poverty

In the post-Reconstruction era, many white and black farmers found themselves locked in a vicious cycle of poverty. Following the war's devastation of the plantation economy, three new forms of agriculture emerged. The most common arrangement for landless rural workers was *sharecropping*, whereby a landlord provided seed, housing, and tools in return for a share of the resulting crop. The constraints of sharecropping—the landowner retained control over when and how crops would be planted, tended, harvested, and sold—evoked bitter memories of slavery. It was viewed as a last resort by impoverished black farm workers.

Share tenancy was an option for farmers who had a little money to invest. Landlords provided the housing but tenants chose the crop, provided their own seed, and set their own schedule for harvesting and selling. This system

Jim Crow

Frustrated by the South's intransigence during Reconstruction, federal officials by the early 1880s felt less and less inclined to invest time, effort, and money in southern freedmen. The Supreme Court began vacillating between expanding the rights of black Americans and whittling them away. In 1875, the Court's civil rights rulings struck down state laws that discriminated against African Americans in public accommodations, but in 1883 the Court declared the 1875 Civil Rights Act unconstitutional, stating that while Congress might bar *states* from discriminating, it had no authority to prevent *individuals* or private entities from doing so. In *Stauder* v. *West Virginia* (1880), the Court flip-flopped again, concluding that the Constitution prohibited the exclusion of black Americans from juries.

But the tide was clearly turning against black freedom. In a series of 1883 cases, the Court ruled more broadly that Congress could not declare "by law that all persons shall have equal accommodations in all inns, public conveyances, and places of public amusement." In *Hall* v. *Cuir* (1887), it specifically decreed that states could legislate segregation on public transportation. Once the protection afforded by federal laws slipped away, the new category of state and local statutes known as *Jim Crow* took root, restricting African Americans' rights. Probably named for a minstrel character who mocked black people, Jim Crow laws helped institute racial segregation across the land.

In the early 1880s, Jim Crow policies became more formalized. In 1881, Tennessee passed a law requiring black and white people to ride in separate railroad cars. Other southern states quickly followed suit. Many rewrote their constitutions to mandate separate schools and to ban black patrons from white-run hotels, barbershops, restaurants, and theaters. However, it was years before most states systematically enforced the new laws. (South Carolina and Virginia did not pass Jim Crow laws until the early twentieth century.) Even after passage of such statutes, black and white people often attended church and other public events together—but the laws laid the legal foundation for racial separation and exclusion.

Such segregation of the races was rare in the old slave South. Black and white people had long lived together in close proximity. House slaves often slept in owners' bedrooms, and slaves frequently attended public celebrations with or without their masters. But now that all southerners were free citizens, Jim Crow laws required black Americans to defer to white people in public places. In bars and public eating places, where black and white workers had once shared leisure time, new laws required separate seating and strict rules governing how much alcohol and what kinds of food could be served to black patrons.

Jim Crow was not limited to the South. In response to the 1883 Supreme Court cases revoking African Americans' civil rights protections, more than a dozen northern states passed their own civil rights laws. However, these proved ineffectual and short-lived. By 1890, most northern states

■ Though the beach was segregated, this photograph by New Jersey black photographer John Mosely (a descendant of Underground Railroad organizer William Still) shows that black Americans followed the fad to Atlantic City. Carrying packed lunches because no public facility would serve them, they strolled along the boardwalk and admired the new buildings.

also had laws and customs segregating black people from white people.

The Rise of Booker T. Washington

As federal protection for black Americans waned in the 1880s, the old national black leadership faded as well. In the antebellum years, black leaders focused on one thing: ending slavery. Now the venerable Frederick Douglass, who reached his seventy-third year in 1890, was slowing down. When Sojourner Truth died in 1883, black communities lost their best-known women's suffrage lecturer. The deaths of Henry Highland Garnet and Martin Delany silenced the most persuasive voices advocating African colonization. With the end of slavery, black communities searched for new leaders who understood the plight of southern freed people.

By the mid-1880s, Booker T. Washington emerged as one such leader. After a year of teaching at Hampton, Washington joined Olivia Davidson in Tuskegee, Alabama, where she was helping organize a teachers' training school. Davidson reported that the state "agreed to aid in the purchase of a farm with a view to having an industrial school, where students can work to pay their expenses and at the same time pursue their studies."

■ Wishing to project an air of dignity and learnedness, Booker T. Washington always dressed formally and preferred to be photographed holding a book.

Drawing on the habits of hard work and perseverance developed at Hampton, Washington and Davidson, persuaded local white residents to support the school financially. The Tuskegee founders assured their supporters that education would turn ex-slaves into well-trained, cooperative workers who would accommodate the white-controlled society. Washington indicated that Tuskegee's black graduates would perform menial work and would not challenge the southern system of social segregation.

Under Washington's leadership, Tuskegee flourished. Using student labor, Washington renovated the building, beginning an enduring tradition of student involvement in maintaining and upgrading the school. By July 1881, Tuskegee opened with thirty students. Within three months, the school had outgrown its building. Washington married Davidson in 1885, and at the time of her death four years later, the school had more than 400 students. Over the next two decades, Tuskegee grew to over 2,000 acres, dozens of buildings, and a faculty of nearly 200. In the next century, it sent forth thousands of graduates who possessed agricultural, craft, or industrial skills as well as a strong work ethic and the commitment to inspire others to lift themselves out of poverty.

Washington shaped his understanding of southern poverty into a broad social philosophy. Even with black representatives in Congress, no African American leader had yet crafted a sweeping remedy for freed people's relief from the economic and social deprivation Washington personally witnessed daily. In his travels, he saw large families sharing one-room houses with dirt floors. Parents and children had little access to medical care. As under slavery, the cotton crop dominated their lives as they scraped together meager meals to consume while working the fields. With planters devoting their land to cash crops, fresh fruits and vegetables were scarce and malnutrition common. Even the typical diet of pork fat and cornbread, which offered only minimal nutrition, was often procured on credit. Washington worried that black politicians had not grasped the urgency of the situation.

Washington felt convinced that racial integration and the power of the franchise could come only after black people acquired work skills that made them indispensable to the southern economy and literacy levels that made them informed voters. In his view, frugality combined with mastery of skills such as carpentry, blacksmithing, bricklaying, housekeeping, and efficient farming techniques would enable black people to rise out of poverty.

But often the freed people Washington met were not ready for these next steps. Many seemed to view themselves

Blanche K. Bruce on American Indians

Booker T. Washington was not the only black leader who compared education for black people with that for Native Americans. In a statement before Congress in 1880, Mississippi Senator Blanche K. Bruce advocated using education and citizenship to "civilize" Indians. Bruce hinted that when education made all races alike, America's racial problems would disappear.

The Indian is human, and no matter what his traditions or his habits, if you will locate him, . . . and hold him in contact, with the forces of our civilization, his fresh, rugged nature will respond, in his civilization and development, will be the more permanent and enduring because his nature is so strong. . . . When you have no longer made it necessary for him to be a vagabond and a fugitive; when you have allowed him to see the lovable and attractive side of our civilization as well as the stern military phase; when you have made the law apply to him as it does to others, so that the ministers of the law shall not only be the executors of its penalties but the administrators of its saving, shielding, protecting provisions, he will become trustful and reliable . . . savage life will lose its attractions, and the hunter will become the herdsman.

. . . When rightful conceptions obtain in the treatment of the red race, the Indian question, with its cost, anxieties and wars, will disappear.

—from Congressional Record, *46th Congress, 2nd Session, Part 3, 2195–96 (1880).*

To view a longer version of this document, please go to *www.ablongman.com/carson/documents.*

eracy to children and adults. Still others were makeshift classrooms developed by local black communities.

Like Hampton and Tuskegee, many of these schools taught manual labor. Practical skills, teachers argued, would enable freed people to find jobs, protect themselves from exploitation, and build schools for the next generation. Booker T. Washington believed learning to make a living should take precedence over protest and agitation for social equality.

However, more and more black people insisted their schools include subjects like literature, art, and music. These disciplines would help them develop academic skills and demonstrate that black people were intellectually and morally able to be good citizens. Moreover, appreciation of liberal arts enabled black people to make a life, not just a living.

Among the best known of these academic schools was the AMA's Colored High School. Founded in the 1860s, the institution grew into Fisk College in Nashville, Tennessee. By the 1880s, it was turning out graduates who became lawyers, ministers, civil service workers, teachers, and college professors. But like many other schools—most of which did not survive—Fisk struggled financially during its first few years. The AMA planned to close it in 1871, but its music teacher organized students who "began to help our school by going Fridays and Saturdays to neighboring towns to give concerts."

One of those students was Ella Sheppard. A professor selected Sheppard to go "with his little band of singers to sing the money out of the hearts and pockets of the people." Sheppard recalled that initially slave songs "were never used in public, [because they] were associated with slavery and the dark past, and they were sacred to our parents, who used them in their religious worship." However, after "two or three slave songs were sung at the close of a concert," the group found that "the demand of the public changed this. Soon the land rang with our slave songs."

Traveling to England and Russia in 1871, the Fisk Jubilee Singers raised money to pull their school out of debt and take on new liberal arts faculty members. The Fisk Jubilee Singers inspired pride in black Americans and earned admiration from some white people.

The accomplishments and loyalty of Fisk's students and faculty inspired the founding of hundreds of similar schools elsewhere. Some offered an ambitious array of courses; others, little more than reading lessons. Virginia

State College, near Petersburg, began offering courses in liberal arts and agriculture in 1882—the first black college established under an 1862 congressional provision granting tracts of public land on which states could build agricultural schools. When the college opened with one hundred students and seven black faculty, Ohio lawyer John Mercer Langston served as its first president before winning election to Congress in 1888. In Greensboro, black and white congressmen sponsored another land-grant school, North Carolina Agricultural and Technical Institute, which accepted its first students in 1897. In Topeka, Kansas, black teacher E. H. White founded a night school in 1881 so that "mothers, fathers, young men and ladies whose opportunities . . . have not been such that they could acquire an education" could have a "regular program" of instruction.

Believing education prepared individuals for success, some white liberals supported schools for poor people, including Hampton and Tuskegee. In their view, these experiments might demonstrate whether education could help raise the prospects of the disadvantaged. Cynics accused congressmen and northern white philanthropists of supporting southern black schools only to ensure that black people remained trapped in menial jobs in the South. Indeed, many upper-class northern white people wanted to keep their distance from black people. Regardless of motivation, money from northerners was often matched by southern white donors eager for trained workers. These supporters envisioned a South whose factories competed with northern industries—processing cotton into textiles, producing finished goods from metal ore, and developing railroad networks to transport these goods to market. If black laborers could learn to do this work, perhaps the region could rise again. As long as state schools like Elizabeth City Institute in North Carolina and Delaware State College in Dover (both opened in 1891) focused their programs on workplace skills, the private donations poured in.

Some northern philanthropists, such as Andrew Carnegie and Julius Rosenwald, helped establish southern schools with an academic curriculum. Spelman College, a liberal arts school for black women, opened in Atlanta, Georgia, in 1881. Hartshorne College, a liberal arts school for women in Richmond, Virginia, soon followed. New northern schools included Philadelphia's Berean Institute, which began taking students in 1884.

Both manual-skills and academic schools fostered personal and black pride. Faculty encouraged students to excel, reminding them their successes brought honor to the entire race. As the school song of the M Street High School in Washington, DC, expressed it, black schools aimed to "strengthen and hearten and quicken with life / minds fettered by darkness, hearts deadened by strife." Despite the black pride instilled by both types of schools, Booker T. Washington insisted that practical training should form the core of freedmen's education. He worried that liberal arts students at schools like Howard University and Washington, DC's M Street High School "knew more about Latin and Greek when they left school, but they seemed to know less about life and its conditions as they would meet it in their homes." The education of liberal arts graduates, he declared, would make them too self-centered to perform community service. In Washington's view, education was less about academic subjects than about the development of self-esteem, the improvement of home life and health, and dedication to community progress. With lessons in hygiene, nutrition, and home economics along with integrity, self-discipline, and long-range planning, Tuskegee turned out healthy, industrious, thrifty, and well-mannered graduates. Equally important, Washington pointed out, these young men and women dedicated themselves to improving economic and social conditions for *all* African Americans—not just themselves.

Segregated or Integrated Schools?

"The subject of race pride is to my mind one of the most important and worthy to be considered at this time," black Boston lawyer Edward Everett Brown told an audience in 1888. Brown compared African Americans with German, Hungarian, and Irish immigrants, among others. "Why should any man of African descent be ashamed of his race?" he asked. "In every department of industry in its higher scientific branches, the Negro is proving . . . beyond any question that he is the equal and in many cases the superior of his Anglo-Saxon brother." Other African Americans also used racial pride as a defense against Social Darwinism and eugenics. But black educators pondered how best to develop their students' minds and confidence. Would students fare best competing in integrated schools or in all-black institutions?

> "Why should any man of African descent be ashamed of his race?"
> —*Edward Everett Brown*

Advocates of integrated schools insisted the only way for black citizens to gain access to the resources of mainstream

Alexander Crummell Pleads for Black Women of the South

Alexander Crummell (1819–1898) spent more than four decades promoting the American Colonization Society. He believed African women, especially those who had adopted Christianity, were superior to black American women in "sweetness, gentleness, and maternal solicitudes." A northern, free-born graduate of England's Oxford University, Crummell had firm notions of how women should behave. In the 1888 essay excerpted below, Crummell outlined what he saw as the "neglects and needs" of former slaves.

The lot of the black *man* on the plantation has been desolate enough; but the fate of the black woman has been awful!

In her girlhood all the delicate tendencies of her sex have been rudely outraged. In the field, in the rude cabin, in the factory, she was thrown into the companionship of coarse and ignorant men. . . . All the virtues of her sex were utterly ignored. . . .

I ask for the equipment and the mission of "sisterhood" to the black women of the South. I wish to see large numbers of practical Christian women, women of intelligence and piety, . . . well-trained in domestic economy; women who combined delicate sensibility and refinement with industrial acquaintance . . . to go South; . . . to visit Uncle Tom's Cabin; to sit down with "Aunt Chloe" and her daughters; to show and teach them the ways and habits of thrift, economy, neatness and order . . . and by both lectures and talks guide these women and their daughters into the modes and habits of clean and orderly housekeeping.

. . . The effect must be made immediately, in *this* generation . . . and it is to be done at their own homes, in their own huts.

—*from* The Black Woman of the South: Her Neglects and Needs *(Washington, DC, 1883).*

To view a longer version of this document, please go to *www.ablongman.com/carson/documents*.

America was to learn the ways of white society. These supporters believed prejudice would evaporate if people from different races got to know each other, as Washington had experienced with his Indian students at Hampton. They also felt that by competing with white students while young, African Americans would not be intimidated by white people as adults. Well-off black families sent their children to integrated, white-operated schools and colleges, such as New England boarding schools, Oberlin College in Ohio, Harvard and Amherst in Massachusetts, Wesleyan College in Connecticut, and the University of Pennsylvania.

Other educators advocated all-black schools. Philadelphian Jacob C. White, principal of Roberts Vaux Consolidated School, believed that by "educating ourselves, by and through ourselves," African Americans would acquire the confidence and independence of mind to resist racial injustice. Dedicated black teachers would serve as role models for black youth. Educated in the Quaker-sponsored Institute for Colored Youth, White himself had both black and white teachers. He mastered Latin and mathematics, literature and pedagogy, and chess and baseball. Like Booker T. Washington, he promoted industrial education and attention to cleanliness and integrity. Yet White also advocated liberal arts training.

Some African Americans believed black schools offered a higher-quality education than their white counterparts. In particular, they appreciated educational institutions that taught black students about their own heritage and instilled personal pride, self-confidence, and commitment to uplift the race. For example, many elite upwardly mobile black families moved to Washington, DC, to take advantage of the black public schools there, especially the M Street High School. Some wealthy African American parents took advantage of exclusive black boarding schools such as the Allen Normal (teacher training) Institute in Thomasville, Georgia. Allen Normal prepared students to become gracious and sophisticated members of American society when segregation ended.

The debate over the merits of separate and integrated schools soon became moot. By century's end, Jim Crow laws brought segregated schools and neighborhoods to both the

North and the South. A few urban public schools in Boston, New York, Chicago, and New Orleans remained integrated, but this too would change in the early decades of the twentieth century.

TABLE 12.2 Black Americans Move to the Cities, 1880–1900

In the last two decades of the nineteenth century, the black population mushroomed in many northern, southern, and western cities.

	Number and Percentage of Total Pop., 1880		*Number and Percentage of Total Pop., 1900*	
Washington, DC	48,300	33	86,000	28
Baltimore	53,716	16	79,000	15
New Orleans	57,600	27	77,000	26
Philadelphia	32,700	4.5	63,000	5
New York [Manhattan]	19,600	0.1	60,000	3.2
Atlanta	16,000	43	35,000	33
Charleston	27,300	57	31,000	56
Chicago	6,480	1	30,000	2
Boston	5,873	.01	11,590	2
Los Angeles	102	1	6,000	2
Denver	1,046	0.3	5,000	2
Topeka	3,648	23	4,807	14
Detroit	2,821	2	4,000	1
Seattle	19	0.6	2,000	1

Education and Gender Identity

Believing education should shape pride in one's gender as well as one's race, numerous black women set out to prove themselves to black men as well as to white America. Many drew inspiration from Howard University Law school graduate Charlotte Ray, who passed the Washington, DC, bar in the 1870s and became the nation's first black woman lawyer. Mary Ann Shadd Cary completed Howard's law program in 1883 at the age of sixty. In the same year, Lucy Moten became the first woman to head Washington's Miner Normal School. During her two decades at Miner Normal, she encouraged young teachers to embrace a mission of expanding minds rather than simply training workers.

Studying at Fisk and then at Harvard during the 1880s and 1890s, young scholar W. E. B. Du Bois also connected education to gender identity. Du Bois concluded that only a liberal arts curriculum could shape young African American boys into men. The importance of manhood surfaced many times in the rhetoric of black Americans. Whether it involved the franchise, owning land, earning a good wage, or protecting black women from exploitation, manhood increasingly gained importance among African Americans as a primary goal of racial justice and black education.

THE LURE OF CITIES

In the post-Reconstruction era, many black Americans turned to cities for new opportunities. Edward Booker, for example, established a gambling operation in Detroit. He enjoyed the dynamism and excitement of urban life, and he profited from the temptations it offered. Starting out as a saloonkeeper, Booker used his earnings to buy a building in which he hosted gambling and prostitution. Then he expanded his operation by purchasing a racehorse, a gaming rooster, and a fighting tomcat. By 1887, he was earning $30,000 a year in a time when the average black man might earn less than $100 per year. But Booker died penniless, a victim of debt and his own passion for gambling. His story illustrates both the economic possibilities and pitfalls of urban life.

Urban Community Life

African Americans constituted less than 10 percent of northern urbanites during the 1880s, yet those who ventured to northern cities found considerable economic and social opportunities. When enough black people settled near each other, they developed viable black businesses. Earning cash wages, black city-dwellers also began using banks. In 1888, Maggie Lena Walker responded to this new development by opening the nation's first black bank in Richmond, Virginia.

During the 1880s, black communities thrived in cities along the waterways that once had served the Underground Railroad. Before the Civil War, old river cities such as New Orleans, Cincinnati, Chicago, Detroit, and Pittsburgh, and newer towns like Topeka and Denver, had offered work opportunities to southern black migrants. Now towns along the newly built railroads offered employment as well. Many black people found jobs loading freight cars and ships, repairing wharves and railbeds, and serving as cooks, stewards, and porters on boats and train cars. After railroad baron George Pullman was embarrassed by newspaper coverage of the Fisk Jubilee Singers' experience with racial discrimination on his trains in 1869, he pledged to integrate Pullman cars (sleeping cars on trains) and guarantee work for black porters. At eastern railroad hubs like New York, Philadelphia, and Baltimore, black people found plentiful service and domestic jobs.

Urban work also allowed for leisure time. Domestic workers got days off to use as they chose. And when white employers left the cities during the summer, black laundresses, theater doormen, and caterers visited friends or relatives in the South or took summer jobs at resorts in Saratoga, New York, and Newport, Rhode Island. These opportunities enabled them to combine a change of scene with seasonal service work in hotels.

Urban life enabled black churches to flourish. Community members gathered to worship and to celebrate weddings, holidays, and other special events. Black churches also served as venues in which to discuss politics and raise money for charities. They hosted picnics, dances, and the offices of burial insurance and savings and loan institutions. Through churches, black urbanites learned about upcoming concerts, debates, lectures, and professional black baseball games. In these ways, places of worship nurtured both religious and secular life. Leadership in church activities also prepared many men and women for leadership in business, politics, and the arts.

The influx of black newcomers made many urban communities highly stratified. Philadelphia's black society, for example, had distinct layers. The several hundred black families who had settled in the city before the Civil War often enjoyed social privileges that separated them from more recent arrivals. Black politician Gilbert Ball owned a comfortable house in an integrated neighborhood. But the majority of black newcomers had few financial resources. They crowded into mostly black neighborhoods characterized by high crime, dirty streets, polluted water, and high rates of illness and mortality—a situation that foreshadowed the all-black ghettoes soon to come. In 1880, the majority of Philadelphia's 32,700 black residents (an increase from 22,100 a decade before) could not read. They lived from hand to mouth, relying on churches or other social agencies to help them find housing, employment, and access to reading and food programs.

Newer cities such as Topeka, Kansas, were also divided by class. Between 1865 and 1880, migrants from border states and the Lower South more than tripled Topeka's black population. When the Exodusters poured into Kansas during the early 1880s (see Chapter 11), Topeka's population grew to almost one-quarter black. Black Topekans established their own stores, churches, schools, recreation clubs, and newspapers, even though more than two-thirds of black men and one-third of black women worked in unskilled occupations. The city's First African Baptist Church welcomed the poor, while the Second Baptist Church was home to most middle-class black Topekans. Many southerners who had come to Kansas hoping for a plot of land to farm had found instead only urban unemployment and racial hostility. When Sojourner Truth visited Kansas in 1879 and saw widespread poverty, she was so distressed that she traveled through other urban black communities to raise money for relief.

Those fortunate enough to find employment often gained middle-class status through the practical occupations espoused by Booker T. Washington. Henry Clay Wilson was one such person. Starting out as a housepainter in Topeka, Kansas, Wilson saved his money and soon owned a fifteen-chair barbershop. His business served white customers primarily, and the profits enabled him to purchase a controlling interest in a nearby recreation park where black churches held their outings. Wilson was part of a small social circle that included Topeka's black real-estate agent, doctor, lawyer, restaurant owners, and newspaper publisher. More than two-thirds of these black leaders could read, a proportion twice as high as in the general black population. Their experience helped confirm African Americans' conviction that education was the way out of poverty.

Despite a legacy of Reconstruction race riots, black Memphis was thriving by the 1890s, thanks to the leadership of black saloon-owner Robert Reed Church. The son of a black woman and a white riverboat captain, Church learned the liquor business while working on his father's steamship. When yellow fever swept through the region in 1878, the epidemic precipitated a mass exodus from Memphis. Church remained in the city, buying up vacated property. Over the next twelve years, Memphis grew from a town of 20,000, of whom two-thirds were black, to a sprawling city of 100,000, of whom half were African American. With financial help from Robert Reed Church, Memphis residents installed sewers, which reduced the incidence of disease.

Federal Appointments

On February 27, 1885, Laura Hamilton Murray "went down to Washington on ten Oclock train, [and] saw President [Grover Cleveland] going to Capitol to take [his] oath." Cleveland was the first Democratic president elected since the Civil War. Like many other black Americans, Murray felt apprehensive about the Republican Party's loss of power. "Well we are now living under a new administration," Murray wrote in her diary. "How it will terminate who can tell."

Since Reconstruction, Washington, DC, had attracted many black men and women with its abundance of federal jobs. The capital city became even more of a magnet in 1883, when Congress passed the Pendleton Act. Prompted by a public outcry against favoritism in federal appointments, the act

Henry Ossawa Tanner, son of a middle-class black Philadelphia minister, studied art with white painter Thomas Eakins. In a career spanning four decades, Tanner painted classical religious works as well as scenes that celebrated—and romanticized—African Americans. In this 4-foot-tall painting, *The Banjo Lesson* (1893),Tanner used the meagerness of black possessions to dignify African Americans' music, domestic tidiness, family tenderness, and the transmission of cultural wealth from older generations to the young.

established a merit-based civil service open to black and white applicants alike. Murray's husband, a native of Ohio, was one of hundreds of black people from across the country who passed the civil service exam. Landing a clerkship in the War Department, he moved with his family to Washington. There, Laura Murray kept her eye on Washington politics. The federal government, she reminded herself, had initiated constitutional amendments protecting black people's access to jobs, education, and the possibility of acquiring land. Thus only federal authority could prevent local leaders in the North and South from rescinding black Americans' right to vote or block their access to the courts.

Under President James Garfield, black men obtained numerous federal appointments: Henry Highland Garnet became minister to Liberia; Frederick Douglass, District of Columbia Recorder of Deeds; Blanche K. Bruce, Registrar of the Treasury; and John Mercer Langston, minister to Haiti. Former congressman Robert Brown Elliott worked in the Treasury Department. Even though the number of African Americans in Congress steadily declined after 1876, these federal positions continued to be open to African Americans for decades to come.

Black Towns

As discussed in Chapter 8, black and white Americans alike had established utopian settlements designed to cure society's ills. One such town was New Philadelphia, an isolated agricultural village peopled by black fugitives. Frank McWhorter, a former slave who bought his own and his family's freedom, was the organizer of this town. He moved with a few dozen other former bondspeople to a location in Illinois, across the Mississippi River from St. Louis.

After the Civil War, black towns could survive only if their residents had access to a rail connection and a nearby industry where there was work. The most successful post–Civil War black towns, then, became black suburbs, such as Brooklyn, Illinois, which lay a few miles from New Philadelphia. Home to black railroad employees and workers in nearby coal mines and the sprawling St. Louis National Stock Yards, Brooklyn offered a haven from white intrusion.

Stimulated by the emergence of enough free black people to settle and sustain them, black towns flourished after the Civil War, often with the cooperation of white capital-

Long accustomed to handling livestock, black trainers and riders worked alongside white stable workers as Kentucky became a center for horse breeding and racing. In 1875, at the first running of the Kentucky Derby, black jockey Oliver Lewis bested fourteen competitors—thirteen of whom were African American. During the next sixteen years, black jockeys rode in every Derby, winning six times.

ists and black leaders. Mound Bayou, Mississippi, was one such town. Established in 1888, the town was led by Isaiah Montgomery, the black farmer who lost his plantation but not his vision of an independent black economy. When the owners of the Louisville, New Orleans, and Texas Railroad sought to create a rail hub, Montgomery served as liaison between black settlers and white investors. He noticed the railroad hub lay at the convergence of two Mississippi River bayous and several Indian burial mounds. Thus he named the hub Mound Bayou. A modest down payment and a five-year mortgage was all a family needed to move in. Within a decade, Montgomery had sold 15,000 acres in the town and its surrounding area to almost 2,000 black settlers. As the new residents cleared land to build their homes, Montgomery helped them turn the excess timber into railroad ties and other salable wood products.

Booker T. Washington praised Mound Bayou as a model of black enterprise and leadership, and he raised financial support for its continued development. The town thrived for several years after Montgomery's death in 1934, despite a foundering cotton market and the subsequent demise of the railroad.

Though most of the nation's three dozen black towns lay within 500 miles of Mound Bayou, a few were scattered through New Jersey, Florida, Oklahoma, Kansas, Illinois, Colorado, Iowa, California, Tennessee, Texas, and Virginia. Founded on dreams of rural life and values, most of these towns could not keep pace with industrializing America. Small local stores could not compete with the rise of large mail-order houses like Sears & Roebuck and Montgomery Ward, which offered much more variety and often delivered purchases by mail for less than they cost locally. By 1930, when automobiles began to make the rail junction irrelevant, many black towns were abandoned or absorbed into other municipalities.

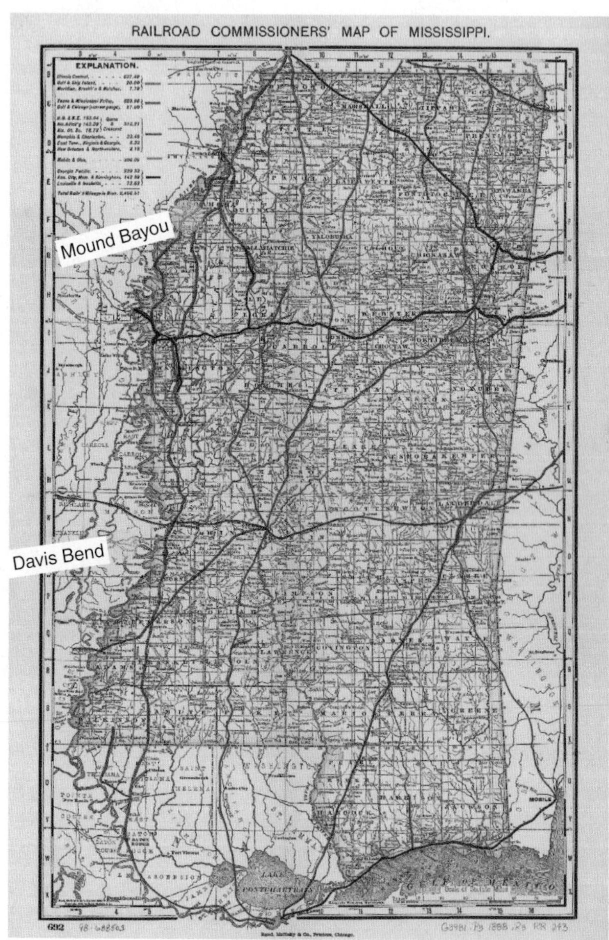

MAP 12.2 Isaiah Montgomery's Mississippi

This 1895 map of Mississippi shows Mound Bayou's location along railroad routes that bisect the northwest corner of the state. Hurricane Plantation, at Davis Bend, lies more than 100 miles to the south, just below Vicksburg. By the end of the twentieth century, Mississippi's major transportation routes had changed little. Vast sections of the state still had only secondary roads.

THE ECONOMICS AND POLITICS OF UNITY

"One of the objects of [the Knights of Labor] is the abolition of distinctions that are maintained by class, creed, color, or nationality," proclaimed New York African American labor leader Frank Ferrell to an audience in Richmond, Virginia, in 1886. In the last decades of the century, the New South began industrializing as northern investors saw the potential in southern natural and human resources. Unions like the Knights of Labor, which sought to unite black and white workers, helped usher in this new era. Northern white workers had engaged in organized strikes since at least the 1830s, but black people helped lead labor organizing in the post-Reconstruction South. In 1881, for example, a group of black laundry women in Atlanta initiated a successful strike for higher wages.

Established in 1869, the Knights of Labor was the first lasting national union. This union promoted the idea that all laborers, shopkeepers, and farmers had a common interest in replacing capitalism with a system in which workers owned the means of production. Its members wanted to see sweeping reforms enacted for banking and tax systems and advocated the outlawing of child labor. By the mid-1880s, the Knights of Labor had drawn thousands of southern workers to its membership.

In most industries, black men and women worked alongside their white counterparts in menial jobs. Ferrell, a New York post office worker and skilled machinist, hoped to help all these workers see that their class as laborers had far more importance than their racial differences.

Many southern black people who could break free of farm work headed for the cities to find industrial jobs. With 200,000 people, New Orleans remained the South's only big city for several decades. But growth in other southern urban centers also gave African Americans access to semiskilled and service jobs that mostly did not fall under union influence: dock and rail-yard work, food and domestic service, and work as well-diggers and sewer-line builders.

Unions

Like Frank Ferrell, southern white workers began to realize that class unity mattered more than racial disunity. As modern capitalism seemed to force workers into longer days and shrinking wages, tensions between laborers and captains of industry sometimes cut across racial lines even where Jim Crow laws worked to keep the races separate. Around the country, labor unions sprang up to unify industrial wage earners who worked long hours under dangerous conditions for low pay. Sometimes, as in the Chicago and Omaha stockyards that housed farm animals awaiting shipment, the interests of farmers and laborers merged into political coalitions.

By 1886, the Knights of Labor had 700,000 members nationwide, 60,000 of whom were black. Many state chapters, such as Virginia's, met in segregated units. Learning that Richmond hotels would not accommodate their union's black members at the national conference, the New York Local 49ers of which Ferrell was a member, protested by housing themselves in their own tents. The New Yorkers brought black members to a segregated theater and opened the convention's picnic to local black residents. They also insisted their white president, railroad machinist Terence Powderly, support their protest by sharing the podium with Frank Ferrell. But Powderly felt ambivalent about the black members. Though he did share the stage, he hastened to assure the public he did not advocate equality between the races. On southern speaking tours, Powderly usually addressed black members in segregated meetings. Nonetheless, most black workers stuck with the union, hoping bargaining power would come with membership. After the Richmond convention, African American membership in the Knights of Labor increased.

Across the nation, union locals followed the New York example, treating their black peers as allies in the economic struggle, and promoting new black leaders. Among them was Lucy Parsons, a light-skinned African American with Mexican American and Native American ancestors. Parsons was an anarchist—that is, a person who aimed to overthrow a government that was unresponsive to workers' needs. There were enough disgruntled laborers in 1880s America that her speeches found ready ears. In Texas, Lucy married Albert Parsons, a white former Confederate Army scout who became the outspoken pro-black Republican editor of the Waco *Spectator*. After Albert Parsons was shot in the leg and threatened with lynching for promoting black equality and mixed-race marriages, the couple fled Texas.

In the 1870s, the Parsons settled in Chicago, where they edited the radical labor newspaper *The Alarm,* published by the Knights of Labor. They also helped organize Chicago's participation in a nationwide workers' strike on May 1, 1886 in support of the eight-hour workday. During the strike, confrontations among strikers, strikebreakers, and police left several people dead and others wounded. Tensions rose when workers initiated a mass protest against police brutality three days later in Haymarket Square.

The so-called Haymarket Riot unleashed bloody mayhem. A dynamite explosion and the death of seven policemen led to murder convictions for protest organizers, among them Albert Parsons. He went to prison, and his wife

Timothy Thomas Fortune's View of Labor

Timothy Thomas Fortune, the son of Florida politician Emanuel Fortune, worked as a New York newspaper editor through the 1880s and 1890s. In April 1886 he spoke before the Brooklyn, New York, Literary Union, a union of printers. Known as "T. Thomas" Fortune, he was strongly influenced by the revolutionary ideas of German political philosopher Karl Marx and American political economist Henry George. Both these thinkers contended that capitalism always benefited owners at the expense of laborers. Fortune believed black and white workers had to unite to defeat the capitalist powers oppressing both races.

I do not exaggerate the gravity of the subject [labor relations] when I say that . . . the wall of industrial discontent encircles the civilized globe.

Organized society, as it obtains today, based as it is upon feudal conditions. . . .

. . . [T]he inspiration of all conflict has been that of capitalist, landowner and hereditary aristocracy against the . . . disinherited proletariat of the world. . . .

Capital, in the first instance, is the product of labor. . . . [D]estroy the brawn and muscle of the world and it could not be reproduced by all the gold ever delved from the mines of California . . . and the fabulous gems from the diamond fields of Africa. In short, labor . . . is the producing agency, while capital has been and is the absorbing or parasitical agency. . . .

. . . I believe in the divine right of man, not of caste or class.

—*from* New York Freeman, *May 1, 1886.*

To view a longer version of this document, please go to *www.ablongman.com/carson/documents.*

continued to organize workers while raising funds to appeal his case. Before a Kansas City audience in December 1886, Lucy Parsons called for the federal government to intervene on behalf of those she called "the unemployed, disinherited and miserable." Though Albert Parsons was executed in November 1887, Lucy Parsons remained committed to their cause. For the next fifty years she edited labor newspapers, demonstrated for the unemployed and homeless, and raised money for "a common humanity, the same red blood whether that of African or Caucasian." Many black organizers criticized Parsons' approach, urging her to place more emphasis on racial issues than on class concerns. But she persisted in agitating on behalf of the dispossessed regardless of race or background. In her fiery speeches, she equated race discrimination with class discrimination. At the 1905 founding convention of the Industrial Workers of the World (IWW), an international and colorblind union, Parsons was the only female speaker.

T. Thomas Fortune, black editor of the *New York Age,* spoke for many African Americans when he praised labor unions for uniting the races in pursuit of economic justice, but in the wake of the Chicago violence, union loyalties fell apart. Many Knights of Labor members who disliked direct confrontation and strikes dissociated themselves from the union and Terence Powderly. The American Federation of Labor (AFL) soon eclipsed the Knights of Labor. This new union also courted black members. Led by New York cigar maker Samuel Gompers, the AFL united those workers who still believed strikes and boycotts could force employers to provide better hours, wages, and workplace conditions.

Interracial Alliances and Populism

Urban labor union action was mirrored by farmers who established alliances or cooperatives. As farmers sought to protect themselves against economic exploitation, they created cooperative ventures that could bypass—or stand up to—overcharging suppliers and high-priced shipping. Established in Texas in 1886, the Colored Farmers' National Alliance and Cooperative Union represented thousands of black farmers in a dozen states. The Alliance negotiated lower rates from suppliers and shippers. Soon members of the white National Farmers' Alliance made overtures to their black peers. As with the Knights of Labor, white farmer unions did not favor full

Lucy Parsons, whose revolutionary rhetoric included racial, class, and gender issues, refused to be hemmed in by black leaders who felt she should focus on race only.

racial equality. But allying with black farmers enabled both groups to negotiate favorable transportation and marketing agreements and bulk purchase prices. These deals proved especially valuable when the cost of supplies to bale cotton suddenly shot up. Members of white farmers' alliances understood that by including black cotton growers in their sales agreements, they could prevent black farmers from undercutting wholesale cotton prices by selling their cotton at lower prices.

These new class loyalties had profound political implications. United in their resentment of landowners, black and white sharecroppers in North Carolina teamed up with local Knights of Labor units to elect black and white state legislators who pledged to protect small farmers. This same coalition sent a black congressman to Washington to champion workers' rights. These efforts gave rise to the populist movement, in which black and white activists worked for federal protection of farmers and workers.

Populism spread throughout the rural South. In 1890, Georgia fruit growers supported the populists in the fight against railroad monopolies. Furious at the railroads' sudden hike in freight prices, they helped elect white lawyer Tom Watson to Congress. Watson, in turn, lobbied for legislation to restrain railroad monopolies. He shook the halls of Congress with his radical oratory: "Every laborer [should] understand that the cause of labor is the same everywhere; . . . every farmer, white and black [should] understand that the cause of the farmer is the same; . . . every producer, white and black, [should] understand that the cause of the producer is the same; and thus [they should] march shoulder to shoulder to the redress of grievances, demanding laws [to] . . . insure justice to all." In Texas, Florida, South Carolina, and Virginia, poor black and white people also joined forces against high freight costs. By February 1892, Tom Watson's prophecy was realized. Representatives from the integrated Knights of Labor, the Colored Farmers' Alliance, and the Dakota Alliance joined to form the Populist Party. The new organization included not only farmers but also women's suffrage advocates and urban reformers with radical ideas for redistributing wealth and restricting the power of corporations and railroads. The Populists chose James Beard Weaver from Iowa as their 1892 presidential candidate. Rural midwestern support for populism ran strong, and Weaver won more than 1 million popular votes, which secured him twenty-two electoral votes. But on Election Day, many white southerners gave their support to the Democratic Party, fearing that splitting the white vote might endanger white dominance in the South.

Thus, the populist tide turned almost as soon as it crested. That same November, Tom Watson was voted out of Congress. By the following spring, the economy deteriorated as rail companies went bankrupt, banks failed, 15,000 businesses closed, and agricultural prices plummeted. During the severe depression that soon hit, many white workers began seeing black people as competitors, not allies. Watson retracted his pro-black rhetoric, and many other populists accepted the southern argument that even a poor white person was racially superior to any black person. In northern cities, populists refused to join unions that had African American members. AFL leaders gradually withdrew their commitment to black laborers—first by forming separate local organizations and then by sponsoring completely segregated black unions. Indeed, this 1890s pattern of retreat from interracial unionism had begun even before the 1892 elections. In San Francisco, where in 1883 the Pacific Coast Cooks and Waiters Union had tried unsuccessfully to ban black waiters, the support of the all-white bakers' union helped drive black waiters out of the workforce five years later.

After endorsing Democratic candidate William Jennings Bryan in 1896, the Populist Party faded away. Local pockets of populists lingered for decades, yet most white organizers had all but forgotten that they had briefly envisioned racial cooperation.

the army or railroad gangs. After the war, some black Americans stayed on as soldiers and homesteaders in the West.

Beginning in the late 1860s, the federal government formed new military units to fight Indian wars and serve as local police. The Ninth and Tenth cavalries, created in 1867, merged with the Twenty-fourth and Twenty-fifth infantries in 1869. Over the next half-century, 20,000 black soldiers made western military bases their home, staffing more than a dozen army posts in Texas, Nebraska, Iowa, Montana, California, and the New Mexico Territory. These troops included both northern and southern recruits as well as seasoned Civil War soldiers who had never been discharged. Following military service, some veterans helped lay track or build roadbeds. Thus, military installations and railroad stops sometimes became the seeds of nascent black communities.

Military life brought adventure and steady pay, but in some respects it resembled slavery. Black soldiers often found themselves in service roles: cooking, building camps, or hauling supplies and water for white soldiers. Sometimes the Native Americans against whom they fought jeered at them, calling for the black soldiers to join forces against white men.

Despite hardships and discrimination, soldiers like Thomas Boyne, Henry Johnson, and John Alexander made a career of the army. A member of the Ninth Cavalry's Troop C, Boyne in 1882 received a Congressional Medal of Honor for bravery in New Mexico's Indian wars. Johnson earned the rank of sergeant in the Tenth Cavalry's F Troop and served in several other units. Owing to his ready temper, Johnson lost and then re-earned his stripes several times during his thirty-one-year military career. But he received a Medal of Honor for his part in the campaign against the Ute Indians on Colorado's Milk River in 1879. The Ninth Cavalry was also home to Alexander, West Point's second black graduate. Arriving in Nebraska in 1887, Alexander was promoted to first lieutenant in 1893—one of only a handful of black officers. His experience, unique among his peers, nevertheless inspired other black men to pursue a military life.

Opportunities to work with livestock or to help build frontier towns drew other black people west. White ranchers in Texas, Montana, Wyoming, and Colorado, desperate for help driving cattle to the Kansas stockyards, recruited an estimated 8,000 black, Indian, Mexican, and mixed-race

Frederic Remington, a white painter from New York, sought to capture the romance of the West in his art. He "saw the living, breathing end of three American centuries of smoke and dust and sweat." Remington included many Indians and African Americans among his 2,000 depictions. In this work, he dramatized the military action of the Ninth Cavalry in the 1870s. These black soldiers were sent to risk their lives protecting white miners near Colorado's Milk River. The miners had broken federal laws by trespassing on Ute Indian lands, provoking an attack by the Utes.

Source: Frederic Remington, Capt. Dodge's Colored Troops to the Rescue, ca. 1890, Courtesy The Flint Institute of Arts, Mrs. Charles S. Mott Collection.

cowboys. These newcomers, who made up about one-quarter of all cowboys, sometimes became ranchers in their own right. In isolated western towns, black men also found work in laundries, post offices, freight concessions, and blacksmith shops, while women (often single, widowed, or abandoned) worked as midwives, laundresses, shopkeepers, or prostitutes.

Western towns also offered work in mining. Helena, Montana, had a small band of black gold miners. African Americans were particularly welcomed in the mining town of Buxton, Iowa. A group of Quakers had founded Buxton as a multi-ethnic model community with substantial homes instead of the makeshift shacks often found in mining towns. The town also had churches of several denominations for both black and white residents. Work in gold, coal, copper, lead, and silver mines was backbreaking, dirty, dangerous, and confining, but for many miners, the pay made it worthwhile.

Oklahoma Territory presented opportunities to acquire land and set up businesses and homesteads. With the Dawes Act of 1887, Congress reassigned Indian communal lands to individual families. Creek and Chickasaw lands previously protected by the federal government became fair game for homesteaders. Ten thousand African American settlers joined the land rush. Civil War veteran David Franklin and his family, for example, established a prosperous ranch near the Washita River. The Franklin family sent their seven children to college. One son, Buck Colbert Franklin, became a lawyer who fought Jim Crow laws and lived to see his own son, John Hope Franklin, become a world-renowned historian.

During these same years, a young black man named George Washington Carver traveled the Midwest. Hearing of the new all-black towns, Carver left his Missouri birthplace and hitched a ride to Kansas. After witnessing the lynching of a black man accused of raping a white girl, he decided to move on. He settled in Minneapolis, where he opened a laundry, bought land, and taught himself to read, hoping to go to college. But in 1885, white admissions officers turned him away from a Presbyterian college in Kansas because of his race.

Carver eventually gained admission to a white agricultural college in Iowa, where he studied chemistry and botany. When Booker T. Washington persuaded Carver to join Tuskegee in 1895, Carver became Tuskegee's only faculty member with an advanced degree from a white institution. Tuskegee now had an accomplished scientist to enhance the school's rising reputation. It also had an able artist: Carver's paintings had been displayed at the Chicago Columbian Exposition in 1893.

After an odyssey typical of black men in his generation, Carver made Tuskegee his home. For more than four decades, he trained black scientists and carried on agricultural research, proposing solutions to the South's problems of boll weevil infestation, tobacco diseases, and overworked soil. His work with peanuts, which gained him wide recognition from white agriculturalists, inspired many black men to study science.

Antidiscrimination laws also drew black people west. Admitted to the Union in 1889, the new state of Washington protected interracial marriage and integrated schools. Of the few hundred African Americans who lived there in 1890, most clustered in Seattle. There they worked in hotels, restaurants, and shipyards while building a close-knit community with their own AME church. The state's franchise laws gave black women the vote and permitted them to serve on juries. Thanks to the vigorous advocacy of the Knights of Labor, black Washingtonians faced less discrimination on the job than did workers in other states.

Seattle had a few black leaders who built community institutions. William Bush made substantial financial contributions to build the region's roads and bridges. In 1889, he won election to Washington's first legislature. Horace Cayton, a former Mississippi slave, established the *Seattle Republican,* which promoted black rights and Republican loyalty.

Rethinking Africa

During the 1880s, a few black Americans looked once more toward Africa as a new home. Black scholar George Washington Williams poured years of research into *The History of the Negro Race from 1619–1880 . . . As Slaves, As Soldiers, and As Citizens* (1883). His book focused on the three subjects that defined his life: Christianity, Africa, and Christianity *in* Africa. Williams was part of a small circle of late-nineteenth-century black Americans who sought liberation through African colonization.

After an early career that included military service and travel in Mexico, Williams studied at Howard University before moving on to Newton Theological Seminary near Boston in 1870. By 1874, when the twenty-four-year-old Williams spoke before his white Harvard-educated classmates about Christianity in Africa, he had solidified his African strategy. Volunteering to help Belgium's king Leopold Christianize Africa's Congo region, he traveled to Africa in 1885.

Williams returned to the United States in 1889 to rally American support for a central African railroad Leopold had decided to build. He traveled to Washington, DC, hoping to enlist the help of the federal government in sending African Americans to work on this project. When President Benjamin Harrison rebuffed him, Williams unsuccessfully petitioned Europeans before finally returning to Africa. There he soon saw that Leopold's railroad scheme was nothing but "fraud and trickery." The Belgian king had cheated tribal leaders out of their land, while white foremen brutalized Congolese workers.

In a long "Open Letter to Leopold II," Williams criticized the Belgian monarch for failing to keep his promise of "fostering care, benevolent enterprise, [and] honest and practical effort" to "secure the welfare" of the Africans. Meanwhile, he tried to convince black Americans that establishing Christian missions in Africa would enable them to reclaim their lost racial heritage. Williams continued writing about Africa until his death in August 1891, but his ideas appealed to only a minority. Most black Americans had little interest in Africa during the late nineteenth century.

Nevertheless, other intellectuals also tried to focus black Americans' attention on Africa. Writer Edward Blyden, for many years associated with the biracial American Colonization Society, published *Christianity, Islam, and the Negro Race* in 1887. In it he acknowledged African American ties to the Muslim faith, but he believed by adopting Christianity—the religion of Europe—Africans would have a more powerful foundation for resisting a European takeover. Blyden's program, known as *Ethiopianism,* recommended calling European attention to the biblical story in which Ethiopia commanded a divinely protected empire.

Henry McNeal Turner also dreamed of Africa. After an unsuccessful repatriation attempt in 1879, he made his first trip to the vast continent in 1891. But Turner lamented that he had waited too long to make the voyage: "I have just strolled as far out in the direction of Boporo—the Eden of West Africa—as my strength would permit. I have seen the African in his native town and hut, rather dwellings, and I have just had a long weep or cry at the grand field for missionary operation here, and that I am too old now to engage in it." The fifty-seven-year-old Turner returned to the United States to launch *The Voice of the Mission*, a newspaper promoting missionary work. Over many years, his entreaties inspired a steady trickle of black Americans to Liberia. Individually and in organized groups, a few thousand black Americans crossed the Atlantic to Africa.

"I have seen the African in his native town and hut." —*Henry McNeal Turner*

TERROR AND ACCOMMODATION

"If you will kill us, turn our faces to the West." These were the last words of Thomas Moss just before a mob of white men lynched him and two other black men near Memphis, Tennessee, in the spring of 1892. Historians do not know whether Moss was making a spiritual allusion or suggesting that black people migrate west in search of justice. However, his death riveted international attention on Memphis and on lynching.

Lynching has a long history in Western society. For centuries, Europeans used public humiliation, hanging, and execution to remind people of what could happen if they broke society's rules. In the post–Civil War years, however, lynching in the United States was heavily used to enforce racial inequality. Moreover, it escalated in frequency as states passed laws curtailing black people's citizenship rights. Particularly in the South, African Americans who ran successful businesses, stood up to white people's insults, ran for office, or voted, risked incurring white people's wrath. Mere friendliness or eye contact with white women could get a young black man killed.

A year after Moss's death, his friend Ida B. Wells told his story to a Boston audience. "On the morning of March 9, the bodies of three of our best men were found in an old field horribly shot to pieces. These young men had owned and operated the 'Peoples Grocery.'" Wells recounted how a local white storeowner, displaced by the successful Peoples Grocery, incited a confrontation between the black store owners and police officers. During the melee, black men shot and wounded several policemen. When it became clear the officers would live and therefore the black storekeepers would not receive death sentences, an angry white mob dragged the three men from their jail cells. As Wells put it, the mob set out to "do what the law could not be made to do . . . [teach] a lesson to the Afro-American that he must not shoot a white man,—no matter what the provocation." The three black men did not go easily. They fought back, trying to wrench a gun from their attackers. In retaliation, their killers mutilated their bodies and gouged their eyes out.

"On the morning of March 9, the bodies of three of our best men were found in an old field horribly shot to pieces." —*Ida B. Wells*

Campaign Against Lynching

Ida B. Wells knew how to get heard. Her 1893 Boston speech was not the first time she called attention to racial injustice. In 1884, she refused to leave the Ladies Coach reserved for white women on a Jim Crow train in Tennessee. She sank her teeth into the arm of the first conductor who tried to remove her; it took three men to haul her out of the car. Moss's death unleashed the full extent of her fury. In the newspaper she had co-owned since 1889, she wrote a long account of his murder—the first of many such articles she eventually published over the years in her campaign against lynching. The piece was printed in her Memphis paper, *Free*

Speech and Headlight, while Wells was in New York visiting fellow black journalist T. Thomas Fortune. In her absence, white supremacists vandalized her office. Fortune told her, "I'm afraid you will have to stay in New York."

So Wells went to work for Fortune's *New York Age*, launching a war of words and rallying 250 women to raise funds to publish a report on lynching. Money came from as far away as Seattle, where women in the tiny AME church had recently formed a Women's Christian Temperance Union chapter. Investigating the circumstances of more than 700 southern lynchings in the previous decade, Wells published a detailed study in 1893. The report concluded that lynch mobs frequently targeted successful black men, and many black men who were lynched for rape had been involved in relationships into which white women had invited them. In 1889, 150 black lynchings were reported across the country. In 1892, the year Thomas Moss lost his life, there were 250 such murders.

Wells's campaign galvanized black communities. Frederick Douglass helped her plan a sustained campaign. Wells admired Douglass, often quoting his vision of America as a "composite" nation of many peoples and cultures. Douglass, in turn, valued Wells's focus on women's rights and social justice. He encouraged her to hire detectives to investigate a lynching in Paris, Texas, and she took her findings on a European speaking tour. He also wrote an introduction to *A Red Record*, her 1895 report on lynching. Wells persuaded British merchants to pressure their American cotton suppliers to stop the lynchings. Though black politicians failed to pass federal anti-lynching laws, the number of lynch mob attacks in Memphis and around the country declined after 1893. Ida B. Wells had exerted a measurable impact.

The Atlanta Compromise

Organizers of the 1895 Cotton States and International Exposition in Atlanta, Georgia, invited Booker T. Washington—a speaker they hoped would please both black and white audiences—to address the crowd. In his address, he did not publicly decry lynching or challenge white racism. Instead, he presented a blueprint for southern progress he hoped his black and white audience could accept. Hoping to inspire black dreams and allay white fears, he repeated his hope that black people would stay in the South, accommodate themselves to racial discrimination, build their economic strength, and bide their time.

"One third of the population of the South is of the Negro race. No enterprise seeking the material, civil or moral welfare of [the South] can disregard this element of our population and reach the highest success," Washington began in the speech for which he is best remembered. Describing ex-slaves as "ignorant and inexperienced," he apologized that "in the first years of our new life we began at the top instead of at the bottom; that a seat in Congress or the state legislature was more sought than real estate or industrial skill; that the political convention or stump speaking had more attractions than starting a dairy farm or a truck garden."

Washington advocated accommodation because he believed the destinies of black and white southerners were intertwined. A number of black politicians had expressed this same belief during Reconstruction, and now Washington articulated it in a lyrical philosophy. Using a metaphorical story of passengers dying of thirst on a ship lost at sea, he reminded his audience that when told to "cast down your bucket where you are," the passengers did so and discovered fresh water in the midst of the salt ocean. Urging patience, he encouraged black Americans to "cast down your bucket in making friends of the people by whom we are surrounded." Suggesting black southerners should "cast it down in agriculture, mechanics, in commerce, in domestic service, and in the professions," he implored them to accommodate racial segregation.

"Cast down your bucket in making friends of the people by whom we are surrounded."—*Booker T. Washington*

Washington attempted to dissuade white southerners from hiring new immigrants so as to make more jobs available to black Americans. "To those of the white race who look to the incoming of those of foreign birth and strange tongue and habits for the prosperity of the South . . . I would repeat what I say to my own race, 'Cast down your bucket where you are.' Cast it down among the eight millions of Negroes whose habits you know." He reminded them of loyal black workers who "without strikes and labour wars, tilled your fields, built your railroads, and helped make possible the progress of the South." He promised the white South that black workers would be "the most faithful, law-abiding and unresentful that the world has seen." He advocated racially separate social circles, where black and white workers would be "separate as the fingers, yet one as the hand in all things relating to mutual progress." Widely publicized, the speech catapulted Washington to a position of influence and power never before held by even so revered a black American as Frederick Douglass, who had black and white admirers in the North and in the South.

Some black leaders applauded Washington's speech. New York journalist T. Thomas Fortune praised Washing-

Booker T. Washington Predicts a "New Heaven"

In his speech at the Atlanta Exposition in 1895, Booker T. Washington's rhetoric and cadence were as spellbinding as his message. With passionate delivery, he outlined a prescription for cooperation between white and black southerners.

Nearly sixteen millions of [black] hands will aid you in pulling the load upward, or they will pull against you the load downward. We [black people] will constitute one third and more of the ignorance and crime of the South, or one third its intelligence and progress; I pledge that in your effort to work out the great and intricate problem which God has laid at the doors of the South, you shall have . . . the patient, sympathetic help of my race. . . . This, coupled with our material prosperity, will bring into our beloved South a new heaven and a new earth.

—*from Booker T. Washington,* Up From Slavery *(1901).*

To view a longer version of this document, please go to *www.ablongman.com/carson/documents*.

ton as "the best equipped of the lot of us to be the single figure ahead of the procession." Fortune had previously exhorted African Americans to push assertively for black progress. In an 1883 editorial, he had written, "From Denmark Vesey to Nat Turner, from the flight of Frederick Douglass and Henry Highland Garnet from the bloodhounds of Maryland, to the present time, the voice of the race has been heard . . . protesting against injustice." Now Fortune echoed Washington's request for patience. Isaiah Montgomery of Mound Bayou, one of Mississippi's delegates to Atlanta's Cotton States Exposition, was also inspired by Washington's speech.

But many African Americans distanced themselves from Washington and his ideas. "It is supreme folly to speak of Mr. Washington as the Moses of the race," wrote one black Atlanta newspaper. "If we are where Mr. Washington's Atlanta speech placed us, what need have we of a Moses? . . . Let us pray that the race will never have a leader, but leaders. Who is the leader of the white race in America? It has no leader, but leaders. So with us." African American leaders who favored more immediate and direct demands for equal political rights labeled this speech "Washington's compromise."

In his Atlanta address Washington also hinted of a future in which black people were full citizens, even while he acknowledged the current grim realities. He assured his listeners that black workers valued "the opportunity to earn a dollar in a factory . . . infinitely more than the opportunity to spend a dollar in an opera-house." Recognizing the competition from immigrant workers, Washington sought to bind southern white employers to black labor. At the same time, he reminded both black and white listeners that black enterprise would eventually bring equality. "No race," he said, "that has anything to contribute to the markets of the world is long in any degree ostracized."

TABLE 12.4 Rural and Urban African Americans, by State, 1890

In the South, African Americans remained rural, but those who could leave the South had more chance to find work and community in the cities.

	Population	*Rural*	*Urban*
Mississippi	750,000	95%	5%
Texas	487,000	83%	17%
Pennsylvania	107,000	29%	71%
New York	69,000	27%	73%
New Jersey	47,000	47%	53%
Oklahoma	27,000	99.7%	0.3%
Massachusetts	21,700	8%	92%
Connecticut	12,300	14%	86%
Maine, Vermont, New Hampshire, Rhode Island	10,100	15%	85%
Iowa	10,000	40%	60%
Nebraska	8,800	20%	80%
Minnesota	3,600	12%	88%

CONCLUSION

The first generations of African Americans born into emancipation struggled to find a hospitable place to establish families, make a living, and educate themselves in a society controlled by hostile white Americans. The Civil War had left the South with social, economic, and political problems Reconstruction could not solve. After 1877, black and white southerners tried to rebuild their economy and forge a new relationship with each other. Poverty mired black and white workers in a cycle of debt and a mood of despair. Jim Crow laws bound African Americans to menial jobs and subjected them to racial discrimination. Pseudoscientific theories of Social Darwinism and eugenics prompted white people to shun African Americans. Against a backdrop of racial violence, migration, and relocation, black Americans struggled to forge enduring alliances with white farmers and industrial workers. All of these made it even more difficult for black people to move away from the slave past.

Out of this climate of hopelessness, Booker T. Washington rose up to lead African Americans into the twentieth century. He urged his followers to use education to gain work skills and to remain in the South as they lifted themselves above their "discouraging surroundings." Hoping to reduce the violence against southern black people, Washington assured white southerners that black workers would accommodate old racial hierarchies. He opposed aggressive leaders like Ida B. Wells and W. E. B. Du Bois, who argued that education should include the liberal arts, lay the foundation for what Du Bois called the development of men, and encourage students to stand up to racial injustice. For these leaders, "manhood"—which included personal dignity, and economic and political power—seemed to be missing from Washington's goals. Though Washington and the Tuskegee Institute dominated black strategies in the early decades of the twentieth century, black people left the rural South in droves. They headed for southern and northern cities, all-black towns, the western frontier, and Africa. As soldiers, rail workers, radical political activists, missionaries, and journalists, they plowed fresh ground in new places.

In 1896, the election year following Washington's Atlanta Compromise speech, a political movement known as Progressivism emerged. Black and white intellectuals came together to design solutions to what one observer described as "the problem of the twentieth century . . . the problem of the color line."

FURTHER READING

Ashbaugh, Carolyn. *Lucy Parsons, American Revolutionary* (Chicago: Charles Kerr, 1976).

Barr, Alwyn. *Black Texans: A History of African Americans in Texas, 1528–1995* (Norman: University of Oklahoma Press, 1996).

Billington, Monroe Lee. *African Americans on the Western Frontier* (Boulder: University Press of Colorado, 1998).

Borchet, James. *Alley Life in Washington: Family, Community, Religion, and Folklife in the City, 1850–1970* (Urbana: University of Illinois Press, 1980).

Brownell, Blaine, and David R. Goldfield. *The City in Southern History: The Growth of Urban Civilization in the South* (Port Washington, NY: Kennikat Press, 1977).

Cha-Jua, Sundiata Keita. *America's First Black Town: Brooklyn, Illinois, 1830–1915* (Urbana: University of Illinois Press, 2000).

Clanton, Gene. *Congressional Populism and the Crisis of the 1890s* (Lawrence: University Press of Kansas, 1993).

Franklin, John Hope. *George Washington Williams* (Chicago: University of Chicago Press, 1985).

Franklin, John Hope, and John Whittington Franklin, eds. *My Life and an Era: The Autobiography of Buck Colbert Franklin* (Baton Rouge: Louisiana State University Press, 1997).

Gatewood, Willard. *Aristocrats of Color: The Black Elite, 1880–1920* (Bloomington: Indiana University Press, 1990).

Hamilton, Kenneth Marvin. *Black Towns and Profit: Promotion and Development in the Trans-Appalachian West, 1877–1915* (Urbana: University of Illinois Press, 1991).

Hochschild, Adam. *King Leopold's Ghost: A Story of Greed, Terror, and Heroism in Colonial Africa* (Boston: Houghton Mifflin, 1998).

Jenkins, Edward Sidney. *To Fathom More: African American Scientists and Inventors* (Lanham, MD: University Press of America, 1996).

Junne, George H. *Blacks in the American West and Beyond—America, Canada and Mexico: A Selectively Annotated Bibliography* (Westport, CT: Greenwood Press, 2000).

Liftwack, Leon. *Been in the Storm So Long: The Emergence of Black Freedom in the South* (New York: Knopf, 1998).

McKee, Margaret. *Beale Black and Blue: Life and Music on Black America's Main Street* (Baton Rouge: Louisiana State University Press, 1981).

McMath, Robert C. *American Populism: A Social History, 1877–1898* (New York: Hill and Wang, 1993).

Ravage, John W. *Black Pioneers: Images of the Black Experience on the North American Frontier* (Salt Lake City: University of Utah Press, 1997).

Saville, Julie. *The Work of Reconstruction: From Slave to Wage Labor in South Carolina, 1860–1870* (New York : Cambridge University Press, 1996).

Schechter, Patricia Ann. *Ida B. Wells-Barnett and American Reform, 1880–1930* (Chapel Hill: University of North Carolina Press, 2001).

Schubert, Frank N. *Black Valor, Buffalo Soldiers, and the Medal of Honor, 1870–1898* (Wilmington, DE: Scholarly Resources, 1997).

Schweninger, Loren. *Black Property Owners in the South, 1790–1915* (Urbana: University of Illinois Press, 1990).

Taylor, Quintard. *In Search of the Racial Frontier: African Americans in the American West, 1528–1990* (New York: W. W. Norton, 1998).

Ward, Andrew. *Dark Midnight When I Rise: The Story of the Jubilee Singers Who Introduced the World of Black Music to America* (New York: Farrar, Straus, Giroux, 2000).

Watkins, William H. *The White Architects of Black Education: Ideology and Power in America, 1865–1954* (New York: Teachers College Press, 2001).

CHAPTER 13

In the campaign to make lynching a national concern, the NAACP resorted to dramatic measures such as this banner hung above a busy New York city street.

"Colored" Becomes "Negro" in the Progressive Era

Mary Church Terrell and the NACW

The applause was deafening. As Harriet Tubman, now in her seventies, entered the Washington, DC, meeting hall in the spring of 1896, a crowd several hundred strong rose to its feet. Tubman had arrived to help launch the National Association of Colored Women (NACW), a federation of forty urban black women's clubs from around the nation. Inspired by Ida Wells Barnett's antilynching campaign, which demonstrated women's power to unite and finance a common cause, the NACW planned to focus on children and home life. Members envisioned black families creating the cornerstone of a strong national community, teaching children to seek personal success while helping others. The NACW adopted the motto "lifting as we climb," echoing Booker T. Washington's credo.

As NACW members honored Tubman for her leadership in the slave past, they chose Mary Church Terrell to serve as their president to lead into the future. Wealthy and well educated, Terrell had developed her worldview amid the hope and violence of the Reconstruction South. Her father, Memphis businessman Robert Reed Church, born the enslaved son of a white master, eventually became one of America's wealthiest black men. After white ruffians shot him while ransacking his saloon, Church testified in the courts against his attackers. His actions defined him as a "race man"—one determined to defend the possessions and honor of all African Americans. Through her childhood, Mary Church absorbed her family's commitment to struggle for racial justice.

CHAPTER OUTLINE

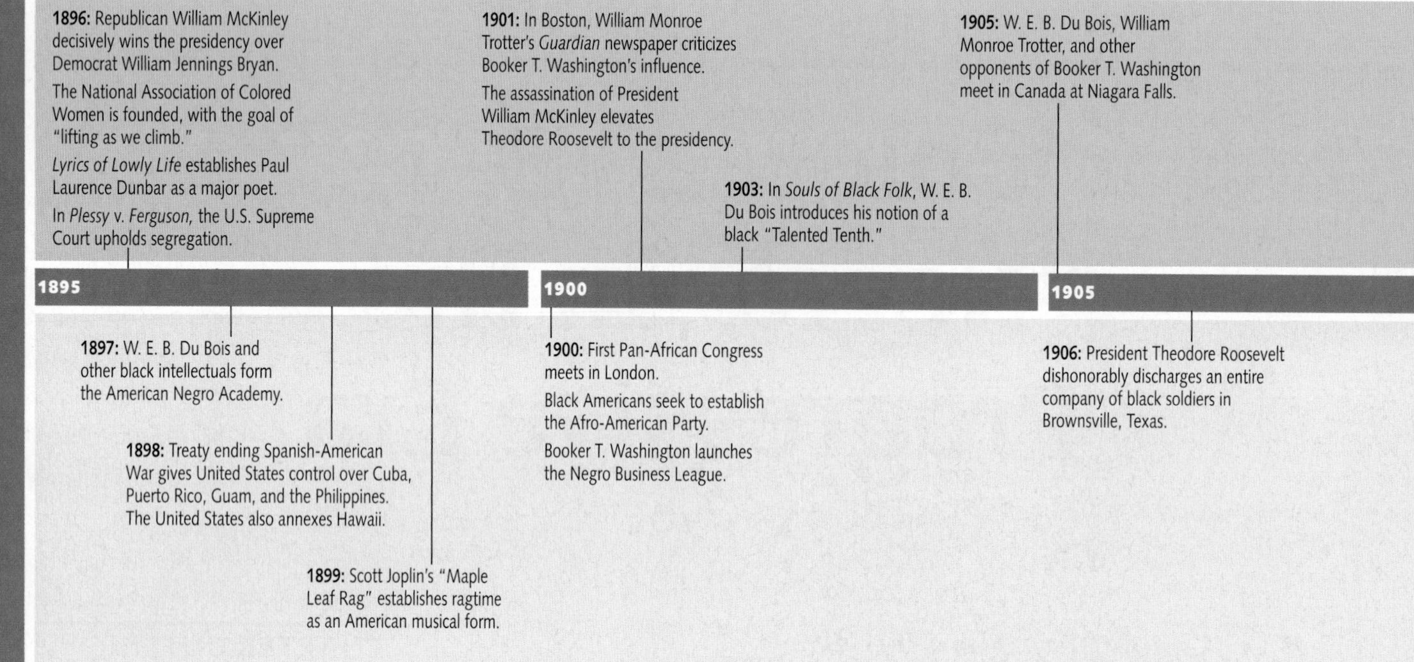

Mary Church Terrell attended Oberlin College and completed a course of classical studies in 1884. After teaching at Wilberforce College in Ohio and at the M Street High School in Washington, DC, she returned to Oberlin and obtained a master's degree. Next she embarked on a two-year European tour before returning to marry Robert Heberton Terrell, who held a law degree from Howard University. The couple settled in Washington, DC, where Mary Church Terrell got to know both established social reformers and struggling young black people.

Mary Church Terrell's commitment to resist racial injustice strengthened the NACW. In her first speech as president, she proclaimed, "In Union there is strength . . . the colored women of the United States [have] banded together to fulfill a mission." African American women needed their own organization, she said, "because our peculiar status in this country . . . demand[s] that we stand by ourselves in the special work for which we have organized." She maintained that "only through good homes . . . [can] people . . . become really good and truly great."

Because most white Americans viewed colored women as intellectually and morally inferior, NACW members resolved to go beyond charity work and cultivate "fine, cultured, women" with "better homes, purer homes." The organization shared Booker T. Washington's concern for teaching hygiene, home economics, and self-discipline. Members urged personal grooming, good manners, and practices such as reading to children and disciplining them with reason rather than with corporal punishment. Eventually representing more than 50,000 black women in 1,000 clubs across the United States, the NACW also promoted kindergartens and childcare facilities at which black children could learn while their mothers earned a living.

Improving colored Americans' lives was also part of the Progressive movement that swept America in the last decade of the nineteenth century. Progressives, who came from all races and political parties, sought to perfect society. Progressive ideas influenced everything from political and scientific theories to architectural design and religion, sparking schools of social work, city planning organizations, and urban community centers for the disadvantaged. The NACW's mission and strategy included some Progressive ideas, including an emphasis on women's rights. Like white female reformers, black female reformers disputed women's supposed inferior-

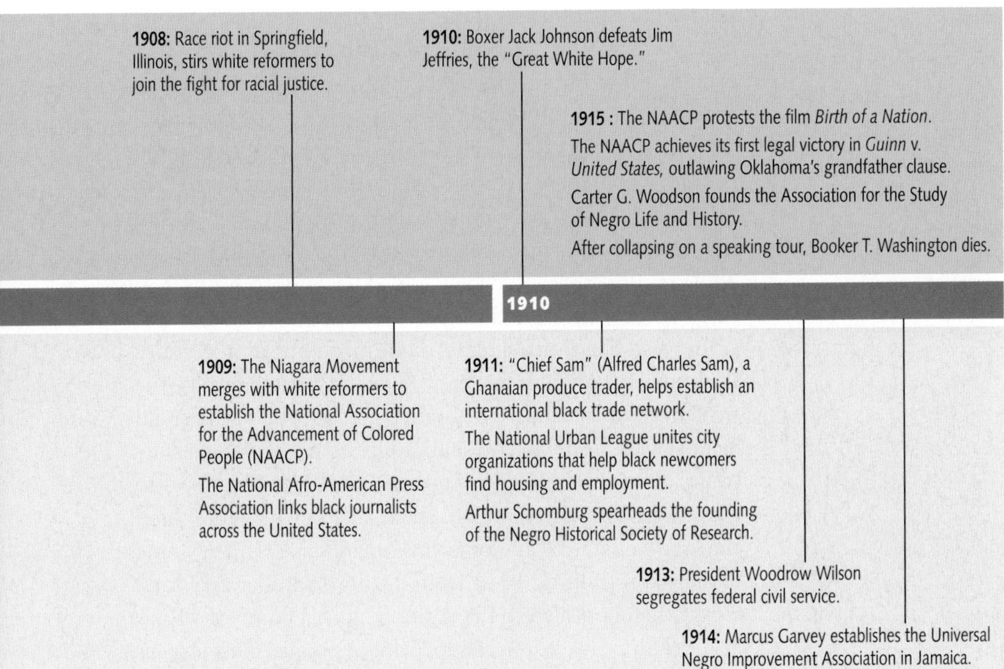

ity. They declared that colored women's dual oppression of race and gender made them "the most interesting women in the country." One NACW founder described broad goals: "The old notion . . . that woman was intended by the Almighty to do only those things that men thought they ought to do is fast passing away. In our day and in this country, a woman's sphere is just as large as she can make it."

NACW leaders represented the new intellectual black leadership. Born after Emancipation, well educated, and sometimes economically independent, such women faced the future with optimism and confidence. But as we will see in this chapter, they encountered staggering challenges. With its *Plessy* v. *Ferguson* decision upholding racial segregation, the Supreme Court led a backlash against federal protections for black citizens. Convinced by pseudoscientific racism that defined African Americans as inferior, state and local governments initiated new laws and customs—often enforced by violence—increasingly restricting black freedom and opportunity.

New leaders launched a variety of legal and cultural counterattacks. Seeking to accommodate or combat racial segregation, they promoted unity and racial pride. Some hoped to earn their country's respect through military service in the Spanish-American War. Others supported the National Association for the Advancement of Colored People (NAACP) and the Urban League to improve their lot.

In cities such as New York a proud black identity emerged, often encouraged by the churches and enhanced by arts, literature, and sports. By 1915, powerful ideological and social pressure from the white majority prevented many black Americans from achieving social or economic progress. As World War I erupted, the NAACP led the campaign to end accommodation.

RACIAL SEGREGATION

"Another Jim Crow Car Case, Arrest of a Negro Traveler Who Persisted in Riding with the White People," announced the New Orleans *Daily Picayune*, which reported Homer Plessy's challenge to segregation laws. Plessy boasted he would "sooner go to jail than leave the spirit of the Thirteenth and Fourteenth Amendments." On June 7, 1892, this black shoemaker violated the 1890 Louisiana Separate Car Act, which used race to assign people to "white" or "colored" passenger train cars. He boarded a train in New Orleans and sat down in the car reserved for white people for the 30-mile ride to Covington, Louisiana. Plessy might have gone unnoticed, since the heritage that defined him as colored—one black great-grandfather—hardly showed on his pale skin. But Louisiana law declared that any person who had "one drop of Negro blood" was "colored." A railroad employee responsible for keeping track of local family relationships identified Plessy and had him arrested. Plessy welcomed the arrest, for he wanted to confront the unjust law. A $500 bond, posted by supporters, kept him out of jail while his case proceeded through the courts.

Mary Church Terrell, the first president of the National Association of Colored Women, saw a strong home life, education, self-discipline, and good hygiene as essential to improving the lives of African Americans. This image shows Terrell in her typically impeccable attire.

"Separate But Equal"

Supported by a group called the New Orleans Citizens Committee that had been formed specifically to test the legality of separate train cars, Plessy and his allies aimed to use public opinion and the courts to force the federal government to protect the right to equal access to public services. Like Plessy, many black people in New Orleans had a mixed heritage. Called Creoles, they had French or Native American as well as black ancestors. One such person was newspaper editor and lawyer Louis Martinet, whose *Crusader* was the only New Orleans black newspaper financially secure enough to publish daily throughout the 1890s. The *Crusader* advocated opening the Louisiana polls to black men and poor white southerners. Like many black men, poor white men were subject to local "grandfather clause" laws that excluded them from casting a ballot because their landless grandfathers had not been allowed to vote. The franchise, the *Crusader* argued, was an issue "in which all the common people, whether colored or white, are vitally interested." To Martinet, "Once the wealthy [white] classes get the laws as they want them," only people who supported upper-class white candidates would be allowed to vote. In July 1892, Plessy's lawyers argued before the New Orleans District Court that the Fourteenth Amendment prohibited states from making or enforcing "any law which shall abridge the privileges or immunities of citizens." But the court ruled against Plessy, saying the state's right to regulate intrastate trade allowed it to require separate cars. Plessy's appeal to the Louisiana Supreme Court also failed. This court ruled that the Separate Car Act treated black and white people equally, prohibiting both from sitting in integrated cars. Plessy then appealed to the nation's highest court.

The appeal failed. In 1896, eight Supreme Court justices ruled against Plessy. The justices concluded that though the Fourteenth Amendment guaranteed "absolute equality of the two races before the law, . . . in the nature of things it could not have been intended to abolish distinctions based upon color, or to enforce . . . a commingling of the two races upon terms unsatisfactory to either." Upholding Louisiana's 1890 law segregating public transportation, the Supreme Court stated that as long as "equal" services were provided for black citizens, states could legislate that those services be "separate." The judges did not rule on how *equal* would be defined, and indeed train cars and other services for colored patrons were seldom of equal quality. The justices noted that "the enforced separation of the races [does not mark] the colored race with a badge of inferiority."

The sole Court dissenter in the *Plessy* case was Justice John Marshall Harlan, a former slaveholder. Harlan warned that the *Plessy* decision would stir up political trouble, as the *Dred Scott* decision had nearly four decades earlier. Moreover, he noted that the *Plessy* ruling would erode the Fourteenth Amendment constitutional guarantees that had overturned *Scott*. Harlan cautioned that court rulings that reduced black Americans to inferior status would "stimulate [white] aggressions, more or less brutal, upon the admitted rights of colored citizens." But few white Americans heeded these warnings; the *Plessy* ruling encouraged many states to pass segregation laws.

The *Plessy* decision shaped American racial policies and limited black people's civil rights for more than a half-century. Now that states and local governments had legal approval for racial segregation, the New Orleans Citizen's

Robert James Harlan, the mixed-race half-brother of Justice John Marshall Harlan, accumulated a fortune during the California gold rush, which he invested in Cincinnati real estate. In 1875, after raising a black regiment that became the Ninety-fourth Ohio battalion, he was commissioned as a colonel by President Rutherford B. Hayes. Serving in the Ohio Legislature in the 1890s, Harlan worked to repeal Jim Crow laws.

"It was better to suffer in silence than to attract attention to their misfortune and weakness." —*New Orleans Citizens Committee*

Committee dissolved. "It was better," committee members said, for African Americans "to suffer in silence than to attract attention to their misfortune and weakness." Changing his plea to guilty, Plessy paid the $25 fine for riding in the "wrong" car. The militant *Crusader* ceased publication. Many African Americans came to believe in this era that continuing political agitation "would not only be fruitless but decidedly dangerous."

Across the nation, state and local laws segregated more and more facilities. In the South, public transportation and public services were divided, as were schools, with middle-class white children separated from schools that served African Americans, immigrants, and the poor. The New Orleans Catholic diocese divided its parishes into black and white. In at least one Mississippi town, the body of a black person was dug up from a cemetery and reburied in a segregated burial ground. Even in the North, communities segregated schools, libraries, prisons, hospitals, and cemeteries. Hotels, theaters, and restaurants followed. Northern urban neighborhoods rapidly became all black or all white, with African Americans typically concentrated in older areas. White workers moved to new suburbs and used the new electric streetcars and rail lines to commute to their city jobs.

Jim Crow laws also affected the political process. In 1898, when the Supreme Court upheld Mississippi's poll tax, many southern states adopted some combination of grandfather clauses, poll taxes, literacy tests, and "understanding clauses" that required a potential voter to interpret parts of the Constitution. These tests were applied unequally; white applicants might be given nursery rhymes to interpret, while black would-be voters might be asked to read the Bible in Latin. Such restrictions quickly erased the black franchise. In Louisiana, the number of black voters dropped from 130,000 in 1890 to just 1,300 in 1900. Some southern states prevented black candidates from getting on the ballot by passing laws such as the "white primary," which banned African Americans from running or voting in primary elections. By limiting the franchise to upper-class white men—and black men who voted for designated white candidates—southern politicians completed their resurrection of the hierarchy of pre–Civil War America.

For many black people, the *Plessy* ruling bolstered Booker T. Washington's view that African Americans had best concentrate on economic progress, not legal and political equality. Frugality, integrity, and job skills, Washington argued, would bring success in the only areas in which black Americans could control their destiny. Though publicly withdrawing from antisegregation efforts, some Louisiana Creoles continued to smolder privately. One Plessy supporter, Rodolphe Desdunes, waited ten years before again speaking out. Colored people, he said, should continue protesting, lest white Americans assume they no longer care about racial injustice. "It is more noble and dignified to fight, no matter what," he said, "than to show a passive attitude of resignation."

"It is more noble and dignified to fight, no matter what, than to show a passive attitude of resignation." —*Rodolphe Desdunes*

Progressivism and White Supremacy

The decline of Populism (see chapter 12) coincided with the rise of Progressivism in the early twentieth century. Fueled by the social dislocation that came from rapid industrialization, urbanization, and the arrival of many new immigrants, the Progressive movement united a disparate group of

Pan-African Conference in London, Du Bois proclaimed that "the question [was] how far differences of race . . . will hereafter be made the basis of denying to over half the world the right of sharing . . . the opportunities and privileges of modern civilization." Expressing unity with the "millions of black men in Africa, America and the Islands of the Sea, [and] the brown and yellow myriads elsewhere," Du Bois predicted that "if by reason of carelessness, prejudice, greed and injustice the black world is to be exploited and ravaged and degraded, the results must be deplorable, if not fatal—not simply to them, but to the high ideals of justice, freedom and culture which a thousand years of Christian civilization have held before Europe." Seeking to arrest imperialism—the process by which Western nations extended control over Africa, parts of Asia, and the Pacific—Du Bois called on the United States, Great Britain, Germany, and France to "respect the integrity and independence" of the "darker peoples."

Before the Pan-African Conference, the mixed-race Du Bois had spent more than a decade developing his vision of an international alliance of colored peoples. Drawing on his own life and the experiences of other African Americans, he concluded that the color line—the line that divided black people and white—was a global problem. It served to hold people back in every way, and in the United States that line was becoming more and more deeply pronounced.

Pan-Africanism

The term *Pan-Africanism* had been coined by a Trinidadian organizer of the conference to embrace a broad spectrum of men and women who shared the idea of an international stand against racism. Du Bois interpreted it to mean that the world's colored peoples should unite to challenge white imperialism at home and abroad. "In this the closing year of the nineteenth century, there has been assembled a congress of men and women of African blood, to deliberate solemnly upon the present situation and outlook of the darker races of mankind," he said. Conference funding and speakers came from many black organizations, including the NACW. They envisioned goals ranging from full inclusion in American democracy to temporary or permanent separation of the races. Even Booker T. Washington initially backed the Pan-African Conference, though he and Du Bois would soon fall into a bitter rivalry.

James Holly, who had left his native United States to live in Haiti, proposed during the conference that the United States purchase West Indian islands to establish a black confederacy. Du Bois felt the rising tide of racism was part of an international mood sanctioned in 1884–1885 at Berlin, where European nations had agreed to invade Africa and divide it among themselves. Supported by eugenic ideas, Europeans and Americans justified imperialism by arguing that white people were superior to the world's darker peoples and thus needed to rule them. Du Bois was concerned that even religion was being used for imperialist ends. He cautioned, "Let not the cloak of Christian missionary enterprise be allowed . . . to hide the ruthless economic exploitation . . . of less developed countries."

Du Bois's experiences at Fisk, Tennessee's renowned black college, opened his eyes in many ways. Growing up in western Massachusetts with few black peers, he had moved comfortably among white classmates. But in his teen years, a white girl's refusal to exchange visiting cards with him took him by surprise. The incident reminded him that he was "shut off from their world by a vast veil." At Fisk, where Du Bois had his first experience with a black institution, he was deeply moved by the sight of Jubilee Hall, built with money raised by the Jubilee Singers. It "seemed ever made of the songs themselves, and its bricks were red with the blood and dust of toil. . . . [It] was full of the voices of my brothers and sisters, full of the voices of the past." He felt "thrilled to be for the first time among so many people of my own colour or rather of such extraordinary colours, who it seemed were bound to me by new and exciting external ties." Du Bois later recalled: "Into this world I leapt with enthusiasm: henceforth I was a Negro."

For Du Bois, being Negro was as much a mission as an identity. He shared some of the ideas of the intellectuals of his day—for example, that membership in a given race implied common characteristics. But he rejected the notion that white people were more intelligent or morally superior. Determined to bring honor to his race, he earned in 1895 the first history doctorate ever awarded a black man by Harvard University. Soon after, Booker T. Washington invited the young scholar to teach at Tuskegee. Du Bois declined, accepting a position at Wilberforce College in Ohio. He was then hired by the University of Pennsylvania to produce a study evaluating black potential. *The Philadelphia Negro: A Social Study* (1899) profiled 40,000 black Americans in the industrial city. Du Bois's study showed how black people defied huge odds to build vibrant communities through their churches and educational institutions. But "color prejudice" impeded economic progress. Without the intervention of a white protector, he said, "it is next to impossible for a Negro to get regular employment in most of the trades." *The Philadelphia Negro* reflected the Progressive idea that poor people could fashion better lives if social planners helped improve their environment. Lacking employment and the franchise, Du Bois argued, struggling black families had few prospects.

After publishing *The Philadelphia Negro,* Du Bois joined the faculty at Atlanta Baptist College (soon to become Morehouse College), the South's premier black liberal arts school. There he continued to study black business, education, labor unions, churches—even prison life. He also joined with other black intellectuals to establish the American Negro Academy to promote lectures, meetings, and publications of black scholars. He believed an academic education and the franchise would give African Americans the stature and self-confidence to master economic challenges. Liberal arts education, he contended, would soon enable them to be good citizens and to make wise choices for themselves and their society. By the time he spoke before the Pan-African Conference in 1900, Du Bois's reputation as a scholar and teacher gave him an authoritative voice on the subject of worldwide racism.

Black Americans and the Spanish-American War

In his London speeches, Du Bois drew a connection between "the problem of the color line" in the United States and America's recent war with Spain. That venture had won for the United States control over Cuba, Puerto Rico, Guam, and the Philippine Islands in the South Pacific. American officials saw the dark-skinned native peoples of these islands as incapable of governing themselves. Insisting they wanted to improve the lives of the native peoples, the American occupiers made sweeping changes in these places—establishing missionary schools and hospitals and introducing new forms of agriculture and commerce. But Du Bois knew that in return for these advances, Americans seized mines, farmlands, and other resources, consigning local colored residents to menial jobs.

The World.

MAINE EXPLOSION CAUSED BY BOMB OR TORPEDO?

Capt. Sigsbee and Consul-General Lee Are in Doubt—The World Has Sent a Special Tug, With Submarine Divers, to Havana to Find Out—Lee Asks for an Immediate Court of Inquiry—260 Men Dead.

The Spanish-American War erupted in February 1898. The American battleship U.S.S. *Maine,* which had been dispatched to Cuba, a Spanish colony, to protect American citizens there, exploded and sank, killing dozens of American soldiers. Political tensions between the United States and Spain had been mounting for several decades, and the *Maine* incident gave American imperialists a fresh opportunity to push the United States to declare war against Spain, ostensibly to help liberate Cuba and the Philippines from Spanish rule.

Thousands of black soldiers fought in the Spanish-American War, which lasted three months. For many African American men, the call to service highlighted their conflict between loyalty to their race and loyalty to their country. As Kansas City's black newspaper *American Citizen* put it, "Uncle Sam [should] keep his hands off other countries till he has learned to govern his own." Black Republicans such as Calvin Chase, editor of the Washington *Bee,* announced, "The Negro has no reason to fight for Cuba's independence. . . . He is as much in need of independence as Cuba is." But other black journalists urged loyalty to the U.S. government. "America is the land of our birth," said the Cleveland *Gazette.* "As citizens and patriots, let us be ready and willing to do our part . . . our full duty, and to do even more than others in the hour of the nation's peril." Other African Americans echoed Du Bois's conviction that racial issues in United States reflected an international pattern. "The dark-skinned inhabitants of these islands will be the victims of race prejudice," predicted Richmond's black newspaper, *The Planet.* Events in the Philippines justified the comparison. When U.S. troops arrived, Filipinos welcomed their assistance in ending Spanish rule. But when the Filipinos realized the U.S. government intended to replace Spanish control of the Philippines with American control, they mounted a resistance that lasted five years. More than 14,000 dark-skinned Filipinos lost their lives in the war, as some white soldiers relished the opportunity to slaughter them. It was "like killing the niggers back home," wrote one soldier from the South, "more fun than a turkey shoot."

> "The Negro has no reason to fight for Cuba's independence. . . . He is as much in need of independence as Cuba is."
> —*Calvin Chase*

Racism reverberated at home. Barely a week after twenty-two black American soldiers lost their lives on the *Maine,* a white mob in Lake City, South Carolina, torched the home of black postmaster Fraser Baker, killing Baker and his child and wounding several others. When the murders went unpunished, Ida Wells Barnett took Baker's case to the White House. Pointing out that the U.S. government had compensated Italy and China when Americans lynched those nations' citizens, Barnett argued that the United States should "do as much for its own." North Carolina's George Henry White, the only black representative in Washington, made a similar case before Congress. Both Congress and President William McKinley dismissed the appeal.

When a race riot in Wilmington, North Carolina, the following year left dozens of black Americans dead or wounded,

McKinley again remained silent. A black refugee from Wilmington condemned the irony of race murders "while the nation was on its knees thanking God for having enabled it to break the Spanish yoke from the neck of Cuba."

The Spanish-American War wrested Caribbean and South Pacific islands from Spain and led to the United States annexing Hawaii in 1898. To ensure its influence over these countries, the American government dispatched troops and officials to "establish system where chaos reigns." But black Americans understood that white Americans' attempts to impose new ways of life on these foreign peoples meant that the chaos was far from over. Local residents in these places would surely show their resentment.

The Brownsville Incident

Du Bois returned from the Pan-African Conference to an America where the political influence of black people was declining. Representative George White, completing his term in 1901, would be the last African American to serve in Congress for more than three decades. With the Democrats outspokenly racist, many black voters halfheartedly cast their ballot for Republican presidential candidate William McKinley. In 1901, McKinley's assassination put Vice President Theodore Roosevelt in the Oval Office. A Progressive New Yorker, Roosevelt sought Booker T. Washington's advice about African Americans. When the president crossed the color line, inviting Washington to dine at the White House, many black Americans dared to hope the federal government might again support black rights. In 1904, they helped reelect Roosevelt.

But two years later, the president dishonorably discharged the entire Twenty-fifth Infantry regiment, many of them recently returned from the Philippines. These black soldiers were stationed near Brownsville, Texas, where local white residents resented their presence. On August 14, an unidentified band of men fired dozens of shots, wounding several white Brownsville residents. The presence of military rifle cartridges led the federal investigators to blame the black soldiers. Roosevelt dismissed the regiment with no trial and no possibility of appeal. (In 1972, a black Congressman successfully petitioned President Nixon for a pardon and honorable discharge for the Twenty-Fifth. This allowed the one surviving soldier to receive a $25,000 pension.)

In Boston, black journalist William Monroe Trotter described the mass discharge as "meanness, injustice, and unwarranted cruelty." Privately, Booker T. Washington also condemned it. "There is no law, human or divine," Washington told his friends, "which justifies the punishment of an innocent man." But Washington refrained from public condemnation. Instead, he made excuses for Roosevelt and discouraged his followers from "going too far" in protesting.

ACCOMMODATION OR AGITATION?

The Brownsville incident provided both a sharp reminder of African Americans' political powerlessness and of divisions within the black community. More and more black people refused to accept Washington's admonitions about "going too far." Washington's passivity in response to Brownsville marked the beginning of the end of his singular influence among black people. One-time followers such as Mary Church Terrell and Ida Wells Barnett now sought leaders who would openly condemn racism.

Until the Pan-African Conference, Du Bois and Washington had been allies, but they disagreed about how to achieve racial progress. Washington's tepid response to the Brownsville incident only deepened their enmity. Thus, as the twentieth century dawned, black people faced a dilemma: Should they follow Washington's strategy, accommodating racial injustice and waiting patiently for white people to see them as worthy, or should they confront injustice head-on, agitating for immediate equality?

Opposition to Washington

"We have come to protest forever against being shut off from equal rights with other citizens, and shall remain forever on the firing line in defense of such rights," wrote William Monroe Trotter in 1901. A proponent of direct resistance to racial injustice, the twenty-nine-year-old black journalist was in Boston producing the first issues of *The Guardian*, a news weekly that focused on black political concerns. Occupying the building in which William Lloyd Garrison had launched the *Liberator* in 1831, Trotter, like Garrison, passionately advocated full and immediate equality for African Americans. The son of a Boston realtor,

> "We have come to protest forever against being shut off from equal rights with other citizens, and shall remain forever on the firing line in defense of such rights."—*William Monroe Trotter*

Trotter graduated from Harvard in 1895, where he met Du Bois. He shared the older man's disdain for Booker T. Washington's political patience and emphasis on vocational education. In *The Guardian,* Trotter criticized Washington's programs while promoting the immediate dismantling of segregation.

Though he admired Washington's accomplishments, Du Bois felt slave origins had narrowed the southern leader's vision. African Americans, Du Bois argued, should insist on immediate full inclusion in the society their labor had built. The small but vocal group of intellectuals who followed Du Bois and Trotter viewed Washington's accommodation strategy as shortsighted. Despite these criticisms, Washington continued to publicly espouse caution and patience. He and his followers worried that Du Bois and Trotter encouraged poor black Americans to pursue unrealistic goals. When Washington spoke in Boston in 1903, Trotter and others publicly challenged his conciliatory style. Washington had the hecklers arrested and encouraged his allies to withhold advertising from any newspaper that refused to endorse the Tuskegee approach. His loyal friend T. Thomas Fortune, editor of the powerful *New York Age,* supported him.

Living daily among southerners scarred by slavery, Washington continued to focus on helping them acquire survival skills. By ingratiating himself with wealthy white philanthropists and vilifying African Americans who stood in his way, he reaped results. Hundreds of southern black people from disadvantaged backgrounds benefited from education at Tuskegee Institute. Demonstrating the value of Washington's strategy, they made a respected place for themselves in black communities. But to the minority of black Americans who followed Du Bois—most coming from privileged backgrounds—respect in the black communities was not enough. Far removed from black southerners, Trotter and Du Bois agitated for a world where black men and women did not have to compromise their dignity to make a living.

The rivalry between Washington and Du Bois dominated black discourse between 1900 and 1915. The year that Trotter heckled Washington, Du Bois published a collection of essays, *The Souls of Black Folk,* describing Washington as leading a "cult" that had an ignorant, "unquestioning following." Du Bois conceded that Washington, "beginning with so little, has done so much." But the southerner's limited vision, argued Du Bois, which discouraged African Americans from seeking political power and publicly protesting injustice, perpetuated cowardice and passivity. Vocational education, Du Bois added, could make workers, but it could not make men. Du Bois also noted the inconsistency in Washington's educational philosophy: "He advocates common school and industrial education, and deprecates institutions of higher learning, but neither the Negro common schools, nor Tuskegee itself, could remain open a day were it not for teachers trained in Negro [liberal arts] colleges."

In *The Souls of Black Folk,* Du Bois presented the idea that the color line stunted black Americans' "spiritual strivings." Capturing the dilemma of black people's divided loyalties, he described how the American Negro "ever feels his Twoness—an American, a Negro . . . two warring souls in one dark body whose dogged strength alone keeps it from being torn asunder." Du Bois dedicated himself to understanding and dignifying the "spiritual strivings" of African Americans—a group whom he felt shared a special racial consciousness with other "darker peoples of the world."

> The American Negro "ever feels his Twoness—an American, a Negro . . . two warring souls in one dark body whose dogged strength alone keeps it from being torn asunder."
> —*W. E. B. Du Bois*

For Du Bois, black consciousness had a lyrical and almost religious quality. Born out of suffering and an African mysticism stretching back through centuries, black consciousness gave dark-skinned peoples a unique depth of soul. People of "Negro blood," he proclaimed, had "a message [of spirituality and high morality] for the world." Influenced by Darwinist ideas, he also suggested that a small minority of African Americans were socially and intellectually superior to the rest. He suggested that the race should unite to develop the talents of these few, who would become the race's leaders. "Negroes," he argued, "must first of all deal with the Talented Tenth . . . developing the Best of this race that they may guide the Mass away from the contamination . . . of the Worst, in their own and other races." Du Bois later recanted this arrogant notion.

Chicago Democrat Julius Taylor, the black editor of the *Broad Axe,* felt Republican patronage politics—with which Washington allied himself—worked against black people. Patronage jobs, he felt, went to favored white applicants, rarely to well-qualified black people. Meanwhile, the Republican Party did little to ensure the franchise for African Americans, or to help them gain access to other than menial jobs. In 1899, Taylor predicted that "the time is not far distant when Booker T. Washington will be repudiated as the leader of our race, for he believes that only mealy-mouthed Negroes like himself should be involved in politics."

Despite intensifying opposition, in 1905 Washington was one of the most powerful men in America. A central operator among national Republicans, often helping black workers secure service jobs in Republican homes and businesses, and a savvy strategist for black enterprise, he had secured the loyalty of rising urban black entrepreneurs (many of them Tuskegee graduates) by establishing the Negro Business League in 1900. Consulted by presidents and white capitalists, and supported by their charity, he affected the lives of thousands of black Americans, most of whom idolized him. Former slave Daniel Dowdy of Oklahoma City recalled, "He is the father of industrial education and you know that sho' is a great thing."

The Niagara Movement and the NAACP

Washington's stranglehold on black leadership prompted a backlash. In July 1905, William Monroe Trotter, W. E. B. Du Bois, and Morehouse College president John Hope invited two dozen black leaders—mostly northerners—to meet at Niagara Falls in Ontario, Canada. There they formalized their opposition to Washington's idea of gradual progress for black people. Soon 400 strong, the Niagara Movement, as the group came to be known, agitated for national legislation guaranteeing equal rights for black citizens.

Sensing the threat to his power, Booker T. Washington tried to undermine the Niagara Movement by sending spies to meetings and warning that federal workers who supported Du Bois would lose their jobs. He also discouraged both black and white financiers from backing the movement. But a 1908 race riot in Springfield, Illinois—Abraham Lincoln's birthplace—catalyzed support for the movement among some influential white Progressives. Distressed by the murder of eight African Americans and the wounding of dozens more, white Kentucky-born socialist William E. Walling called for a national organization of "fair-minded whites and intelligent blacks" to speak out boldly against racial violence and injustice.

Heirs to the nineteenth-century abolitionist movement responded. In the spring of 1909, journalist Oswald Garrison Villard (grandson of William Lloyd Garrison) joined Walling and a committee of other white Progressives, including settlement house founder Jane Addams, to establish the National Negro Committee Conference. Booker T. Washington refused their invitation, but Du Bois and John Hope attended the conference as representatives of the Niagara Movement. Poet Alice Ruth Moore, antilynching crusader Ida Wells Barnett, and NACW leader Mary Church Terrell also attended.

The conferees called for government intervention to protect Fourteenth Amendment rights and southern black voters, to ensure African Americans' physical safety, and to provide fair access to education. Black members also passed a resolution opposing Tuskegee's policy of focusing on industrial and manual training.

The committee met again in 1909 to establish the National Association for the Advancement of Colored People (NAACP), of which white lawyer Moorfield Storey was elected president. The organization flourished as more white Progressives joined, including *Harper's* editor William Dean Howells. W. E. B. Du Bois inaugurated the NAACP's magazine, *Crisis,* and remained its editor until 1934.

The NAACP had a compelling mission: to ensure that African Americans be "physically free from peonage, mentally free from ignorance, politically free from disfranchisement, and socially free from insult." To accomplish this, it aimed to design test cases forcing the courts to dissolve racial segregation. Led by an interracial board of directors, the NAACP soon expanded to encompass fifty branches and more than 6,000 members. Booker T. Washington declined to join. So did Ida Wells Barnett. Preferring to be out in the streets with working people, Barnett found the NAACP's legalism too slow-moving.

A few black Americans sought a middle ground between Washington and Du Bois. One such person was John Hope, who cofounded the Niagara Movement. Though he had witnessed racial violence and deprivation firsthand as a child, Hope's horizons were broadened by his education at Rhode Island's elite Brown University. In 1906, when he became the first black president of Morehouse College, Hope urged both vocational and liberal education. He inspired others who sought black unity. Buck Colbert Franklin, who studied at Morehouse, even named his son John Hope Franklin in honor of the great educator. The grandson of a slave, Buck Franklin had grown up in Oklahoma and had Choctaw Indians in his extended family. After graduating from Morehouse, Franklin returned to Oklahoma and became a lawyer, turning his attention to repealing Oklahoma's grandfather clause restricting the franchise to men whose grandparents were voters—which excluded most black people, whose grandparents had been slaves. Though he chose to live in Rentiesville, an all-black town, Franklin agitated against segregated schools.

Franklin embodied the ideals of both Du Bois and Washington. Like Du Bois, he supported the NAACP. Like Washington, he dedicated himself to hard work. Near the end of his life, Buck Franklin wrote in his autobiography: "At best, the road ahead for the American Negro is going to be rough, and there will be no way for the weak or timid to make it. Those with strength, with creative genius, potential, courage, faith and hope, will make it if they are willing to work hard. They must be clean and presentable, for outer cleanliness advertises inner cleanliness. If you live across the tracks and have something the other fellow needs, he will come to you for it."

BLACK CULTURE

"He was kind to all of us musicians that would just, as I say, 'flock' around him, 'cause he was an inspiration to us all. We always treated him as 'daddy' to the bunch of piano players." So Arthur Marshall remembered composer Scott Joplin. Marshall had studied with Joplin in the early 1890s, when Joplin was playing in Sedalia, Missouri, at the black Maple Leaf Club. Joplin had traveled through Texas and Missouri singing with his friends and his brother, playing piano and cornet and developing the Queen City Cornet Band and the Texas Medley Quartette.

> "The Maple Leaf Rag will make me the king of ragtime composers."—*Scott Joplin*

While in Sedalia, Joplin also composed music. "The Maple Leaf Rag will make me the king of ragtime composers," he told Marshall. In October 1896, Joplin registered the copyright for his first musical score, "Crush Collision March." Joplin called his music "rag" because it had a "ragged rhythm." He soon would be "daddy" to ragtime, a musical form that captured the imagination of both white and black Americans.

Black culture crossed the color line. International audiences had thrilled to performances of the Fisk Jubilee Singers when they traveled abroad in the 1870s. Penetrating the African interior, European imperialists had been captivated by the local sculpture. After Du Bois attributed a mystical spirituality to black Americans, many white intellectuals developed the romantic notion that the world's colored peoples were naturally artistic. White audiences also admired black athletic talent.

Black artistic and athletic ability were not new. What was new was white America's growing appreciation of black expression, especially when it blended with the familiar. Joplin's mixture of classical European music, the complex African rhythms, and his own north Texas heritage proved an enticing blend.

Music, Poetry, Composition

The son of a free mother and a father who had been enslaved, Scott Joplin grew up determined to bring honor to his race. Encouraged by his mother to study piano with a German musician, he had a firm grounding in European music traditions as well as his mother's memories of southern black modes of expression. He also studied music at George R. Smith College in Sedalia, Missouri, which was run by the Freedmen's Bureau and the Methodist Church. A few months after publishing "Crush Collision March," Joplin published "Maple Leaf Rag," the composition that indeed made him the king of ragtime composers. White music publisher John Stark, who liked ragtime's intricate rhythms and dramatic orchestration, gave Joplin a five-year contract for royalties on the sales of "Maple Leaf Rag." By 1900, the thirty-two-year-old Joplin had become the first black American to earn a living writing music.

Just as Joplin's music caught the nation's attention, so too did the lyrical poetry of Paul Laurence Dunbar. Like Joplin, Dunbar had grown up hearing southern black rhythms in his mother's voice. Dunbar's mother encouraged her son to master the speech styles of white Americans as well as the sounds of black America. Also like Joplin, Dunbar never lost sight of a racial mission.

During high school, Dunbar submitted poems and essays to newspapers across the country. Several black newspapers printed his advice that black Americans should settle in the West. Frederick Douglass saw great promise in the young poet when he heard Dunbar read his poem "Ode to Ethiopia," which offered "a pledge of faith unwavering" to "the Mother Race" of African Americans who "have the right to noble pride." Dunbar felt deeply honored when Douglass accepted the gift of a book, promised to buy more, and invited the poet to stay with him in Washington: "It would do me good to have you up there in my old study just working away on your poetry."

In his work, Dunbar embraced both patriotism and race pride. In "A Columbian Ode," he memorialized Christopher Columbus's voyage to America and proclaimed his allegiance to the American flag. He also soon made friends with other black artists, writers, and musicians who helped him hone his skills. The 1898 musical *Clarindy, or the Origin of the Cakewalk,*

Paul Laurence Dunbar Tells an African American Story

As a child, Dunbar absorbed his mother's dignity, resolve, and appreciation for stories handed down from her Kentucky slave family and friends. Sometimes, as in this poem, published in 1896 in Lyrics of Lowly Life, *Dunbar told an African American story in classical English verse. For generations to come, black parents read his work to their children.*

We Wear the Mask

We wear the mask that grins and lies,
It hides our cheeks and shades our eyes—
This debt we pay to human guile;
With torn and bleeding hearts we smile,
And mouth with myriad subtleties.

Why should the world be over-wise,
In counting all our tears and sighs?
Nay, let them only see us, while
We wear the mask.

We smile, but, O great Christ, our cries
To thee from tortured souls arise.
We sing, but oh the clay is vile
Beneath our feet, and long the mile;
But let the world dream otherwise,
We wear the mask!

—from "We Wear the Mask" from The Complete Poems of Paul Laurence Dunbar *(1913).*

To view a longer version of this document, please go to www.ablongman.com/carson/documents.

on which he collaborated with dramatist Will Marion Cook, became the first show by a black person produced on Broadway. Dunbar's approach was simple: "Let the work have a message . . . a story to tell, a living man or woman to present, a lesson to deliver—clear, strong, and unmistakable." The result was a poetic style that appealed both to unschooled audiences and sophisticated intellectuals.

Dunbar often expressed "self-doubts" about his work. He hoped "that there is something worthy in my writings and not merely the novelty of a black face associated with the power to rhyme." When *Harper's Weekly* editor William Dean Howells reviewed Dunbar's third book of poetry, *Majors and Minors,* in 1896, the young artist's success was assured. The review, however, expressed the romantic, naive, and patronizing white view of black art and artists: "There has come to me . . . a little book of verse. I feel a heightened pathos in the appeal . . . [of] the face which confronted me when I opened the volume . . . a young Negro, with the race traits strangely accented: the black skin, the woolly hair, the thick outrolling lips, and the mild, soft eyes of the pure African type. . . . I hope that the love of dramatic contrasts has not made me overvalue it . . . because it is the work of a man whose race has not hitherto made its mark in art. . . . I do not forget what the race has done in other arts."

Nevertheless, Howells did "not remember any English-speaking Negro" who was Dunbar's equal. He compared Dunbar to the venerated eighteenth-century Scottish poet Robert Burns. "I have sometimes fancied that the Negro *thought* black and *felt* black, that they were racially so utterly alien and distinct from ourselves that there could never be common intellectual and emotional ground." But in Dunbar's writing, Howells found "white thinking and white feeling in a black man." He speculated that through art, others might discover that "God hath made of one blood all nations of men." From then on, Dunbar reaped handsome royalties from the sales of his poetry. His readings and royalties made him the first black American to support himself entirely with a literary career.

Dunbar never lost sight of his own modest beginnings, and his writing celebrated both slave dialect and formal European writing styles. In an 1895 letter to black poet Alice Ruth Moore (whom he married three years later), he asked "whether or not you believe in preserving by Afro-American—I don't like the word—writers those quaint old tales and songs of our fathers . . . or whether you, like so many others think we should ignore the past and all its . . . literary materials." Explaining that "characters in fiction should be . . . the embodiment of a principle or idea," Dunbar walked a fine line between preserving his ancestors' expressiveness and making them a laughingstock. In his writing, he celebrated a variety of black and white leaders, including Haitian revolutionary slave Toussaint L'Ouverture

ONE OF THE SUREST WAYS
TO SUCCEED IN LIFE IS TO
TAKE A COURSE AT

The Touissant Conservatory of Art and Music

253 West 134th Street
NEW YORK CITY

The most up-to-date and thoroughly equipped conservatory in the city. Conducted under the supervision of

MME. E. TOUISSANT WELCOME
The Foremost Female Artist of the Race

Courses in Art

Drawing, Pen and Ink Sketching, Crayon, Pastel, Water Color, Oil Painting, Designing, Cartooning, Fashion Designing, Sign Painting, Portrait Painting and Photo Enlarging in Crayon, Water Color, Pastel and Oil. Artistic Painting of Parasols, Fans, Book Marks, Pin Cushions, Lamp Shades, Curtains, Screens, Piano and Mantel Covers, Sofa Pillows, etc.

Music

Piano, Violin, Mandolin, Voice Culture and all Brass and Reed Instruments.

TERMS REASONABLE

■ This advertisement in the NAACP's *Crisis* magazine reflected black intellectuals' desire to promote black art and entrepreneurship. Jennie "Mme. E. Toussaint" Welcome, born Jennie Louise Van Der Zee, was the daughter of General Ulysses Grant's maid and butler. She had private lessons in art and music before establishing her conservatory in Harlem. Her brother James became a noted New York photographer.

■ Black artists were supported by philanthropists like Sarah Breedlove "Madam C. J." Walker, America's first black woman millionaire. One of twenty children in a Mississippi family, Walker established an international network of beauty parlors. Walker had a worldwide payroll of 5,000 black women by 1910, when she turned forty-three years old. When she died nine years later, she bequeathed most of her wealth to charity. She also left instructions that her company always be run by a woman.

and eighteenth-century New England black poet Phillis Wheatley, and white heroes like President Theodore Roosevelt and Robert Gould Shaw, the Civil War commander of the Massachusetts Fifty-fourth Regiment.

When Dunbar died in February 1906, black bicycle racer Major Taylor voiced the impact of Dunbar's literary success: "I am thinking seriously of taking up this work [writing verse] where poor Paul Laurence Dunbar had to leave off." Taylor had achieved his own success as an athlete. Yet inspired by Dunbar, he dreamed of becoming a poet.

Thanks to Dunbar's literary trailblazing, other black artists began finding appreciative audiences. In 1900, James Weldon Johnson and his brother J. Rosamond Johnson signed a contract with musical producer Joseph W. Stern, thereby becoming the first black songwriters on Broadway. Many of their so-called "coon songs" mocked black and foreign characters alike. Unlike Dunbar, the Johnson brothers seemed to care little whether art expressed dignity or had a "message." At first, the popular black press proved surprisingly tolerant of caricatured portrayals of black people, believing any successful black performer was an inspiration to the race. However, black journalists soon grew critical of black dialect and the degrading "coon songs." Beginning in the late 1890s, several journals defined a new mission for black music. Best-known was the *Negro Music Journal*, started by pianist J. Hillary Taylor. Published in Washington, DC, the journal extolled music's power to teach young musicians "how to be industrious, studious, patient, benevolent, loving, unselfish, and refined."

tenants, then purchased other rental properties nearby. Extended families and groups of friends were able to afford the desirable location by sharing housing. By 1915, about 50,000 black people lived in more than a thousand buildings in Harlem's twenty-three square blocks. By 1930, the majestic, elegant Harlem brownstones were home to roughly 200,000 black Americans who had come to improve their lot.

Black institutions followed. The NAACP moved its national office to Harlem by 1915. T. Thomas Fortune relocated his *New York Age* to the neighborhood. Black churches bought property, and social service agencies set up their offices there. Indeed, Harlem became known as the place where African Americans could expect a warm welcome. It was a magnet for black Americans of every class, providing them with their first chance to live in modern, attractive city residences.

One of the most enduring improvement organizations spawned by Harlem's dramatic growth was the National Urban League. In contrast to the NAACP, with its focus on court battles, the Urban League tackled issues of working-class city life, from negotiations with police and public officials to mediation with employers or landlords to neighborhood organizing.

Like the NACW and the Negro Business League, the Urban League started out as a national organization linking local community centers, child care facilities, and employment programs. One such organization that affiliated itself with the Urban League was the White Rose Mission. This group provided temporary housing, child care, and job counseling to newcomers—similar to the services that urban settlement houses offered European immigrants. The founder of the White Rose Mission, Georgia-born Victoria Earle Matthews, was motivated by "the history of [my] race lifting itself out of . . . helplessness." Matthews also believed that "the Afro-American woman . . . deserves . . . active sympathy and cooperation." Poet Alice Ruth Moore taught evening classes at White Rose, adding a cultural component to the mission's programs.

Other cities offered similar services. In Philadelphia, an interracial coalition organized the Armstrong Association, which provided temporary housing and job counseling. Lugenia Burns Hope, wife of educator John Hope, helped establish the Atlanta Neighborhood Union, with nurseries, playgrounds, and a tuberculosis care center. Chicago's Negro Fellowship League, started by Ida Wells Barnett, helped

Networked by 1911 in dozens of cities, the National Urban League absorbed Philadelphia's Armstrong Association. In this cover photo for its 1915 annual report, it showcased children it had helped equip for school, describing them as "proud to be in the new shoe line."

■ Promoting hygiene, education, and strong families, the Armstrong Association sought to combine the family goals of the NACW with the educational goals of the "Tuskegee Machine."

southern newcomers adjust to city life. All these enterprises came under the National Urban League umbrella.

The National Urban League was the most overtly political of early twentieth-century organizations. Closely linked with the liberal wing of Progressivism, it encouraged black urbanites to vote, join unions, and petition local governments for equal services. Like the NAACP, the Urban League received some support from white Progressives.

But there was an important distinction between the NAACP and the Urban League. Strongest in northern cities, the NAACP was dominated by educated and sophisticated men and women, often of mixed race, and usually from families that had been free before the Civil War. While the NAACP's political agenda included black people of all classes, its membership and social gatherings often did not. By contrast, the Urban League reached out to a broad spectrum of black city-dwellers, welcoming uneducated newcomers and offering them social, medical, economic, and political services. The organization's resources included social workers and settlement houses. By 1915, the League had also begun gathering annual statistics on housing and employment among black urbanites—a tradition it continues today.

Churches and Clubs

In all the urban places where black people clustered, black churches connected them. More than 6,000 AME churches established a network from Atlanta to Seattle, San Francisco to Boston. The Baptist and Methodist churches also flourished, their membership exceeding the AME by the early twentieth century. Many Baptist and Methodist congregations in northern and western cities enabled black migrants to preserve connections to the South. All the denominations had congregations in Philadelphia, New York, or Detroit that linked members with families and friends in "sister churches" in Georgia, Alabama, or Mississippi.

Black churches had a bold social mission as well. They provided places where people could learn to read and write or to feed families. They served as recreation centers, voting information centers, employment agencies, and savings and loans institutions. Incubators of black talent, they sponsored Sunday schools and sports teams and encouraged orators, writers, singers, and athletes. Churches helped send black youth to college and supported entrepreneurship. When Texan Richard Henry Boyd in 1897 established the National Baptist Publishing Board to publish religious literature for black people, local churches supported him. The churches also fortified racial pride by placing ads in *Crisis* for "the Negro doll," designed by Nashville's National Negro Doll Company. Black children finally had a doll that looked like them.

Dominated by "plain American Negroes," the black churches spent little time debating the intellectual merits of various black strategies. Their members gave their loyalties to the Republican Party and to Booker T. Washington, kept their spirits up with Bible study and song, and attended to the day-to-day business of supporting whatever black enterprises sprang up. For example, black churches helped inaugurate the Associated Correspondents of Race Newspapers (ACRN) in 1907 to provide accurate information to black newspapers across the country, with the goal of promoting "the best interests of our race through the press." Soon to become the National Afro-American Press Association, members included T. Thomas Fortune of the *New York Age;* William Sidney Pittman of the *Negro Business League Herald;* Robert Sengstacke Abbott, whose weekly Chicago *Defender* soon reached a circulation of 250,000; and Robert Lee Vann, whose Pittsburgh *Courier* soon became the *Defender's* closest competitor.

In addition to fostering social improvement organizations, the Progressive spirit also gave rise to such institutions as college fraternities and sororities. Alpha Phi Alpha, the nation's

William Bulkley on Race and Economics

Black New Yorkers like William Bulkley decried the economic forces driving black southerners to the North. Born a South Carolina slave in 1861, Bulkley by 1909 had become New York's first African American school principal in a predominately white district. A cofounder of both the NAACP and the Urban League, he spoke before the 1909 National Negro Conference.

[A]ny limitation put on the development of the Negro seriously affects the South's economic development. . . . Any thoughtful student of economics would readily see that the lack of reliable labor is due . . . to the absence of effort on the part of the South to enlighten, to encourage, and to render contented its laboring classes. . . .

. . . [R]ace oppression is driving out of the South a host of best Negroes, best in culture of mind, best in sturdiness of character, best in skill of hand. A census of the Negroes in any city in the North would show that the majority of the most progressive of them, whether in the professions, in business, or in the trades, were more or less recent arrivals from the South. Can the South afford to lose this class? Can any country afford to drive out its best?

If only a small part of the time that is devoted to schemes to restrict, to humiliate and to oppress the Negroes were spent in an effort to study means by which they might be made more intelligent, more thrift as laborers, more skillful as artisans, more content as citizens, there are few spots on the globe that would show so great an industrial awakening [as the South].

—from National Negro Conference, Proceedings *(New York: National Negro Conference, 1909), pp. 39–97.*

To view a longer version of this document, please go to *www.ablongman.com/carson/documents.*

Ultimately, however, epidemics in Africa decimated the settlers there, and Sam's mysterious disappearance in Africa ended the venture. But a few settlers remained in Africa, helping plant Western ideas in established African towns. Like similar back-to-Africa movements, Sam's dream foundered on lack of funds and overreliance on a charismatic leader.

Other black visionaries congregated in Harlem. In the spring of 1911, a small informal group known as the Men's Sunday Club created the Negro Historical Society of Research. Members included established intellectuals like W. E. B. Du Bois, Harvard-educated Carter G. Woodson, and young men like Alain Locke, who five years before had been the first black Rhodes scholar. To raise black Americans' appreciation for their heritage, Woodson established the Association for the Study of Negro Life and History (ASNLH) four years later. In conjunction with ASNLH, Woodson soon began publishing the *Journal of Negro History,* which celebrated the achievements of black Americans. In his efforts to preserve black heritage, Woodson also received encouragement from his friend Jesse Edward Moorland. The grandson of free black Underground Railroad conductors, Moorland had accumulated a large library of books, manuscripts, graphics, and newspaper clippings, which he shared with Woodson and others who aimed to publicize black history. "The achievements of the Negro properly set forth," Woodson said, "will crown him as a factor in early human progress and a maker of modern civilization." Similar groups were launched in other cities. Philadelphia's American Negro Historical Society claimed that "no country can tell its history truthfully until all its scrolls are unrolled."

> "No country can tell its history truthfully until all its scrolls are unrolled."
> —*American Negro Historical Society*

Another member of the Men's Sunday Club was book collector Arthur Schomburg. The child of Puerto Rican immigrants who had settled in Harlem, Schomburg developed an interest in black history when a fifth-grade teacher told him that black people had no past, no heroes, no great moments. Determined to prove otherwise, Schomburg began gathering literary works and examples of visual art by people of African descent. He developed contacts with other collectors in Washington, Philadelphia, and other cities. Schomburg enjoyed the company of his intellectual colleagues, but he distrusted white people and preferred the company of the black working class.

Schomburg and other lay historians were enthusiastic about the work of Jamaican black nationalist Marcus Garvey. Though many intellectuals considered Garvey brash and overbearing, Schomburg eagerly read Garvey's writing in the London-based *Africa Times and Orient Review*. He admired Garvey's focus on Haitian revolutionary Toussaint L'Ouverture and on the writings of Edward Blyden, a former teacher and missionary in Liberia.

Schomburg became an ardent supporter of Garvey when the Jamaican established his Universal Negro Improvement Association (UNIA) in 1914. This organization promoted socially and economically separate American black communities with an orientation toward Africa. With racial separation, the UNIA aimed to "have for its object the raising of the standard of the Negro . . . the promotion of a Universal Confraternity; the promotion of the spirit of pride and love; the reclamation of the fallen . . . the civilizing of the backward tribes of Africa." Schomburg also admired Garvey's focus on working class issues. For Schomburg, "Negro improvement" applied to both middle-class and poor black people.

THE "NEW ABOLITION"

In response to race riots in 1915, the Chicago *Defender* counseled its black readership, "If you must die, take at least one with you." This cry of rage, which got the paper banned in many cities, arose from the frustration that underlay black struggles for progress. Black leaders saw their choices limited to emigration, separate communities within the United States, agitation for full civil and political rights, or accommodation of white supremacy. W. E. B. Du Bois chose agitation, using the *Crisis* to stir both black and white Americans to protest disfranchisement and racial violence. In 1912, he and the NAACP began to receive assistance from white New York intellectual Joel E. Spingarn. A man of enormous energies, Spingarn inaugurated what he called "the New Abolition"—a movement promoting the abolition of racial segregation and calling for full and immediate equality for African Americans. Two years earlier, the impulsive Spingarn had purchased the Heart of Hope Club, a suburban New York service organization for destitute black people. Seeking advice about how to manage the club, he had written to Du Bois, initiating a lifelong partnership. Now, criss-crossing the country on "New Abolition" tours, Spingarn spoke before 70,000 people in two dozen cities. His efforts helped establish an NAACP presence in Chicago, Detroit, Indianapolis, St. Louis, and on the Howard University campus. Spingarn also got NAACP literature distributed to white campuses and civic organizations. "There is no such thing as a 'Negro problem,'" Spingarn insisted. "It is an American problem, for while injustice exists, the whole country is in danger."

On "New Abolition" tours, Spingarn and Du Bois reminded Americans of the recent deterioration of black rights. In 1911, Baltimore had been the first city to write legislation mandating segregated neighborhoods, pushing the *Plessy* decision and Progressive ideas about social management to new levels. Fears of race-mixing led northern states such as New York, Massachusetts, and Michigan to consider laws against interracial marriage, violation of which carried stiff jail sentences. State legislators even considered forced sterilization of white people who "tainted" white "blood" by mating with inferior races. Spingarn cited the continuing horror of lynchings—such as the burning alive of a black man in Coatesville, Pennsylvania, in 1911. "All we ask is absolutely fair treatment among men regardless of color." But neither fairness nor physical safety seemed imminent.

The NAACP Legal Assault

But even as frustration intensified, Spingarn contended that if legal obstacles were removed, black Americans could easily become part of mainstream America. He cited the NAACP's success in pressing important legal cases. These efforts enabled black student Carrie Lee to petition for a room in Smith College's dormitories, helped a black boy gain admittance to New York's Central Preparatory School, successfully challenged housing discrimination in Louisville, Kentucky, and desegregated a New York theater. In *Guinn* v. *United States* (1915), the Supreme Court outlawed Oklahoma's grandfather clause.

But Spingarn and the NAACP also met with legal defeats. The NAACP was unsuccessful in overturning President Woodrow Wilson's 1913 order mandating segregation in federal employment facilities. Spingarn also spearheaded the NAACP's unsuccessful campaign to persuade the National Board of Censorship to ban the movie *Birth of a Nation* (1914), which depicted the Ku Klux Klan as heroes and black Americans as brutes. Wilson showed the film in the White House, praising it as "history written with lightning." As black Americans expressed outrage, Springarn denounced Wilson, declaring that "reformers and prophets are always ahead of politicians."

> "Two years ago you were thought to be a second Lincoln. Have you a New Freedom for white Americans and a new slavery for 'your Afro-American fellow citizens'?"—*William Monroe Trotter*

Although most black leaders continued to reluctantly support Republican candidates, Du Bois had used the *Crisis* to back Democrat Woodrow Wilson in 1912, believing the president would protect black rights. William

W. E. B. Du Bois Eulogizes His Rival

Upon Booker T. Washington's death, W. E. B. Du Bois published his assessment of his rival's contributions. In this excerpt from the NAACP's magazine, Crisis, *Du Bois praised aspects of Washington's life, but he also continued to criticize Washington's strategies.*

He was the greatest Negro leader since Frederick Douglass, and the most distinguished man, white or black, who has come out of the South since the Civil War. His fame was international and his influence far-reaching. Of the good that he accomplished there can be no doubt: he directed the attention of the Negro race in America to the pressing necessity of economic development; he emphasized technical education and did much to pave the way for an understanding between the white and darker races. [But] he never adequately grasped the growing bond of politics and industry; he did not understand the deeper foundations of human training. . . . We may then generously lay on the grave of Booker T. Washington testimony of our thankfulness for his undoubted help in the accumulation of Negro property and land, his establishment of Tuskegee and spreading of industrial education and his compelling of the white South to at least think of the Negro as a possible man. On the other hand, in stern justice, we must lay on the soul of this man a heavy responsibility for the consummation of Negro disfranchisement, the decline of the Negro college and public school, and the firmer establishment of [racial discrimination].

—from Crisis, *December 11, 1915, p. 82.*

To view a longer version of this document, please go to www.ablongman.com/carson/documents.

Monroe Trotter also supported Wilson, albeit reluctantly. The child of a black politician, Trotter had grown cynical about national politics. Even before the inauguration, he wrote Wilson, "As your inauguration approaches, the clouds are lowering and a feeling of foreboding is creeping over the Colored people."

In 1914, Trotter met with Wilson in the White House to protest racial segregation in federal offices. "Two years ago you were thought to be a second Lincoln," Trotter admonished the president. "Have you a New Freedom for white Americans and a new slavery for 'your Afro-American fellow citizens'? God forbid."

The End of Booker T. Washington and Accommodation

Despite the changes swirling around him, Booker T. Washington continued to promote accommodation. To him, fulfilling white America's expectations offered African Americans their best hope for physical safety and economic success. But more and more black men and women disagreed. Years later, George Conrad, an ex-slave from Oklahoma, recalled his reaction to Washington: "He argued for our people to stay out of town and stay in the country. . . . He was a smart man but I think a man should live wherever he chooses. . . . I never stopped working to go and see him when I'd hear he was coming to town to speak."

In November 1915, Washington collapsed during a speaking tour in New York. A man of provincial tastes—he seldom left the South and was uninterested in African heritage—he asked to be taken home to die. "I was born in the South," he said, "I have lived and laboured in the South, and I expect to be buried in the South." He died at Tuskegee a few days later. After his death, it was revealed that the man who had promoted accommodation also had harbored a white-hot rage at racial injustice. Washington secretly contributed to efforts challenging grandfather clauses that kept black men from voting in the South. He also had quietly met with industrialists to improve conditions for black train travelers and had donated money for court battles against segregation and disfranchisement. He had even written an essay citing reasons why segregation was "ill-advised," including that it was "unjust" and "embitters the Negro and harms the moral fiber of the white man." In a telling comment, Washington

> "That the Negro does not express this constant sense of wrong is no proof that he does not feel it."
> —*Booker T. Washington*

remarked, "That the Negro does not express this constant sense of wrong is no proof that he does not feel it."

With Washington's death, the day of the docile, accommodating colored person drew to a close. Increasing numbers of Negroes—who now insisted on a capitalized N—would soon confront injustice head on.

The Amenia Conference

With the death of Booker T. Washington in 1915, Du Bois set out to ease the tension between those who sought an immediate end to segregation and racial injustice and those who counseled patience and accommodation. He joined white reformer Joel Spingarn to host a meeting at Spingarn's summer estate near Amenia, New York. With Du Bois, Spingarn, and Tuskegee representative Emmett J. Scott at Amenia in August 1916 were many NAACP supporters and old allies of Washington.

An upbeat mood infused the Amenia Conference. The delegates drafted a statement affirming both liberal and industrial education for young black people. The statement also recognized the "peculiar difficulties" of black southerners who supported Booker T. Washington's philosophy of pursuing economic progress but postponing the goal of integration to avoid incurring the wrath of white southerners. The delegates ended by pledging to support African Americans in any plan that sought racial progress.

Boston's William Monroe Trotter, publisher of *The Guardian,* chose not to attend the conference, but he felt cheered by its outcome. "In this celebration the big chiefs buried the hatchet and smoked together the pipe of Peace," he wrote. Trotter predicted black leaders, "with a united front and unbroken ranks," would "turn to renew the warfare against race discrimination, segregation, and lynching." He decided that "this is the spring-time of the race's hopes in America."

CONCLUSION

During the Progressive era, the first generation of African Americans born after emancipation reached adulthood. They hoped to erase the color line and to choose how and where they would live and how they would be identified—colored, Afro-American, negro, Negro. Through government and military service, economic endeavors and artistic pursuits, community building, and protest, the men and women of this new generation sought to educate their children and gain white Americans' respect. Though they faced daunting challenges, new black leaders and everyday African Americans built organizations dedicated to progress and improvement.

Supported by their churches and publications, African Americans sought to improve themselves and the world they lived in through confrontation or accommodation. While Booker T. Washington urged restraint as he sent forth thousands of Tuskegee graduates trained in manual skills, W. E. B. Du Bois called for immediate full political and legal equality. But a few successes in the courts and a new dignity in the name *Negro* were not enough to offset the blow dealt by Plessy's legal defeat. Jim Crow laws remained alive and well. In the coming decades, as thousands of black Americans left the South, the organizations and ideas born in the Progressive era would gain momentum. The NAACP would chip away at legal restrictions. Organizations like the NACW, Urban League, YWCA, and YMCA would help a growing minority of black Americans climb painstakingly into the American middle class—even while the great majority still barely eked out an existence. But the big gains for African Americans in the years after 1915 would come with the development of black culture and arts romanticizing ancient Africa in a rebirth—a renaissance—of black poetry, fiction, and music.

FURTHER READING

Berlin, Edward A. *King of Ragtime: Scott Joplin and His Era* (New York: Oxford University Press, 1994).

Franklin, John Hope, and John Whittington Franklin, eds. *My Life and an Era: The Autobiography of Buck Colbert Franklin* (Baton Rouge: Louisiana State University Press, 1997).

Gaines, Kevin. *Uplifting the Race: Black Leadership, Politics and Culture in the Twentieth Century* (Chapel Hill: University of North Carolina Press, 1996).

Hamilton, Kenneth Marvin. *Black Towns and Profit: Promotion and Development in the Trans-Appalachian West, 1877–1915* (Urbana: University of Illinois Press: 1991).

Hawkins, Mike. *Social Darwinism in European and American Thought, 1860–1945: Nature as Model and Nature as Threat* (Cambridge: Cambridge University Press, 1997).

Higginbotham, Evelyn Brooks. *Righteous Discontent: The Women's Movement in the Black Baptist Church, 1880–1920* (Cambridge: Harvard University Press, 1993).

Hirsch, Arnold R., and Joseph Logsdon. *Creole New Orleans: Race and Americanization* (Baton Rouge: Louisiana State University Press, 1992).

Malcolmson, Scott L. *One Drop of Blood: The American Misadventure of Race* (New York: Farrar, Straus, Giroux, 2000).

Pride, Armistead S., and Clint C. Wilson. *A History of the Black Press* (Washington, DC: Howard University Press, 1997).

Ravage, John W. *Black Pioneers* (Salt Lake City: University of Utah Press, 1997).

Ritchie, Andrew. *Major Taylor: The Extraordinary Career of a Champion Bicycle Racer* (San Francisco: Bicycle Books, 1988).

Taylor, Quintard. *In Search of the Racial Frontier: African Americans in the American West, 1528–1990.* (New York: W. W. Norton, 1998).

Wintz, Cary D. *African American Political Thought, 1890–1930: Washington, Du Bois, Garvey, and Randolph* (Armonk, NY: M.E. Sharpe, 1996).

CHAPTER 14

■ Helping to popularize the new musical form of improvisational jazz, Louisiana-born Louis Armstrong became an ambassador for black creative expression.

The Making of a "New Negro": World War I to the Great Depression

Thomas Edward Jones to the European Front

In June 1918, First Lieutenant Thomas Edward Jones crossed the Atlantic Ocean to serve as an American soldier in France. The previous year, the United States had entered Europe's Great War to support Britain and France against Germany and Austria. Struck by the magnitude of what lay ahead, Jones began keeping a diary. "Day clear and cool. Saw my first whale after many days of watching," he wrote on June 21. Fearing German submarine attacks, soldiers slept in life preservers, and Jones quoted black poet Paul Laurence Dunbar to describe the anxiety: It felt as if they were sleeping with "one eye shet [shut] and one eye open." Assigned to medical duty in the infirmary, Jones reported a night with "about 30 cases of acute gastritis, cause undetermined, Both white and colored."

A child of slaves, Jones had left the South and earned a medical degree at Howard University in 1912, becoming one of 3,000 licensed black physicians in the United States. But his rural southern experience, education, and his ocean crossing could not prepare him for what he experienced during World War I: a warm welcome by the French people, the horror of trench warfare, and the vicious racism of white American comrades-in-arms. Arriving in France in June 1918, Jones found the "French people extremely courteous," and he enjoyed dinners at a "swell hotel." With a degree of freedom he had never experienced before, he visited a French mineral-water spa and used his medical skills to treat a white baby.

Jones's diary entries took on a more ominous tone beginning on August 21, 1918. That day, he wrote, he was "busy preparing to leave for the trenches" in

CHAPTER OUTINE

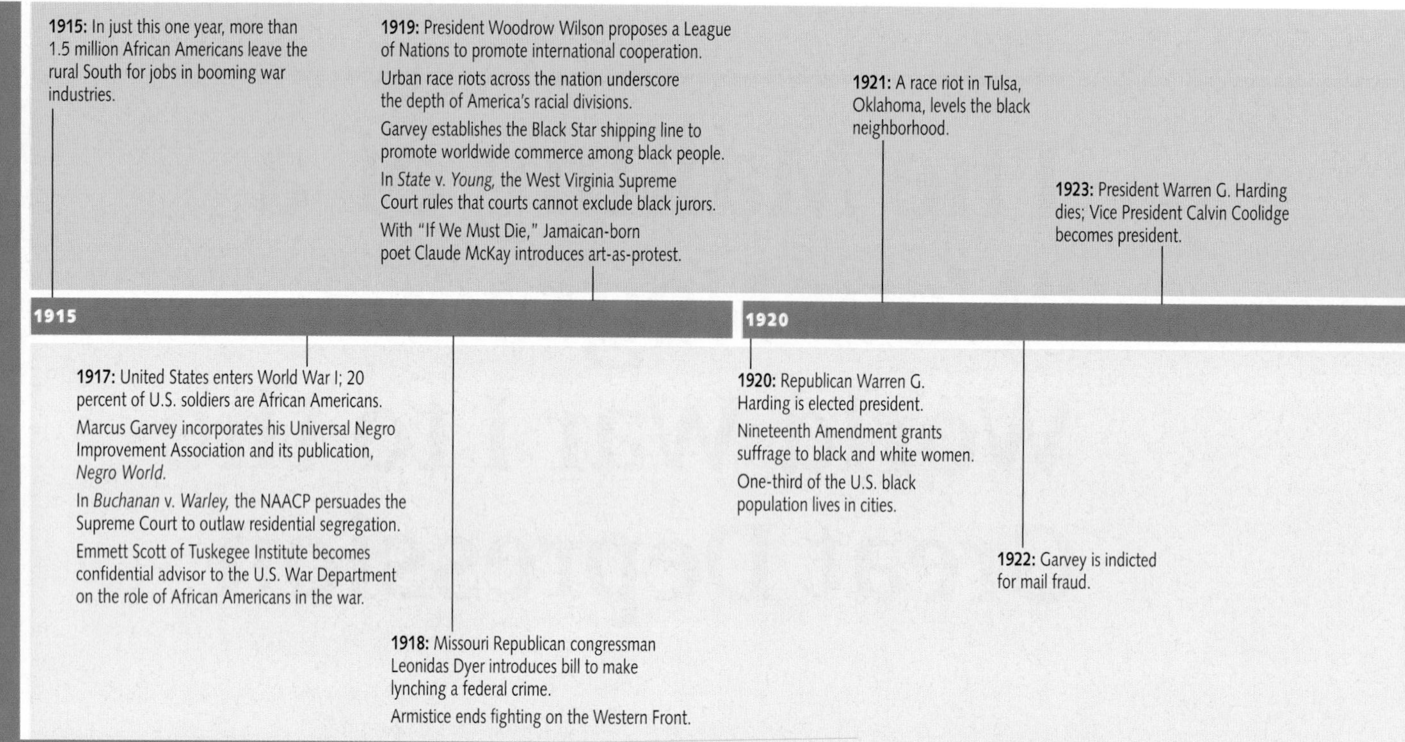

the critical battle zone of the Argonne Forest. Until October 4, when his all-black 368th Infantry "left Argonne forest . . . cold, hungry and weary," Jones's notes were brief and grim. "Took our positions in line at Argonne . . . quite a few casualties due to . . . shells"—including Jones's own shell wound. The mission failed, and his unit was labeled as cowards. Later investigations, however, uncovered the 368th's bravery in the Argonne Forest mission, and the cowardice of their white officers. The unit was commended, and Jones was rewarded with a promotion, the French Croix de Guerre, and the American Distinguished Service Cross. He also returned home with a lifelong friendship with an Italian-American soldier whose life he saved.

Often American racism followed black troops abroad. Though they shared the battlefield with white soldiers, black soldiers were relegated to segregated regiments, and their white comrades-in-arms constantly reminded them of the meaning of race in America. Jones recalled one white "captain who called our boys God Damned Niggers."

Though Jones's background was similar in some ways to that of his fellow soldiers, he had unique experiences as well. At age nineteen, having graduated from Lynchburg High School in Virginia, he moved to Washington, DC, where he supported himself with odd jobs. He joined the volunteer National Guard and worked his way up to first lieutenant. Twenty years older than the typical soldier, Jones was almost thirty-seven in 1917 when the United States declared war on Germany. After the Argonne Forest Campaign, he earned a promotion to captain and become one of a few dozen black soldiers in World War I decorated for bravery.

Upon his return from the war, Jones joined the staff of Freedmen's Hospital, the federal black hospital in Washington, DC. There his war record, professional accomplishments, and participation in the local National Association for the Advancement of Colored People (NAACP) eventually brought him to the attention of the White House. Secretary of State Harold Ickes appointed Jones to head the hospital in 1939. But despite this recognition, Jones remained acutely aware of the persistent mistrust white Americans felt toward black people.

This chapter examines how World War I and its aftermath reshaped black Americans' lives. On the front lines, black soldiers encountered the horrors of war while facing racism from white soldiers. On the home front, the war accelerated African Americans' exodus from the rural South to northern and

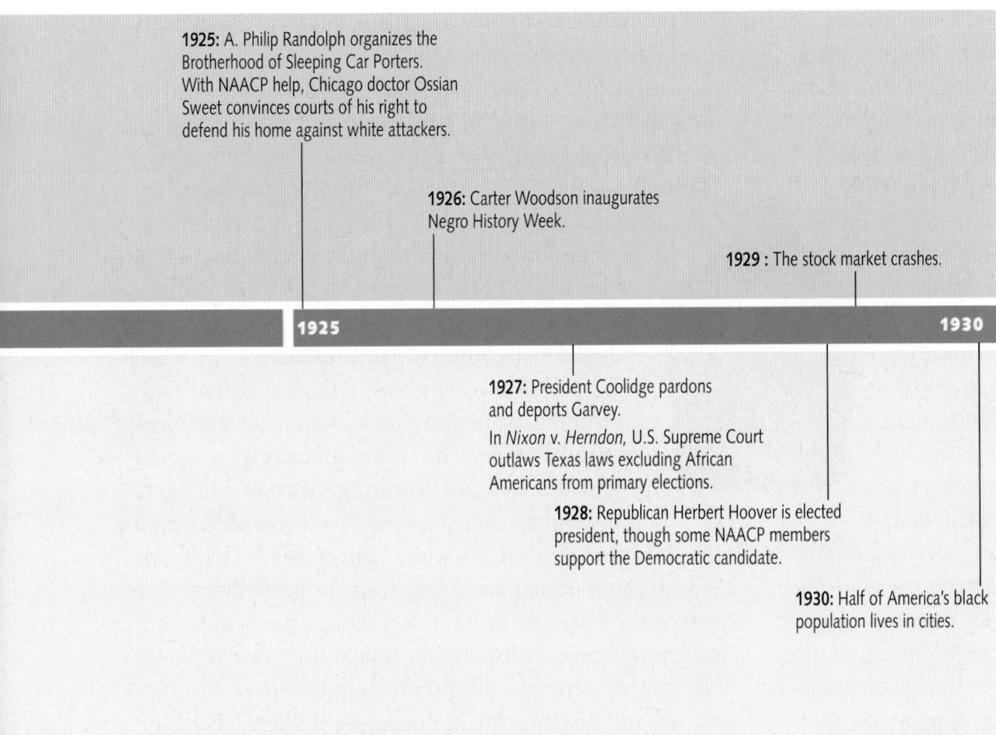

southern cities, where they found plentiful jobs because of the booming war industry and decreased competition from the many young white and black men who went off to fight.

The postwar era saw the growth of a large and influential black movement. Charismatic Jamaican immigrant Marcus Garvey argued that black people construct an economy separate from that of white Americans. His message appealed to poor and working-class black people, many of whom used his ideas to build their own confidence, pride, and economic self-sufficiency.

The Harlem Renaissance, a flowering of black artistic expression nourished by black entrepreneurs, artists, writers, and intellectuals, reverberated in black neighborhoods across the nation. Out of Harlem also came black musical innovations such as ragtime and jazz—new styles all Americans embraced.

"OVER THERE" . . . AND BACK HERE

"On account of our meeting, the Negro race was more united and more ready to meet the problems of the world than it could possibly have been without these beautiful days of understanding." With these words, W. E. B. Du Bois recalled the 1916 Amenia Conference that brought together his supporters and those of Booker T. Washington. But with the United States' entry into the world war one year later, "these beautiful days of understanding" and black unity evaporated in the face of international conflict and white Americans' ingratitude toward black servicemen.

Black Americans and World War I

What black journalist William Monroe Trotter called "the springtime of hope" was soon followed by a storm that shattered black unity. While European nations had been embroiled in war since 1914, U.S. president Woodrow Wilson had struggled to keep America neutral. But in April 1917, spurred by German attacks on U.S. ships sailing through the war zone, the United States declared war on Germany. As in the Spanish-American War two decades before, African Americans were divided over how to respond to their country's military call. While a new popular song warned Europeans that "the Yanks"—American soldiers—were coming to straighten out politics "over there," many black people were wary. They questioned whether black men should go to war and join a segregated military that claimed it would make the rest of the world "safe for democracy" when they did not have full political and social rights at home.

> "As this nation goes forth to fight the 'natural foe of liberty,' let Americans highly resolve that all shall have liberty within her borders."—*William Monroe Trotter*

Du Bois supported the NAACP's position that patriotism and national unity should come first. "Let us, while this war lasts," he wrote in the *Crisis*, "forget our special grievances and close our ranks shoulder to shoulder with our own white fellow citizens and the allied nations fighting for democracy." He hoped African Americans' military service abroad would win them respect and legal equality at home. Others opposed sending black soldiers overseas. In the *Guardian*, William Monroe

Trotter urged black Americans to boycott the military until it agreed to integrated units and black officers. "As this nation goes forth to fight the 'natural foe of liberty,' let Americans highly resolve that all shall have liberty within her borders," he insisted. Eventually Du Bois came to share Trotter's view.

In the early months of the war, more than 400,000 black volunteers and draftees joined the army, constituting 20 percent of America's military force. But their hopes for respect soon dissolved. Even as the first black servicemen landed in France in the summer of 1917, dozens of Twenty-fourth Infantry soldiers in Texas were court-martialed and sentenced to death for disobeying Houston's Jim Crow laws. That August, a riot broke out in Houston after a black soldier tried to prevent a white policeman from beating a black woman. More than a dozen white men died in the melee. Secretary of War Newton D. Baker concluded the underlying cause of the uprising was the "so-called Jim Crow laws." Yet he could persuade President Woodrow Wilson to reverse just ten of the nineteen execution sentences handed down by the court martial. Stung by the irony that the Twenty-fourth Infantry was the same outfit that had served with distinction during the Spanish-American War, Howard University professor Kelly Miller lashed out at Wilson: "The Negro, Mr. President, in this emergency, will stand by you and the Nation. Will you and the Nation stand by the Negro?"

> "The Negro, Mr. President, in this emergency, will stand by you and the Nation. Will you and the Nation stand by the Negro?"—*Kelly Miller*

Secretary of War Baker took steps to raise black troops' morale. He established new training sites for black officers and recruited Tuskegee's Emmett J. Scott to be a "confidential advisor" to the War Department on issues regarding black troops. However, racial tensions mounted among troops in Europe. The problem had several sources. First, some black regiments drew criticism because the poor training and preparation of some recruits decreased the unit's performance. Second, the white officers put in charge of black units often ridiculed their own troops. Third, military leaders could not always impose strict segregation in the movement and housing of troops, so white recruits sometimes lived in close quarters with people of a race they customarily shunned. Indeed, First Lieutenant Thomas Jones reported open hostility between black and white soldiers aboard the ship that transported his unit to and from Europe. Name-calling, jeering, and practical jokes as well as assignment to the worst quarters reminded black soldiers that they were not viewed as respected team members. Finally, unreliable supply lines meant delays in the delivery of provisions, further damaging troop morale.

Despite these difficulties, the first black units to arrive in France fared well. They included the 369th Infantry, which Secretary of War Baker praised as the best all-round regiment sent to France. The 369th later won the French Croix de Guerre, France's highest military honor, for helping capture a railroad junction in the fall of 1918. Throughout the Great War, the 369th never lost a foot of ground and never had a man captured. The unit included baseball hero Spottswood Poles, who is credited with planning exhibition games that introduced baseball to France. The 371st Infantry also served with distinction, capturing German prisoners and weapons and shooting down several German airplanes near Verdun. Its white commander, southerner William Hayward, reported that his men "never flinched or showed the least sign of fear. They will go down in history as brave soldiers." Admiring the men's discipline and dedication, U.S. general John J. Pershing declared, "I cannot and will not discriminate against these soldiers." Pershing ordered field officers to ensure that black troops had comfortable quarters as well as the freedom to visit nearby towns and socialize with local people.

By the time Jones and the 368th Infantry reached France in June 1918, the attitude toward black soldiers had shifted. Field officers as well as officials back in Washington began to worry that black soldiers would grow accustomed to a level of respect and authority they would not receive once they returned home. Despite the praise for the 369th and 371st, orders came down that no black man would be promoted above the rank of captain. Scott protested, but his complaints fell on deaf ears. As officer vacancies came up in black units, they were filled with white men. By August 18, when Jones's unit hunkered down in the trenches, the black officer staff had dwindled by more than 30 percent.

Reports pouring into the United States seldom acknowledged black soldiers' bravery. Instead, the American press emphasized stories of black inferiority and cowardice. The 368th Infantry experienced the consequences of these attitudes firsthand. After two weeks in battle, fifty deaths, and several hundred more casualties, the 368th was summarily recalled from the Argonne campaign. Commanders far from the front had deemed their mission a failure. But when Scott pressed for an investigation, the 368th's bravery came to light. It turned out the unit had captured a crucial German stronghold and had pushed the battle line 6 miles into enemy territory amid heavy artillery and sniper fire. Investigators reported that one white commander had deserted the 368th under fire and another had retreated without notifying his

In this painting, artist Alan Werner uses photographic images and impressionistic symbols to capture defining aspects of Thomas Jones's life: his graduation from Howard University, his military uniform with its Distinguished Service Cross and Buffalo Soldier insignia, his installation by Eleanor Roosevelt as medical director of Freedmen's Hospital in 1939. The backdrop of this painting depicts the farm Jones purchased in Maryland. As a resident of Washington, DC, he was disenfranchised; in Maryland, he could—and did—vote.

black troops. Meanwhile, a nearby white unit had broken ranks and fled, and the French artillery support had never arrived. Convinced by the evidence, the investigators recommended the 368th for commendation, not punishment. In January 1919, the 368th Infantry was awarded the Distinguished Service Cross, America's second-highest military honor. As part of what Jones described as "a gala day" of celebration, the troops were "decorated with flowers by ladies."

The new mood of appreciation for black soldiers caught on in many quarters. After the war in Europe ended with an armistice signed on November 11, 1918, black soldiers returning home often received a hero's welcome. Crowds of black and white spectators turned out to welcome them in New York, Cincinnati, St. Louis, and many other cities. When Jones, now promoted to captain, entered Washington's Asbury Methodist Church, the congregation rose and sang "Praise God from Whom All Blessings Flow." In New York, the jazz band of the black Fifteenth Regiment also came home to acclaim. When they played for the victory parade along New York City's streets in the fall of 1918, the response was so enthusiastic the band cut twenty-four records in the spring of 1919. Both war and jazz helped gain respect for black Americans at home.

Despite honoring black war heroes, white America was not yet ready to embrace racial equality. When the victory celebrations ended, American race relations resumed their prewar tension. White mobs rioted against black veterans and civilians in cities across the nation. In *Crisis,* Du Bois summarized black soldiers' challenge to America: "We return. We return from fighting. We return fighting. Make way for Democracy." Jamaican Claude McKay, soon to rank among the nation's best-known black poets, used his artistic talent to mount political protest. In a poem entitled "If We Must Die," he advised black people to resist their attackers. "If we must die, let it not be like hogs / Hunted and penned in an inglorious spot," he began one poem. "Like men we'll face the murderous, cowardly pack / Pressed to the wall, dying, but fighting back!"

The Great Migration

Arriving in Philadelphia by 1916, Hughsey Childs was part of a group that decided to "name a church after Morris Chapel in Greenwood [South Carolina]." Typical of the black migrants streaming out of the South to northern cities after 1915, he intended to keep his connections to his

"The Flags of the Fighting 15th." Color Bearers of the 369th, marching up Fifth Avenu with Regimental Colors bearing the decoration presented to the entire Regiment b the French Government. These flags were given to the Regiment by the Union Leagu Club of New York, and returned to the Club at the close of the war. The Regimenta Standard has the distinction of being the only State flag carried into action by a

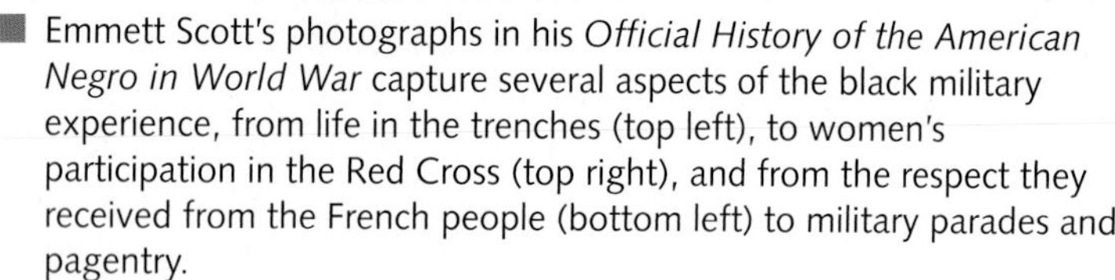

■ Emmett Scott's photographs in his *Official History of the American Negro in World War* capture several aspects of the black military experience, from life in the trenches (top left), to women's participation in the Red Cross (top right), and from the respect they received from the French people (bottom left) to military parades and pagentry.

southern family and friends. He was joined by George Bailey, described by the group as "a very ambitious man [who] opened his first community market [in 1916], and by 1922, he was the second Negro member of the Frankford Grocers' Association." Bailey married a Greenwood woman, and together they made his store the news center linking black Philadelphians and their South Carolina relatives. In 1916, an article in the AME *Christian Recorder* described such new migrants as "vigorous, active, ambitious men and women . . . [who] will equal the best we've got here; for all of us are immigrants."

Southern migrants came for economic opportunity, but many also felt they were running for their lives. One New Orleans resident said he came north to escape "the lynchman's noose and the torchman's fire." A Macon, Georgia, woman reported that black men were "shot down here like rabbits for every little offence." A black newspaper predicted African American immigrants would "suffer in the North.

Some of them will die . . . [but] any place would be paradise compared with [the danger in] some sections of the South."

Even before the United States entered World War I, African Americans had begun migrating. Beginning just after the Civil War, the black exodus accelerated during the 1920s in what historians call the Great Migration. By 1930, half of black Americans had left the southern countryside. During the first phase of the Great Migration, which had unfolded between 1900 and 1915, most migrants simply moved from the South's rural areas to its cities. Owing to depleted soil and agricultural pests such as the boll weevil, which swept out of Texas and destroyed cotton crops throughout the Southeast, white and black farmers alike were thrown out of work. They sought new employment in industrial southern cities such as Atlanta, Birmingham, Memphis, New Orleans, and San Antonio. In these urban hubs, they found steady wages in the railroad, furniture, and metal industries.

When the war began in Europe in the summer of 1914, northern U.S. factories stepped up production of ammunition, food, and textiles to aid Britain and France. These factories also recruited workers from the South to meet the increased demand for labor. Northern factory owners welcomed black workers who, because of their limited employment opportunities, would toil for lower wages than white people. Poor white people also fled rural areas in search of factory work in the cities. Typically, a small group (or just one person) moved to a town easily accessible by rail or river. When they found jobs, friends and family joined them. Whole urban neighborhoods thus cropped up comprising family, church, or community members from a particular rural area.

Black urbanites built communities through their participation in churches, clubs, businesses, and schools. Barbershops, hairdressers, and bars distributed local gossip and black newspapers. Atlanta's black Decatur Street neighborhood sprouted vaudeville theaters, Charleston supported numerous dockworker organizations, and New Orleans became home to poor black men who joined together to make music. In these ways, urban black southerners developed a vigorous social life. Moreover, as long as they observed racial boundaries, some achieved the economic gains Booker T. Washington had predicted. However, many discovered that city life had an ugly underside. Jim Crow laws brought constant assaults on their dignity, and the Ku Klux Klan posed a constant threat.

Thus began the second phase of the Great Migration, during which many black Americans left the South entirely. Between World War I and 1930, an estimated 2 million black people departed the South. Some headed for border states such as Missouri and Illinois. Others traveled farther north or west. Still others formed separate black communities in far-flung sections of the United States or even abroad. Large cities, such as Chicago, Detroit, New York, Washington, and Los Angeles, together absorbed more than 800,000 black newcomers in this period.

On the rise since the 1880s, black towns now reached new heights of popularity and prosperity. In Alabama, Elmore and Macon each boasted more than 700 residents. Snow Hill, New Jersey, had 1,200. Another 100 black townspeople lived in Whitesboro, New Jersey, near Cape May. In Oklahoma, 7,000 African Americans inhabited thirteen all-black communities, while in Mississippi, Mound Bayou remained one of the most prestigious black towns.

Race Riots and Revival of the Klan

Despite the optimism infusing some black towns, the problem of racial hatred persisted for most African Americans. In cities outside the South, black workers found jobs at factories, railroads, and docks—but they also bore the brunt of resentment and competition from poor white people also desperate for work. Often the tensions between the two groups erupted in urban riots. For example, in the summer of 1916, striking white workers attacked newly arrived black workers in St. Louis, Missouri, who had come to fill vacant jobs at the city's Aluminum Ore Company. Similar antagonisms sparked anti-black riots in East St. Louis, Illinois. There, four days of rioting from late May into early June ended with the deaths of eight white people (some killed by bullets intended for black targets). A Missouri senator reported that "over 100 Negroes were mangled or beaten to various degrees of helplessness." But President Woodrow Wilson, who viewed racial separation as the best way to manage American society, refused to meet with a delegation of riot refugees. With the Great Migration, black Americans found the old white attitudes of discrimination and intimidation traveled with them to their new urban homes.

Throughout the nation, people died in street confrontations. One riot broke out in Philadelphia when a black woman moved into a white neighborhood. A 1921 uprising in Tulsa, Oklahoma, where oil drilling had attracted a large black community, became one of the most notorious of these conflicts. The riot erupted when a

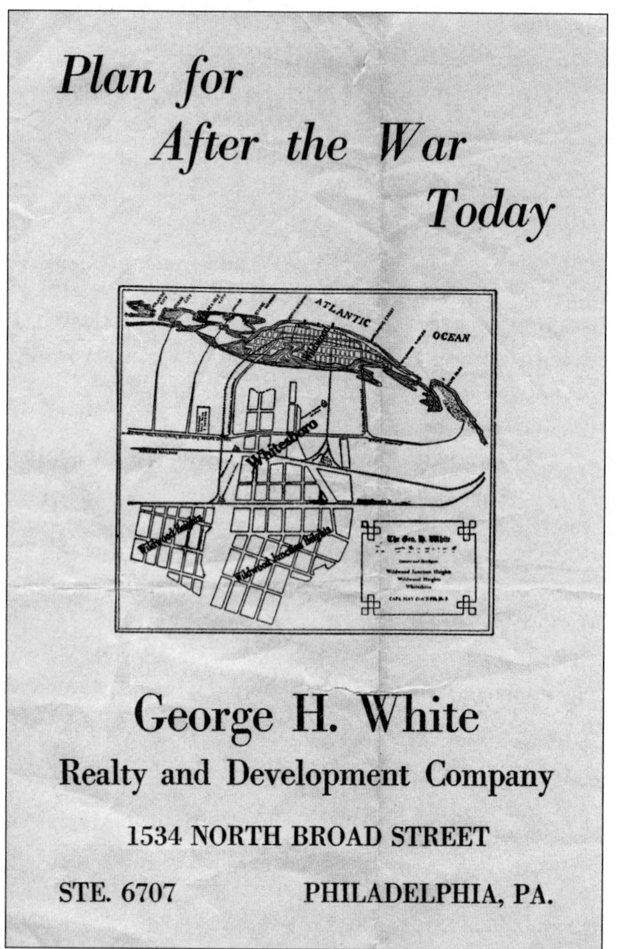

A Few Interesting Facts about Whitesboro, Wildwood Junction Heights and Wildwood Heights, N. J.

WHITESBORO, N. J., was founded in 1901 by George H. White, the first colored Congressman to be elected from North Carolina to the United States House of Representatives.

WHITESBORO is about four and a half miles from Wildwood, and seven miles from Cape May, world famous seashore resorts.

WHITESBORO, WILDWOOD JUNCTION HEIGHTS and WILDWOOD HEIGHTS adjoin each other.

The State Highway (Routes No. 4 and 9) passes directly through our tract.

Philadelphia is only 90 minutes away and New York is 3 hours from here.

WHITESBORO has an excellent elementary public school, the children being instructed by colored teachers.

There are four churches in Whitesboro; Baptist, Methodist, Holiness and Seven Day Adventist.

There are about eight hundred (800) inhabitants living here and approximately two hundred (200) homes.

Home sites are 25 feet by 100 feet. Most clear and some wooded.

The tax rate is very low, about $1.00 per lot, per year.

The ground is high, dry and level, and clear of all encumbrance.

Transportation facilities are provided by speedy buses, and passenger train services which stop at Wildwood Junction Heights.

Fishing, crabbing, clamming, boating and bathing can be enjoyed in the Delaware Bay which is only two and one half (2½) miles from our tract, or in the Atlantic Ocean which is only six (6) miles from Whitesboro.

WHITESBORO has gas, electric, telephone service, a post office and a large supply of artesian well water.

The soil is admirably adapted to poultry raising, hog breeding; fruits, berries, garden truck, all kinds of vegetables being easily tilled and abundantly productive.

There are vast markets in nearby resorts for these products.

You will be pleasantly surprised how little it costs to own a home site. Prices start as low as $49.00 per lot. Now is your chance to become the owner of one of these beautiful lots as prices and terms are within reach of any one.

Conditions here are desirable. The people are friendly and living is economical. A visit to Whitesboro will convince you.

You are dealing with a reliable company, one having been in business continuously for over forty (40) years.

Our company owns every foot of ground we sell, and when you finish paying for your home site we give you a warrenty deed.

Our titles are such that can be insured with any reputable title company.

And last of all ask yourself this question, "What am I, and all of us fellows working on defense, going to do when the emergency is over?"

Write to us for any further information you may desire. Don't delay, do it now, before it is too late.

To many African Americans, black towns were as much a symbol as a place to live. Thomas Jones was one of dozens of black people who bought property in towns like Whitesboro. Yet he never lived in this tiny outpost, which remained a black town into the 1950s.

policeman accused a black man of assaulting a white woman and threw him in jail. Young Buck Franklin witnessed the subsequent tragedy. He recalled that a group of black military veterans "fired up the crowd by telling . . . how they spent nights in foxholes and how winning a battle [depended on good] strategy." Incited by these men who had fought for democracy abroad, several people barricaded the courthouse to protect the prisoner from a gathering lynch mob. Franklin and hundreds of others were arrested. Released from jail several days later, Franklin returned to find his neighborhood a smoking ruin. The accused attacker was ultimately found innocent, but more than fifty black people had perished in the riots. Upwards of a thousand residents of Greenwood, Tulsa's black neighborhood, suffered property losses their insurance companies refused to reimburse. Appeals to President Warren Harding went unanswered.

The threat of lynching accompanied the riots. On the decline since Ida Wells Barnett's 1890s campaign, lynching picked up again during the first years of the Great Migration. Fifty-eight black people lost their lives to lynch mobs in 1916—most in the South, but a few in the North as well. In 1919, more than seventy people perished in similar attacks. Some of the victims were in military uniform. Wives warned husbands and parents cautioned sons about traveling alone. Every family knew of men who had mysteriously disappeared, only to be found drowned, hanged, or beaten. Black women or girls considered "uppity" (disrespectful to white people) risked rape by white men as well as lynching.

Horrified by the violence, Missouri congressman Leonidas Dyer introduced a bill in 1918 to make lynching a federal crime. Most of his fellow representatives showed little interest in his proposal. Though President Wilson eventually denounced lynchers as "betrayers" of

TABLE 14.1 Black Americans Move to the Cities, 1910 and 1930

By 1930, Chicago, New York, and Philadelphia were America's "black" cities, with the highest number of black residents. In some northern cities, the African American population grew by more than 300 percent, increasing both the number and proportion of black residents. The southern urban black population also mushroomed.

	1910		*1930*	
	Black Population	*Percent of total population*	*Black Population*	*Percent of total population*
Chicago	44,000	2	234,000	6
New York [Manhattan]	61,000	2	225,000	11
Philadelphia	84,000	5	220,000	11
Baltimore	85,000	15	142,000	17.6
Washington, DC	94,000	28	132,000	27
New Orleans	89,000	26	130,000	28
Detroit	6,000	1	120,000	7
Atlanta	52,000	33	90,000	32
Los Angeles	15,500	2.6	38,900	3
Denver	6,000	2	7,200	2.5
San Francisco	2,400	4.7	3,800	6
Seattle	2,894	9	3,300	9

democracy, Congress took no action on the Dyer anti-lynching bill. Recognizing that local law enforcement officers almost never prosecuted the murder of a black person, the NAACP lobbied in support of the Dyer Bill. Though it never passed, rising outrage and increasingly strict neighborhood segregation led to a decrease in lynching over subsequent decades.

In 1915, the dormant Ku Klux Klan came alive again. The organization continued to target African Americans primarily, but now it stepped up attacks on Jews, Catholics, and dark-skinned immigrants from eastern and southern Europe. Its terrorist tactics spread quickly across the nation. With 3 million members nationwide by the mid-1920s, the Klan strengthened its presence in southern cities as well as rural areas. In any location where disgruntled southerners had migrated after the Civil War—including Pittsburgh, Los Angeles, and Seattle—the Klan gained a foothold. Several of its members were elected to political office in Denver, Colorado; Dallas, Texas; and Portland, Oregon. Though nearly every city across the country had at least a small Klan membership, the organization flourished particularly in the Midwest in areas where white and black southern refugees were concentrated in towns along the Mississippi River. From Indianapolis, home to at least 12,000 members, the Klan published its newsweekly, *The Fiery Cross*. The publication touted the group's conviction that darkness (and dark-skinned people) signified sin, and that all nonwhite residents from the United States should leave the United States.

Eugenics—the old Progressive notion that racial characteristics indicated a person's intellectual and social worth—added fuel to the Klan's revival. In 1920, the Government Printing Office published *Defects Found in Drafted Men*, a study of physical dimensions and markings gathered when the Surgeon General's staff examined military recruits. The study gave legitimacy to the Klan by attributing negative meanings to the physical characteristics of black and immigrant men. "Swarthy skin" and "slanty eyes" were among the descriptions used to label those whom eugenicists considered sinister and prone to drunkenness and crime. While most Klan members probably could not quote from this or similar works, these ideas circulated widely through the white population.

Black Americans and the Red Scare

Though interracial violence peaked in the summer of 1919, most white Americans remembered the violence as being aimed at "Reds" rather than black people. In 1917, as Russian troops retreated from the Germans on the Eastern Front, Russian laborers overthrew their aristocratic government and established a communist or "Red" regime (named after the color of the revolutionaries' flag). Promising equality to the dispossessed and proclaiming their intention to unite the workers of the world in a new political and economic order, the revolutionaries abolished private property and replaced it with collective ownership of factories and fields. They aimed to end capitalism, unequal profits, and labor exploitation. Worried that low-paid U.S. workers would make ripe targets for revolutionary organizers, Attorney General A. Mitchell Palmer stirred up a "Red Scare" against socialists, anarchists, and labor radicals in American cities that had large immigrant populations. To implement the scare, he encouraged U.S. citizens to ostracize people they suspected of harboring revolutionary ideas. In the summer of 1919, in outright violations of constitutional rights, federal agents kicked down doors and barged into homes and offices, intimidating and arresting thousands of citizens and deporting hundreds of noncitizens.

A. Philip Randolph Demands a New Ministry

The black churches– New York had about 200 of them in the 1920s—have always been a mainstay of African American communities. Though two-thirds of black churches were led by ministers with little formal theological training, these institutions found their real mission as not only places of worship but also recreation centers, savings and loan associations, childcare facilities, employment agencies, educational institutions, and cradles of leadership. But some black Americans felt the churches impeded black progress. In a Messenger *editorial in October 1919, A. Philip Randolph admonished the churches for not creating the right kind of leaders.*

YES, the Negro church has failed. It has failed in a great crisis. Its failure is patent and apparent. The only question before us then is: Why and How?

The chief cause of the failure of the Negro church is economic. That is to say, the church has been converted into a business and the ruling characteristic of a business is that it is run primarily for profits.

. . . There is that class of Negro churches that is directly dominated by white capitalists. These are the Episcopal, Congregational, Presbyterian and Methodist Episcopal. Their policies are molded and handed down from the white ecclesiastical oligarchy [which is] controlled by the "money power" of the country. It is a matter of common knowledge that Trinity church, situated at the head of Wall Street, is one of the biggest corporations in America. It controls a large number of apartment houses from which it reaps . . . extortionate rents from the working people. . . .

The Negro minister is ignorant of the modern problems of capital and labor. It is disinterested in unionism as a means of securing higher wages, shorter hours and better working conditions for Negro workers. It regards the discussion of politics in the church as sacrilegious unless some good old Abraham Lincoln Republican desires the vote of the Negro, and is willing to pay for educational propaganda. It has failed to use its power to rouse the Negro against disfranchisement and lynching. No conference of Negro churches has ever gone on record as endorsing the principle of unionism.

The Negro ministry . . . needs less Bible and more economics, history, sociology and physical science. . . . The New Negro demands a new ministry—an educated, fearless and radical ministry.

—from The Messenger, *October 1919.*

To view a longer version of this document, please go to www.ablongman.com/carson/documents.

Prejudice against outsiders hardened into public policies. Believing the United States should maintain the dominance of white Protestant people, most congressmen voted in favor of bills that set strict limits on admitting immigrants from places other than northern Europe.

Black Americans were not immune from this treatment. In Congress, a South Carolina senator insisted that southern black farm and factory workers were "happy and contented and will remain so if the . . . [revolutionaries] . . . of Russia, and the misguided theorists of other sections of this country will let [them] alone." Still, the Justice Department launched an investigation of *Crisis* and several other black periodicals, seeking evidence of disloyalty to the United States. A few African Americans did read radical publications and supported communist programs. Indeed, A. Philip Randolph, who established a New York Socialist club in 1917, claimed that "capitalism [is] the cause of

> "The New Negro demands a new ministry—an educated, fearless and radical ministry."—*A. Philip Randolph*

lynching." Randolph was convinced racism would persist until black and white workers achieved economic equality. Randolph and his wife, Lucille, repeatedly—and unsuccessfully— ran for political office on a Socialist Party ticket.

Frustrated with exclusive white unions, Randolph sought to improve the lot of black workers. He organized the Brotherhood of Sleeping Car Porters (BSCP) in 1925. The union's membership was comprised of hundreds of black men who carried baggage, made beds, and served meals on sleeping-car trains. The unionized porters' demands included higher pay and more control over their working conditions. After a decade of agitation, the Brotherhood and its women's auxiliary, the Hesperus Club of Harlem, succeeded in gaining recognition from the American Federaion of Labor and concessions for their demands from the Pullman Company, which owned and managed railroad sleeping cars.

Gradually a few white unions, including the International Ladies Garment Workers' Union (ILGWU) and the longshoremen's unions, also opened up to black workers. Though refusal to protest unequal pay and other forms of racial discrimination sometimes crept into union policies, membership in these organizations did bring benefits. In particular, union members had increased wage protection and gained a sense of solidarity and dignity for themselves and their families. In many unions, the members embraced the communist belief that socioeconomic differences posed a far greater problem than racial differences did.

THE CHALLENGE OF GARVEYISM

"We never heard one syllable from the lips of Woodrow Wilson, touching anything relative to the destinies of the Negroes of America or England or of the world," Marcus Garvey told a Baltimore audience in 1918. He was reminding his listeners that the president's concern for the self-determination of oppressed minorities in Europe did not extend to American Negroes. Many black Americans knew of Garvey even before he arrived in Harlem in 1916. The dynamic young Jamaican had already published political tracts and organized laborers in Central America, the Caribbean, and England. Now he spoke out to white America and challenged African Americans with a bold new program of racial unity: the Universal Negro Improvement Association (UNIA).

Impressed by Booker T. Washington's book *Up From Slavery,* Garvey had written to the Tuskegee leader about establishing an industrial school in his native Jamaica. After Washington's death, he contacted Washington's successor, Robert Russa Moton, and visited Tuskegee in the spring of 1916 to learn more about its manual skills curriculum. Garvey told Moton of his hope for black economic independence, outlining "many large schemes . . . for the advancement of my people." Garvey next traveled north to Harlem. Du Bois announced in *Crisis:* "Mr. Marcus Garvey, founder and president of the Universal Negro Improvement Association of Jamaica, is now on a visit to America. He will deliver a series of lectures on Jamaica to raise funds for the establishment of an industrial institution for Negroes in Jamaica." Finding a welcoming audience in the United States, Garvey extended his tour.

Du Bois promoted Garvey's fundraising, but soon a bitter rivalry divided the two men. Garvey envisioned separate black nations in many locales across the world. If geographic separation were not possible, black people should at least maintain racially separate and independent economic and social institutions. Du Bois, in contrast, wanted to gain equal access for black Americans within America's existing economic, political, and social framework. Though both men advocated Pan-Africanism—the idea that people of African heritage from around the world should unite—they had different ideas about how it should be achieved. Garvey's bold programs, which brought successes that astonished even Garvey himself, challenged traditional black leaders even as they defied notions of white supremacy. Perhaps most important, while Du Bois found a following among black intellectuals, Garvey appealed to poor black people desperate for a ray of hope.

The Universal Negro Improvement Association

Bustling with black-owned businesses serving nearly 200,000 black residents, Harlem was the ideal setting in which Garvey could develop his ideas and recruit for the universal improvement movement. But Harlem was only the beginning. By 1917, Garvey had publicized his plan for a separate black economy in thirty-eight states. African American newcomers to northern cities responded enthusiastically to his call for racial separation. One observer described Garvey as a powerful speaker who could "throw his voice around three corners." Crowds as large as 100,000, by some estimates, heard him describe the East St. Louis riots as evidence of a "conspiracy" to exterminate black people. (The idea of genocide conspiracies resurfaced in black protests for decades to come.)

■ Marcus Garvey hired James VanDerZee, Harlem's premier black photographer, to create an extensive portfolio promoting the UNIA's activities. VanDerZee took many photographs like this one, which captures the Garveyites' power to dominate a neighborhood. Week after week, thousands of listeners poured into the streets to hear Garvey speak. Garvey organized parades of men and women who wound through the streets on foot, on horseback, or in motorcades, dressed in military-style uniforms or the white garb of the Black Cross nurses. For Garvey, the martial dress and parading conveyed the message that "we Negroes have fought and died enough for white people; the time has come to fight and die for ourselves."

At the end of 1917, Garvey set aside his plan to establish an industrial training school in Jamaica and instead moved his headquarters to Harlem. He incorporated the UNIA as an umbrella under which to shelter economic, philosophical, social, and even religious enterprises. He started a weekly newspaper, *The Negro World*, whose international circulation eventually topped 200,000. With English, Spanish, and French editions, it became the world's most widely circulated paper devoted to black issues.

"We Negroes have fought and died enough for white people; the time has come to fight and die for ourselves."—*Marcus Garvey*

"The Universal Negro Improvement Association advocates the unity and blending of all Negroes into one strong, healthy race," the organization proclaimed. Its program combined the Urban League's goals of acquiring jobs and decent housing with the entrepreneurial spirit of Booker T. Washington's Negro Business League. Establishing outposts in Europe, Africa, and the Caribbean, the UNIA welcomed black people around the world. Garvey's message also contained a religious element. Redefining Christianity to make God black and the Devil white, Garvey encouraged his followers to reenvision religion to reinforce race pride. He promoted self-help and self-reliance, chastising those whom he feared would "depend upon the other races for a kindly and sympathetic consideration of their needs, without making the effort to do for themselves."

The UNIA gained its power both from its goals (autonomy for black peoples) and its methods (appealing to ordinary people who felt excluded by black intellectual organizations). Garvey aimed to attract the masses and to bludgeon them into self-discipline and united action. He solicited donations from black people to finance his projects of independent enterprises, promising jobs and returns on investments. Through investments and contributions from some of the poorest African Americans, the UNIA soon controlled assets worth hundreds of thousands of dollars in dozens of cities. By 1925, the organization claimed a membership of 6 million in 900 branches across the United States, Central and South America, Britain, and West and South Africa. Black people around the world recognized the UNIA—and Garvey.

"Negro Nation"

Garvey styled himself the heir to the Tuskegee tradition. He frequently quoted Booker T. Washington, and the UNIA letterhead echoed Washington's challenge of "Up, you mighty race!" Using the same rhetoric of racial superiority voiced by eugenicists, he told black American soldiers: "It was you, the superman, that brought back victory at the [World War I Battle of the] Marne." Like the eugenicists, Garvey advocated racial separatism to promote the "purity of the Negro race and the purity of the white race." Consistent with his commitment to racial purity, he refused to take advertisements for the hair straighteners and skin bleachers that sustained most black publications. The UNIA, Garvey bragged, did not need such help to shape "men and women who are able to create, to originate and improve, and thus make an independent racial contribution to the world." Garvey's ideas were consistent with the mood of his day. He opposed "rich blacks marrying poor whites" and "rich or poor whites taking advantage of Negro women."

Garvey developed an ambitious plan for the world's black people. "The Negro," he said, "must plant the banner of freedom on the battle plains of Africa." He declared himself called to "redeem Africa" and designated himself "Provisional President of the African Republic"—a political entity he envisioned resulting from his Pan-African movement. He imagined leading a bold transformation of the entire African continent: "Steamships must be bought and built. . . . In Liberia railroads must be built. Industrial plants must go up." He assured his audiences that the UNIA "Declaration of the Rights of the Negro Peoples of the World" would "take its place alongside of the Declaration of Independence of the United States of America and the Magna Charta of England." In short, Garvey exhorted "Negroes [to] get busy building a nation of your own." He further imagined that the Negro nation stretching across international borders would inspire black people to think of "race *first* in all parts of the world."

Setting a goal of "Negro producers, Negro distributors, Negro consumers," Garvey conceived this "Negro nation" as a global political and economic network. In 1919, he incorporated the Black Star Line, a commercial shipping operation headquartered in Harlem, to develop trade with African nations. By 1924, the company had grown into the Black Cross Navigation and Trading Company, which transported emigrants to Africa and promoted international commerce. Under the Negro Factories Corporation, Garvey turned out uniforms for the UNIA's recruiters and its Black Cross Nurses. A thriving laundry kept two delivery trucks busy. Next came black doll factories, Caribbean grocery stores, restaurants and a hotel, tailoring shops, and a printer that served most of Harlem's publication needs. The UNIA also acquired property in Philadelphia, Chicago, Pittsburgh, Detroit, and other locations around the world. By 1920, it had more than 300 employees and plans to set up a bank.

The Second Pan-African Conference

While sharing Garvey's commitment to making Africa a central component in black American identity, Du Bois pushed specifically for African self-government, and he denounced Garvey's arrogant self-promotion as "Provisional President." "Africa belongs to the Africans," Du Bois said. "They have not the slightest intention of giving it up to foreigners, white or black. Liberia is not going to allow American Negroes to assume control and direct her government. Liberia . . . is for Liberians."

Nevertheless, inspired by plans for a League of Nations that had emerged from the Versailles Peace Conference after World War I, Du Bois organized the Second Pan-African Congress in 1919. Delegates from fifteen countries, meeting in Paris, proposed an international committee to assume control of Germany's African colonies and an international code of laws to protect all peoples from imperialism. Subsequent Pan-African congresses, contesting treaty arrangements that gave Germany's African colonies to European war victors, called for "the development of Africa for the Africans and not merely for the profit of Europeans." However, Du Bois's Pan-African agenda had fewer followers than Garvey's. Du Bois's agenda included the independence of colonial India, China, and Egypt, and few black Americans viewed these countries as relevant to their situation.

Garvey's Decline

Garvey was not above collaborating with his adversaries if he believed black people might gain by it. For example, he put aside his reluctance to work with white allies in order to petition the League of Nations for African independence. He sometimes teamed up with the NAACP, falsely claiming credit when the NAACP helped bring the Dyer antilynching

Marcus Garvey Reconceives Christianity

All black leaders had to work with the church, the strongest black institution. Historians have described Garveyism as combining "various elements of black nationalism—religious, cultural, economic and territorial—into one distinctive philosophy." Building on his youth in the Methodist Church in St. Ann's Parish, Jamaica, Garvey imagined Christ as the leader of a mass movement of oppressed peoples, and he saw himself in a similar messianic role. Convinced of the importance of African "redemption," Garvey preached that African peoples must re-envision themselves as a "mighty race." Black people around the world, he added, must break both their economic and their psychological dependence on white people.

Since the white people have seen their own God through white spectacles, we have now started to see our God through our own spectacles. We Negroes believe in the God of Ethiopia, the everlasting God—God the Father, God the Son, and God the Holy Ghost—but we shall worship him through the spectacles of Ethiopia. . . .

The Negro is now accepting the religion of the real Christ, not the property-robbing, gold-stealing, diamond-exploiting Christ, but the Christ of Love, Justice, and Mercy. The Negro wants no more of the white man's religion as it applies to his race, for it is a lie and a farce; it is propaganda pure and simple to make fools of a race and rob the precious world, the gift of God to man, and to make it the exclusive home of pleasure, prosperity and happiness for those who have enough intelligence to realize that God made them masters of their fate and architects of their own destinies.

—*from* Negro World, *November 3, 1923.*

To view a longer version of this document, please go to www.ablongman.com/carson/documents.

bill to Congress. But even while threatening to "whip" the Ku Klux Klan, he built alliances with white segregationists to secure land for separate black colonies in Africa. In his most outrageous move, Garvey met with Klan leader Edward Young Clarke to seek Clarke's aid in establishing such colonies. Describing this 1922 meeting in Atlanta, Garvey reported, "I was speaking to a man who was brutally a white man, and I was speaking to him as a man who was brutally a Negro." As both men advocated racial purity and a ban on interracial marriage, Clarke promised economic support for Garvey's plans. But this sort of tactic initiated Garvey's downfall; some UNIA members resisted taking racist money to be forced to leave America.

Though none of Garvey's rhetoric suggested armed revolution, many white officials were alarmed by his defiant posture and his economic power. As early as 1917, federal immigration officials were watching Garvey, hoping to spot an opportunity to oust him from the country. By 1919, they worried that "a doctrine of [independence] of the Negro, for the Negro" might incite revolution among "those elements of our population that have a just cause of complaint." Immigration officials transcribed and studied Garvey's public speeches, and they established contacts in Europe, Africa, the West Indies, and Latin America to track his travels, enterprises, and connections. They also used the Black Star's stockholders' list to solicit complaints from disgruntled investors.

Following Garvey's meeting with Clarke, outraged black leaders and the black press joined the federal government's campaign to bring down Garvey's empire. With declining memberships, the NAACP and the Urban League shared white America's disdain for the charismatic Jamaican. Du Bois mocked Garvey as "a little fat black man, ugly but with intelligent eyes and a big head." The Urban League's newspaper, *Opportunity*, called Garvey's financial programs "a gigantic swindle." One-time Garvey admirer A. Philip Randolph launched his own campaign "to drive Garvey and Garveyism in all its sinister viciousness from the American soil."

At first, Garvey dismissed his critics with a victor's bravado. "My first political enemies in Harlem . . . fought me until they smashed the first organization and reduced its membership to about fifty. I started again, and in two months built up a new organization of about 1,500 members." Garvey considered middle-class black leaders "big Negroes . . . doctors and lawyers and other professionals . . . [who] feel they are not part of the other negroes . . . who call themselves 'aristocrats' and 'gentlemen.'" Taunting the NAACP, Garvey reported he had "visited some of the so-called negro leaders, only to discover that they had no program, but were mere opportunists living off their so-called leadership while the poor people were groping in the dark." He bragged about his influence over people he termed "the small negroes."

But as Garvey's flamboyance united his white and black enemies, that influence began dwindling. In the early days of the UNIA, Garvey had claimed just enough of Booker T. Washington's legacy and following to give legitimacy to his movement. But his plan for complete and permanent segregation differed from Washington's view of temporary segregation as an interim step on the way to full acceptance. Few black Americans believed permanent segregation of the races would bring them economic progress. As Garvey kept sounding a permanent segregation note, many of his followers turned away.

In 1922, the U.S. government convicted Garvey of mail fraud. The UNIA leader spent five years in jail. President Calvin Coolidge—hoping that if Garvey left the country the UNIA would wither away—pardoned him on the condition that he depart the United States. After Garvey left for England in 1923, small pockets of UNIA members remained, continuing to hold property and to promote segregationist programs in many cities for decades to come. However, they were only vestiges of the largest and most powerful mass movement of black Americans the nation would see until the midcentury civil rights movement.

The NAACP and the Urban League in the 1920s

Garvey's meteoric rise temporarily caused long-established black organizations to lose momentum. The NAACP's experience offers an apt example. The NAACP's membership peaked in 1920, with 300 branches and 50,000 members in the United States and abroad. But by the time writer James Weldon Johnson was named executive secretary in 1921—the first black man to hold this position—the UNIA boasted a far larger membership.

To be sure, the NAACP won some dramatic successes in the courts and had the support of imaginative and committed workers like the biracial, blond, blue-eyed Walter White. Still, the organization's influence began waning. White tried to revive the NAACP by traveling through the South and infiltrating white supremacist groups, while Du Bois summarized his reports in *Crisis*. But by 1930, membership had shrunk to about 30,000. Meetings were sparsely attended, and the organization struggled financially.

Many NAACP supporters found these developments deeply discouraging. Retired bicycle racing star Major Taylor, for example—who regularly read *Crisis* and was a friend of Du Bois—began distancing himself from politics. Typical of many Americans, he focused his energies instead on day-to-day affairs. He attended his local Baptist church, managed his bike and auto repair shop, and raised his daughter.

Despite dwindling support and limited means, the NAACP continued its legal assault on segregation and discrimination in the United States. Chipping away at segregated courts, schools, and neighborhoods, it sought to make racial exclusion so morally reprehensible and expensive that white Americans would back away from the policy. In its first decade, NAACP lawyers had won rulings against residential segregation in Kentucky and Chicago (*Buchanan* v. *Warley*, 1917) and against all-white juries (*State* v. *Young*, 1919). In 1923, in *Moore* v. *Dempsey*, it won protection of the right for all perspectives to a fair hearing in a courtroom, and not have black voices suppressed. In 1927, in *Nixon* v. *Herndon*, the courts upheld the right of African Americans to participate in election primaries.

Drawing on the talents of white counsel and dedicated black lawyers like Tulsa's Buck Franklin and Howard University law school dean Charles Houston, a World War I veteran of the 368th Infantry, the NAACP inaugurated what became a decades-long campaign among middle-class black people: integrated neighborhoods. Since poor people and African Americans were often consigned to the oldest housing in deteriorating neighborhoods, middle-class black people who could afford it sought access to modern neighborhoods. Houston insisted that only concerted and consistent legal pressure would dismantle restrictive covenants—private agreements among homeowners not to sell to so-called unacceptable buyers. In one California case, the NAACP successfully defended Booker T. Washington Jr. from the threat of having his San Gabriel Valley home forcibly sold out from under him.

Across the nation, white people also used violence to keep black Americans out of their neighborhoods. When black physician Ossian Sweet moved into a white Detroit neighborhood, a mob attacked his home. A shot from Sweet's house killed one of the attackers, and Sweet was indicted for murder. In 1925, his NAACP legal team, including white lawyer Clarence Darrow, convinced a local judge the Sweet family had acted in self-defense. But other victims of racial violence were less fortunate, and the NAACP suffered numerous legal defeats. Over and over, the courts declared themselves powerless to prevent

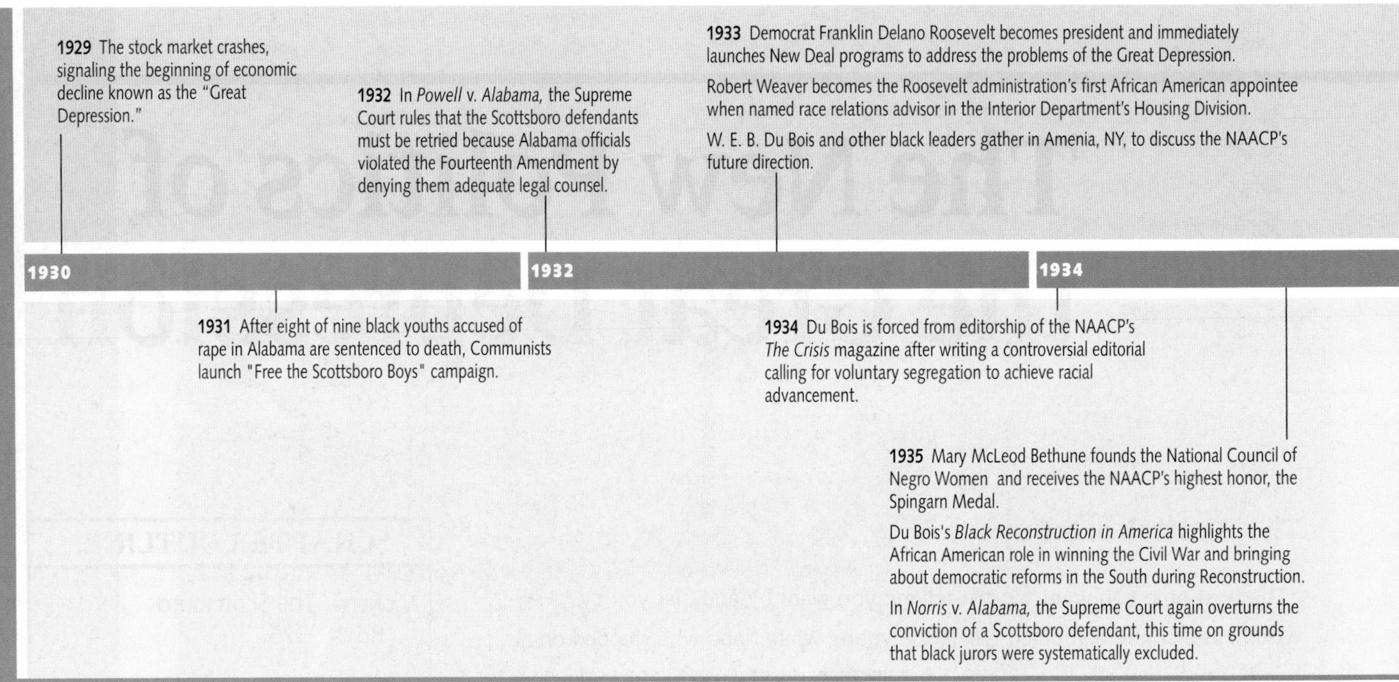

moving train. Then they complained to local authorities that a gang of blacks wielding knives and guns had assaulted them.

When the train arrived in Paint Rock, the next stop in Alabama, the sheriff was waiting with an armed posse. By this time, some of the black riders had already gotten off the train. But deputies roped Patterson and eight others together and took them to the county jail in Scottsboro. The arrestees would soon be known as "the Scottsboro boys," though the oldest was nineteen years old. Two were thirteen. All nine were poor, illiterate or barely literate, and bewildered by the allegations against them. A deputy initially told Patterson, who knew two of the other arrestees, that the group would be charged with assault and attempted murder. Yet only after the inmates had languished in jail for hours did they learn the true seriousness of their situation.

Patterson recalled that two young white women were brought to the jail. He had paid little attention when he had seen them in Paint Rock standing with the white hobos and wearing men's clothing.

"Do you know these girls?" a deputy asked the prisoners. Patterson and the others said no.

"No? You damn-liar niggers! You raped these girls."

Charged with rape, a capital offense in Alabama, the Scottsboro defendants now faced the possibility of the electric chair—that is, if they managed to avoid being lynched by the mob of whites who gathered as lurid accounts of the alleged crime spread. There had been twenty-one reported lynchings in the United States the previous year, nearly all involving southern black men who were murdered before they could stand trial. Fearing bad publicity for the state, Alabama's governor and the local sheriff agreed to call in the National Guard to ensure that the defendants received a formal trial.

The trials began in Scottsboro on April 6, just twelve days after the arrest. They unfolded in a climate of mob vengeance that made it clear the defendants had no chance. Angry white people gathered inside and outside the courtroom. Some insisted that the trials were a waste of taxpayers' money, given that the defendants must certainly be guilty. The headline of a *Huntsville Times* editorial read, "DEATH PENALTY PROPERLY DEMANDED IN FIENDISH CRIME OF NINE BURLY NEGROES." The sixty-nine-year-old white defense attorney who reluctantly agreed to accept the cases had little time to prepare and was hesitant to challenge the stories of the white accusers.

Yet the testimony of Victoria Price and Ruby Bates contained numerous inconsistencies and improbabilities. Like the defendants, the two women were unemployed vagrants. They claimed that armed black men had brutally raped them, but medical examinations revealed no evidence of sexual assault. No weapons were found on the defendants. But such considerations did not deter the prosecutors. Within four days, all-

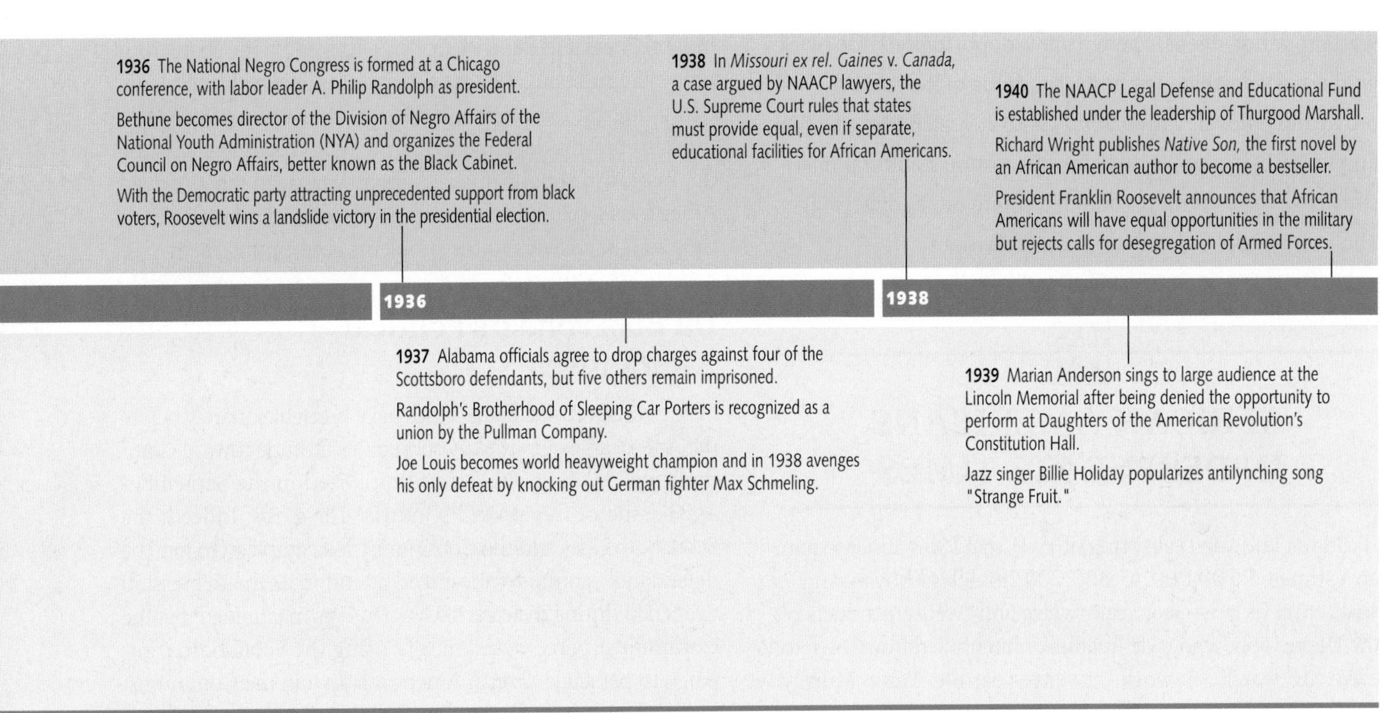

white juries had convicted eight of the nine defendants, who were then sentenced to death. Jurors deadlocked in the case of the youngest defendant, Roy Wright. A mistrial resulted in his case when eleven of the twelve jurors insisted on the death penalty after the prosecutors asked only for life imprisonment.

In previous years, the Scottsboro case might have attracted little attention outside the South, and the defendants would have been promptly executed. But in 1931 economic catastrophe was reshaping American politics. People of all races had begun questioning their country's political and economic institutions and considering radical solutions to their problems. Insisting that the depression demonstrated the failure of capitalism, members of the United States Communist Party saw the Alabama case as a chance to unite workers of all races against what they called the Scottsboro Frame-Up. Though few African Americans embraced revolutionary socialism, the Communist-led Scottsboro campaign spurred various forms of black militancy, especially in urban areas. During subsequent years, black non-Communists worked with communists to stage numerous mass protests—rallies, marches, rent strikes, union organizing, economic boycotts—to try to vanquish discrimination. The Scottsboro campaign also catalyzed heated debates about the future of the National Association for the Advancement of Colored People (NAACP), the nation's oldest and largest civil rights organization.

Presidential politics also influenced the fate of the Scottsboro defendants and the lives of most African Americans. Franklin D. Roosevelt's New Deal offered an alternative to radicalism. Although Roosevelt's first priority after winning the presidency in 1932 was to restore confidence in the economic system, his administration provided relief assistance to ease the anguish of joblessness and hunger. New Deal employment and job training programs brought hope to those without work. Despite racial bias in the administration of some of these programs and Roosevelt's failure to support civil rights legislation, most African Americans appreciated the New Deal and some benefitted from it. In the 1936 election, many black voters switched allegiances from the Republican party of Abraham Lincoln to the Democratic party of Roosevelt. Moreover, Roosevelt's black appointees—often called the Black Cabinet—testified to the gradual incorporation of African Americans into the New Deal coalition, which came to include numerous black workers who joined the expanding industrial union movement.

The cultural explosion of the Harlem Renaissance could not survive the economic downturn. Yet black writers, artists, and entertainers of the 1930s still managed to reach large multiracial audiences and influence the nation's mass culture as never before. By the early 1940s, mobilization for a new war in Europe further transformed American race relations, as wartime labor needs opened new opportunities for black workers. Meanwhile, the bestseller status of Richard Wright's provocative novel *Native Son* (1940) revealed the growing impact of black intellectuals on the nation's cultural mainstream—even as Wright's doomed young protagonist, Bigger Thomas, symbolized persistent racial divisions.

AFRICAN AMERICANS IN DESPERATE TIMES

"I did not know in that spring of 1931 that I was about to join an estimated 200,000 to 300,000 homeless boys—and a smattering of girls—between twelve and twenty, products of the Depression, who rode freights or hitchhiked from town to town in search of work," twenty-year-old Pauli Murray recalled. Unlike the Scottsboro defendants, Murray's time as a hobo was limited to one cross-country trip that ended without misfortune. She was a college student at New York's Hunter College at the time of the 1929 stock market crash, but had been forced to quit school when laid off from her restaurant waitress job. "I became one of those marginal workers who felt the first shocks of the Depression."

Although Americans of all races and backgrounds were profoundly affected by the worsening economic crisis of the 1930s, black Americans such as Pauli Murray experienced special hardships due to the added burden of racial discrimination. African Americans who had fewer employment opportunities than whites even during the best of times were especially hard hit by the crisis. As the overall unemployment rate reached 25 percent of the nation's entire workforce, the black unemployment rate was over twice that high in many cities. In once-thriving Detroit, the center of automobile production, the unemployment figure for black workers exceeded 60 percent in the early 1930s. One of thousands of African American migrants who had flooded into New York during the Harlem Renaissance, Murray and other black people encountered the intensified competition for urban jobs as the economy deteriorated.

While conditions worsened throughout the nation, rural black southerners experienced even more dire conditions, exacerbated by boll weevil infestations and floods. At the beginning of the 1930s, one of every two African Americans lived on farms, most of whom were tenants working on land owned by others. The fall in cotton prices—from twenty cents per pound in the early 1920s to five cents by 1933—added to the hardship. Ned Cobb, a tenant farmer in Alabama, struggled to acquire and hold onto land despite indebtedness and dependency encouraged by the sharecropping system. Though illiterate, Cobb was finally able to secure a low-interest loan through a federal government program that lessened his dependence on the white landowner. As the depression dramatically reshaped American life, African Americans explored a wide range of political alternatives as they sought answers to the problems confronting them.

Du Bois Ponders Political Alternatives

"The Scottsboro, Alabama, cases have brought squarely before the American Negro the question of his attitude toward Communism," W. E. B. Du Bois editorialized in the September 1931 issue of the NAACP's journal *The Crisis*. Indeed, the Scottsboro cases and the Communist-led campaign to free the defendants captured widespread attention as the depression deepened during the early 1930s. Du Bois maintained that the Communist party was cynically using the Scottsboro campaign to persuade African Americans "to join the Communist movement as the only solution to their problem." At the same time, his loyalty to the NAACP, which he had helped found two decades earlier, was being tested by his growing conviction that the organization needed to shift its direction to combat both economic deprivation and racial discrimination.

Du Bois had stirred controversy when he urged black voters to support the Socialist party's presidential candidate in the 1928 election. But just three years later, he found himself on the defensive as Communist organizers spearheaded efforts to organize industrial workers and increasingly competed with the NAACP for the support of African Americans. In his editorial, Du Bois conceded that Communists had "made a courageous fight against the color line among the workers." But he doubted whether white workers would ever turn toward socialism or ally themselves with black workers. Throughout the history of the Negro in America, white labor has been the black man's enemy, his oppressor, his . . . murderer," Du Bois insisted. White workers, after all, had joined the Scottsboro mob "demanding blood sacrifice."

> "Throughout the history of the Negro in America, white labor has been the black man's enemy, his oppressor, his . . . murderer."
> —*W. E. B. Du Bois*

Du Bois concluded that the NAACP's strategy of achieving *gradual* reform held greater promise for African Americans than the Communists' radical effort to overthrow capitalism. "Negroes know perfectly well that whenever they try to lead revolution in America, the nation will unite as one fist to crush them and them alone," he wrote. Though most African Amer-

Ella Baker and Marvel Cooke Describe "The Bronx Slave Market"

During the 1930s, employment opportunities for African American women were largely restricted to domestic service. The following article, prepared in 1935 by black activists Ella Baker and Marvel Cooke, indicates that many women were forced each day to sell their labor under degrading conditions reminiscent of slavery.

Rain or shine, cold or hot, you will find them there—Negro women, old and young—sometimes bedraggled, sometimes neatly dressed—but with the invariable paper bundle, waiting expectantly for Bronx housewives to buy their strength and energy for an hour, two hours, or even for a day at the munificent rate of fifteen, twenty, twenty-five, or, if luck be with them, thirty cents an hour. If not the wives themselves, maybe their husbands, their sons, or their brothers, under the subterfuge of work, offer worldly-wise girls higher bids for their time.

Who are these women? What brings them here? Why do they stay? In the boom days before the onslaught of the depression in 1929, many of these women who are now forced to bargain for a day's work on street corners, were employed in grand homes. . . . Some are former marginal industrial workers, forced by the slack in industry to seek other means of sustenance. In many instances there had been no necessity for work at all. But whatever their standing prior to the depression, none sought employment where they now seek. They come to the Bronx, not because of what it promises, but largely in desperation.

—from Ella Baker and Marvel Cooke, "The Bronx Slave Market," The Crisis, *November 1935. Reprinted by permission of the Crisis Publishing Co., Inc.*

icans shared Du Bois's skepticism about the Communist party, a small minority found the party a source of hope in a time of desperation. Exerting influence far beyond their numbers, these black Reds provided the spark that ignited an unprecedented period of African American political militancy.

Black Reds

"WOULD YOU RATHER FIGHT OR STARVE?" Seventeen-year-old Angelo Herndon spotted this provocative headline on a leaflet he found on a Birmingham street as he walked home from work in June 1930. At first he guessed the leaflet was a call to military service. But when he read it more closely, he learned it was an invitation to attend a meeting of Birmingham's Unemployment Council. Herndon had a job. Nevertheless, he had struggled to survive since leaving home at age thirteen to work as a coal miner, as his father had done for most of his life. Lying about his age, Herndon had labored in the mines of Kentucky and northern Alabama before landing a job in Birmingham loading coal onto railway cars. He found the working conditions harsh. The racism of white foremen and bosses—who often assigned the most dangerous and lowest-paying jobs to black workers—only worsened matters.

Conditions for workers everywhere had deteriorated rapidly after the stock market crash of 1929. Detroit's automobile assembly lines had long symbolized American prosperity, but by 1930 automobile plants were laying off workers and canceling orders for Birmingham's steel. The depression hit the nation's farmers hard as well—in their case, by continuing the long-term decline in prices for their products. Farm foreclosures as well as depressed economic conditions in Europe undermined confidence in the nation's banks. "Mines and factories were closing down; businesses failed, banks crashed," Herndon recalled. "Workers who had never been out of jobs before suddenly found themselves tramping vainly in search of new employment."

> "Workers who had never been out of jobs before suddenly found themselves tramping vainly in search of new employment." —*Angelo Herndon*

At the meeting sponsored by the Unemployment Council, Herndon listened to Communist organizers, both black and white, calling on workers to unite to fight "the bosses." Ignoring warnings from relatives about associating with "Reds," Herndon attended other such meetings. Within a few months he became a Communist organizer, urging other workers to join unions to fight exploitation. Herndon had once admired "big Negro leaders" such as Du Bois, but now he decided that such "self-appointed leaders" were "lined up on the side of the capitalist class." Though Herndon had dropped out of school to become a miner, he struggled to read Karl Marx's *Communist Manifesto* "over and over with pained concentration." He knew the risks of affiliating with a revolutionary group; nevertheless, he decided that the Communist party offered a vision of a "radiant future" that gave him "a purpose in living, in doing, in aspiring."

The Communist party's success in recruiting black workers such as Herndon resulted from its decision during the 1920s to combat racial discrimination as well as economic oppression. In the first decade after its founding in 1919, the party had attracted only a handful of black members. Notable among them were the Harlem Renaissance writer Claude McKay (who soon abandoned radical politics) and a few black nationalists affiliated with the secretive African Blood Brotherhood. The party scored greater successes, however, in the late 1920s, when it followed the lead of the Communist International—the institution, dominated by the Soviet Union, that provided ideological guidance for the worldwide Communist movement—declared that African Americans were an oppressed national group with the right of self-determination in the South's "Black Belt," where they formed a majority. The party stepped up recruitment of African Americans and established the League of Struggle for Negro Rights to fight lynching and other forms of racism.

Shortly before the Scottsboro arrests, the Communist party's racial policies were put on display at a well-attended mock trial in Harlem. The trial resulted in the expulsion of a white Communist who failed to defend a black worker being harassed at a dance. Even in the South, Communist organizers stressed that racial divisions undermined the power of workers. Herndon was impressed that the party "fought selflessly and tirelessly to undo the wrongs perpetrated upon my race. Here was no dilly-dallying, no pussyfooting on the question of full equality for the Negro people."

The Scottsboro Campaign

The Scottsboro trials in 1931 gave the Communist party an opportunity to demonstrate its commitment to protecting black workers' rights. Within days of the verdicts, William Patterson, the African American head of the Communist-sponsored International Labor Defense (ILD), and no relation to defendant Haywood Patterson, sent the ILD's lead attorney and other representatives to meet with the defendants and their parents. A graduate of the University of California's law school, Patterson had risked his successful legal practice in Harlem to join the Communists. After receiving instruction in Marxist theory during a stay in the Soviet Union, he quickly became one of the party's most influential black members.

The NAACP also sent lawyers to Alabama, but the ILD team argued convincingly that its strategy of combined legal appeals and mass protests offered the best chance for saving the defendants. Du Bois and NAACP executive secretary Walter White complained that the Communists were manipulating the poorly educated defendants, but the defendants saw things differently. Explaining his decision to place his fate in the hands of Communists, Haywood Patterson noted that the ILD representatives "were the first people to call on us, to show any feelings for our lives, and we were glad."

The Communist party launched a nationwide "Free the Scottsboro Boys" campaign. As the defendants awaited execution, which was scheduled for July 1931, Communists in Harlem held boisterous rallies and led marchers along Lenox Avenue demanding "Death to Lynch Law" and "Smash the Scottsboro Frame-Up." Several demonstrations featured appearances by Janie Patterson, Haywood Patterson's mother, and Ada Wright, mother of two other defendants. Angelo Herndon, who had relocated to New Orleans to escape harassment by Birmingham police and vigilantes, enthusiastically joined the Scottsboro effort. He assembled a mass meeting of workers and helped form a Provisional Committee for the Defense of the Scottsboro Boys. Speakers at these gatherings not only called on workers of all races to prevent the "legal lynching" but also praised the Communist party at the expense of the "reformist" NAACP. Denouncing NAACP leaders for believing that the Scottsboro defendants could receive a fair trial in Alabama, the ILD-sponsored newspaper *Liberator* remarked, "Anyone who says otherwise is trying to deceive." ILD lawyers insisted that only mass protests could free the defendants. Yet they also appealed the convictions, thereby staving off the executions and buying time to mobilize support for the Scottsboro campaign. In *Powell* v. *Alabama* (1932), the Supreme Court ruled that the Scottsboro defendants be retried because they had been denied adequate legal counsel.

Much to the dismay of NAACP leaders, the Communist party's enthusiastic support of the Scottsboro defendants proved to be its most effective recruiting tool in black communities. Although some black ministers barred Communist organizers from churches because of their atheist views, the Scottsboro campaign attracted support from many sources. Early in 1932, the black poet Langston Hughes visited Alabama's Kilby Prison, where the defendants waited. The experience inspired Hughes to spread the news about "eight black boys and one white lie." He quickly crafted a one-act play titled *Scottsboro, Limited* that portrayed black workers uniting to smash an electric chair. When the play was later performed in Los Angeles, the aroused audience rose in unison at the end to chant "Fight! Fight! Fight! Fight!" Though Hughes did not join the Communist party, the Scottsboro campaign brought him into close contact with party activists, and he agreed to serve as president of the party's League of Struggle for Negro Rights.

Haywood Patterson (seated) and seven other "Scottsboro Boys" facing death sentences confer with defense lawyer Samual Liebowitz in March 1933, shortly before the beginning of Patterson's second trial on rape charges.

Clamping Down on Black Radicalism

Langston Hughes risked his career as a writer by associating himself with the Communist-led Scottsboro campaign, but black Communists working in the South, such as Angelo Herndon, took far more serious risks. Even without the Red label, black political activists in the region often came under violent attack from the Ku Klux Klan. Moreover, southern police and thugs hired by employers to combat unions had long targeted labor organizers. Herndon recalled finding a Klan handbill lying at his front door warning black Birmingham residents against attending "Communist meetings." The document read: "Alabama is a good place for good negroes to live in, but it is a bad place for negroes who believe in SOCIAL EQUALITY." Raymond Parks, a barber in Montgomery, Alabama, discovered that simply attending Scottsboro defense meetings exposed him to the potential for violent retribution. "I didn't go to meetings because it was dangerous," his wife, Rosa, remembered. "Whenever they met, they always had someone posted as a lookout, and someone always had a gun."

Herndon found that the threat of violence loomed the largest in rural Alabama, where the Croppers and Farm Workers Union (later known as the Sharecroppers Union) had established a foothold. Despite massive black migration from the countryside to cities during World War I and the decade afterward, most African Americans still lived in the rural South at the start of the 1930s. Three out of four black farmers in the region did not own the land they worked. Such tenant farmers had to acquire staples—seed, fertilizer, farm equipment, and other items—on credit from their white landlords or from merchants, with the aim of paying off those debts after harvesting the crops. Tenants who sharecropped had to give landlords part of the harvest—usually a third or a half. This system forced most tenants to grow commercial crops, such as cotton, rather than the grains and vegetables they needed for their own use. For this reason, members of the Croppers Union demanded the right to sell their own crops rather than hand them over to their creditors for sale. They also wanted their children to be able to attend school for nine months, instead of helping with planting and harvesting most of the year.

Just two months after the Scottsboro trials, a violent clash outside a union meeting near Camp Hill, Alabama, revealed the vulnerability of black tenants to violent intimidation. When a county sheriff and his deputies tried to break up a gathering of about 150 sharecroppers, they exchanged gunfire with Ralph Gray, a union member posted to guard the meeting. Both the sheriff and Gray were wounded. Later, the white posse tracked Gray to his home and killed him. During the next few days, vigilantes discouraged further union activity by attacking black farmers and arresting dozens of union members on charges of conspiracy to murder. The ILD immediately publicized the Camp Hill tragedy and eventually secured the release of most of those arrested by arguing that there was insufficient evidence of wrongdoing. The following year, Ned Cobb's decision to join the union caused him to become involved in another bloody clash between union supporters and sheriff's deputies sent to confiscate a black farmer's property. Cobb would later recount his decision to join the union and his subsequent imprisonment in *All God's Dangers,* a vivid autobiography (dictated under the pseudonym Nate Shaw).

Herndon moved to Atlanta in 1932 to continue his organizing activities and soon became the central figure in another major protest campaign. After he led a thousand black and white workers to Atlanta's courthouse to demand increased funding for economic relief, police arrested him for "attempting to incite insurrection." Facing a possible death sentence, Herndon defiantly turned his 1933 trial into a forum on injustice. He proclaimed to the jury, "If the State of Georgia and the City of Atlanta think that by locking up Angelo Herndon, the question of unemployment will be solved, I say you are deadly wrong. If you really want to do anything about the case, you must go out and indict the social system."

Like the Scottsboro trials, Herndon's plight provided a rallying point for Communists, who began organizing demonstrations on his behalf. Black attorney Benjamin J. Davis Jr., the son of a wealthy Republican realtor and a graduate of Morehouse, Amherst, and Harvard Law School, volunteered to defend Herndon at no charge. Though lacking in trial experience, Davis devoted all his energies to the case. When Herndon was nonetheless convicted and sentenced to twenty years on a Georgia chain gang, the undaunted Davis appealed the conviction and resolved to continue working on behalf of workers. (The Supreme Court overturned Herndon's conviction in 1937.) As Davis later explained, "I entered the trial as [Herndon's] lawyer and ended it as his Communist comrade." Davis later became editor of the *Harlem Liberator* and began a rise to political prominence that culminated in 1943, when he won election to the New York City Council—the first Communist to hold such a position in the United States.

Election of 1932

Herndon's imprisonment revealed the considerable obstacles facing Communist organizers in the South. Yet even in northern cities, the party found it difficult to garner mass support in black communities. As the 1932 presidential election approached, the Communist party attempted to strengthen its black support by running a black vice presidential candidate—James W. Ford, a Fisk graduate radicalized by his military experiences in World War I. Still, few African Americans felt comfortable casting their vote for a controversial party that had no chance of winning a national election.

Though Republican candidate Herbert Hoover had presided over the economic tailspin of the previous three years, many black voters despaired at the thought of breaking their traditional Republican ties. Others viewed the Democratic candidate, Franklin D. Roosevelt, with skepticism. Roosevelt's record as governor of New York had shown him to be liberal on many issues, but he had never supported civil rights reforms. Furthermore, the Democratic party had historically allied itself with labor unions that excluded black workers.

Roosevelt swept the election, capturing more than 57 percent of the votes cast. Although the Republican party still retained the support of most black voters, Democrats made substantial gains in northern black communities. The Communist ticket received slightly more than 100,000 votes, less than 1 percent of the total turnout. This was less than one-eighth the votes cast for the Socialist Party's Norman Thomas, the candidate favored by Du Bois as a nonrevolutionary alternative to the major candidates.

As his first priority on taking office in March 1933, Roosevelt set out to restore confidence in the economic system. He said nothing about addressing racial problems. In addition to regulating the banking system and securities trading, the new president quickly won passage of a series of measures that became known as the New Deal. The National Recovery Administration (NRA) established codes to stabilize prices in certain industries. Although these codes helped some workers by setting minimum wages, the menial job categories containing most black workers were not covered by minimum wage regulations. The Federal Emergency Relief Administration provided funding for local agencies that provided food and shelter for unemployed African Americans. Since federal programs sometimes provided alternatives to extremely low-wage jobs, some agencies, particularly those in the South, did their best to discourage black applicants. Yet, as the New Deal gradually shifted its focus from reviving capitalism to providing jobs and training for those in need, increasing numbers of black workers benefited from federal programs such as the Public Works Administration (PWA), the Civil Works Administration (CWA), and the Civilian Conservation Corps (CCC). In time, these programs affected the lives of many black Americans and prompted them to adopt more favorable views regarding Roosevelt and the Democratic party. For the first time since the days of the Freedmen's Bureau, established after the Civil War, the federal government undertook new assistance programs that provided tangible benefits and hope to millions of African Americans. The Communists had promised more than the Democrats, but Roosevelt demonstrated that he could deliver.

BLACK MILITANCY

For the NAACP, the upsurge of Communist agitation and the launching of Roosevelt's New Deal posed a dilemma. Under the leadership of executive secretary Walter White, the nation's largest civil rights organization struggled to build a mass following in black communities while also attracting the support of powerful white people. White's initial reluctance to involve the NAACP in the controversial Scottsboro case drew criticism from African Americans who saw the group as overly cautious. W. E. B. Du Bois, editor of the NAACP's journal *The Crisis,* initially agreed with White's view that the Communists were exploiting the Scottsboro case and rejected allegations that the NAACP was unwilling to assist the defendants. "Whatever the NAACP has lacked," he wrote, "it is neither dishonest nor cowardly." Nevertheless, Du Bois came to agree with the Communists' view that merely providing legal assistance to the Scottsboro defendants "will never solve the larger Negro problem but that further and more radical steps are needed."

A New Course for the NAACP

As the economy continued spiraling downward in the early 1930s, Du Bois and other NAACP members grew increasingly dissatisfied with White's dedicated but uninspiring leadership. At the organization's annual convention in 1932, Du Bois insisted that the NAACP would never achieve its goals unless it abandoned the notion of working "*for* the black masses but not *with* them." While rejecting calls for revolution, Du Bois was drawn to Marxist notions of class struggle. He urged delegates to seek economic as well as political change and to view America's racial problems through an international lens. In 1933, he provoked debate within the NAACP by publishing an essay in *The Crisis* titled "Marxism and the Negro Problem."

Du Bois also promoted a gathering of some of the best-educated black leaders—whom he called the "talented tenth"—to define economic as well as civil rights goals for the NAACP. He handpicked the thirty-three people who met in Amenia, New York, at the estate of NAACP board chairman Joel Spingarn in August 1933. Du Bois made certain that invitations went to up-and-coming professionals and academics, most of them just half his age. The select group included eleven women. Several of these, such as Anna Arnold Hedgeman, were affiliated with the Young Women's Christian Association, one of the few national interracial organizations in which black women held leadership positions. A brashly confident contingent from Howard University exerted considerable influence over the discussions, sometimes even pushing Du Bois toward a greater emphasis on economic rather than racial concerns. This group included political scientist Ralph Bunche, economist Abram Harris, and Howard Law School dean Charles Houston. Fisk sociologist E. Franklin Frazier, a brilliant young scholar who would soon join Howard's faculty, also participated.

Like Du Bois, these scholars had studied at leading research universities (Bunche and Houston at Harvard, Harris at Columbia, and Frazier at University of Chicago). They shared the leftist views of many white intellectuals of the period and hungered to devote their skills to the cause of social justice. Most of them agreed with Du Bois's dismissal of Communist calls for violent revolution. Yet they saw enormous promise in interracial efforts to unionize industrial workers.

The young intellectuals at the Amenia Conference proved unable to shift the NAACP's direction—a failure that disappointed Du Bois. At the same time, he had his own doubts about the feasibility of working-class unity in the United States, where white laborers had long victimized black workers. Instead, Du Bois urged Pan-African unity and the building of strong institutions within black communities. A decade earlier, he had denounced Marcus Garvey as "either a lunatic or a traitor" for promoting similar ideas, but Du Bois placed his faith in locally based institutions rather than a single national organization such as Garvey's Universal Negro Improvement Association (UNIA). In a January 1934 *Crisis* editorial titled "Segregation," Du Bois questioned the NAACP's single-minded devotion to integrationist policies. He feared that these policies implied a "distaste or unwillingness of colored people to work with each other, to cooperate with each other, to live with each other." Instead, he wrote, "it is the race-conscious black man cooperating together in his own institutions and movements who will eventually emancipate the colored race."

White and other NAACP leaders worried that some readers might mistake the *Crisis* editor's views for the organization's official position. Du Bois added fuel to the fire he had lit when he questioned the fair-skinned White's ability to comprehend racism: "He goes where he will in New York City and naturally meets no Color Line, for the simple and sufficient reason that he isn't 'colored.'" Soon the NAACP board ordered Du Bois to stop using *The Crisis* to criticize the organization's politics. Du Bois defiantly published his resignation letter in the August 1934 issue. "If I criticize within, my words fall on deaf ears," he complained. "If I criticize openly, I seem to be washing dirty linen in public." Du Bois then left New York for Atlanta University, where he had already accepted President John Hope's invitation to teach.

At this point, Du Bois might have retired; he was sixty-six years old. Instead, he began a new, remarkably productive period of study, scholarship, and activism that would last almost three decades. In 1935 he published *Black Reconstruction in America*. This important and controversial historical study challenged the conventional view of the Civil War era by suggesting that a "general strike" by slaves had contributed to Union victory and that the black masses had influenced the democratic reforms of Reconstruction. During the

downtown Atlanta, and he later orchestrated an effort to raise the salaries of black public school teachers to the levels of their white counterparts. He expressed the basic social gospel message when he advised other ministers: "Quite often we say the church has no place in politics, forgetting the words of the Lord, 'The spirit of the Lord is upon me, because he hath anointed me to preach the Gospel to the poor; he hath sent me to heal the broken-hearted, to preach deliverance to the captives, and the recovering of sight to the blind, to set at liberty them that are bruised.'"

Harlem's Adam Clayton Powell Jr. similarly combined religious and political leadership after a privileged childhood as the son of the well-known pastor of Abyssinian Baptist Church. While an undergraduate at Colgate, Powell briefly passed for white, drawing a stern rebuke from his father. But after succeeding to his father's pulpit in 1937, he became a crusader for social justice. Powell helped form the Greater New York Coordinating Committee for Employment, which used picketing and boycotts to pressure businesses to hire more black workers.

■ During the Great Depression, Harlem minister Adam Clayton Powell Jr. established himself as a civil rights leader, campaigning to feed the poor and gain better employment opportunities for African Americans in New York City.

As the large urban black churches turned increasingly to college-educated ministers such as King and Powell for leadership, others without educational credentials also played important roles in African American religious life. One of the most unconventional of the religious leaders to gain prominence in the 1930s was the largely self-educated, charismatic preacher George Baker, better known as Father Divine. After arriving in New York shortly before World War I, Divine convinced a growing number of white as well as black followers that he was "the true and living God." In 1932, officials of the Long Island community where he had purchased a house prosecuted him for disturbing the peace by holding integrated gatherings of his Peace Mission. When the judge who sentenced him to a year in jail suddenly dropped dead three days afterward, Divine added to his legend by asserting, "I hated to do it."

Many self-serving cult leaders simply enriched themselves at the expense of gullible followers. But Divine's movement, which reached as far as California, proved a complex blend of idealism and hucksterism. While stressing spiritual enrichment rather than political activism, Divine nonetheless encouraged his followers, most of them female, to support the Scottsboro and Herndon defense campaigns and similar causes. Despite being embroiled in frequent financial and sexual scandals, he developed self-help programs, such as Peace Kitchens, that responded to the material as well as spiritual needs of his "angels." Even Du Bois grudgingly acknowledged Divine's achievements: "As a social movement there can be no question but that it has helped many people who need help." When Divine submitted to an interview by Claude McKay during the mid-1930s, he insisted that his programs had a longer reach than even those of the Communist party. McKay reported that Divine was "willing to cooperate in his own way with the Communists or any group that was fighting for international peace and emancipation of people throughout the world and against any form of segregation and racial discrimination." McKay added: "He had come to free every nation, every language, every tongue, and every people. He did not need the Communists or any other organization, but they needed him."

Activist Black Intellectuals

Charles Houston's transformation of Howard's law school provided but one example of what made the university an exciting intellectual center during the 1930s. Most college campuses buzzed with political activism during the depression. But black students at black colleges in the South were discouraged from political expression by college presidents—who had to answer to white trustees. Even at Howard, Mordecai Johnson, the university's first black president, suppressed student protests. Nonetheless, Johnson worked to attract talented black faculty

Adam Clayton Powell Jr. and the Fight for Jobs

As African Americans endured the general decline in the American economy, they also attacked employment discrimination with a new sense of militancy. In New York, as in many other cities, boycotts provided an effective weapon against retail stores that had black customers but few or no black employees. As pastor of a church with more than ten thousand members, Adam Clayton Powell Jr. became a major figure in Harlem's campaign to end employment discrimination. Later, he built on this success when he launched a long political career.

The Coordinating Committee for Employment is beginning a serious business in Harlem. It is beginning a fight for jobs. It has asked for work. It has pleaded for work. It has held conferences. It has utilized every means at its disposal to get the employees of New York City to stop starving the Negroes of New York. These means have failed. The Committee is now inaugurating a mass boycott and picketing of every enterprise in Greater New York that refuses to employ Negroes. The Gas and Electric Company has seen the light, the telephone company must also. The big department stores must follow suit. If Negroes can work at Ovington's, Wanamaker's, Macy's and Bloomingdale's, then an appreciable percentage must work at Gimbel's, Klein's, Hear's, Saks and other stores. The milk companies are next. No more subterfuges, no more passing the buck, but black faces must appear on Harlem milk wagons immediately or the milk concerns shall be boycotted. Three hundred and fifty thousand consumers are not anything to be sneezed at and if anyone dares try to sneeze, we are killing him with the worst cold he ever had. The same thing goes for the Metropolitan Life. As long as we have Negro insurance companies there is no reason why Negroes should pay one cent to any other insurance company that refuses to employ Negroes.

—Adam Clayton Powell Jr., "Soap Box" (regular column) New York Amsterdam News, *May 7, 1938, p. 11.*
Reprinted by permission of the publisher.

To view a longer version of this document, please go to *www.ablongman.com/carson/documents.*

members. Many of them had scholarly credentials that would have gained them teaching positions at leading, predominantly white universities—if racial barriers had not existed in academia.

Writer Alain Locke, a distinguished contributor to the Harlem Renaissance, was already on the Howard faculty when Johnson took over in 1926. During the next ten years, the university raised standards and faculty salaries to attract other major scholars. These included Rayford Logan in history, Sterling Brown in literature, and Charles Drew in medicine, as well as Amenia Conference participants Abram Harris, Ralph Bunche, and E. Franklin Frazier. Several of these professors tested Johnson's constraints on political activism. For example, Bunche joined the Scottsboro Defense Committee. With help from Howard law professor William Hastie, he also founded the New Negro Alliance to launch boycotts against businesses that discriminated against black workers.

International events, especially the rise of fascism in Europe and the stirrings of anticolonialism in Africa, further intensified political militancy among black intellectuals. During these years, Bunche—who wrote his doctoral dissertation on French colonialism in Africa—met with many African leaders, including Kenya's Jomo Kenyatta, who would later lead an independence movement in his country. In 1936, Bunche's influential *World View of Race* predicted that racial conflict would soon give way to "the gigantic class war which will be waged in the big tent we call the world."

> "The gigantic class war . . . will be waged in the big tent we call the world."—*Ralph Bunche*

The success of Roosevelt's New Deal eventually confirmed the view of Bunche and other activist intellectuals that the United States could solve its economic problems without revolution. By the mid-1930s, some of the outspoken intellectuals who had attended the Amenia Conference had considered or accepted positions in New Deal agencies. Even some Communists gladly took federal jobs as the Roosevelt administration began providing jobs and other direct aid to the unemployed. Federal employment programs—most notably those under the Works Progress Administration (WPA)—restored hope to millions of Americans and contributed to Roosevelt's growing support in black communities.

Although New Deal programs addressed economic rather than racial problems, they forced African Americans to rethink their political views. Instead of revolutionary activism or mass protest, it was the Roosevelt administration that emerged as the most significant new political force of the 1930s. In addition, it was a Roosevelt appointee who emerged as the most influential African American of the period.

A NEW DEAL FOR AFRICAN AMERICANS?

"Don't you realize this is the first such post created for a Negro woman in the U.S.?" pleaded Aubrey Williams, head of the National Youth Administration (NYA). Williams was attempting to persuade Mary McLeod Bethune to join his New Deal agency, which provided training and part-time jobs for students to enable them to stay in school. Two weeks earlier, Bethune had caught President Roosevelt's attention when he heard her present a report concluding that NYA wages of $15 to $20 per month "meant real salvation for thousands of Negro young people" and brought "life and spirit" to people "who for so long have been in darkness." In the report, Bethune had added that she was speaking not for herself but "as the voice of 14,000,000 Americans who seek to achieve full citizenship." After concluding her moving testimony, Bethune recalled "a stillness in the room" and tears flowing from the president's eyes. Impressed by Bethune's accomplishments as an educator and by her forthright manner, Roosevelt decided she had to join his administration as director of the NYA's Division of Negro Affairs.

Mary McLeod Bethune

Initially, Bethune hesitated to leave her position as founding president of Florida's Bethune-Cookman College, but she recognized the historic significance of her decision and finally accepted Roosevelt's invitation. "I visualized dozens of Negro women coming after me, filling positions of high trust and strategic importance." When Aubrey Williams took Bethune to the White House to discuss her new role with Roosevelt, she assured the president, "I shall give it the best that I have." Roosevelt observed to Williams, "Mrs. Bethune is a great woman. I believe in her because she has her feet on the ground; not only on the ground, but deep down in the ploughed soil."

Even before she accepted the position that would make her Roosevelt's most influential black appointee, Bethune had demonstrated remarkable perseverance and leadership skills. Born in 1875 in Mayesville, South Carolina, the fifteenth child of former slaves, she had left cotton farming to gain a formal education, eventually training to become a missionary in Africa. But she then realized, "Africans in America needed Christ and school just as much as Negroes in Africa." After teaching in various places including Chicago's slums, she used her savings of $1.50 to found a small girls' school in Daytona Beach, Florida. Yet it was her shrewd appeals to white businessmen vacationing in Florida and to black entrepreneurs—such as hair-care distributor Madame C. J. Walker—that enabled Daytona Normal and Industrial Institute to flourish. In 1923, the school merged with nearby Cookman Institute to become Bethune-Cookman College.

The following year, Bethune's prominence expanded when she was elected president of the National Association of Colored Women (NACW). Walking the middle ground between racial militancy and accommodation, she emerged as the most revered black educator of the period after Booker T. Washington's death. She also became a major figure in the NAACP and the National Urban League. Republican presidents Calvin Coolidge and Herbert Hoover sought her advice on racial issues.

As Bethune's national influence grew, organizations around the country jockeyed to invite her to speak. Known for her distinctive flair for fashion—long capes, colorful jewelry, and a cane carried for "swank"—and her strong sense of racial pride, she often said of herself, "Look at me, I am black, I am beautiful." Her down-to-earth, direct manner enabled her to get along with a wide range of people. These included Langston Hughes, who came to appreciate Bethune when he accepted her invitation to travel through the South in 1931. Hughes recalled that Bethune "was a wonderful sport, riding all day without complaint in our cramped, hot little car, jolly and talkative, never grumbling." During the trip, Bethune's many friends and admirers provided housing and food. Their generosity prompted Hughes to remark that chickens fled upon Bethune's arrival: "They knew some necks would surely be wrung in her honor."

> "Look at me, I am black, I am beautiful."—*Mary McLeod Bethune*

In 1935 Mary McLeod Bethune founded the National Council of Negro Women in New York. Franklin D. Roosevelt appointed her director of the Division of Negro Affairs of the National Youth Administration, a position she occupied from 1936 to 1943. She was particularly well suited to this role because it allowed her to reach the nation's black youth with her zeal for education. Roosevelt also considered her one of his foremost advisers in the unofficial "Black Cabinet" in his administration.

Bethune's ability to collaborate with people who held differing views served her well as a New Dealer. For example, she jauntily deflected racial slights as she carried out her duties. When a White House guard called her "Auntie," she quipped, "Which one of my brother's children are you?" She realized that Roosevelt himself was no racial liberal, at least at the start of his presidency, but instead was a patrician accustomed to seeing blacks in subordinate roles. He even used the epithet "nigger" in private conversations. The president was also reluctant to support civil rights reforms that would offend the southern segregationist politicians, nearly all of them Democrats, who provided crucial support for his New Deal programs.

But Roosevelt did select a few white proponents of racial equality—such as Bethune's boss, Aubrey Williams—for important posts in his administration. Secretary of the Interior Harold Ickes, a progressive who once headed the Chicago NAACP, appointed the New Deal's first black official, Harvard-trained economist Robert Weaver. Bethune and Weaver, both "advisors for Negro affairs," became visible symbols of racial progress. Rather than setting New Deal policies, even on racial issues, they instead persuaded powerful whites to follow their recommendations. The talented black professionals joining the Roosevelt administration also included William Hastie, who left the Howard law faculty to become assistant solicitor of the Interior Department.

Among the dozen or so black appointees of the Roosevelt administration, Bethune quickly became the most visible and most effective black advocate. Although previously a Republican, Bethune soon developed an intense loyalty to President Roosevelt. She not only gained the president's confidence but also forged strong ties with the president's politically active wife, Eleanor Roosevelt, whom she had met in 1924 while attending a luncheon of women leaders at the Roosevelt family home in New York. As this relationship deepened during the 1930s, Bethune encouraged the First Lady's growing commitment to racial equality and often influenced the president through her. By 1935, when the NAACP honored Bethune with its annual Spingarn Medal, she had become the nation's best-connected black leader. Drawing on her rich array of contacts, she brought together all the major black women's organizations to form a new umbrella group, the National Council of Negro Women.

Realizing that African Americans had mixed opinions about the New Deal, Bethune urged the president to tackle racial discrimination even as she defended him against his harshest black critics. Yet despite her pleas, Roosevelt refused to support the NAACP's proposed antilynching legislation. He also did little to address complaints of racial discrimination in the distribution of Federal Employment Relief Administration funds in southern communities, where relief payments were seen as encouraging black laborers to turn down low-wage jobs.

Black Critics of the New Deal

Despite her own doubts about New Deal programs, Bethune sometimes served as a restraining influence on more critical black appointees, such as Robert Weaver and William Hastie. Weaver, an Harvard-educated expert on labor policies, was aware of the limitations as well as the benefits of the New Deal with respect to African Americans. In a 1935 article published in the Urban League's journal *Opportunity*, he noted that there had been racial "abuses" in the distribution of relief payments. "We can admit that we have gained from the relief program and still fight to receive greater and more equitable benefits from it," he wrote. Weaver's concerns were shared by other black intellectuals, both inside and outside the Roosevelt administration. In 1935 John P. Davis, a black economist who had collaborated with Weaver to monitor the impact of fed-

T. Arnold Hill and the Negro Worker in the 1930s

As executive secretary of the Chicago Urban League and then as director of the National Urban League's Department of Industrial Relations, T. Arnold Hill was well placed to study the New Deal's impact on African Americans. The following excerpt from a report published in 1937 draws on the many surveys conducted by federal and state governments as well as private organizations.

No group suffered more severe devastation in the depression period than did the workers in agriculture and household employment—the two major classifications in which Negroes predominate. Government reports teem with evidence of unemployment and dire want throughout the agricultural regions of the country. The number of workers in the domestic service classification who found themselves on relief during the whole period of unemployment, was greatly out of proportion to the rest of the workers. . . .

Fully 90 percent of Negro workers in industry fall into the marginal or unskilled class. This accounts for the terrific amount of unemployment among Negroes in cities; which, as is commonly known, is out of proportion to their actual numbers in the population.

—from T. Arnold Hill, The Negro and Economic Reconstruction *(Washington, DC: Associates in Negro Folk Education, 1937).*

To view a longer version of this document, please go to *www.ablongman.com/carson/documents.*

eral programs on African Americans, persuaded Bunche to call a conference at Howard University billed "The Status of the Negro under the New Deal." Although most participants in this conference supported the New Deal, the discussions at Howard made clear that many black intellectuals were becoming increasingly vocal in their criticism of Roosevelt's policies.

Early the following year, as Roosevelt began preparing his reelection campaign, Benjamin Davis, Ralph Bunche, and other black critics of the New Deal convened a major gathering that drew more than 800 representatives of 585 black organizations to Chicago. This conference inspired the formation of the National Negro Congress, with black labor leader A. Philip Randolph as president and Davis as executive director. Although internal disputes between Communists and non-Communists soon weakened the new organization, during its initial years, the group strengthened bonds between established African American organizations, such as the NAACP and Urban League, and black activists (including Bunche, Randolph, and Davis) who saw the New Deal as merely the first step toward more far-reaching social change. As Randolph's keynote speech insisted, "The New Deal is no remedy. It does not seek to change the profit system. It does not place human rights above property rights, but gives business interests the support of the State."

Bethune did not participate in the Chicago conference. But later in 1936, she provided a forum for constructive criticism of the New Deal when she invited Weaver and other black officials of the Roosevelt administration to a meeting at her home. This gathering resulted in the formation of the Federal Council on Negro Affairs, an informal group that journalists soon described as the Black Cabinet. Though no member of the group actually held a cabinet position (thirty years later, Weaver would become the first African American to hold such a position), the so-called Black Cabinet enabled the growing number of black New Dealers to exchange views on the racial impact of New Deal programs. Bethune's leading role in the group also enhanced her visibility as a symbol of black participation in the Roosevelt administration.

By the 1936 election, Roosevelt had successfully countered black criticism through his savvy appointments of African Americans. More and more blacks concluded that the New Deal, despite its limitations, constituted their best available political option. Even members of the Communist party shifted their stance regarding the New Deal from open hostility to more measured criticism. Facing the rising threat of German fascism but encouraged by the success of industrial union movements in the United States, American Communists adopted a Popular Front strategy—joining forces with liberals and non-Communist socialists to resist fascism and to seek reforms short of revolution. The party's decision to cede control of the Scottsboro cases to the Scottsboro Defense Committee was part of this strategy.

During the 1936 presidential election, the Communist party again ran its own candidate, with James W. Ford once

TABLE 15.1 African Americans on Unemployment Relief, 1935

From the list of selected cities which follows, the percent of African Americans among employables on relief in 1935 was greatly in excess of the ratio of African Americans to the total population.

City	Percent African Americans in total population: 1930	Percent African Americans among employables on relief:1935
Atlanta, GA	33.4	65.7
Birmingham, AL	38.2	63.3
Charlotte, NC	30.4	75.2
Cincinnati, OH	10.6	43.5
Kansas City, MO	9.6	37.2
New York, NY	4.7	11.2
Norfolk, VA	33.9	81.3
St. Louis, MO	11.4	41.5
Wilmington, DE	11.3	43.9

Source: T. Arnold Hill, "The Negro and Economic Reconstruction," 1937.

more as his black running mate. This time, the party focused its campaign on attacking "ruling class" opponents of the New Deal. In a historic shift of black political allegiance, a majority of black voters abandoned the Republican party to support the Democrat Roosevelt—who won by a landslide. An historian later estimated that Roosevelt captured an overwhelming 81 percent of Harlem's black vote and exceeded his nationwide 61 percent in many other black communities. For the first time, African Americans became part of the northern liberal-labor coalition that competed with southern conservatives for control of the Democratic party.

After the election, Bethune asserted herself as forcefully as she thought prudent against racial bias in New Deal programs. In her view, gradual progress through New Deal reforms offered far more potential than "the quicksands of revolution or the false promises of communism or fascism." Indeed, the early years of Roosevelt's second term marked the high point of New Deal social programs. In addition to providing food and shelter to unemployed men and women, Bethune's NYA, the CCC, and the WPA offered jobs and training to needy individuals of every race. For many black workers, these programs provided the best wages they had ever received.

Still, some black people continued to voice their discontent with racial bias in New Deal programs during Roosevelt's second term. Rather than seeking to muzzle these criticisms, in 1937 Bethune called on black leaders throughout the nation to attend a conference at Howard University to offer recommendations for addressing black Americans' problems. "Until now, opportunities have not been offered for Negroes themselves to suggest a comprehensive program for the full integration of benefits and responsibilities of American democracy," she remarked.

The report that resulted from the National Conference on the Problems of the Negro and Negro Youth provided a balanced assessment of the New Deal's impact on African Americans. In the document, the delegates conceded that black Americans had received unprecedented benefits from the New Deal. But they bluntly acknowledged the New Deal's limitations: "It is a matter of common knowledge that the Negro has not shared equitably in all of the services the Government offers its citizens." The delegates proposed that the federal government take over control of New Deal programs from state and local officials to prevent further racial discrimination. They also urged that minimum-wage and overtime-wage rules as well as Social Security coverage be extended to the two largest categories of black workers—agricultural laborers and domestic servants. Additional recommendations included the enactment of antilynching legislation, reduction of the standard work week to thirty hours in order to create more jobs, and denial of collective-bargaining rights to unions that excluded black workers. The delegates further suggested that the government expand federal employment opportunities for black Americans and purchase farmland and resell it to black tenant farmers or small cooperatives.

In 1938, Bethune went further to address the New Deal's limitations. She persuaded Eleanor Roosevelt to join her at the founding meeting of the Southern Conference for Human Welfare in Birmingham, Alabama. The new group defined a daunting mission: to attack the South's especially severe economic problems, which affected white and black people alike. Bethune and Roosevelt knew that the Jim Crow system hampered the effectiveness of New Deal programs in the South, but they were also hesitant to take steps that would anger southern white Democrats whose support Roosevelt needed. When local sheriff Eugene "Bull" Connor insisted on segregated seating at the meeting, Roosevelt tried to find neutral ground between militancy and caution by sitting in the middle aisle. Press reports of her action impressed many black Americans, but a black Communist organizer who attended the meeting still complained that Bethune and Roosevelt should have "broke the backbone of jim crowism" by openly challenging segregation in seating.

Gains and Setbacks

The criticisms of the New Deal expressed at the Birmingham meeting and at the earlier conference called by Bethune foreshadowed subsequent assessments of historians who have studied the New Deal. These scholars have concluded that Roosevelt did little to confront racism and racial dis-

Augusta V. Jackson on Southern Black School Teachers

A delegate to the second annual meeting of the Southern Negro Youth Congress held in Chattanooga during April 1938, Augusta Jackson would be involved in many of the southern political movements of the 1930s and 1940s. In this excerpt from her account of the meeting, she relates the difficulties faced by young women teaching with few resources in racially segregated schools.

A bright-eyed girl, who in appearance and manner does not differ from any girl seen walking down a city street, tells you that she teaches in a rural community where she conducts a school during the "season," that is during the six months of the year when neither the planting season, or cotton picking, or berry picking has emptied the school of its students. As she describes it, you can see her rough one-room schoolhouse, without enough textbooks, or enough teaching material, where most of her pupils come to school without shoes, where some who came last season must stay out this term so that another two or three from their large family can attend while the first is at work on the farm. Since her salary depends upon the attendance quota, she must walk many miles a week in all weather to recruit absentees. She is teacher, social worker, and the community model in morals, dress, and speech. She earns twenty-five dollars a month—during the season.

Another teacher from a school just in the suburbs of a large southern city tells a tale of different, but almost equal difficulties. She earns twice as much as her colleague in the rural community. . . . She has no trouble in getting her pupils to attend school; many are eager to come for they have no long miles to travel over the countryside. Her room is crowded to the door with sixty-five first grade children whom she must teach to read and write. She is responsible for obtaining teaching materials; she must either "raise" the money or give part of her fifty-dollar wage for this purpose.

—from Augusta V. Jackson, "Southern Youth Marches Forward," The Crisis *(June 1938). Reprinted by permission of The Crisis Publishing Co, Inc.*

To view a longer version of this document, please go to *www.ablongman.com/carson/documents*.

crimination. He sought to appeal to black voters without supporting civil rights reforms that would alienate southern segregationists or northern workers who competed with black people for jobs and housing.

Some of the New Deal's deficiencies had long-term consequences that widened the economic gulf between white and black Americans even further. For example, when the Agricultural Adjustment Administration gave subsidies to farm owners who reduced production and purchased machinery (such as the mechanical cotton picker), the move lessened the need for black tenant farmers, both renters and sharecroppers. Together, these groups included more than one-third of all black workers. Moreover, the failure of new labor legislation to require labor unions to admit black workers allowed some unions to maintain racially exclusive practices. Federal housing programs in urban areas often reinforced existing patterns of racial segregation. Furthermore, these programs could not keep up with the demand for housing caused by large-scale migration of blacks to the cities. In addition, the exclusion of farm workers and domestic servants from the Social Security program had a damaging effect on the very categories in which black workers predominated.

Yet, despite their limitations, government social programs delivered much needed benefits to many African Americans. In addition to providing direct relief, such as food, New Deal programs gave training and jobs to black workers who had previously been unemployed or restricted to menial jobs and domestic service. African Americans also benefited from the rapid expansion of the union movement following passage of the National Labor Relations Act (often called the Wagner Act, after its Senate sponsor). The act protected workers' rights to join unions and bargain collectively. In 1937, the Brotherhood of Sleeping Car Porters won a major victory when the fiercely antiunion Pullman Company recognized the Brotherhood's right to bargain on behalf of porters and maids who worked on the trains. The Brotherhood's president, A. Philip

Randolph, then chose to affiliate his union with the American Federation of Labor (AFL), even though many AFL craft unions excluded black workers. As the AFL's most prominent black labor leader, Randolph became a persistent critic of racial discrimination in the labor movement.

Although the Wagner Act did not prevent unions from excluding black people or prevent employers from firing nonunionized black workers, nonetheless, it did strengthen the new Congress of Industrial Organizations (CIO), which organized semiskilled factory workers rather than the skilled craftsmen favored by the AFL. Recognizing that black replacements (often labeled "scabs") could undermine strikes, CIO organizers energetically recruited black workers, targeting especially those working in Detroit's automobile factories. Previously, Henry Ford had fended off the United Automobile Workers (UAW) union by hiring nonunion black workers carefully screened by black ministers whose friendship Ford had cultivated through donations to churches and other community groups. By the end of the 1930s, however, black workers had participated in successful UAW campaigns at General Motors and Chrysler, and in 1941 black and white workers at Ford Motor Company achieved sufficient unity to win a bitter, prolonged strike.

Such successes strengthened Bethune's conviction that, [illegible] New Deal improved African Americans' [illegible] recall of her decade of service in the [illegible]ration, "More than once I proposed [illegible] to end the hideous discriminations and [illegible]nship that make the South a blot upon [illegible] When she asked Roosevelt "why this [illegible] at once or that done immediately," the [illegible]ned the political realities causing the Democra[illegible] shy away from civil rights: "Mrs. Bethune, if we do that now, we'll hurt [another valuable] program over there." Despite Bethune's awareness that Roosevelt would not take political risks on behalf of African Americans, she remained confident that the president ultimately had good intentions. After his death, she wrote that Roosevelt expected Americans to achieve racial equality in time. "That day will come," she quoted the president as saying, "but we must pass through perilous times before we realize it, and that's why it's so difficult today because that new idea is being born and many of us flinch from the thought of it."

BLACK ARTISTS AND THE CULTURAL MAINSTREAM

In New Orleans, sixteen-year-old Margaret Walker heard her parents discussing an upcoming visit by Langston Hughes. The white president of the college where her mother and father taught had told them that Hughes charged a fee of $100 and that he didn't think one hundred people would pay a dollar apiece to come to hear a Negro poet. But one *thousand* people came. That night, Walker later recalled, "was one of the most memorable in my life." At the reception after the reading, she nervously handed Hughes a manuscript of her poems. He read them carefully, one by one, and explained how each might be improved. "He said I had talent," she recalled, "and urged my parents to send me to school in the North, where I would have more freedom to grow."

Margaret Walker and the Works Progress Administration

After Walker graduated from Northwestern University in 1936, job prospects were not plentiful, but she was nonetheless able to find employment with the WPA's Writers' Project, one of many New Deal programs that provided jobs for people who would otherwise have been unemployed. For many black unemployed artists, actors, musicians, and writers, these federal jobs often offered them their first opportunity to earn a living while developing their craft. Like other WPA programs, the Writers' Project also sought to provide useful work experiences. Walker, for example, was hired to work on a guide to Illinois—part of a nationwide research effort designed to produce touring and historical guides for every state. She was able to support both herself and her sister on her salary of $85 a month.

For Walker, the job meant far more than just a wage. Working for the WPA, she believed, helped end "the long isolation of the Negro artist" and fostered "a great deal of exchange between black and white writers, artists, actors, dancers, and other theater people." At a reading by her mentor Langston Hughes, Walker heard that Chicago writers were planning a South Side Writers' Group to discuss their work. She resolved to join the group. At the first meeting, "I heard a man expounding on the sad state of Negro writing at that point in the thirties, and he was punctuating his remarks with pungent epithets," she recalled. "I drew back in Sunday-school horror, totally shocked by his strong speech, but I steeled myself to hear him out."

The speaker, Walker learned, was Richard Wright, already a leading force in Chicago's black literary community. After hearing Wright read some of his works in progress, Walker marveled, "Even after I went home I kept thinking, 'My God, how that man can write!'" Wright told Walker that he planned to transfer from the Theater Project to the Writers' Project because the Theater Project had rejected his controversial proposal for a play depicting a southern chain gang. The next week, Wright began serving as a supervisor in Walker's office. His salary of $125 a month was the highest he had ever received. Over the next year, the two had many long conversations about their mutual literary ambitions. For Walker, the Writers' Project "turned out to be one of the best writers' schools I ever attended." Her relationship with Wright later soured, but she continued to admire his talent, and she would later write a book about him. Another fellow writer asked her a crucial question—"What do you want for your people?"—that inspired her to finish her most celebrated poem, "For My People," in 1937. "The greatest significance of the WPA," recalled Walker, was that it accomplished what nobody believed was possible at that time: "a renaissance of the arts and American culture, with the appearance of spectacular artists or artistic figures, phenomenal programs, and immortal creative work."

In addition to employing Walker and Wright, the WPA also gave early, crucial support to Ralph Ellison, who would later write the prize-winning novel *Invisible Man* (1952). Zora Neale Hurston, soon to achieve prominence for her novel *Their Eyes Were Watching God* (1937), conducted fieldwork for the Writers' Project in Florida, interviewing former slaves as part of an effort to preserve the fading memories of those once held in bondage. Aaron Douglas created murals for the walls of the New York Public Library, while Jacob Lawrence gained early training as a painter in the federally sponsored Harlem Arts Center. Oberlin graduate Shirley Graham worked for the Federal Theater Project directing plays, including *Swing Mikado* (1939), a jazzy adaptation of the Gilbert and Sullivan play with black actors.

■ As an actor, the charismatic Paul Robeson was one of the first black men to play serious roles in the primarily white American theater. He also performed in a number of films, including a remake, shown here, of *The Emperor Jones* (1933).

Paul Robeson and the Black Role in Hollywood

As federal programs fueled advances in African American culture, the expanding entertainment industry also accelerated the entry of black artists and entertainers into American mass culture. Despite the depression—or perhaps owing to it—large numbers of Americans bought mass-produced novels and records, attended movies, and went to nightclubs and dance halls in the 1930s. Nearly everyone listened to the radio. (By the end of the decade, 90 percent of American homes boasted a radio; many cars had them, too.) More than ever before, black entertainers began attracting white fans. Still isolated in mostly separate social worlds, black and white Americans nevertheless now danced to the same commercially popular variant of jazz and blues called swing. Although white executives dominated the entertainment industry and catered mainly to white consumers, African American musicians, singers, and dancers had reason to hope. Like Langston Hughes, they found that their talents could make them a decent living. As entertainer Paul Robeson sardonically observed in 1935, "In a popular form, Negro music, launched by white men—not Negroes—has swept the world."

Robeson's star shown so brightly that he was willing to accept the risks that came with his leftist political ties. During the 1920s he had earned admiration in Harlem, first as a professional football player. (He had been an All-Ameri-

> "In my music, my plays, my films, I want to carry always this central idea: to be African." —*Paul Robeson*

can football star and a Phi Beta Kappa student at Rutgers.) Then he attracted notice as an actor and singer during the heyday of the Harlem Renaissance. His fame spread quickly following critically acclaimed performances in the Broadway production of Eugene O'Neill's *Emperor Jones* (1925). He also played a starring role in black filmmaker Oscar Micheaux's *Body and Soul* (1925) and had a brief but memorable part singing "Ol' Man River" in the 1929 Hollywood musical *Show Boat*. Despite the onset of the Great Depression, Robeson's continuing success as an entertainer brought him personal wealth, a home in London, and freedom to expand his political and cultural contacts. He became acquainted with leftist radicals, such as the Jamaican Marxist writer C. L. R. James, and with African nationalists, such as Nnamdi Azikiwe (later president of Nigeria) and Jomo Kenyatta (later president of Kenya). By 1934, Robeson had resolved that "in my music, my plays, my films, I want to carry always this central idea: to be African." He took particular pride in *Song of Freedom* (1936). In that film, he played a London dockworker who gets his lifelong wish to visit his ancestral home in Africa when he achieves sudden success as a concert singer. Although the film depicted Africa in simplistic terms, its portrayals were considerably more accurate than those in Hollywood's Tarzan adventures. A 1935 trip to the Soviet Union fostered a lasting affinity for socialism and left him convinced "that of all the nations in the world, the modern Russians are our best friends." Infused with racial pride and a growing commitment to leftist politics, Robeson resolved to accept only those movie roles that portrayed blacks in a positive light.

But he made this decision at a time when Hollywood studios cast black actors in comic bit roles—mainly as servants, porters, or menial laborers—in films whose plots focused on white characters. The popular radio program *Amos 'n' Andy* had shaped the mental image many white Americans had of African Americans, even though the program's lead characters were played by white actors. Stepin Fetchit, who depicted slow-witted, slow-moving racial stereotypes, was the highest-paid black actor in Hollywood. He established a model for subsequent black comics who demeaned themselves to get laughs. In 1935, jazz pioneer Louis "Satchmo" Armstrong clowned and played his trumpet in *Pennies from Heaven* (1936), starring white actor Bing Crosby, and thereafter took similar cameo movie parts. Child actor Shirley Temple's hit films included roles for talented blacks; in *The Little Colonel* (1935), Hattie McDaniel played Mammy and Bill "Bojangles" Robinson danced. Despite the limitations of such roles, the presence of African Americans in Hollywood films attracted black ticket buyers. It also enabled the major studios to quash competition from struggling black film producers such as Oscar Micheaux. Some black performers (and their fans) saw even these stereotypical Hollywood roles as personal and racial breakthroughs. McDaniel, who won an Academy Award for her performance—again as Mammy—in the 1939 epic *Gone With the Wind,* defended her roles emphatically: "I'd rather play a maid than be one."

The Swing Era

Living abroad and performing before largely white concert audiences in Europe, Robeson sustained his career as a singer even as a gulf opened between his own musical preference for traditional music, such as slave spirituals, and the commercially popular music of his day. Trends in the commercial industry disturbed him. He believed that even jazz had lost touch with the African American tradition of "honest and sincere" folk music with spiritual significance. For him, the entry of African Americans into the nation's cultural mainstream represented a loss of cultural integrity. "No Negro will leave a permanent mark on the world till he learns to be true to himself," he warned.

But while Robeson harbored serious reservations about the commercialization of African American music, many African American musicians welcomed the new trends. By the mid-1930s, the swing phenomenon took jazz from the small clubs in the black sections of New Orleans, Chicago, and New York to bigger nightclubs and urban radio stations throughout the nation. While Robeson continued to perform concerts of traditional songs drawn from many cultures, swing musicians, black and white alike, revolutionized popular music in the United States and around the world. As a struggling student in depression-era Harlem, Pauli Murray saw black entertainers as welcome antidotes to hard times. She savored the Apollo Theater as one of the "bright spots." There, she said, "we could sit in the balcony for twenty-five cents and see the great Negro entertainers in the heyday of their youth—Ethel Waters, Jackie (Moms) Mabley, the one-legged dancer Peg Leg Bates, tap dancers Peter, Peaches, and Duke, comedian Galley de Gaston, and the great bands led by such extraordinary musicians as Duke Ellington and Cab Calloway."

The appeal of these performers transcended racial lines. Both Ellington, composer of hit tunes such as "Mood Indigo" and "It Don't Mean a Thing (If It Ain't Got That Swing)", and the flamboyant Cab "Hi Di Ho" Calloway were headliners at New York's Cotton Club. The club had relocated from black Harlem to midtown Manhattan. Louis Armstrong expanded his audience as he moved from the breakthrough exuberant Hot Five

Composer, bandleader, and pianist Duke Ellington was recognized in his lifetime as one of the greatest jazz composers and performers. The unique "Ellington" sound found expression in works like "Mood Indigo" and "Sophisticated Lady."

recordings of the 1920s to the more refined big-band sound inspired by white bandleader Guy Lombardo. By the mid-1930s, the bands of Ellington, Calloway, Count Basie, Fletcher Henderson, and Chick Webb were facing competition from highly popular white bandleaders such as Tommy Dorsey, Glenn Miller, and Benny Goodman. Indeed, Goodman's regular appearances on NBC radio earned him the title King of Swing. Singer Billie "Lady Day" Holiday eclipsed the popularity of her earthier blues predecessors Ma Rainey and Bessie Smith. By the end of the decade, white bandleader Artie Shaw broke racial barriers by hiring Holiday to perform with his band. Holiday subsequently redirected her career when she began performing regularly at New York's Café Society, a hangout for bohemians and leftists of all races. It was there in 1939 that she first performed "Strange Fruit," a haunting anti-lynching song with lyrics written by a white Communist schoolteacher.

The popularity of swing music enabled some black performers to reach white audiences, but, as Robeson's comments make clear, not all performers went along with the new trend. The tradition of southern blues music was kept alive in small clubs and juke joints. Leadbelly and Josh White were among the few blues musicians to have successful recording careers as they spurred interest in traditional blues in the urban North, especially among leftists who appreciated authentic expressions of southern black working-class consciousness. Robeson himself continued to sing traditional African American music, although his film acting increasingly overshadowed his singing career. (He would have one final burst of success as a singer in 1940 when his rendition of the patriotic "Ballad for Americans" became an instant sensation.) The tradition of black sacred music also remained vibrant as gospel singing evolved in new directions in big-city church choirs featuring the upbeat compositions of Chicagoan Thomas A. Dorsey, often called the Father of Gospel Music. Dorsey's "Precious Lord, Take My Hand" and numerous other songs reached large national audiences when recorded by Clara Ward and Mahalia Jackson.

African Americans would continue to debate whether the growing popularity of black musical styles was a positive or negative trend. Many African Americans resented entertainers who perpetuated racial stereotypes while performing before white audiences. Nevertheless, most black entertainers certainly welcomed opportunities to display their talents before white audiences, and those who achieved wealth and fame were often widely admired in black communities. As was true for the writers of the Harlem Renaissance, black entertainers often faced dilemmas as they sought to meet the expectations of both black and white fans. More than ever before, successful black entertainers also became unofficial racial representatives. When the NAACP awarded its annual Spingarn Medal to opera singer Marian Anderson in 1939, the honor signaled that African Americans took pride in the success of a performer who had used singular talent and determination to break through racial barriers. That year, Anderson was denied permission to give a concert at Washington's Constitutional Hall (owned by the Daughters of the American Revolution). Later, at the urging of Eleanor Roosevelt, Secretary of the Interior Harold Ickes invited Anderson to give an open-air concert at the Lincoln Memorial. On a chilly Easter Sunday, 75,000 fans came to hear her.

Native Son and the Decline of Leftist Radicalism

"Generally speaking, Negro writing in the past has been confined to humble novels, poems, and plays, prim and decorous ambassadors who went a-beggin to white America," Richard Wright complained in his 1937 "Blueprint for Negro Writing." Wright's essay concerned literature, but his criticisms of previous writers applied as well to black entertainers and artists who compromised their integrity to gain acceptance in "the Court of American Public Opinion." During his own career as a writer, Wright struggled to break free of constraints that prevented him from honestly depicting "Negro life in all of its manifold and intricate relationships." During his formative years in the South, his ambition had been stifled by the Jim Crow system and his own family. He had found a way out through his exposure to literature that "evoked in me vague glimpses of life's possibilities." After migrating to Chicago during the late 1920s, he still struggled to make a living, but he eventu[illegible]zed that his writings could be his weapons. [illegible]e could make others aware of what black [illegible]en, when he attended meetings of the John [illegible]munist-affiliated group of artists and writ[illegible]alienation gave way to hopes for a united [illegible]t of the magazines I read came a passion[illegible]eriences of the disinherited," he remem[illegible]y: 'Be like us and we will like you, maybe.' It said: 'If you possess enough courage to speak out what you are, you will find that you are not alone.'"

Wright joined the Communist party, but his political views continued evolving during the 1930s as he gained confidence as a writer. He saw himself as a revolutionary, but his writings rarely discussed Marxism. Instead, in his journalistic pieces about Chicago's black community, he avoided the tendency of some Communist writers to see African Americans only as potential working-class allies. He sought to convey the complexities of American race relations—in particular, the ways in which shared experiences shaped African American political attitudes. His description of the massive street celebration that followed Joe Louis's knockout victory in 1935 over former heavyweight champion Max Baer demonstrates his approach. Twenty-five thousand black residents of Chicago's South Side, he wrote, "poured out of the taverns, pool rooms, barber shops, rooming houses and dingy flats and flooded the streets" to celebrate the black boxer's win. For Wright, as for many black Americans, the fight was more than just a sports contest. He saw the enthusiasm displayed on Chicago's streets as a "wild river that's got to be harnessed and directed," for it arose from African American history: "Four centuries of oppression, of frustrated hopes, of black bitterness, felt even in the bones of the bewildered young were rising to the surface. Yes, unconsciously they had imputed to the brawny image of Joe Louis all the balked dreams of revenge, all the secretly visualized moments of retaliation, AND HE HAD WON!"

By the time he wrote "Blueprint for Negro Writing," Wright's political views had evolved to the point that he was

[illegible]nsformed familiar songs with her intensely personal interpretations.

In the face of racial discrimination in Nazi Germany, where beliefs in racial supremacy and destructive actions led to World War II, Jesse Owens achieved world-record success in the 1936 Berlin Olympics. The track star won four gold medals.

willing to criticize openly Communist notions of political propaganda. While urging black writers to match the dedication displayed "in the Negro workers' struggle to free Herndon and the Scottsboro Boys," he also called on them to pay attention to the distinctive "nationalist" aspects of African American culture. That culture, he believed, derived largely from the religious life and folklore of black people rather than just from their work experiences. Black writers, he added, must understand this culture to reach black readers. "Marxism is but the starting point," he continued. "No theory of life can take the place of life." Wright insisted that black writers be more than political propagandists. "Negro writers spring from a family, a clan, and a nation; and the social units in which they are bound have a story, a record," he concluded. In 1937 Wright left Chicago and the WPA to become Harlem correspondent with the Communist *Daily Worker*, edited by former Atlanta lawyer Benjamin Davis. Yet he gradually broke away from the party. Like other black intellectuals of the period, he lost patience with the ideological bickering and pressures for ideological conformity associated with Communist activism.

> "No theory of life can take the place of life."
> —*Richard Wright*

In 1938 Wright sent Margaret Walker an airmail special-delivery letter. In it, he asked her to send him all the news clippings she could about a sensational story then breaking in Chicago. Robert Nixon, a young African American accused of rape and murder, had been captured by the police and forced to confess to five major crimes. Wright saw the accusations against this black youngster not as another Scottsboro-type episode of class and racial oppression but as a basis for a more complex story. Rather than assuming that the young man was innocent, Wright made his character guilty. Then he sought to imagine the circumstances that might have led his black protagonist—Bigger Thomas—to kill a white woman who sympathized with Communist efforts to help African Americans. *Native Son,* published in 1940, became the first bestselling novel by a black author. In 1940 it was a Book-of-the-Month Club selection, and in 1941 Orson Wells directed a stage production of the story.

Many readers of *Native Son* were shocked by Wright's raw language—especially his vivid depiction of the killing of Mary Dalton as seen through the eyes of Thomas. Although Wright did not justify Thomas's crime, he allowed readers to see it as resulting from a series of tragic misunderstandings rooted in racial and class differences. *Native Son* revealed not only the wide gulf that separated Thomas and his employer, Dalton's wealthy father, but also the gulf between Thomas's perspective and that of Communists who saw him solely as a victim of oppression. When Mary Dalton asks Thomas to drive her and her Communist boyfriend, Jan Erlone, to a black restaurant, Thomas becomes increasingly uncomfortable and resentful as Jan's probing questions prod him to reveal that his father was killed in a southern riot.

> "Listen, Bigger," Jan replied,"that's what we want to *stop*. That's what we Communists are fighting. We want to stop people from treating others that way. I'm a member of the Party. Mary sympathizes. Don't you think if we got together we could stop things like that?"
>
> "I don't know," Bigger said; he was feeling the rum rising to his head. "There's a lot of white people in the world."
>
> "You've read about the Scottsboro boys?"
>
> "I heard about 'em."
>
> "Don't you think we did a good job in helping to keep 'em from killing those boys?"
>
> "It was all right."
>
> "You know, Bigger," said Mary, "we'd like to be friends of yours."
>
> He said nothing.

Wright's narrative illuminates the enormous racial barriers that prevented Bigger, Mary, and Jan from seeing one another as individuals rather than as black or white. After returning to the Dalton home, Bigger carries the intoxicated Mary to her bedroom. Sexually aroused by her helpless condition, he also fears that Mary's blind mother will discover him in her daughter's room. He quiets Mary by pressing a pillow over her face, inadvertently suffocating her. Eventually caught after a massive search, he is tried for murder. As in the Scottsboro case, the Communist party provides Thomas with legal assistance. Yet even his well-intentioned lawyer can never fully understand what led Thomas to kill Dalton and then his own girlfriend to avoid getting caught. Condemned to die, Thomas eventually perceives that his crime came not only from racial and class oppression but also from his own choices.

Richard Wright's disenchantment with the Communist party was shared by other black intellectuals who had once been drawn to Communist-led campaigns. Langston Hughes wrote to a friend, "I am laying off of political poetry for a while, since the world situation, methinks, is too complicated." Ralph Ellison, who became Wright's protégé after arriving in New York from Tuskegee Institute, distanced himself from his mentor's Communist friends. A friend of Margaret Walker's advised her to "get to know" leftist writers but to avoid "getting to be a part of them and all they represent."

Much had changed since the early 1930s, when Communists staged massive protests on behalf of the Scottsboro defendants. A decade later, the case had faded from public view. In 1938 Alabama officials quietly released one of the four defendants still in prison, but two of the other defendants would wait until 1944 before they were paroled. Haywood Patterson, labeled a troublemaker by prison officials, would languish in prison cells until 1948, when he escaped and enjoyed a few years of freedom in Michigan before being imprisoned once again on a manslaughter charge. Patterson resembled Bigger Thomas in age and impoverished background, but he was largely forgotten by the time Wright's doomed fictional character captured the nation's attention. Looking back on all that he had endured, Patterson concluded shortly before his death that the Scottsboro campaign had advanced the cause of civil rights. "I guess my people gained more off the Scottsboro case than any of us boys did. It led to putting Negroes on juries in the South. It made the whole country, in fact the whole world, talk about how the Negro people have to live in the South."

CONCLUSION

By the time *Native Son* achieved bestseller status, Communist radicalism had been largely supplanted by New Deal liberalism. Still, the party's attention to civil rights issues and its innovative use of mass militancy made a lasting impact on American race relations. In a broad sense, leftist agitation and publications expanded popular awareness of racial discrimination and encouraged appreciation for African American art, music, and literature. Yet, as New Deal programs moderated some of the hardships of the Great Depression and as Communist leaders turned their attention from civil rights issues to the threat of German Nazism, black militancy continued to evolve in new directions. The outbreak of war in Europe prompted black protests against segregation in the military and discriminatory hiring practices in war-related industries. The NAACP's legal campaign, now under the direction of Thurgood Marshall, moved ahead with increasing confidence. Many African Americans had suffered during the Great Depression, but they had also shared experiences with Americans who were not black. Black Americans still faced widespread discrimination and segregation, but in important ways the political, economic, and cultural changes of the 1930s had brought them closer to the nation's political, economic, and cultural mainstream.

FURTHER READING

Du Bois, W. E. B. *Dusk of Dawn: An Essay toward an Autobiography of a Race Concept* (New York: Harcourt, Brace and World, 1940).

Goodman, James. *Stories of Scottsboro* (New York: Random House, 1994).

Greenberg, Cheryl Lynn. *Or Does It Explode? Black Harlem in the Great Depression* (New York: Oxford University Press, 1991).

Harris, William H. *Keeping the Faith: A. Philip Randolph, Milton P. Webster and the Brotherhood of Sleeping Car Porters, 1925–37* (Urbana: University of Illinois Press, 1977).

Henry, Charles P. *Ralph Bunche: Model Negro or American Other?* (New York: New York University Press, 1999).

Kelley, Robin D. G. *Hammer and Hoe: Alabama Communists During the Great Depression* (Chapel Hill: University of North Carolina Press, 1990).

Kirby, John B. *Black Americans in the Roosevelt Era: Liberalism and Race* (Knoxville: University of Tennessee Press, 1980).

McCluskey, Audrey Thomas, and Elaine M. Smith, eds. *Mary McLeod Bethune: Building a Better World* (Bloomington: Indiana University Press, 1999).

Lewis, David Levering. *W. E. B. Du Bois: The Fight for Equality and the American Century, 1919–1963* (New York: Henry Holt, 2000).

Patterson, Haywood, and Earl Conrad. *Scottsboro Boy* (New York: Doubleday, 1950).

Rowley, Hazel. *Richard Wright: The Life and Times* (New York: Henry Holt, 2001).

Sitkoff, Harvard. *A New Deal for Blacks: The Emergence of Civil Rights as a National Issue, The Depression Decade* (New York: Oxford University Press, 1978).

Sullivan, Patricia. *Days of Hope: Race and Democracy in the New Deal Era* (Chapel Hill: University of North Carolina Press, 1996).

Trotter, Joe William, Jr. *Black Milwaukee: The Making of an Industrial Proletariat, 1915–45* (Urbana: University of Illinois Press, 1985).

Trotter, Joe William, Jr., and Earl Lewis, eds. *African Americans in the Industrial Age: A Documentary History, 1915–1945* (Boston: Northeastern University Press, 1996).

White, Walter. *A Man Called White: The Autobiography of Walter White* (New York: Viking Press, 1948).

Wolcott, Victoria W. *Remaking Respectability: African American Women in Interwar Detroit* (Chapel Hill: University of North Carolina Press, 2001).

Wright, Richard. *American Hunger* (New York: Harper and Row, 1944).

CHAPTER 16

Aaron Douglas, *Corporal Horace Marshall*, 1942. Douglas was a Harlem Renaissance painter who often depicted the solemn pride of his subjects.

Fighting Fascism Abroad and Racism at Home

A. Philip Randolph Challenges President Franklin Roosevelt

"Which class were you in at Harvard?" President Franklin D. Roosevelt asked A. Philip Randolph, head of the Brotherhood of Sleeping Car Porters, as they began their White House meeting on June 18, 1941. Randolph knew the question was small talk—Roosevelt's skillful way of shifting the subject when pressed to make difficult decisions. The attempt at flattery fell flat. Randolph had attended Cookman Institute in Florida and took night classes at New York City College. "I never went to Harvard, Mr. President," he responded. He became increasingly impatient as Roosevelt chatted amiably with Walter White of the NAACP and T. Arnold Hill of the Urban League. "Mr. President, time is running on," Randolph finally interjected. "You are quite busy, I know, but what we want to talk with you about is the problem of jobs for Negroes in defense industries."

This was Randolph's second visit to the White House. The previous September the three black leaders had urged Roosevelt to end racial discrimination in the military and in the booming defense industries that were already supplying weapons to Great Britain and other nations involved in the European war ignited by Germany's invasion of Poland in September 1939. Although war industries, not New Deal programs, were finally ending the Great Depression, black Americans were still being shut out of job opportunities. Busy aircraft factories had few black employees. As head of the nation's largest black union, Randolph was determined to secure jobs for black workers, and when the president declined to act, Randolph took matters into his own hands. Early in 1941 he brashly proposed that African Americans stage a massive march on Washington.

CHAPTER OUTLINE

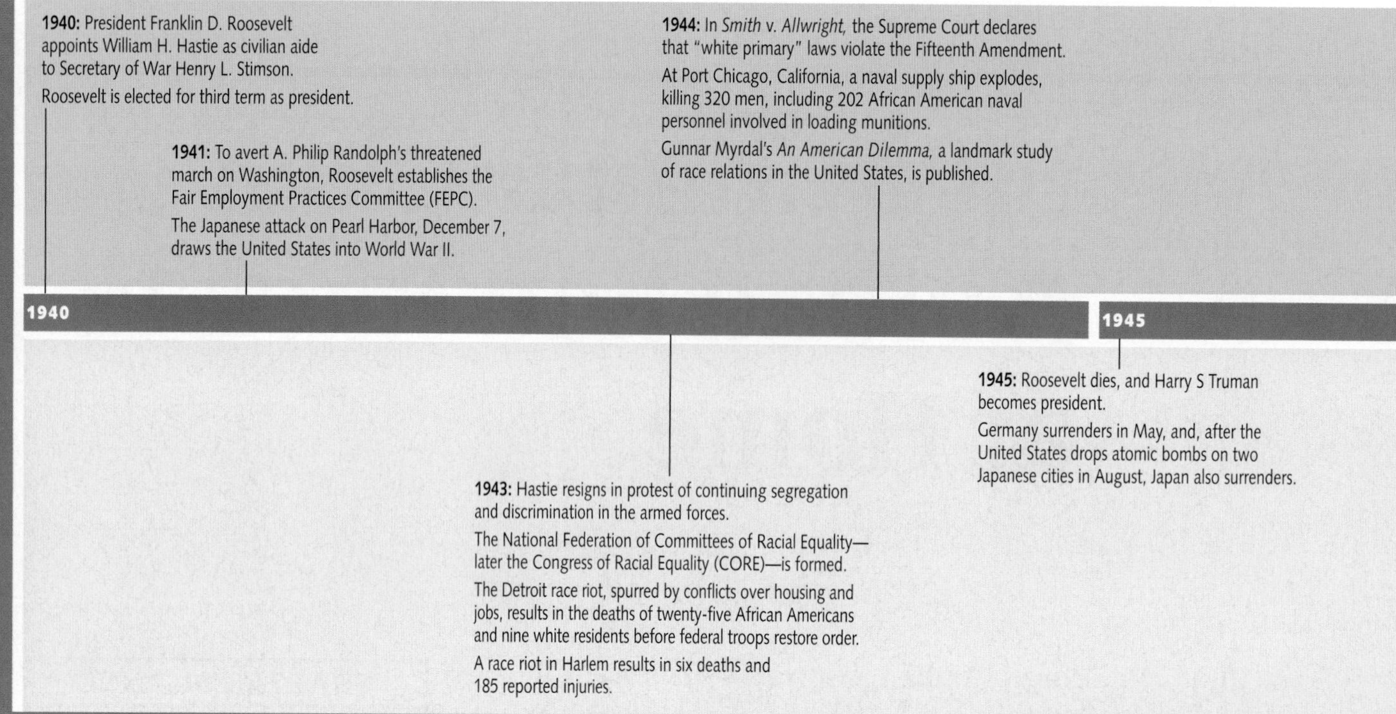

Randolph's idea quickly became a movement, with branch offices mobilizing support in numerous cities. "Black people will not get justice until the administration leaders in Washington see masses of Negroes—ten, twenty, fifty thousand—on the White House lawn," Randolph insisted. Now, seated across from the president, and with the march scheduled for July 1, 1941, just two weeks away, Randolph suggested participation would be even greater—perhaps 100,000. Worried administration officials voiced strong objections, but Randolph refused to call off the march unless African Americans had "jobs, not promises." The meeting at the White House was the last chance for the two sides to reach agreement.

Randolph pressed the president to issue an executive order banning discrimination in defense plants, but Roosevelt objected: "If I issue an executive order for you, then there'll be no end to other groups coming in here and asking me to issue executive orders for them, too. In any event, I cannot do anything unless you call off this march of yours."

"I'm sorry, Mr. President," Randolph firmly replied. "The march cannot be called off."

After further intense discussions, Roosevelt reluctantly agreed to make concessions in return for a promise to cancel the march. On June 24, he issued Executive Order 8802 authorizing a Fair Employment Practices Committee (FEPC) to ensure "full and equitable participation of all workers in the defense industries, without discrimination because of race, creed, color, or national origin." Although some black activists were disturbed that Randolph had not won a promise to end segregation in the military, the threatened march had produced the most significant presidential order on behalf of African Americans since Reconstruction. Randolph, who insisted that mass protests still might be needed, had demonstrated the potential of mass activism to achieve federal civil rights reforms. "A tall, courtly black man with Shakespearean diction and the stare of an eagle," NAACP leader Roy Wilkins later recalled, "had looked the patrician Roosevelt in the eye—and made him back down."

Randolph's confrontation with Roosevelt reflected not only growing African American militancy but also the increasing importance of black voters in the Democratic Party's New Deal coalition. During the previous decade, as the Roosevelt administration mobilized against the economic depression and then in preparation for American involvement in the spreading war, black Americans increasingly expected that federal power would be used to address both racial and economic issues. In August 1941, Roosevelt raised these expectations when he met with British leader Winston Churchill to draft an Atlantic Charter

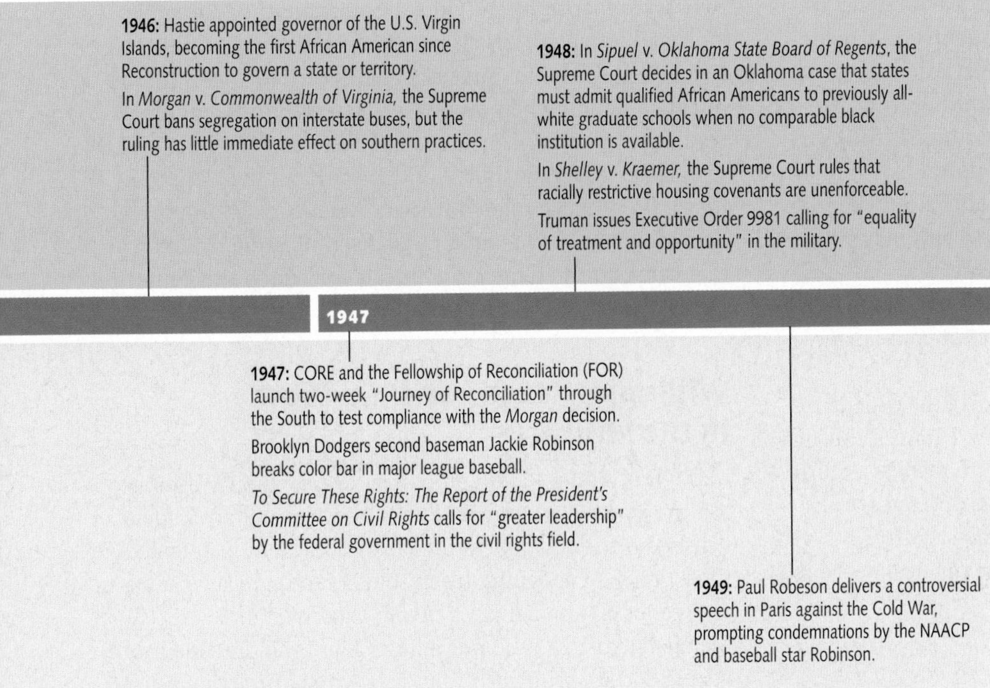

affirming that the war against "Nazi tyranny" in Germany was also intended to achieve democratic principles, such as "the right of all peoples to choose the form of government under which they live." Although Churchill quickly made clear the charter was not intended to apply to Great Britain's colonial possessions, Roosevelt hinted that he supported such an interpretation, feeding the hopes of African Americans that the war would bring democracy not only to Asian and African nations but perhaps also to parts of the United States where black citizens were prevented from voting.

As they had during previous wars, African Americans contributed to the World War II mobilization, but they also challenged segregation and took advantage of the employment opportunities made possible by wartime needs for military personnel and industrial labor. Although wartime civil rights militancy was often locally rather than nationally organized, various national groups attracted significant black support; these included the NAACP, Randolph's March on Washington Movement, and, to a lesser extent, Communist-backed groups such as the National Negro Congress and the Civil Rights Congress.

When the wartime alliance of the United States and the Soviet Union gave way to Cold War hostilities, growing anticommunism fostered bitter ideological divisions among black leaders. While most NAACP leaders identified themselves with the American government's efforts to combat communism at home as well as abroad, black leftists such as W. E. B. Du Bois and Paul Robeson strongly criticized these Cold War policies and tried in vain to push the newly organized United Nations to act not only against colonialism but also against racial discrimination within the United States. The 1948 presidential election proved a crucial turning point in the declining fortunes of black leftists, who backed the unsuccessful campaign of Progressive Party candidate Henry Wallace. In contrast, NAACP leaders and their liberal allies supported the victorious Democratic candidate, Harry S Truman, and they emerged from the election confident that their strategy of litigation and lobbying would soon result in major civil rights reforms.

AFRICAN AMERICANS IN THE ARMED FORCES

On the morning of December 7, 1941, Dorie Miller, a black sailor with the rank of Mess Attendant, second class, was collecting laundry on the battleship USS *West Virginia,* stationed at Pearl Harbor in Hawaii, when he heard the call to battle stations. Japanese planes were attacking American naval forces. He first went to an antiaircraft station amidships, only to find that it had been destroyed by a torpedo. Then he raced to the deck and began to carry wounded sailors to safety, using the strength he had once displayed as a football player in his hometown of Waco, Texas, and as the *West Virginia*'s heavyweight boxing champ. After taking the ship's mortally wounded captain to a first aid station, Miller returned to the bridge and positioned himself behind a 50-caliber antiaircraft machine gun. He had not been trained to use the weapon, but for fifteen minutes he fired at attacking Japanese planes, shooting down at least two and perhaps as many as five. "It wasn't hard," Miller later explained. "I just pulled the trigger and she worked fine." When the ammunition ran out, he was ordered to abandon the heavily damaged ship. For his extraordinary courage in battle, Miller was awarded the Navy Cross. Miller's heroism brought him only fleeting fame, however, and did little to open up opportunities for black sailors, who were limited to noncombat positions. After the Pearl Harbor attack, which led the United States to declare war on Japan and its Axis allies, Germany and Italy, Miller received a promotion—to Mess Attendant, first class, and then to Cook, third class. In November 1943, he was reported missing, then presumed dead, when a Japanese torpedo sank his escort carrier.

Miller's military career is emblematic of the experience of African Americans in the U.S. Armed Forces during World War II. Even as they contributed to the war against fascism—and especially the superior race doctrines of German leader Adolf Hitler—they faced racism within their own ranks. For African Americans whose political perspectives were shaped by the Great Depression, the war and its aftermath offered both new challenges and opportunities. Criticizing the nation's racial policies carried special risks during a period when dissent was often considered unpatriotic and military considerations were accorded priority over other concerns. But World War II and the Cold War that followed also offered African Americans an unprecedented opportunity to fight racial discrimination by linking this cause to the democratic ideals for which the United States claimed to be fighting.

Mess Attendant Dorie Miller was awarded the Navy Cross for his courage in battle aboard the USS West Virginia during the Pearl Harbor attack.

William H. Hastie and Jim Crow in the Military

Though A. Philip Randolph's threat to march on Washington prompted concessions from Roosevelt, military leaders brushed off complaints from black leaders and maintained their policy of assigning black soldiers to segregated units and generally menial roles. Army chief of staff George C. Marshall expressed the prevailing view: "The settlement of vexing social problems cannot be permitted to complicate the tremendous task of the War Department and thereby jeopardize discipline and morale." In the U.S. Navy, African Americans such as Dorie Miller served as stewards and cooks. In the Army, black soldiers were routinely assigned to all-black support or service units, such as the Quartermaster Corps, under white officers—most of them southern, in part because military leaders believed that southern whites had a special understanding of black soldiers. At the beginning of 1940, the United States had only two African American military officers—Colonel Benjamin O. Davis and his son, Lieutenant Benjamin O. Davis Jr., whose desire to train as a pilot had been frustrated by the Army Air Corps' refusal to give flight instruction to black candidates.

Black women who wanted to join the military faced similar obstacles. At the start of the war, black women could volunteer only for segregated units of the Women's Auxiliary Army Corps (WAAC). The Navy's auxiliary, the WAVES (Women Accepted for Volunteer Emergency Service), at first declined to admit black women volunteers in any capacity, a policy that did not change until the final year of the war. Despite a campaign led by Harlem's Mabel K. Staupers to open up opportunities for black nurses, the Army and Navy Nurse Corps refused to recruit black women until President Roosevelt intervened in 1944—just in time to build black support for his reelection. The Coast Guard accepted only five black women during the war, and the Marine Corps held out until 1949.

The Roosevelt administration was forced to make overtures to black voters, however, due to the fallout from a

What Are Our Immediate Goals?

1. To mobilize five million Negroes into one militant mass for pressure.
2. To assemble in Chicago the last week in May, 1943, for the celebration of

"WE ARE AMERICANS – TOO" WEEK

And to ponder the question of Non-Violent Civil Disobedience and Non-Cooperation, and a Mass March On Washington.

WHY SHOULD WE MARCH?

15,000 Negroes Assembled at St. Louis, Missouri
20,000 Negroes Assembled at Chicago, Illinois
23,500 Negroes Assembled at New York City
Millions of Negro Americans all Over This Great Land Claim the Right to be Free!

FREE FROM WANT!
FREE FROM FEAR!
FREE FROM JIM CROW!

"Winning Democracy for the Negro is Winning the War for Democracy!" — A. Philip Randolph

440

■ A. Philip Randolph's March on Washington Movement threatened mass protest to achieve federal civil rights reforms. This leaflet typified the effort to mobilize support in black communities throughout the nation.

racial incident during the 1940 presidential election. On a campaign stop in New York City, Roosevelt's press secretary inadvertently kicked a black policeman who blocked his way as he rushed to catch up with the presidential party boarding a train. To counter the negative publicity that followed, the president ordered Colonel Davis promoted to brigadier general and asked William H. Hastie, dean of Howard University's law school, to join the War Department as civilian advisor on racial issues. Hastie was at first "skeptical" about what "a person with no authority of his own" could accomplish, but he decided to accept the position, hoping he would be able "to work effectively toward the integration of the Negro into the Army and to facilitate his placement, training, and promotion."

Hastie was frustrated from the start, as he could do little to alter military recruitment and promotion policies. Although the 1940 Selective Service Act forbade racial discrimination, military officers assumed that segregation was necessary to maintain white soldiers' morale and applied the *Plessy* v. *Ferguson* logic that racial separation in the military did not constitute discrimination. Secretary of War Henry L. Stimson was adamant about keeping black soldiers under white officers. "Leadership is not embedded in the Negro race," he reflected in his diary. On one occasion he asked Hastie, "Is it not true that your people are basically agriculturalists?"

Although Hastie could not change the military's racial policies or Stimson's racial attitudes, he was well placed to collect large amounts of information about black discontent in the military. One of his former assistants recalled, "Black GIs who thought they were being wronged would say, 'Goddamn it, I'm gonna write to Hastie.'" Write they did. Aeron Bells, a black college graduate from Houston, complained that the army did not accept black candidates for officer training. "I am sure you will agree with me," Bells wrote, "when

I say that the situation is 'Confusing,' for I fail to see why I WILL BE FORCED TO SHED MY BLOOD on Democracy's battlefields as a Private and [not allowed] to volunteer as an officer candidate." Three black soldiers who had qualified as aviation cadets wrote, "It seems, sir, as if we are going from one basic training to another and getting no nearer to the Air Corp[s]." Black soldiers who wanted to contribute to the war effort were, for the most part, prevented from serving in combat roles. "The operative theory in the War Department was that blacks were not adequate soldiers, because they lacked courage and were too stupid to master the intricacies of modern warfare," recalled Coleman Young, the future Detroit mayor, who served in the military from February 1942 to December 1945 but never received an overseas assignment.

> "The operative theory in the War Department was that blacks were not adequate soldiers."
> —*Coleman Young*

When Hastie learned of plans to establish a segregated flight training facility at Tuskegee Army Air Field, he pointed to the foolishness of replicating existing sophisticated facilities: "Why in the name of common sense should all this elaborate special machinery be set up to train Negro flyers?" Although convinced the segregation policy was wrong, he finally acquiesced, relieved that African Americans would finally be accepted for flight training. Benjamin O. Davis Jr. joined the initial group of pilot trainees at Tuskegee.

But discrimination in promotion and training opportunities was not the worst of the complaints Hastie received. A group of black soldiers at Jackson Air Base in Mississippi reported that they were "treated like wild animals here, like we are unhuman. The word Negro is never used here, all they call us are nigger do this, nigger do that." In April 1941, a black soldier at Fort Benning in Georgia was found hanging from a tree with his hands tied behind his back; military authorities dubiously suggested it was a suicide. In one of the most serious incidents, military police at Fort Dix, New Jersey, killed two black privates and wounded five others.

Hastie warned Stimson that such incidents would jeopardize military preparedness. "So long as we condone and appease un-American attitudes and practices within our own military and civilian life, we can never arouse ourselves to the exertion which the present emergency requires," he wrote in September 1941 as American entry to the war seemed imminent. Considerable discontent, he explained, seethed beneath the surface: "Most white persons are unable to appreciate the rancor and bitterness which the Negro, as a matter of self-preservation, has learned to hide beneath a smile, a joke, or merely an impassive face." Hastie argued it was impossible to train a black soldier to be both "a fighting man toward a foreign enemy" and also "a craven" willing to be treated "as less than a man at home."

After the Pearl Harbor attack in December 1941, the United States allied with Britain and the Soviet Union against the Axis alliance of Japan, Germany, and Italy. Hastie again pleaded with Stimson to end racial discrimination. "On every essential front we must be moved to aggressive, far reaching and uncompromising action," he wrote. Soon afterward, a group of black leaders that included Mary McLeod Bethune petitioned Roosevelt to end "the persistent, contemptuous rejection of the earnestly proffered services of the colored American," by ensuring that black representatives served on major defense policy boards. But Hastie's experience demonstrated that black advisors had little impact on white leaders unwilling to remove racial barriers in the military and defense industries.

His pleas ignored, Hastie decided to resign. He explained early in 1943 that military leaders were unwilling to speed the process of removing racial barriers. "I have not found in the War Department the group will and understanding," he explained. The resignation of the War Department's highest-ranking black official drew attention to racial problems in the military, as did the articles Hastie later published in a pamphlet titled *On Clipped Wings*. Although Hastie's departure briefly embarrassed military leaders and the Roosevelt administration, his complaints were not heeded. Many black Americans, however, admired Hastie's willingness to express his dissent publicly. Later in 1943, the NAACP awarded him its highest honor, the Spingarn Medal, not only for his work in the War Department but also for his earlier contributions to the group's legal effort.

The Double-V Campaign

Early in 1942 the *Pittsburgh Courier,* the most widely circulated black newspaper in the United States, launched the "Double-V Campaign," which called for victory over the Axis powers on the battlefront and victory over racial prejudice on the home front. The campaign sought to push the nation to live up to the democratic principles expressed in the 1941 Atlantic Charter. The NAACP agreed that the war effort should be two-pronged: "We shall not abate one iota in our struggle for full citizenship rights here in the United States. We will fight, but we demand the right to fight as equals in every branch of the military, naval, and aviation services."

Randolph's March on Washington Movement kept alive the spirit of his threatened mass protest. While affirming his commitment to the defeat of totalitarian regimes in Germany, Italy, and Japan, Randolph also urged supporters "to win the peace, for democracy, for freedom and the Brotherhood of Man without regard to his pigmentation, land of his birth or the God of his fathers." During 1942 he hinted that a national campaign of civil disobedience might be necessary. He warned that black Americans were unlikely to respond to the "close ranks" argument that W. E. B. Du Bois had used to mobilize African American support for World War I. "Negroes made the blunder of closing ranks and forgetting their grievances in the last war," Randolph asserted. "We are resolved that we will not make that blunder again."

Du Bois himself refused to second-guess his "close ranks" argument, but he conceded that World War I "did not bring us democracy." Soon after the Pearl Harbor attack, he warned that democracy would not come without struggle: "We close ranks again but only, now as then, to fight for democracy . . . not only for white folk but for yellow, brown and black." Few were as willing as Du Bois to link their cause to that of other oppressed groups, but World War II soon broadened the perspectives of African Americans, who became more aware of the war's impact on Africans and Asians. Langston Hughes predicted the war would "eventually shake the British Empire to the dust. That will shake Dixie's teeth too, and crack the joints of Jim Crow South Africa."

Yet racial gains did not come without struggle. Even as black resentment increased, military leaders stubbornly retained segregation policies despite growing signs of racial conflict, and civilian employers similarly continued to practice racial bias. Only when labor shortages became acute did black employment in defense industries begin to rise, from 3 percent of the total number of employees in 1942 to 8 percent in 1944, an amount still less than the proportion of black workers in the nation's workforce. But even this modest gain came in the face of stiff resistance from some white employers and workers. The FEPC established by Roosevelt in 1941 could investigate discrimination but lacked enforcement powers.

Polls conducted by the *Pittsburgh Courier* during the early years of the war found considerable black discontent over racial discrimination in civilian employment as well as in the military. One poll found that 82 percent of *Courier* readers were unconvinced by statements from U.S. leaders "about freedom and equality for all peoples, including the American Negro." Readers overwhelmingly supported Mahatma Gandhi and other Indian leaders who were demanding an end to British colonial rule of their nation as a price for backing the war. In response to the question "Do you feel that the Negro should soft pedal his demands for complete freedom and citizenship and await the development of the educational process," almost nine of every ten respondents said no. In June 1942, a secret federal survey of black attitudes similarly revealed that more than a third of African Americans placed more emphasis on improving

Antiwar activism led to the arrest of more than eighty black critics of the military draft.

democracy than on winning the war. Nearly one-fifth of black respondents believed they would be treated better under Japanese rule; another third guessed that treatment under Japanese rule would be "about the same."

While most African Americans remained loyal to the United States, black antiwar activism was sufficiently widespread to prompt a crackdown by the Federal Bureau of Investigation (FBI) in 1942. More than eighty black critics of the military draft were arrested. Nation of Islam leader Elijah Muhammad was sentenced to a five-year prison term, and in 1943 black pacifist Bayard Rustin, who had worked with Randolph to encourage nonviolent protests on behalf of the March on Washington Movement, informed his draft board that he would not submit to military induction. He was quickly arrested and sentenced to three years in prison.

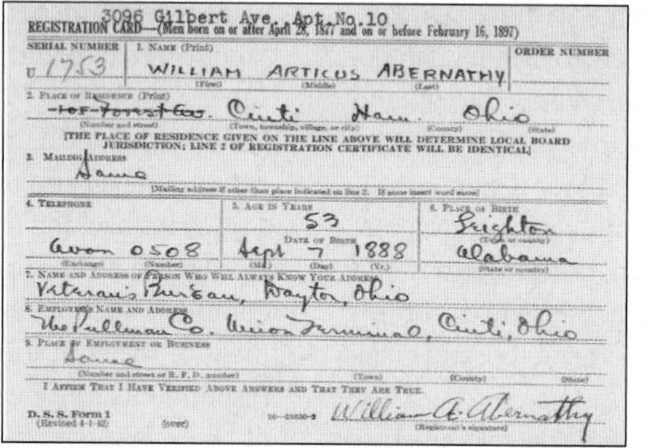

3096 Gilbert Ave. Apt. No. 10
REGISTRATION CARD—(Men born on or after April 28, 1877 and on or before February 16, 1897)

SERIAL NUMBER: U 1753
1. NAME (Print): WILLIAM (First) ARTICUS (Middle) ABERNATHY (Last)
ORDER NUMBER:
2. PLACE OF RESIDENCE (Print): ~~107 Forest Ave.~~ (Number and street) Cinti (Town, township, village, or city) Ham. (County) Ohio (State)
[THE PLACE OF RESIDENCE GIVEN ON THE LINE ABOVE WILL DETERMINE LOCAL BOARD JURISDICTION; LINE 2 OF REGISTRATION CERTIFICATE WILL BE IDENTICAL]
3. MAILING ADDRESS: Same
(Mailing address if other than place indicated on line 2. If same insert word same)
4. TELEPHONE: Avon (Exchange) 0508 (Number)
5. AGE IN YEARS: 53
DATE OF BIRTH: Sept (Mo.) 7 (Day) 1888 (Yr.)
6. PLACE OF BIRTH: Leighton (Town or county) Alabama (State or country)
7. NAME AND ADDRESS OF PERSON WHO WILL ALWAYS KNOW YOUR ADDRESS: Veteran's Bureau, Dayton, Ohio
8. EMPLOYER'S NAME AND ADDRESS: The Pullman Co. Union Terminal, Cinti, Ohio
9. PLACE OF EMPLOYMENT OR BUSINESS: Same
(Number and street or R. F. D. number) (Town) (County) (State)
I AFFIRM THAT I HAVE VERIFIED ABOVE ANSWERS AND THAT THEY ARE TRUE.
D. S. S. Form 1 (Revised 4-1-42) (over)
William A. Abernathy (Registrant's signature)

As the Army increasingly filled its ranks with conscripts rather than volunteers, protests by black soldiers became more frequent. Although Roosevelt issued an executive order in December 1942 banning racial discrimination within the military, black newspapers and leftist periodicals published numerous reports of blacks resisting discrimination at military bases, in nearby communities, and at "camp shows" produced by the United Service Organization (USO) to entertain soldiers. Jackie Robinson, an Army second lieutenant and a former sports star at the University of California, Los Angeles (UCLA), was court-martialed but acquitted during the summer of 1944 when he refused to take a seat in the back of the bus near Camp Hood, Texas. When black film star Lena Horne noticed that German prisoners of war were seated in front of black soldiers for her performance at Fort Riley in Kansas, she pointedly left the stage to sing for her black fans in the rear.

Widespread discontent was particularly evident at Fort Huachuca, a military camp in the southern Arizona desert that housed the largest single concentration of black troops. A riot during 1942 left three soldiers dead and others facing court-martial on mutiny charges. Shirley Graham, who had directed plays for the Federal Theater Project, was brought in as a USO director to raise troop morale at Fort Huachuca, but her constant complaints about conditions at the camp irritated military officials, who forced her dismissal. Even a quickly arranged visit from General Benjamin Davis failed to calm racial tensions.

The worst racial incident of the war occurred at the naval ammunition base at Port Chicago, about 30 miles northeast of San Francisco. On July 17, 1944, a fully loaded ship exploded, killing 320 men, including 202 ammunition loaders, all of whom were black. It was the deadliest single accident of the war, accounting for 15 percent of all black naval casualties. Four days later, the Naval Court of Inquiry concluded the black seamen were at fault, absolving their white supervising officers, who often ignored safety commands and made bets with one another to see whose crew could load the most cargo. The surviving seamen cleaned up the debris and human remains, but 258 refused to obey an order to resume loading bombs, objecting to the fact that no new safety procedures had been implemented. "I wasn't trying to shirk work," one of them recalled. "But to go back to work under the same conditions, with no improvements, no changes, the same group of officers that we had, was just—we thought there was a better alternative, that's all."

Told they could be charged with mutiny and possibly face death by a firing squad, 208 seamen agreed to return to work. They were given bad-conduct discharges and docked three months' pay. The remaining fifty were charged with mutiny, leading to the largest mass court-martial in naval history. Thurgood Marshall, sent by the NAACP to observe the proceedings and support the defendants, remarked, "This is not fifty men on trial for mutiny; this is the Navy on trial for its whole vicious policy toward Negroes." The seamen "just want to know why they are the only ones doing the loading," he explained. "They wanted to know why they are segregated, why they don't get promoted." Despite Marshall's efforts, forty-four of those put on trial were convicted by a military court of organized mutiny, dishonorably discharged, and sentenced to between eight and fifteen years in prison. Only after the war were these sentences reduced.

The Port Chicago explosion dramatically demonstrated the precarious position of black sailors and soldiers, but by the time the deadly accident occurred there were signs that the attitudes of military leaders were changing. Benjamin Davis Jr., who became commander of the 99th Pursuit Squadron, which had trained at Tuskegee, recalled that many questions about the unit's readiness were allayed once the squadron was assigned to combat duty in the Allied push through Italy. "All those who wished to denigrate the quality of the 99th's operations were silenced once and for all by its aerial victories over Anzio on two successive days in January 1944," Davis remembered. Members of the squadron shot down twelve enemy fighters in that combat encounter. "There would be no more talk of lack of aggressiveness, absence of teamwork, or disintegrating under fire," Davis noted.

The 99th and the other squadrons of black pilots that later became known as the Tuskegee Airmen compiled a remarkable record in combat, escorting American bombers on 1,578 missions against German targets without losing a single bomber. Known for their willingness to escort bombers throughout an attack rather than remaining beyond the range of antiaircraft guns, the unit won 900 medals, including a citation for "outstanding performance of duty." Grateful bomber crews called them the "Red-Tailed Angels," a reference to the distinctive bright red paint on the tails of their planes.

The combat successes of the Tuskegee Airmen and the performance of black troops in combat elsewhere persuaded a military advisory committee to recommend in March 1944 that general policy of not assigning black soldiers to combat roles be abandoned. Nonetheless, most black soldiers who participated in the Allied D-Day invasion of Europe two months later served in logistical roles only. A black quartermaster regiment known as the Red Ball Express gained renown for transporting supplies to the front despite heavy enemy fire. As in the Civil War, however, the military's reluctance to use black soldiers in combat receded as casualties mounted in the next year, and African Americans constituted an increasing proportion of available troops. Late in 1944, black soldiers helped repulse the last major German counteroffensive—known as the Battle of the Bulge.

■ Colonel Benjamin O. Davis, the leader of the 332nd Fighter Pilot Squadron (the 99th was added to the 332nd), the only all African American unit in the Army Air Force, at an airbase in Rametti, Italy, in 1945.

During the final months of the European war, Allied Supreme Commander Dwight D. Eisenhower authorized an "experimental" departure from the military's segregation policy when he allowed about forty black soldiers to serve as replacements in white units that had suffered heavy losses. In addition, 2,500 black volunteers were allowed to serve in platoons assigned to predominantly white infantry units. In a subsequent study of this experiment, white officers reported that the black troops performed "very well" in combat, but top military officials belittled the study's conclusions and prevented it from being made public.

As the combat focus shifted from Europe to the Pacific after Germany's surrender in May 1945, segregation remained the military rule, and black soldiers continued to be assigned mainly to noncombat roles. The first black enlistees accepted in the Navy's Marine Corps were sent to guard munitions dumps, although they were pressed into battle at the island of Iwo Jima when their posts came under fire. Thus, for many African-American soldiers, World War II offered more opportunities to fight racism within the military than to engage in combat against fascism abroad.

A protest during the closing months of the war against a segregated officers' club at Freeman Field in Indiana revealed the extent of black militancy and served as a model for postwar civil rights protests. Sixty-nine black officers were arrested as they sought entry to a base club that violated the military's own ban on racial restrictions. More than one hundred were later charged with mutiny for refusing to sign a statement that they had read and understood the regulations governing the officers' club. Coleman Young, who was one of those arrested, recalled that "there was nearly a full-scale mutiny on the base. The black troops refused to gas airplanes or to carry out the basic daily operations of the post." Eventually most of the charges were dropped, the club was integrated, and in August 1995, fifty years later, the Air Force issued an official vindication.

RACIAL ISSUES ON THE HOME FRONT

"We did not plan our arrest intentionally," Pauli Murray wrote to a friend. "The situation developed, and we applied what we

Denied admission to law school at the University of North Carolina in 1938 because of her race, and to Harvard University because of her gender, Pauli Murray worked to dismantle both types of barriers.

knew of *Satyagraha* on the spot." In her autobiography Murray described this technique, which Gandhi had used in India's independence struggle, as "nonviolent resistance coupled with good will." In March 1940, when Murray and a friend found themselves in a Petersburg, Virginia, jail after refusing to obey segregation laws on an intercity bus, they put the idea into practice. They drafted a Statement of Facts, carefully recording the details of their arrest and imprisonment. They also wrote a polite memo to the deputy guarding them, saying they intended to cooperate fully with the prison regulations pasted on the wall of their cell. To keep themselves clean, as the regulations required, each asked the deputy for a sheet, a towel, and one bar of soap, and then thanked him for his kindness and courtesy. Murray remembered that the deputy was unsettled; he knew how to deal with hostility, but not with "courteous behavior which nevertheless revealed a clear demand for justice." The NAACP attorneys who came the next day were also surprised and pleased by the Statement of Facts. "Trained attorneys," the women were told, "could hardly have done a better job." Nevertheless, when the court opened on Tuesday morning, the women were quickly convicted. The subsequent NAACP appeal was also unsuccessful. But for Murray, there was an important lesson: "Although we had lost the legal battle, the episode convinced me that creative nonviolent resistance could be a powerful weapon in the struggle for human dignity."

Pauli Murray and Jane Crow

While teaching in New York for the Works Progress Administration (WPA) Worker's Education Project, Murray had become immersed in Depression-era radicalism and aligned herself with a small socialist—but anticommunist—group. "The study of economic oppression led me to realize that Negroes were not alone but were part of an unending struggle for human dignity the world over," Pauli Murray later wrote of her political education. Fighting for social justice also increased her sense of pride: "Seeing the relationship between my personal cause and the universal cause of freedom released me from a sense of isolation, helped me to rid myself of vestiges of shame over my racial history, and gave me an unequivocal understanding that equality of treatment was my birthright and not something to be earned."

> "Negroes were not alone but were part of an unending struggle for human dignity the world over."—*Pauli Murray*

In 1941 Murray enrolled in Howard University's Law School, where her mentors included Dean William Hastie and others involved in the NAACP's legal campaign. She was excited to be in a place where students helped research the NAACP's key discrimination cases. "When a case was to be presented to the Supreme Court," she recalled, "the entire school assembled to hear dress rehearsal arguments." The experience of Howard Law School, where she was the only woman in her class, made her aware, for the first time, of "the twin evils of discriminatory sex bias, which I quickly labeled Jane Crow." On the first day of class, male classmates laughed when the professor joked that he did not know why women came to law school. Some classmates assumed Murray had nothing important to say, and only male students were eligible to join Sigma Delta Tau, the legal fraternity.

The next year, after the United States entered World War II, Murray expressed her feelings about the war in an article called "Negro Youth's Dilemma." Citing a recent lynching in Mississippi, she compared mob violence to the evils of Hitlerism, explaining "that I and my brothers cannot walk the streets of our native land without fear." She reminded readers that "defense industries had to be threatened with the loss of profitable government contracts before they would employ Negro workers," and even then many blacks were assigned jobs as cleaners and sweepers. Those who did get jobs on production lines found that white employees refused to work with them. She concluded by noting how Japan had used a racial incident at a base in Louisiana to warn "the colored peoples of the world" that beatings and shootings would be their fate if the Allies won the war. "When it is realized that one-half of the population of the New World is non-white, the sinister effect of this propaganda becomes apparent."

Murray joined the Fellowship of Reconciliation (FOR), an international pacifist organization founded in 1914, which promoted its nonviolent strategies on the Howard campus. She was aware that some black members of the group were already beginning to use Gandhian tactics to resist segregation. James Farmer, a graduate of Howard's school of religion who was the FOR's first "race relations secretary," joined with an interracial group of activists in Chicago to form the Committee of Racial Equality. This later became a national civil rights organization, the Congress of Racial Equality (CORE), with Farmer at its head. Murray was even more drawn to Bayard Rustin, another black pacifist who joined the FOR's staff during the early 1940s. Rustin's background in the Depression-era left—he had briefly belonged to the Young Communist League before becoming disillusioned with communism—somewhat paralleled Murray's own political evolution. In addition, as Murray experienced discrimination not only as an African American but also as a woman, Rustin was marginalized as a homosexual in a period before sexual orientation could be acknowledged even within radical political circles.

Murray's growing commitment to Gandhian ideas was put into practice when the Howard campus mobilized to protest the arrest of three female undergraduates for protesting racial discrimination at a lunch counter near campus. Murray became an informal legal advisor for student groups planning nonviolent action, and in the spring of 1943 she joined a student protest at the Little Palace Cafeteria. Outside, picketers carried signs that said, "We Die Together—Why Can't We Eat Together?" Inside, young people who had been refused service at the buffet line took their empty trays to open seats, sat down, and opened books to read. After a few days of these "sit-downs," the restaurant owner agreed to serve African Americans. "We were jubilant," Murray recalled. "We had proved that intelligent, imaginative action could bring positive results." Observing that twelve of the nineteen Howard protestors were female, she also commented, "We women reasoned that it was our job to help make the country for which our black brothers were fighting a freer place in which to live when they returned from wartime service."

Wartime Race Riots

Murray's jubilation over the successful protests against segregated facilities in Washington faded quickly in the summer of 1943, when racial violence exploded in several American cities. Detroit endured the most deadly riot of all. But "few Negroes were surprised," she claimed, as "the racial tensions that produced it had been building steadily throughout the war." The violence brought to the surface the simmering racial antagonism evident wherever black workers competed for the better paying jobs previously monopolized by white people and for the limited supply of decent, affordable housing. But Detroit was a special case, as its booming industrial plants, converted from auto production to the manufacture of tanks and airplanes, attracted 50,000 African Americans between 1942 and 1945. Under pressure, the black-white alliances created by the Congress of Industrial Organizations (CIO) broke down. Thousands of white United Auto Worker (UAW) members walked out at one plant to prevent the promotion of eight African Americans, also UAW members, and Packard employees staged a "hate strike" when three black women were hired as drill operators. In February 1942, three black families attempting to move into the federally funded Sojourner Truth Housing Project in Detroit were menaced by a mob of white people armed with knives, clubs, and guns. National Guardsmen—1,700 of them—restored order, but as more violence threatened, city officials promised that subsequent public housing projects would not disrupt the racial composition of surrounding neighborhoods, a policy soon adopted elsewhere.

These isolated racial clashes set the stage for the widespread violence that broke out in June 1943 following a fistfight between a black man and a white man at a Detroit amusement park. Within hours, rioting had spread to many areas of the city and continued the following day. Black workers were attacked by white people, and white-owned stores were looted by black people. More than 6,000 federal troops were called in, but the city was devastated. Twenty-five African Americans (seventeen shot by police) and nine white people died; at least 700 other people were injured. Property loss was extensive. Murray wrote letters to government officials proposing that a national commission conduct a full investigation noting that President Roosevelt was "strangely silent about the worst racial outbreak to occur in the nation since 1919." When Roosevelt later expressed "regret over the violence," Murray wrote a scathing poem titled "Mr. Roosevelt Regrets," which was published in *The Crisis*.

In an article entitled "Negroes Are Fed Up," Murray predicted further riots. No sooner was it published than the prophecy proved true in Harlem. On August 1, 1943, word that a white policeman had killed a black soldier drew 3,000 residents into the streets. The next day Pauli Murray walked through the area and found it "difficult to believe that human beings could have accomplished such utter destruction so

Walter White on White Supremacy and World War II

In July 1944, the head of the NAACP, Walter White, addressed a War Emergency Conference in Chicago. His remarks on the international significance of the war for Europe's colonial possessions were based on his recent tour of several war zones.

A high official of the British Empire's India Office told me bluntly that Nehru and Gandhi and the other leaders of the fight for freedom of India's three hundred and fifty million people would never be freed from prison until they confessed guilt of treason and insurrection for daring to demand that India's millions receive as well as fight for freedom. Lest he be made a martyr by dying in prison, Gandhi has since been nominally freed. But the brilliant Nehru and other Indian leaders remain in jail to furnish the Japanese propagandists with superb material to convince the one thousand million colored peoples of the Pacific that the white nations of the world are liars and hypocrites when they say that this is a war for the freedom of all men everywhere.

In this shameful program, the United States is doing her full share to create cynicism and scepticism. Every lynching, every coldblooded shooting of a Negro soldier in Louisiana or Mississippi or Georgia, every refusal to abolish segregation in our armed forces . . . builds up a debit balance of hatred against America which may cost countless lives of Americans yet unborn.

Capitalist America and Great Britain fear and distrust Communist Russia, despite all the oleaginous talk nowadays about "our Russian Ally." If they hope to preserve a capitalist economy, would they not be wise enough to stop virtually forcing the oppressed of the world—white, black, brown, and yellow—into desperate alliance with Communism or a racial war which would destroy white and colored peoples?

—from remarks made by Walter White on July 16, 1944.

office was temporary and would disappear once white male lawyers returned from wartime service to claim former jobs. Marshall dashed her hope of working for the NAACP's legal arm, telling her that he had no position available. Murray knew no major law firm would hire a black woman. The elation she felt over the allied victory in World War II was tempered by doubts about her own future.

POSTWAR DILEMMAS

Murray's uncertainty was shared by many African Americans as World War II came to an end. The civil rights gains of the war years were limited. Despite concessions, segregation in the military was still the norm. The FEPC had the power to investigate cases of discrimination but not to compel minority hiring. Roosevelt made no commitment to continuing it after the war. His death on April 12 ,1945 raised a new question regarding racial matters: Would President Harry S Truman be even less responsive to civil rights issues than his predecessor? The signals were ominous when Mary McLeod Bethune's request to meet with the new First Lady was diverted to a White House aide with a query: "Mrs. Truman wants to know whether or not she should see these people."

Racial Understanding and Racist Violence

Despite uncertainties about the future, race relations were better understood at the end of the war than in previous eras, thanks to the work of social scientists who rejected racist assumptions. Gaining the most attention was Gunnar Myrdal's monumental study, *An American Dilemma: The Negro Problem and Modern Democracy,* published in 1944.

Although Myrdal was a Swedish scholar, his book drew on the research of leading black scholars such as Ralph Bunche, E. Franklin Frazier, and Charles S. Johnson. Myrdal's overall theme was that the race problem was solvable if white Americans acknowledged the contradictions between the treatment of black Americans and the nation's democratic ideals, which Myrdal called "the American Creed." Although some leftist intellectuals questioned whether white Americans were willing to uphold ideals that contradicted their interests, Myrdal's work set the optimistic tone for many subsequent studies by black scholars of African American life and black-white relations. Myrdal's associate St. Clair Drake collaborated with Horace Cayton to produce *Black Metropolis* (1944), a classic study of the Chicago black community. Former New Dealer Robert C. Weaver published *Negro Labor: A National Problem* (1946), and Harvard-trained historian John Hope Franklin, then on the faculty of North Carolina Central College, published a pioneering African American history textbook called *From Slavery to Freedom* (1947).

Even as these studies increased popular understanding of the status of African Americans in the United States, the eradication of racial discrimination required more than enlightened scholarship. The demobilization of American society caused considerable disruption. War veterans and workers in the war industries faced new problems as factories shifted from wartime production to meeting civilian needs. The racial conflicts of the war years were compounded as many industrial workers, both black and white, suffered wage cuts and layoffs during the early postwar years. Labor unrest also increased, as nearly 5 million workers participated in nearly 5,000 strikes in 1946. The job prospects for African Americans—historically the last hired and first fired—were also clouded by the introduction of new technology that reduced the need for unskilled labor. Nonetheless, black workers were determined to retain jobs gained as a result of wartime labor shortages, and the more than 900,000 returning black veterans were equally determined to continue the fight against racial discrimination.

In the South, outbreaks of racial violence demonstrated that African Americans, even veterans in uniform, could expect no changes in Jim Crow. The most serious incident occurred in February 1946, when a black veteran in Columbia, Tennessee, defended his mother after a white repairman slapped her in a dispute over charges. After the veteran threw the repairman through a plateglass window, a white mob led by Ku Klux Klansmen and local police retaliated by assaulting black residents (two deaths were reported) and destroying many homes and businesses in the black section of town. A few days later, Columbia police killed two black suspects being held for questioning. When twenty-five black residents who had resisted the violence were charged with attempted murder, Marshall and other NAACP lawyers defended them, convincing an all-white jury to acquit all but two defendants.

Other bouts of violence occured in Georgia. Later in the year, white men in Taylor County, killed Macio Snipes, a veteran who had been the first African American in the county to vote in the Democratic Party primary. On a secluded road near Monroe, a band of several dozen white men assaulted and killed two black married couples. This widely publicized incident prompted sixteen-year-old Morehouse College student Martin Luther King Jr. to write a letter of protest to the *Atlanta Constitution:* "We want and are entitled to the basic rights and opportunities of American citizens: The right to earn a living at work for which we are fitted by training and ability; equal opportunities in education, health, recreation, and similar public services; the right to vote; equality before the law; some of the same courtesy and good manners that we ourselves bring to all human relations."

> "We want and are entitled to the basic rights and opportunities of American citizens."
> —*Martin Luther King Jr.*

Between June 1945 and September 1946, fifty-six African Americans were killed in the wave of racial violence. In February 1946, Walter White of the NAACP led a delegation that called on Truman to inform him of the poor state of race relations. The next day Truman wrote to his attorney general, recounting an incident in which Isaac Woodward, a uniformed soldier discharged from the army just three hours earlier, had been pulled off a bus by police in Batesburg, South Carolina, brutally beaten, and left blinded. "I have been very much alarmed at the increased racial feeling all over the country," Truman remarked.

Colonialism and the United Nations

As southern segregationists sought to sustain white supremacy in the postwar period, so too did European colonialists attempt to preserve their domination of most of Africa and Asia. Soldiers from India, Kenya, Senegal, and many other colonies fought on behalf of the Allied cause, and many of them returned to civilian life with a new determination to realize the democratic ideals of the Atlantic Charter. Political scientist Ralph Bunche was uniquely well placed to understand the relationship between the African American struggle for civil rights and the emerging African and Asian movements for national independence. During the 1930s Bunche became not only

Ralph Bunche at the United Nations Security Council, Paris, 1948.

an outspoken critic of segregation but also an expert on African colonization. As a professor at Howard, he helped form the New Negro Alliance and picketed Washington's National Theater to protest its segregation policies. Through his academic studies, Bunche was aware of the increasing militancy of African nationalists, whom he met in his travels. His 1936 book, *A World View of Race,* insisted that European imperialism was "a product of modern capitalism." As an influential NAACP figure, he questioned the group's emphasis on civil rights to the neglect of economic reform.

Yet Bunche also saw cause for optimism in the anticolonial implications of the Atlantic Charter. During the war, he left academic life to take a position as Africa expert with the Office of Strategic Services (OSS) and ended the war as a State Department advisor on colonial policies. He realized the effort to establish a world body to replace the League of Nations was crucial to the fate of colonized nations. The League had failed to take a stand against colonization, but perhaps the new United Nations would take a different course. When representatives of the world's independent nations met in San Francisco during the spring of 1945 to draft the charter for the United Nations, Bunche was a member of the United States delegation. Although an unofficial NAACP delegation that included Walter White, W. E. B. Du Bois, and Mary McLeod Bethune also came to the conference determined to put the status of dependent peoples on the agenda, Bunche was better situated to influence the deliberations. But he was torn between his belief that decolonization was "the best guarantee of world security" and his awareness that he represented the Truman administration, which was reluctant to put too much pressure on Britain and France. Moreover, the U.S. military wanted to maintain control of some of the Pacific islands it had conquered during the war. In addition, southern Senators who were well placed to block American entry to the U.N. made clear that they opposed giving the world body the authority to intervene in the South to bring about racial equality. American representatives therefore insisted on a clause in the U.N.'s charter forbidding the new organization from intervening in matters "within the domestic jurisdiction" of member states and rejected language calling for an end to colonialism. Although disappointed the charter did not call for an end to colonization and racial discrimination, the NAACP representatives did gain concessions when delegates to the conference agreed to establish a Commission on Human Rights, to be chaired by Eleanor Roosevelt.

Truman's handling of U.N. policies on colonization and racial discrimination was greatly affected by other concerns that were thrust on him after Roosevelt's death. While the war with Japan was still not over, relations between the United States and its communist wartime ally, the Soviet Union, were already deteriorating. The changed international climate had been sharply etched in a 1946 speech by British leader Winston Churchill, who warned Americans that an "Iron Curtain" had descended on Europe, dividing the "free world" from the communist nations aligned with the Soviet Union. Thus, as he focused his attention on foreign policy matters, Truman was also aware that segregation damaged the credibility of the United States as a leader of democratic nations confronting the communist menace. African Americans saw this Cold War, as they had seen World War II, as an opportunity to expose the contradiction between America's ideals and its racial practices, but they also recognized the dangers of black militancy that was out of step with Truman's anticommunist policies.

COLD WAR SPLIT IN AFRICAN AMERICAN POLITICS

In 1946, Pauli Murray found herself in the unexpected position of testifying before the U.S. Senate about the character of one of her Howard professors. President Truman had nominated William Hastie as governor of the U.S. Virgin Islands, but southern segregationist senators, led by Mississippi's James O. Eastland, objected. To discredit Hastie, they implied he had once associated with communists and might be disloyal, pointing to his past ties with leftist groups such as the National Negro Congress. Murray recalled the satisfaction she felt "looking Senator Eastland straight in the eye" and describing Hastie as "a man of principle and not of 'party line.'" Hastie denied any communist affiliation, although he readily acknowledged working with civil rights reformers representing a wide range of views and protesting blood bank segregation during the war. Hastie was confirmed as the first African American governor of a U.S. territory, but his interrogation was an inkling of things to come. As the United States and the Soviet Union faced off in the Cold War, any criticism of America was liable to charges of being "communist inspired," and the intensification of anticommunism brought about major divisions in African American politics.

Loyalty Issues and Internationalist Appeals

In the chilling atmosphere of the emerging Cold War, some African Americans who had associated with the Communist Party in the 1930s found themselves on the defensive. Langston Hughes responded to criticism of his outspoken Depression-era poems by insisting he had never been a communist. Richard Wright published an apologetic article, "I Tried to Be a Communist," in the *Atlantic Monthly*. Others who had no communist connections grew cautious, doing nothing that might make them appear disloyal. NAACP leaders Thurgood Marshall and Walter White carefully aligned themselves with the anticommunist but increasingly pro-civil rights stance of the Truman administration.

W. E. B. Du Bois and Paul Robeson were among those who refused to follow this course because they doubted that Truman would take strong action on behalf of civil rights. The two men believed the United Nations should become a forum for bringing international pressure to bear on U.S. racial policies, even if this proved embarrassing to the Truman administration. In the months after the San Francisco meeting, Du Bois's increasing opposition to Truman's foreign

In 1947 W. E. B. Du Bois presented to the United Nations his "Appeal to the World" document detailing the consequences of racial discrimination against African Americans.

policies became a source of irritation for White, who had forced Du Bois to resign as editor of *The Crisis* during the 1930s and then consented to rehire him in 1944 to head the NAACP's research office. White appreciated Du Bois's exceptional expertise even while resenting his tendency to see himself as the NAACP's principal spokesman rather than as White's subordinate. In 1946 he initially approved when Du Bois proposed drafting an appeal to bring the issue of racial discrimination in the United States to the attention of the U.N. Human Rights Commission, but he became worried as Du Bois began to act with greater independence.

Early in 1947, Du Bois submitted to the United Nations an *Appeal to the World,* a document detailing the consequences of racial discrimination against African Americans. The document benefited from contributions by many experts on racial matters, including Bunche, Hastie, and Rayford Logan of Howard University. American officials, however, were determined to prevent Du Bois from gaining action on his petition, especially when the Soviet Union agreed to sponsor it. Eleanor Roosevelt and other American officials were able to convince other commission members to reject it. Du Bois denied that the petition played into the hands of the Soviet Union, but the controversy over the *Appeal* produced serious infighting within the NAACP. Roosevelt threatened to resign her position on the NAACP's board in protest. White removed Du Bois instead. Eighty years old, Du Bois soon moved on to a position as vice chairman of the Council on African Affairs, which Paul Robeson had cofounded in the late 1930s to aid national liberation struggles in Africa.

The considerably younger Robeson emerged as the most energetic and popular proponent of an African American leftist perspective during the early postwar years. Since the 1930s, his career as a singer and actor was laced with political activism. Ironically, he had achieved his greatest success as an entertainer when he recorded the patriotic "Ballad for Americans" on the eve of World War II, and during the war his public stands in favor of CIO unions, civil rights, and the Soviet Union—America's ally—attracted little public notice. But after the war, he quickly became the focus of controversy. In 1946 he largely abandoned his Hollywood and Broadway careers to sing and speak at civil rights rallies, often on behalf of the Council on African Affairs and the Crusade Against Lynching, a protest group he also helped organize.

At a massive September rally against lynching held at Madison Square Garden, Robeson shared the podium with Henry A. Wallace, Roosevelt's vice president until he was displaced by Truman at the 1944 Democratic Convention, and later secretary of commerce until Truman fired him. While Wallace denounced America's "get tough with Russia policy," Robeson denounced lynching, pointing to the irony of having Nazis on trial for crimes against humanity in Germany while America ignored its own crimes. Soon afterward, when the Crusade Against Lynching held a rally in Washington, Robeson expressed his shame "that here in the capital of the world's first genuine democratic government, it is necessary to seek redress of a wrong that defies the most fundamental concept of that precious thing we call democracy." Then he led a delegation to the White House, where he bluntly contradicted Truman's contention that the United States and Great Britain represented "the last refuge of freedom in the world." When Robeson warned that African Americans might have to defend themselves if the government would not, Truman abruptly announced that the meeting was over.

> "It is necessary to seek redress of a wrong that defies the most fundamental concept of that precious thing we call democracy."
> —*Paul Robeson*

By this time, Truman had already decided to step up his efforts to combat communism both at home and abroad. Increasingly concerned that communist governments would assume power in Greece and other European nations, Truman announced in a March 1947 joint session of Congress that the U.S. government would counter communist gains by providing military and economic aid to Greece, Turkey, and other imperiled nations. The new Truman Doctrine was accompanied by policies designed to combat communist subversion within the United States, including ordering the Justice Department to prepare a list of "subversive organizations." The list included not only the Communist Party but also the National Negro Congress, the Civil Rights Congress, the Council on African Affairs, and many other groups devoted to civil rights reform. Truman not only put leftist civil rights advocates on the defensive by labeling them as subversive but also strengthen his appeal among African Americans by backing the far-reaching recommendations of his Civil Rights Commission, released early in 1947 as a report titled *To Secure These Rights.*

By the time Truman announced these pro–civil rights policies, Robeson was already under investigation by the FBI and the House Committee on Un-American Activities (HUAC), which turned its attention to communist influences in various areas of American life, including the movie industry. Robeson had already resigned himself to being denied opportunities in Hollywood, but the HUAC investigation led to a period of blacklisting that adversely affected the careers of many in the industry, including some black

Ralph Bunche on Peace in Our Time

For his work in mediating peace between Israel and Arab nations to end the war of 1948 on behalf of the United Nations, Ralph Bunche was awarded the 1950 Nobel Peace Prize, the first African American to be so honored. Excerpts from his Nobel lecture follow. One commentator noted that this address brings together "all the themes Bunche had worked on separately at different stages in his past career, as well of most of the goals he was to pursue at the United Nations for the next twenty years."

Peace must be paced by human progress. Peace is no mere matter of men fighting or not fighting. Peace, to have meaning for many who have known only suffering in both peace and war, must be translated into bread or rice, shelter, health and education, as well as freedom and human dignity—a steadily better life. If peace is to be secure, long-suffering and long-starved forgotten peoples of the world, the under-privileged and the under-nourished, must begin to realize without delay the promise of a new day and a new life.

In the world of today, Europe, like the rest of the West, is confronted with the urgent necessity of a new orientation—a global orientation. The pre-war outlook is as obsolete as the pre-war world. There must be an awakening to the incontestable fact that the far away, little known and little understood peoples of Asia and Africa, who constitute the majority of the world's population, are no longer passive and no longer to be ignored. The fury of the world's ideological struggle swirls about them. Their vast numbers will prove a dominant factor in the future world pattern of life. They provide virgin soil for the growth of democracy, but the West must first learn how to approach them understandingly and how to win their trust and friendship. There is a long and unsavory history of western imperialism, suppression and exploitation to be overcome, despite the undenied benefits which the West also brought to them. There must be an acceleration in the liquidation of colonialism. A friendly hand must be extended to the peoples who are laboring under the heavy burden of newly-won independence, as well as to those who aspire to it. And in that hand must be tangible aid in generous quantity—funds, foodstuffs, equipment, and technical assistance. . . .

—from Nobel Lecture, "Some Reflections on Peace in Our Time," by Ralph Bunche, December 11, 1950. © The Nobel Foundation 1950.

actors. During the communist "witch hunts," as these investigations came to be known, entertainers were not the only ones under suspicion. As pressures for political conformity increased, investigative agencies turned their attention to any black leader with a leftist background.

The 1948 Election and the Decline of the Black Left

At the end of 1947, Henry Wallace announced he would run for president on the Progressive Party ticket, and Robeson immediately announced his support, as did Du Bois. As White and other NAACP leaders remained loyal to Truman and the Democrats, the campaign further split black political leadership. Truman responded to the Progressive Party challenge by portraying himself as a staunch opponent of communism, both at home and abroad. Recognizing that he needed the black vote to overcome his principal Republican opponent, New York governor Thomas Dewey, Truman recruited Hastie to campaign on his behalf in black communities, and early in 1948 he announced wide-ranging civil rights proposals that included antilynching legislation and a permanent FEPC.

But even as Truman formulated his reelection strategy, A. Philip Randolph entered the fray by launching a campaign to desegregate the armed forces. When Truman proposed reviving the military draft as a Cold War measure, Randolph saw an opportunity to push the president to act on an issue

TABLE 16.2 Supreme Court Cases, 1944–1950

***Smith* v. *Allwright* (1944):** In a Texas case, the Supreme Court declares that "white primary" laws violate the Fifteenth Amendment.

***Morgan* v. *Commonwealth of Virginia* (1946):** The Supreme Court bans segregation on interstate buses, but the ruling has little immediate effect on southern practices.

***Sipuel* v. *Oklahoma State Board of Regents* (1948):** The Supreme Court decides in an Oklahoma case that states must admit qualified African Americans to previously all-white graduate schools when no comparable black institution is available.

***Shelley* v. *Kraemer* (1948):** The Supreme Court rules that racially restrictive housing covenants are unenforceable.

***Sweatt* v. *Painter* (1950):** The Supreme Court rules that states must make equal educational facilities available to black professional students.

that was unresolved since the war. Leading a delegation of black leaders that included Charles Houston, he met with Truman in March 1948 and bluntly warned, "Mr. President, Negroes are in the mood not to bear arms for the country unless Jim Crow in the Armed Forces is abolished."

"I wish you hadn't made that statement," Truman retorted with a flash of anger.

Houston calmed the president by explaining that Randolph's statement simply reflected the feelings of many African Americans.

"We have fought and bled in every war," Randolph continued, yet "have not gotten adequate recognition and consideration."

> "We have fought and bled in every war."
> —*A. Philip Randolph*

As he had with Roosevelt seven years earlier, Randolph urged Truman to issue an executive order, this time banning segregation in the Armed Forces. When Truman failed to act, Randolph kept up the pressure. He told the Senate Armed Services Committee that he would call on African Americans to refuse to serve in a segregated military. When Congress passed legislation instituting a military draft without banning segregation, Randolph joined Bayard Rustin, his former colleague in the March on Washington Movement who had become the Fellowship of Reconciliation's race relations secretary, to found the League for Nonviolent Disobedience to encourage black draft resistance.

Faced with Randolph's threat of civil disobedience, Truman offered more civil rights concessions, but his willingness to support a civil rights plank in the Democratic Party platform at the national convention in the summer of 1948 split his own party. Southern Democrats led by South Carolina's Strom Thurmond walked out to form the States' Rights party, or Dixiecrats. Ironically, this split gave Truman a freer hand on civil rights issues, as he now had no chance of appeasing the Dixiecrats. Ten days later he strengthened his black support by implementing two recommendations from *To Secure These Rights*—issuing Executive Orders 9980 and 9981 banning racial discrimination in federal employment and in the armed forces. As Randolph had called off the March on Washington after gaining concessions from Roosevelt, he also agreed to call off threatened civil disobedience after gaining them from Truman. The first presidential candidate to campaign in Harlem, Truman kept up his attacks on Wallace supporters by charging that the Progressive Party was dominated by communists and communist sympathizers.

The 1948 presidential campaign thus became a decisive confrontation between the moderate approach to civil rights reform favored by Truman and his black supporters and the more far-reaching changes sought by Robeson, Du Bois, and Wallace. Most black voters opted for Truman as far more able than Wallace to deliver on his civil rights promises, because Truman was more likely to win the election. Black votes in several key northern states gave the president his razor-thin victory over Dewey. Wallace attracted only 2 percent of the vote, slightly less than the segregationist candidate Thurmond received.

In the aftermath of Wallace's overwhelming defeat, the ideological boundaries of African American politics—and American politics in general—narrowed. The exceptional conditions of the depression era and World War II had encouraged a black political militancy and experimentation that could not be sustained during the Cold War. The internationalism and fervent Pan-Africanism of Robeson and Du Bois were increasingly obscured by their communist ties, which made them targets of anticommunist zealots and government prosecutors. By the end of the decade, eleven prominent Communists, including New York City's only black councilman, Benjamin J. Davis, had been convicted of violating the Smith Act, which outlawed membership in the Communist Party. The Civil Rights Congress, headed by veteran Communist activist William Patterson, also came under government attack. Du Bois himself was prosecuted in 1950 for his efforts to end the Cold War, but he was ultimately acquitted of the charges brought against him.

While noncommunist activists such as Randolph and Rustin were not persecuted in comparable ways, they did not thrive in the Cold War political climate. Disbanding the League for Nonviolent Civil Disobedience, Randolph increasingly concentrated on pressing white union leaders to combat discrimination in the labor movement, while Rustin became increasingly active in pacifist protests against nuclear arms.

Era of NAACP Dominance

As urban black voters began to affect state and local elections as well as presidential contests, significant civil rights reforms were achieved in some areas. In addition to electing liberal white politicians who favored civil rights, black voters elected two African Americans to Congress—New York's Adam Clayton Powell and Chicago's William L. Dawson. By the end of the decade, both gained sufficient seniority to influence national legislation affecting African Americans. The NAACP increased its effectiveness by forging ties with liberal politicians, labor unions, and Jewish organizations in an alliance formalized in 1950 with the creation of the Leadership Conference on Civil Rights.

The NAACP was still unable to achieve its longstanding goal of gaining passage of antilynching legislation (or any other federal civil rights legislation), but Marshall's legal efforts produced some highly visible victories. In 1946, the Supreme Court accepted the arguments of NAACP lawyers that Irene Morgan had been denied her constitutional rights when she was arrested for refusing to accept segregated seating on an interstate bus (the same issue that had resulted in Pauli Murray's arrest earlier in the decade). The *Morgan* v. *Commonwealth of Virginia* (1946) ruling was far from a complete victory, however, as Rustin and others were arrested the following year for taking part in bus rides to test enforcement of the decision. Next, Marshall supported leftist activist Heman Sweatt's challenge to the racial barriers that prevented him from attending the University of Texas Law School and Ada Lois Sipuel's similar challenge at the University of Oklahoma Law School. These two complaints became the basis for the NAACP-backed suits—*Sweatt* v. *Painter* (1947) and *Sipuel* v. *Oklahoma State Board of Regents* (1948)—that forced states to make equal educational facilities available to black professional students. Marshall also took on cases initiated by black home buyers and renters challenging racial covenants that excluded them from many neighborhoods. The Supreme Court's decision in *Shelley* v. *Kraemer* (1948), which outlawed court enforcement of restrictive housing covenants, was a major victory in this area.

Marshall's Legal Defense and Education Fund (LDF) not only undermined the legal foundations of the separate-but-equal doctrine but also provided a substitute for mass protest, thus playing an increasingly crucial role in civil rights reform. With growing support from white liberals and foundations, Marshall was able to match the resources of his segregationist opponents, tapping the expertise of civil rights veterans such as Howard legal scholars Charles Houston, William Hastie, and Spottswood Robinson and working closely with legal experts from other liberal and Jewish groups. By 1948, his talented staff had grown to include several other graduates of Howard Law School: Robert Lee Carter, a World War II veteran who became his chief aide; Oliver Hill, Marshall's law school classmate; and Constance Baker Motley, the first woman attorney on the NAACP staff. Although Pauli Murray did not gain a position on the NAACP staff, Marshall and his legal team moved closer to the position she had urged while at Howard: a direct attack against the separate-but-equal doctrine of *Plessy* v. *Ferguson*.

RACIAL DIMENSIONS OF POSTWAR POPULAR CULTURE

In a 1949 article published in Russian in the Soviet Union, Paul Robeson described the enormous influence of "Negro folk music" on American culture. He drew particular attention to his own repertoire of spirituals, work songs, and "songs of protest . . . directly calling the Negroes to the struggle for their rights, and against lynch-law, against their exploiters, against capitalists." Robeson's dismay was evident as he contrasted modern African American musical trends with the folk music and protest songs he performed before audiences of leftists and labor activists. He acknowledged that these traditional music forms had been displaced in popularity by jazz and blues, which Robeson saw as expressing "the emotional state of the individual" rather than the collective concerns of black people. Robeson saw ominous political implications in the rise of "commercial jazz," which, he said, had "prostituted and ruthlessly perverted many splendid models of Negro folk music and has corrupted and debased many talented musicians in order to satisfy the desires of capitalist society."

Although some black artists and performers of the period shared Robeson's perspective, a much larger number pursued success within the constraints of the capitalist system and Cold War liberalism he denounced. Even within the African American cultural world, others who were more willing to adjust to postwar trends in American mass culture had already displaced Robeson. Langston Hughes now offered far gentler social criticisms in his humorous *Chicago Defender* columns, which he reprinted in 1950 as *Simple Speaks His Mind*. Richard

Wright moved from Marxism toward existentialism (a philosophical movement focusing on individual existence) by the late 1940s, increasingly interpreting his sense of alienation in individual rather than class terms.

Decline of Swing and the Rise of Rhythm and Blues

The commercialized jazz that Robeson derided was itself being displaced in popularity during the late 1940s. The big bands of the swing era found it difficult to survive in the postwar period (Duke Ellington was among the few to continue performing into the 1950s), although popular singers such as Ella Fitzgerald, Nat "King" Cole, Sarah Vaughn, and Billie Holiday sustained their careers as individual recording stars. The increasing blandness of heavily orchestrated swing music provoked a revolt by talented young jazz musicians—notably saxophonist Charlie Parker, trumpeter Dizzy Gillespie, and pianist Thelonious Monk—who left the big bands to form small ensembles playing a more intense and experimental jazz style known as bebop.

■ Considered by many to be the quintessential female jazz singer, Ella Fitzgerald displayed remarkable vocal range. Her career, which began in the 1930s, spanned six decades.

But neither swing nor bebop generated as much enthusiasm among large numbers of black recent urban migrants as did gospel and "race music," the name initially applied to the rhythm and blues that began to be played on city radio stations. While Robeson condemned the commercialization of African American culture, others saw opportunities in this trend. In 1948, WDIA Memphis became the first radio station to switch to all-black programming, and the following year, Atlanta's WERD became the nation's first black-owned radio station. Many other stations responded to the growth of black purchasing power by hiring black disc jockeys. In Chicago, black disc jockey Arthur Bernard Leaner achieved wealth and fame when he changed his on-air name to the more mundane Al Benson and developed a more down-to-earth patter. His "jive talk" and awareness of the changing music tastes of black listeners gave him recognition and authority and made him an effective pitchman for advertisers: "I used to say 'And that's for real' to let my audience know that what I was selling them was good merchandise and no crap." Other black disc jockeys used colorful names like Chicago Daddy-O Daylie and Austin's Doctor Hep Cat Durst in Austin. A few politically engaged artists and intellectuals sought to develop uplifting radio programs on African American history, but in the aftermath of depression and war, black urban workers often preferred rhythm-and-blues entertainers such as Memphis Slim, the Staple Singers, and B. B. King.

Black Americans in Hollywood

If Robeson's political views had little impact on the recording industry, they had even less impact on the Hollywood film studios, where opportunities expanded for black actors willing to accept the limited roles offered them. Former Cotton Club singer Lena Horne's scenes in films such as *Panama Hattie* (1942) and *Swing Fever* (1943) made her a favored pinup girl for black soldiers during the war, but her brief appearances were cut by southern censors so as not to offend white audiences. When Hollywood studios responded to government pressure to produce films to boost homefront morale, the result was two 1943 films, *Cabin in the Sky* and *Stormy Weather,* featuring all-black casts that included Horne, Ethel Waters, Eddie Robinson, Butterfly McQueen, and Bill Robinson. These performers often chafed at having to play racially stereotyped roles, but they were also seen as racial pioneers and sources of racial pride. Most of them avoided taking public stands on political issues, but some paid the price for being identified with left-wing groups. Canada Lee, for example, was among the most successful of the black actors of the 1940s—starring not only in films such as *Lifeboat* (1944) and *Body and Soul*

(1947) but also in the Broadway adaptation of the novel *Native Son*—until he was identified as having communist ties. Blacklisted in Hollywood, Lee could find roles only in films made outside the United States, such as *Cry the Beloved Country* (1950), an anti-apartheid film made in South Africa.

Jackie Robinson and the Major Leagues

It was hardly surprising that outspoken entertainers such as Canada Lee and Paul Robeson would find it hard to thrive in a political environment encouraging conformity. More surprising was the sudden emergence of another black personality—Jackson "Jackie" Robinson—who achieved enormous popularity just as the careers of Lee and Robeson began to decline. Indeed, the contrasting career paths of Robeson and Robinson, who broke the color barrier in Major League Baseball in 1947, crossed during the late 1940s as the two men became symbolic figures in the contentious political conflicts of Cold War.

Although Robeson and Robinson were quite different in important ways, they were similar in that both began adulthood as exceptional athletes. Robeson was an All-American football player at Rutgers and a varsity athlete in three other sports, while Robinson earned honorable mention All-American honors as a UCLA football player, led his league in scoring for two years as a basketball player, and excelled as a broad jumper in track. Both men had pursued sports careers after leaving college. Robeson played two seasons as a professional football player at a time when black players were still accepted. The imposition of racial bars in the National Football League restricted Robinson to occasional semiprofessional football games before he was drafted into the military in 1942.

Robeson, however, was not only an exceptional athlete but also an outstanding student and a gifted orator, while Robinson struggled in the classroom and left UCLA before graduation. Robeson's multifaceted intellectual interests as well as his extensive travels abroad contributed to his cosmopolitan outlook, his connection to left-wing politics, and his deep interest in African culture. In contrast, Robinson was more singularly focused on athletics, and his experiences in the Army and then as a baseball player for the Kansas City Monarchs of the Negro National League shaped his adult outlook.

Although both chafed at racial restrictions—as evidenced by Robinson's challenge to bus segregation while in the military during World War II—by the late 1940s they had arrived at differing conclusions about how to respond. Robeson increasingly sacrificed his performing career to immerse himself in radical politics, while Robinson agreed to suppress his aggressiveness in order to participate in the desegregation experiment of Brooklyn Dodgers executive Branch Rickey. "I'm looking for a ball player with guts enough not to fight back," Rickey explained when he signed Robinson to a contract. In 1943, Robeson had pleaded in vain with major league club owners to sign black baseball players, but Rickey carefully orchestrated Robinson's entry into the major leagues while insisting he was not giving in to black protesters and political leaders. He saw desegregation as making moral and economic sense, given the untapped talent of black athletes and the need to attract black fans. He understood that black players in the major leagues would ultimately end competition from the Negro leagues.

Robinson spent a year playing for the Dodgers farm team in Montreal before playing his first game with the Dodgers on April 11, 1947. As Robeson had once won the admiration of teammates and opponents through his skill as a player, so did Robinson gradually gain acceptance from white players. He followed Rickey's instructions to ignore racist taunts and provocations while proving himself on the field, leading the team in runs scored and total bases during his first year. He also led the league in stolen bases during his first season and was named Rookie of the Year.

The significance of Robinson's achievement extended beyond baseball. He attracted enormous attention from the press and appeared on the cover of *Time* magazine. His success in overcoming racial barriers in the "nation's pastime" caused many African Americans to see him as a hero, while his talent and his refusal to retaliate against the provocations of opposing players led large numbers of white people to admire him. He demonstrated to other black Americans that opportunities were expanding and confirmed to white people that the nation was living up to its ideals of fair play. Like heavyweight boxing champ Joe Louis, Robinson became a reassuring racial symbol, talented in his field—yet, unlike Robeson, untainted by radicalism and political militancy.

Robinson's career symbolized broad social trends that enabled a few African Americans to experience success while collective racial gains remained modest and gradual. Those who went to the ballparks to cheer for Robinson returned after the game to mostly segregated neighborhoods. While some observers cited the willingness of white Americans to accept Robinson as a harbinger of broader racial tolerance, he also served as a model for gradual or token racial reform that did not touch the lives of the vast majority of African Americans; even most black athletes who

As a player for the Brooklyn Dodgers, Jackie Robinson was named Rookie of the Year in 1947 and won the National League batting title and Most Valuable Player award in 1949.

were qualified to play in the major leagues were still excluded. Some teams, especially in the American League, continued to resist change, and twelve years passed before the Boston Red Sox became the last team to sign a black player.

Robinson's ascendancy during the late 1940s contrasted dramatically with Robeson's decline. The National League's Most Valuable Player of the 1949 season, Robinson led the Dodgers to the World Series (they lost to the New York Yankees) and led the league in batting percentage and stolen bases. Robeson, for his part, endured a torrent of criticism after he attended the Congress of World Partisans of Peace in April 1949 and suggested that African Americans would "not make war on the Soviet Union." When reports of his comments appeared in the press, black leaders such as A. Philip Randolph, Bayard Rustin, Roy Wilkins, and Mary McLeod Bethune mobilized to denounce his views as unrepresentative. The NAACP's *The Crisis* magazine came close to denying Robeson's racial identity: "Robeson has none except sentimental roots among American Negroes. He is one of them, but not with them."

In the midst of this controversy, HUAC contacted Robinson to invite him to offer testimony regarding Robeson's controversial statement. In remarks he prepared with the help of Rickey and Urban League head Lester B. Granger, Robinson disassociated himself from Robeson's reported comments but also insisted that racism was a real problem rather than "a creation of Communist imagination." He affirmed his loyalty to the United States and expressed confidence that black Americans could win their struggle against racial discrimination "without the Communists and we don't want their help." White patriotic organizations showered Robinson with praise for his repudiation of Robeson. Film footage of this testimony was later included as the climax to a Hollywood film biography, *The Jackie Robinson Story* (1950), in which Robinson depicted his own struggle for white acceptance of his exceptional skills as a baseball player.

By the end of the decade, Robinson had emerged as a major black spokesman. Robeson, in contrast, faded from public view after a mob disrupted his Peekskill, New York, concert in September 1949, and news of the riot led to cancellations of his scheduled appearances. Denied the right to perform in the United States, the State Department also stripped him of his passport to travel.

If Robeson's descent to obscurity represented the fate of the black left during the early years of the Cold War, Robinson's sudden fame represented a type of racial progress that soon emerged in place of leftist political activism. With the exception of his congressional testimony, Robinson steered clear of political controversy during his initial years in the major leagues, but he opposed racial discrimination in his own way. By the late 1950s, a revival of mass black activism pushed him toward a public role outside sports (Robeson, after all, had not been a political activist when he was a star athlete in the early 1920s). Robinson found ways to use his fame to support the civil rights movement, especially once his playing career ended. He became a Republican rather than a leftist radical, but he spoke out on racial issues and even expressed regret that his testimony had been used against Robeson. His extraordinary success in baseball gave him a platform to influence public opinion and perhaps lessened white resistance to desegregation in arenas of American life other than sports.

The decades following Robinson's breakthrough became an era of First Negroes—pioneers in fields from which the race had previously been excluded. Other African Americans who rose to prominence during the 1950s followed Robinson's model of overcoming prejudice through excellence and cautious militancy that stayed within the confines of Cold War anticommunism. Thus, even as Robeson's star faded, Robinson and other African Americans came to prominence and contributed to new civil rights struggles that were different, yet ultimately more powerful than any previous ones.

CONCLUSION

The social stresses of World War II transformed African Americans, affecting them in ways that fed discontent and political militancy as well as producing rising expectations. During the war, A. Philip Randolph, William Hastie, Pauli Murray, and other civil rights activists pressed for racial reform. They discovered, however, that winning a world war was more readily accomplished than overcoming long-standing racial barriers. After the war, the United States seemed at a crossroads. African American scholars, political leaders, and cultural stars struggled to bring home the democratic ideals for which the nation had fought abroad. The Cold War fueled both the leftist agitation of W. E. B. Du Bois and Paul Robeson and the more conventional litigation strategy of Thurgood Marshall and his staff of NAACP lawyers. Moreover, the increasing political power of African Americans and the growing effectiveness of the NAACP brought about significant gains such as President Truman's presidential order to end segregation in the military.

By divorcing itself from the left and adhering to President Truman's loyalty program, the NAACP secured its position as the dominant African American organization on the national political scene. Its legal victories encouraged optimism that African Americans could achieve gains by identifying the cause of civil rights with the fight against communism. The success of a few talented individuals offered promise of progress for all African Americans. By the early 1950s, Jackie Robinson was playing in baseball's major leagues, Ralph Bunche had won a Nobel Peace Prize for his diplomatic work at the United Nations, William Hastie had become the first African American federal appeals court judge, Gwendolyn Brooks had become the first African American poet to win the Pulitzer Prize, and Ralph Ellison had published *Invisible Man,* the first novel by an African American to win the National Book Award. Yet major civil rights legislation and collective racial advancement remained elusive. During the 1950s, the NAACP's continuing legal victories had the ironic effect of encouraging grassroots activism to implement new legal rights. This activism would ultimately pose growing challenges to the group's dominance in the civil rights field.

FURTHER READING

Abdul-Jabbar, Kareem, with Anthony Walton. *Brothers in Arms: The Epic Story of the 761st Tank Battalion, World War II's Forgotten Heroes* (New York: Broadway Books, 2004).

Anderson, Carol. *Eyes Off the Prize: The United Nations and the African-American Struggle for Human Rights, 1944–1955* (New York: Cambridge University Press, 2003).

Berman, William C. *The Politics of Civil Rights in the Truman Administration* (Columbus: Ohio State University Press, 1970).

Biondi, Martha. *To Stand and Fight: The Struggle for Civil Rights in Postwar New York City* (Cambridge: Harvard University Press, 2003).

Chateauvert, Melinda. *Marching Together: Women of the Brotherhood of Sleeping Car Porters* (Urbana: University of Illinois Press, 1998).

Davis, Benjamin O., Jr. *Benjamin O. Davis, Jr., American: An Autobiography* (Washington, DC: Smithsonian Institution Press, 1991).

Duberman, Martin. *Paul Robeson: A Biography* (New York: Knopf, 1989).

Haygood, Wil. *King of the Cats: The Life and Times of Adam Clayton Powell, Jr.* (New York: Houghton Mifflin, 1993).

Henry, Charles P. *Ralph Bunche: Model Negro or American Other?* (New York: New York University Press, 1999).

Horne, Gerald. *W. E. B. Du Bois and the Afro-American Response to the Cold War, 1944–1963* (Albany: State University of New York Press, 1986).

McGuire, Philip, ed. *Taps for a Jim Crow Army: Letters from Black Soldiers in World War II* (Lexington: University Press of Kentucky, 1993).

Murray, Pauli. *Song of a Weary Throat: An American Pilgrimage* (San Francisco: HarperCollins, 1987).

Rampersad, Arnold. *Jackie Robinson: A Biography* (New York: Alfred Knopf, 1997).

Savage, Barbara Dianne. *Broadcasting Freedom: Radio, War, and the Politics of Race, 1938–1948* (Chapel Hill: University of North Carolina Press, 1999).

Von Eschen, Penny M. *Race Against Empire: Black Americans and Anticolonialism, 1937–1957* (Ithaca, NY: Cornell University Press, 1997).

Ware, Gilbert. *William Hastie: Grace Under Pressure* (New York: Oxford University Press, 1985).

Williams, Juan. *Thurgood Marshall: American Revolutionary* (New York: Crown, 1998).

CHAPTER 17

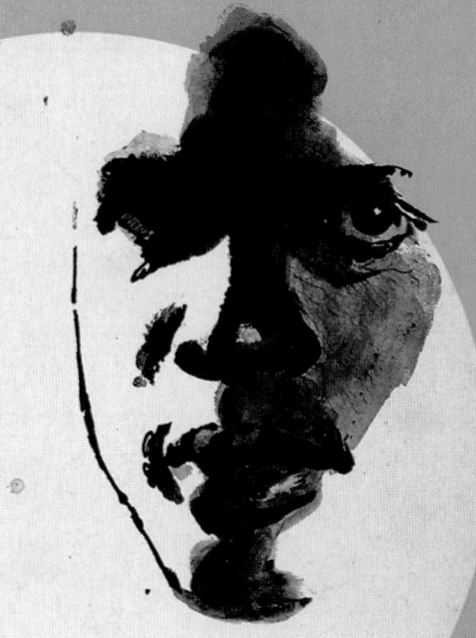

■ Lorraine Hansberry's *A Raisin in the Sun* made its debut on Broadway in 1959. Starring Sidney Poitier, the play focused on the Younger family's effort to build a better life for themselves.

Emergence of a Mass Movement Against Jim Crow

CHAPTER OUTLINE

Barbara Johns Leads a Student Strike

Just before 11:00 A.M. on April 23, 1951, the phone rang in the principal's office at Robert R. Moton High School in Farmville, Virginia. In a muffled voice, the caller said that two Moton students were in trouble at the bus terminal and then hung up. The call—a ploy to lure Principal Boyd Jones away from the building—succeeded. As soon as he headed to the bus station, a student delivered forged notes to the school's teachers, signed with a facsimile of the principal's characteristic *J*, saying that all teachers and students were to report to the auditorium immediately for an assembly. Moton's 450 students filed into the central hall, which doubled as the auditorium. After they took their seats, the stage curtain swung open, revealing a group of student leaders. At the rostrum stood sixteen-year-old Barbara Rose Johns, who announced that the assembly was for students only; emphasizing her point, she rapped her shoe on a bench while shouting to the teachers, "I want you out of here!"

Then Johns began what one of the student leaders called "her soliloquy." Moton's school buildings were totally inadequate, Johns told the students. The white high school in Farmville had a gymnasium, cafeteria, locker rooms, infirmary, and an auditorium with fixed seats; Moton had none of these. When Moton's student body outgrew the building's 180-student capacity, the Prince Edward County school board put up three temporary structures covered with tarpaper. Some people said the "tarpaper shacks" looked like a poultry farm. Teachers had to stop teaching to stoke the sometimes dangerous woodstoves that made close-by students too hot but left those farther away too cold. "We will not accept these conditions," Johns told the students. "We will do something. We will strike."

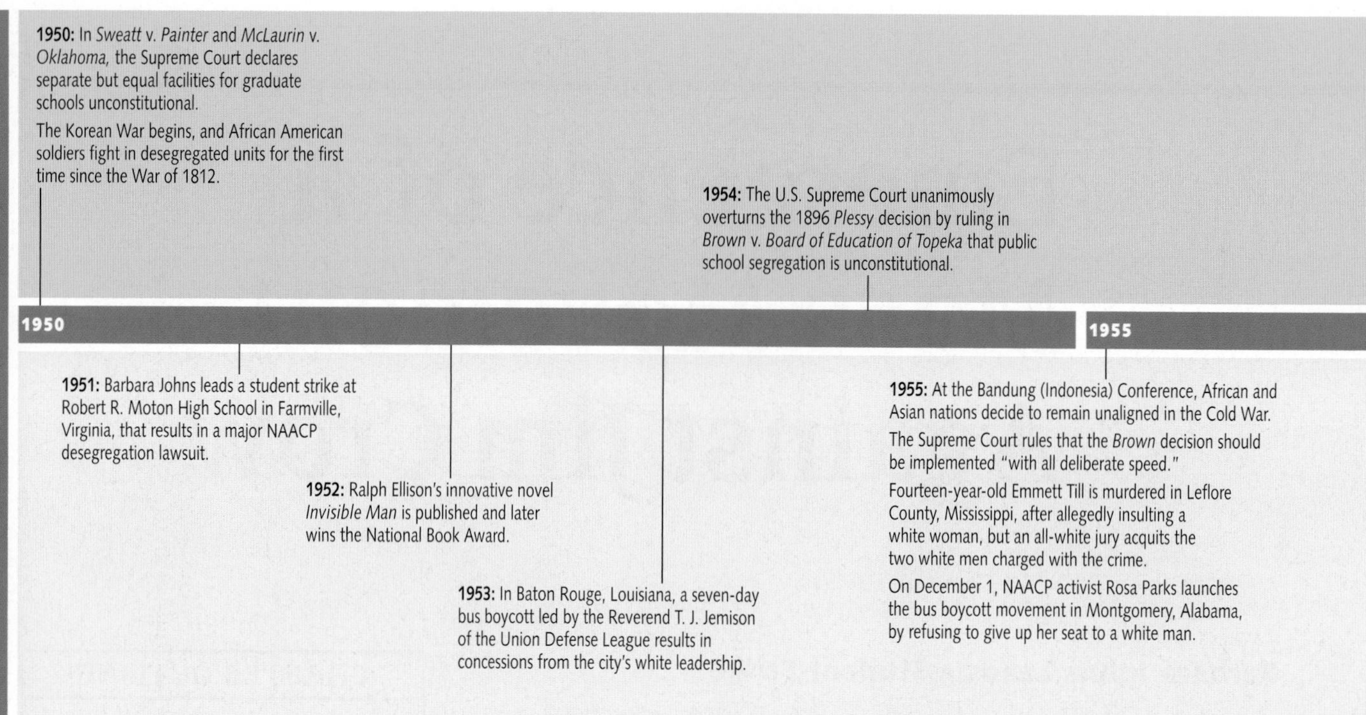

Johns assured the students that none of them would be punished if they stuck together because the local jail was not big enough to hold them all. They paraded outside the school with placards that had already been made and hidden in the school shop. When asked why they were not in school, they blamed the inadequate facilities. The students overwhelmingly decided not to consult their parents first but to act on their own. They marched off the school grounds with placards: "We Are Tired of Tar Paper Shacks—We Want a New School." The next day they rode buses to school but stayed outside, protesting on the school grounds.

According to her family, Johns had always been quiet and studious rather than outspoken before she took charge of the student protest. She had read widely—notably Booker T. Washington's *Up from Slavery,* Richard Wright's *Native Son,* and other books she found in the library of her uncle, Vernon Johns, an outspoken pastor who had once been president of Virginia Seminary. The Reverend Johns had inspired his young niece's rebelliousness before he left Farmville to become pastor of a church in Montgomery, Alabama. "I used to admire the way he didn't care who you were if he thought that something was right," Barbara Johns remarked about her uncle. As she became increasingly angered by Moton's makeshift facilities, a teacher challenged her to do something, and she did.

In the hectic first day of the strike, the students called the NAACP office in the state capital of Richmond. Johns and Carrie Stokes, president of the Moton student council, followed up with a letter to veteran NAACP lawyer Spottswood Robinson: "We hate to impose as we are doing, but under the circumstances that we are facing, we have to ask for your help." Two days later, Robinson and his longtime NAACP associate Oliver T. Hill stopped by Farmville to meet with the students, who were told to bring their parents. "I had a horror of talking to a group of these kids with no adults around," Robinson recalled. After the meeting, the two attorneys were sufficiently impressed by the students' determination to agree to help them, if they agreed to seek desegregation rather than merely better facilities. "What made us go ahead," Robinson explained later, "was the feeling that someone would have to show them something before they would go back to school."

The strike at Moton was planned and led by students. When other students suggested they should defer to the adults who had been working for years to get the county school board to approve a new black school, Johns rejected the advice, quoting scripture: "A little child shall lead them."

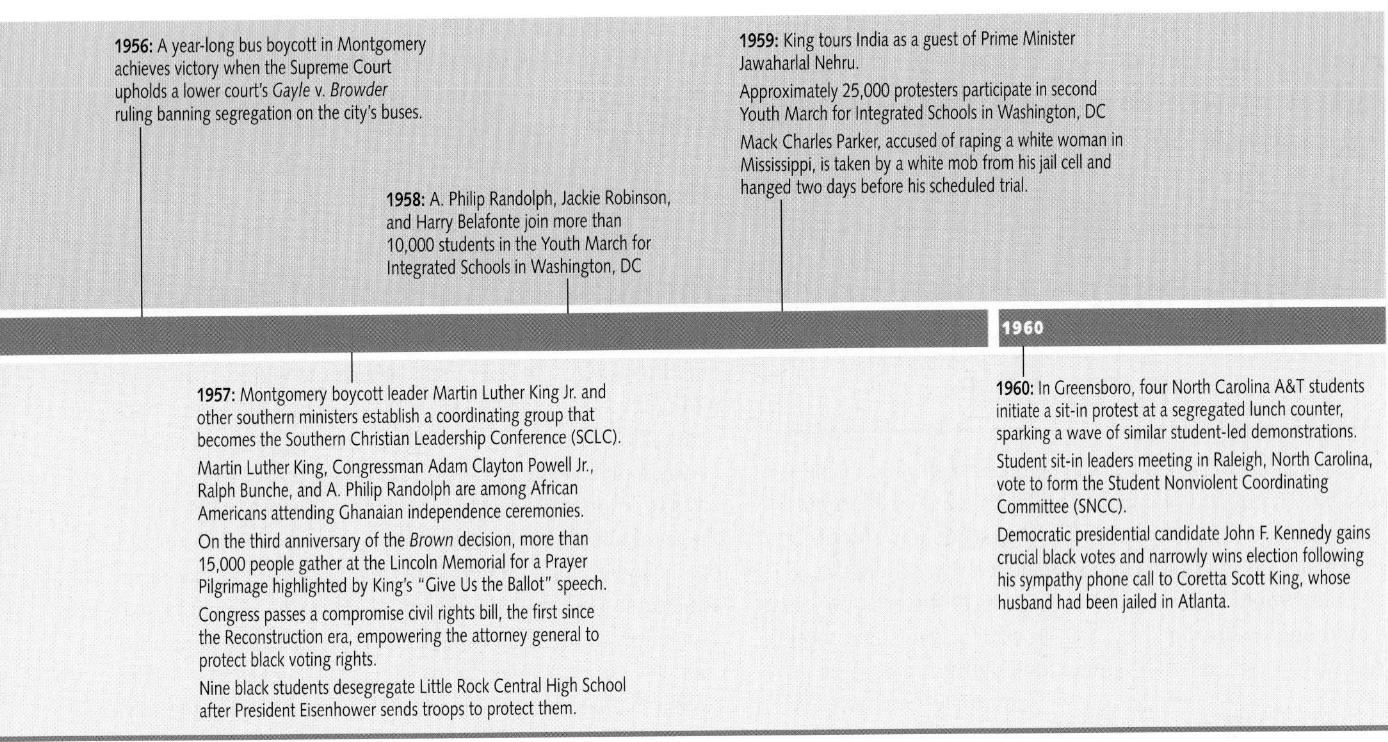

In a later interview, she said, "We knew we had to do it ourselves, and if we had asked for adult help before taking the first step, we would have been turned down." One student leader recalled Johns predicting, "We could make a move that would broadcast Prince Edward County all over the world." Events proved that Johns was right, as the strike at Moton became a lawsuit that was combined with other desegregation cases to become *Brown* v. *Board of Education of Topeka,* the most important and successful suit in the NAACP's long effort to end segregation in schools.

But Johns was not a party to the suit she helped initiate. After threats to her and a cross burning on the school grounds, her parents feared for her safety and sent her to live with her Uncle Vernon in Montgomery, where she finished high school. Her leadership, however, left a legacy of student activism that continued to grow in the following years.

Johns and the Moton students bypassed their parents to appeal directly to the NAACP, which during the early 1950s dominated African American politics at the national level. Under Thurgood Marshall's leadership, the NAACP Legal Defense and Education Fund achieved major victories, most notably the Supreme Court rulings against segregated graduate and professional schools. The NAACP, with more than a thousand local branches, was the leading force in African American activism. Its reliance on litigation and lobbying won the group major legal and legislative victories.

Within the NAACP, however, some members were dissatisfied with the slow pace of civil rights reform. Local black activism eventually posed a challenge to the NAACP at the national level, as impatient members were eager to experiment with new protest tactics.

The year-long Montgomery bus boycott movement that began late in 1955 was an important turning point because it demonstrated the readiness of many African Americans for new forms of militancy. The boycott also revealed that a black community could remain united in struggle for more than a year. Although Martin Luther King Jr. was but twenty-six years old at the start of the boycott, he emerged as a nationally known civil rights leader and the head of his own regional organization, the Southern Christian Leadership Conference (SCLC). But still younger activists soon pushed him as well as the NAACP toward greater militancy. The students who braved mobs to desegregate Little Rock Central High School in 1957 and the black college students who launched a wave of sit-in demonstrations in 1960 inspired an upsurge in grassroots protests through the South. By the spring of 1960, when student protest leaders formed the Student Nonviolent Coordinating Committee (SNCC), it was apparent that the southern freedom struggle was beyond the control of any single leader or organization.

THE ROAD TO *BROWN* V. *BOARD OF EDUCATION OF TOPEKA*

"The complete destruction of all enforced segregation is now in sight," Thurgood Marshall confidently announced in June 1950, about ten months before the student walkout in Farmville. Although Marshall recognized that school desegregation would require many more years of struggle, he was elated and encouraged by the Supreme Court's favorable rulings on two NAACP suits challenging segregation in graduate and professional schools. The first case involved George W. McLaurin, a black man in his sixties who had been admitted to the formerly all-white University of Oklahoma graduate school of education but forced to sit apart from other students, even in the school's library and cafeteria. The second case involved Heman M. Sweatt, a Houston mail carrier who had applied to the University of Texas Law School. Although Sweatt had received outstanding grades at all-black Wiley College in Texas and had done graduate work at the University of Michigan, Texas officials rejected his application, referring him instead to a hastily established black law school located in a basement and affiliated with Texas State University for Negroes (later Texas Southern University).

"The complete destruction of all enforced segregation is now in sight."—*Thurgood Marshall*

Presenting expert testimony from social scientists to support their position, Thurgood Marshall and other NAACP lawyers argued that under such conditions neither McLaurin nor Sweatt could receive educational opportunities equal to those of white students. In June 1950, the Supreme Court ruled in the cases of *McLaurin* v. *Oklahoma State Board of Regents* and *Sweatt* v. *Painter* that the black plaintiffs should be treated the same as other students. Marshall was exuberant as he pondered the rulings. He saw the McLaurin case as particularly important because the court held that, even if a black student could use school facilities, being separated from other students violated the Fourteenth Amendment's equal protection provision. The Court held that "such restrictions impair and inhibit his ability to study, engage in discussions and exchange views with other students, and, in general, to learn his profession." Marshall saw broad implications in the Court's finding that racial isolation hindered the education of black students, as the same reasoning could be applied to the elementary and high school levels.

The Attack on "Separate But Equal"

Soon after the *McLaurin* decision, Marshall convened a meeting of NAACP lawyers to determine whether the time had come for a frontal attack on the separate-but-equal doctrine. Thus far, the NAACP had challenged the *Plessy* v. *Ferguson* precedent piecemeal, forcing states on a case-by-case basis to improve educational facilities—that is, to live up to the *equal* side of the equation. Now Spottswood Robinson and others argued for a new legal strategy maintaining that racial separation itself violated the Fourteenth Amendment's equal protection clause. In a decisive meeting of Marshall and his staff, Robert Lee Carter, the astute legal tactician who served as Marshall's top assistant and whose quiet demeanor contrasted with Marshall's outgoing personality, noted that in a California case involving Spanish-speaking children, *Mendez* v. *Westminster School District* (1946), the Supreme Court had accepted the idea that segregating students implied that they were inferior and thus violated their right to equal treatment. Carter also cited the research demonstrating the psychological damage caused by racism. By the end of the meeting, Marshall was convinced. Acknowledging that schools provided children with their "most important contact with organized society," he announced to reporters, "We are going to insist on nonsegregation in American public education from top to bottom—from law school to kindergarten."

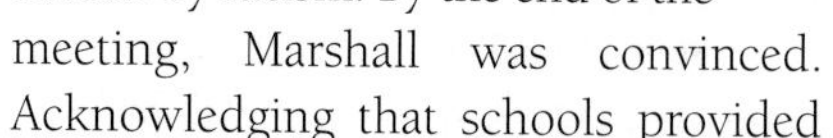

For Marshall, the decision to attack the separate-but-equal doctrine was a crucial turning point in his career as head of the NAACP Legal Defense and Education Fund. Previously, he had steered a moderate course. He had cooperated with FBI director J. Edgar Hoover to purge anyone suspected of communist ties from the NAACP's ranks, but he had also gained Hoover's enmity for criticizing the performance of the bureau's agents in the South. Moreover, soon after American-led United Nations forces intervened in 1950 to prevent a communist takeover of Korea, Marshall took a political risk when he investigated implementation of President Harry Truman's 1948 executive order banning segregation in the military. General Douglas MacArthur, the commander of U.S. military forces in Korea, initially refused to permit Marshall's

Anne Moody Recalls the Murder of Emmett Till

Anne Moody grew up poor and black in rural Mississippi. She was the first in her family to go to college. Once at Tougaloo College, near Jackson, Mississippi, she found a place in the civil rights movement. She worked with the NAACP, SNCC, and CORE for many years and in 1968 published a poignant account of her early years that includes her personal memory of the murder of Emmett Till, who was just her age.

On my way to Mrs. Burke's [Moody's white employer] that evening, Mama's words kept running through my mind. "Just do your work like you don't know nothing." "Why is Mama acting so scared?" I thought. "And what if Mrs. Burke knew we knew? Why must I pretend I don't know? Why are these people killing Negroes? What did Emmett Till do besides whistle at that woman?" . . .

Mrs. Burke called me to eat. I took a clean plate out of the cabinet and sat down. Just as I was putting the first forkful of food in my mouth, Mrs. Burke entered the kitchen.

"Essie, did you hear about that fourteen-year-old boy who was killed in Greenwood?" she asked me, sitting down in one of the chairs opposite me.

"No, I didn't hear that," I answered, almost choking on the food.

"Do you know why he was killed?" she asked and I didn't answer.

"He was killed because he got out of his place with a white woman. A boy from Mississippi would have known better than that. This boy was from Chicago. Negroes up North have no respect for people. They think they can get away with anything. He just came to Mississippi and put a whole lot of notions in the boys' heads and stirred up a lot of trouble," she said passionately.

"How old are you, Essie?" she asked me after a pause.

"Fourteen, I will soon be fifteen though," I said.

"See, that boy was just fourteen too. It's a shame he had to die too so soon." She was red in the face, she looked as if she was on fire.

When she left the kitchen I sat there with my mouth open and my food untouched. I couldn't have eaten now if I were starving. "Just do your work like you don't know nothing" ran through my mind again and I began washing the dishes.

I went home shaking like a leaf on a tree. For the first time out of all her trying, Mrs. Burke had made me feel like rotten garbage. Many times she had tried to instill fear within me and subdue me and had given up. But when she talked about Emmett Till there was something in her voice that sent chills and fear all over me.

—from Coming of Age in Mississippi *by Anne Moody, copyright © 1968 by Anne Moody. Used by permission of Doubleday, a division of Random House, Inc.*

To view a longer version of this document, please go to www.ablongman.com/carson/documents.

fact-finding trip in Korea, citing FBI reports that Marshall was once involved with the National Lawyers Guild and other leftist groups and would be a threat to national security if allowed an inside look at the military. But Truman quickly overturned MacArthur's decision. Within a month, Marshall collected extensive evidence of discrimination against black soldiers and of MacArthur's foot-dragging on desegregation. Marshall's critical report spurred implementation of military desegregation, although MacArthur continued to obstruct the process. Desegregation of the military gained momentum after Truman fired MacArthur in April 1951 for resisting presidential directives on military strategy in the Korean conflict.

Even with these achievements behind him, however, Marshall knew the frontal attack on *Plessy* might not succeed. Oliver Hill, Marshall's friend since their student days at Howard Law School, recalled that Marshall was "cautious" about risking the gains that had been achieved by forcing southern states to increase black teachers' salaries and improve segregated educational facilities for black students. "His prevailing sense, I think, was that we just couldn't

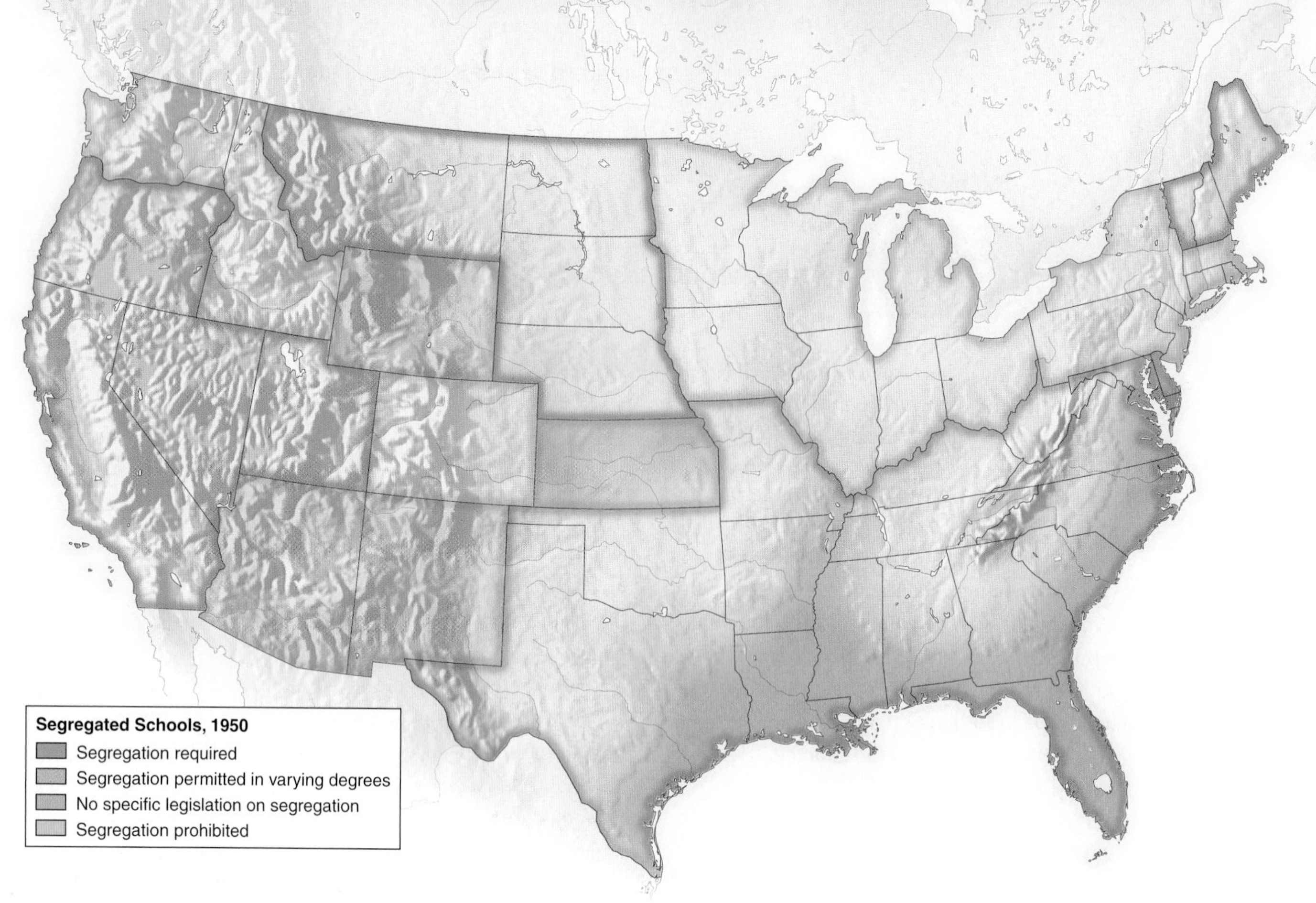

MAP 17.1 Segregated Schools, 1950

In 1950, twenty-one states, including several outside the South, maintained segregated public schools.

afford to lose a big one," Hill remembered. What if black teachers and administrators lost their jobs when public schools were desegregated? Nonetheless, NAACP officials were convinced that most African Americans saw equalization efforts as ineffective and enforced segregation as wrong. "They were just fed up with what we called 'doghouse education,'" Judge William Hastie observed, "and it was clear that the segregation fight was going to be pushed at the secondary- and elementary-school level."

The NAACP's School Desegregation Suits

The conditions endured by Moton High students were not unusual; about two of every five African American children attended classes in schools that were segregated by law and that were rarely equal in quality to the schools provided for white children in the same area. In 1950, twenty-one states, many of them outside the South, maintained segregated public schools (see Map 17.1). Marshall and his colleagues had to select the right cases, however, in order to launch a frontal attack on *Plessy*. As in Farmville, they had to find black plaintiffs—students as well as their parents—willing to take the risks associated with challenging racial segregation. At first the NAACP lawyers focused most of their energies on *Briggs* v. *Elliott,* a case initiated in the late 1940s in predominantly black Clarendon County, South Carolina. As in Virginia's Prince Edward County, the black plaintiffs from Clarendon at first sought to improve facilities for black students, some of whom were forced to walk as much as seven miles to dilapidated black schools while buses were made available to white students. Racial disparities in South Carolina's spending for the 1949–1950 school year were stark: $179 per white student; $43 per black student. When the case first reached court in 1949, a sympathetic white South Carolina judge, J. Waties Waring, privately indicated to Marshall that a suit seeking desegregation rather than equal facilities might succeed. Thus, when the NAACP's revised suit was heard by a three-judge panel in May 1951, Marshall used the opportunity to argue that, even if funding were equalized, racial inequalities would persist.

At the request of the NAACP, social psychologist Kenneth Clark traveled to Clarendon County to study the psychological effects of segregation by administering a test he and his wife, Mamie, had developed. The Clarks consistently found that black children who were shown two dolls—one black and one white—generally considered the white doll prettier and smarter than the black doll, indicating that feelings of racial inferiority had been instilled at an early age. Eleven of the sixteen black children who took this test in Clarendon County said the black doll looked "bad." Clark was most disturbed when the children were asked to select the doll that was most like themselves. "Many of the children became emotionally upset when they had to identify the doll they had rejected," Clark recalled. He testified in the *Briggs* case that segregation caused black children "to reject themselves and their color and accept whites as desirable." He concluded they had been "definitely harmed in the development of their personalities."

Although, as expected, the NAACP lawyers lost the case in a 2–1 decision (Waring was the dissenting judge), they believed the trial record would prove useful on appeal because it included Clark's powerful testimony regarding the psychological damage caused by enforced segregation. Even though worried South Carolina officials rushed to improve school facilities for black children in order to head off further litigation, Marshall was now confident he could demonstrate that Jim Crow education inevitably stigmatized black students.

Meanwhile, still another case had made its way through federal courts. In Topeka, Kansas, the parents of third-grader Linda Brown had sought to enroll her in the white school four blocks from her home instead of the black school twenty-one blocks away. The facts in *Brown* v. *Board of Education of Topeka* differed greatly from those in the South Carolina and Virginia cases because the facilities for black and white children in Topeka, even the plaintiffs agreed, were substantially equal. All children went to the same schools from junior high on; only Topeka's elementary schools were divided by race. The case put the constitutionality of segregation front and center. Carter wrote to Marshall, "The more I think about this case, the more importance I think it will have." In the summer of 1951, federal judges ruled against Brown, but evidence presented in the case supported Clark's contention that segregation retarded "the education and mental development of Negro children" and deprived them of "some of the benefits they would receive in a racially integrated school system."

In June 1952, the Supreme Court announced it would hear appeals in the *Briggs* and *Brown* cases in October, but then they accepted an appeal of the *Davis* case involving Moton High students and postponed oral arguments on the three cases until December. In November, the court added a case from the District of Columbia—*Bolling* v. *Sharpe*, which had been initiated by veteran NAACP lawyer Charles Hamilton Houston before his death in 1950. Three days later it added still another case—*Belton* v. *Gebhart*, from Delaware. Faced with five cases that raised similar issues, the Court decided to consider them together. "We felt it was much better to have representative cases from different parts of the country," one of the justices explained, "so we consolidated them and made *Brown* the first so that the whole question would not smack of being a purely Southern one."

The *Brown* Decision

Marshall had to work fast to keep pace with the Court's additions. At the NAACP headquarters in Manhattan, he pushed himself and his staff to prepare a 256-page legal brief that brought together years of legal, historical, and social science research. "When we were preparing for the *Brown* decision, sometimes we slept there," one staffer recalled. The responsibility weighed heavily on Marshall. He realized he would

George W. McLaurin, the first African American student at the University of Oklahoma's Graduate School of Education, is forced to sit apart from white students. Although permitted to eat in the school's cafeteria, he was also assigned to a separate table there. In 1950 the Supreme Court ruled that such discriminatory treatment violated the Fourteenth Amendment's "equal protection" guarantee.

The Montgomery boycott demonstrated that African Americans, even though often poor, could be a powerful force when united. Not only did the boycott hurt the bus company, but a related MIA boycott of Montgomery's stores put pressure on the city's merchants. Montgomery city officials nonetheless refused to make concessions that would satisfy black residents. Finally, an NAACP-sponsored suit against segregation on city buses prevailed in the courts. In November, as MIA leaders were in a Montgomery courtroom seeking to prevent local officials from shutting down carpool operations, the Supreme Court ruled in *Gayle* v. *Browder* that segregated seating on city buses was unconstitutional. Although the names of Parks and King would become famous as a result of the boycott, the lawsuit had been filed on behalf of four little-known women, including the teenagers Claudette Colvin and Mary Louise Smith, who had acted on their own months before Parks's arrest. On the morning of December 21, 1956, after a protest that had lasted 381 days, King, Nixon, and Abernathy became the first black bus riders to sit legally in the front section of a Montgomery bus.

The Founding of SCLC and King's Widening Influence

"Old Man Segregation is on his death bed," King announced at the MIA's Institute on Nonviolence and Social Change, held as the boycott came to its end. "But history has proven that social systems have a great last-minute breathing power, and the guardians of a status-quo are always on hand with their oxygen tents to keep the old order alive." King added that segregation still existed, not only "in the South in its glaring and conspicuous forms" but also "in the North in its hidden and subtle forms. But if democracy is to live, segregation must die." Thus, even as he celebrated the success of the boycott, King turned the energies of MIA members toward new objectives, such as voter registration and desegregation of educational and recreational facilities.

Grassroots protests against segregation were springing up all over the South, outside the control of any national organization or leader, including King himself. In May 1956, students at Florida A&M University launched their own bus boycott, which soon spread to the city of Tallahassee under the leadership of the Reverend C. K. Steele and the Tallahassee Inter-Civic Council. The following month, black activists in Alabama reacted to that state's banning of the NAACP by forming a new protest group, the Alabama Christian Movement for Human Rights, with fiery Birmingham minister Fred Shuttlesworth as leader. On December 24, 1956, three days after the Montgomery boycott ended, Steele and other activists were arrested for attempting to ride the Tallahassee buses on a desegregated basis. A few days later, Shuttlesworth's home was bombed. The next day King telegraphed Shuttlesworth's supporters, urging them to carry on and, "if necessary, fill up the jails of Birmingham."

King and other leaders recognized the need for a new regional organization to sustain the momentum of the Montgomery movement. With Rustin's behind-the-scenes help, King, joined by Shuttlesworth and Steele, organized a conference of southern black leaders that was held in January 1957 in Atlanta. Although the gathering was disrupted when King and Abernathy rushed back to Montgomery following the bombing of four churches, including Abernathy's, the sixty participants formed the Southern Negro Leaders Conference, which later became the Southern Christian Leadership Conference (SCLC). King was selected to head the new group and help draft a "Statement to the South and Nation" that linked the southern black struggle to global politics:

> Asia's successive revolts against European imperialism, Africa's present ferment for independence, Hungary's death struggle against communism, and the determined drive of Negro Americans to become first class citizens are inextricably bound together. They are all vital factors in determining whether in the Twentieth Century mankind will crown its vast material gains with the achievement of liberty and justice for all, or whether it will commit suicide through lack of moral fibre.

King's growing international prominence became evident when African independence leader Kwame Nkrumah invited him to attend Ghana's independence ceremonies in March 1957. As the leader of the first sub-Saharan African nation to free itself from colonialism, Nkrumah had personal ties to African Americans, having attended college in the United States during the 1930s and 1940s. King traveled to the ceremonies as part of an American delegation that included older and more established black leaders such as A. Philip Randolph, New York Congressman Adam Clayton Powell Jr., and United Nations official Ralph Bunche. The midnight celebration that followed the lowering of the

■ TABLE 17.2 Supreme Court Cases, 1950–1956

***Sweatt* v. *Painter* and *McLaurin* v. *Oklahoma State Regents* (1950):** The Supreme Court declares racially segregated facilities for graduate schools unconstitutional.

***Brown* v. *Board of Education of Topeka* (1954):** The Supreme Court unanimously overturns 1896 *Plessy* decision by ruling that public school segregation is unconstitutional.

***Gayle* v. *Browder* (1956):** The Supreme Court upholds lower court ruling banning segregation on Montgomery, Alabama, buses.

British flag and the raising of the Ghanaian brought tears of joy to King's eyes. "I knew about all of the struggles, and all of the pain, and all of the agony that these people had gone through for this moment." Afterward, King enjoyed a private lunch with Nkrumah and also encountered Vice President Richard Nixon, who was representing the U.S. government. "Mr. Vice President, I'm very glad to meet you here," King gently chided, "but I want you to come visit us down in Alabama where we are seeking the same kind of freedom [Ghana] is celebrating." Nixon responded by arranging a meeting with King in Washington.

Upon his return, King found himself much in demand. He agreed to support a campaign against South Africa's white government and its harsh apartheid policies. He also participated in the Prayer Pilgrimage held at the Lincoln Memorial in May 1957 to mark the third anniversary of the *Brown* decision. Although Randolph, Wilkins, and other established leaders were responsible for organizing the event, the 25,000 demonstrators in attendance gave their most sustained applause to King's rousing closing. "Give us the ballot, and we will no longer plead to the federal government for passage of an anti-lynching law," he proclaimed. "We will by the power of our vote write the law on the statute books of the South and bring an end to the dastardly acts of the hooded perpetrators of violence." The *New York Amsterdam News* reported after the pilgrimage that King had become "the number one leader of sixteen million Negroes in the United States."

Yet King's rapid rise to prominence was accompanied by uncertainties about the roles that he and the SCLC should play in the civil rights movement. SCLC's Crusade for Citizenship, which King announced after he met with Nixon in June 1957, began with the ambitious goal of registering 3 million black voters. But this effort made only modest progress in overcoming racial barriers in voting, including literacy tests and poll taxes. Even the Civil Rights Act of 1957, which passed despite a filibuster by Strom Thurmond and other segregationist senators, did little to stimulate SCLC's voting rights campaign. By the end of 1957, King faced complaints even from within his own organization. Birmingham's Shuttlesworth, who had been beaten by chain-wielding segregationists when he tried to enroll his daughters in an all-white school, urged the SCLC to take the initiative against civil rights opponents "rather than waiting to defend ourselves." Moreover, as King considered the responsibilities and expectations that had been thrust upon him, he wavered between his sense of divinely inspired mission and nagging self-doubt. "One of the frustrations of any young man is to approach the heights at such an early age," he admitted to a reporter. Fearful of "fading from the screen at a time you should just be starting to work toward your goal," King speculated that "no crowds will be waiting outside churches to greet me two years from now when someone invited me to speak."

King's prediction was mistaken, but impetus for continued militancy in the southern civil rights struggle would not come from King or the SCLC. Instead, just as in Farmville, Virginia, and in Montgomery, Alabama, the first stirrings of revolt were localized acts of rebellions, and black teenagers once again took the lead in challenging segregation. Films focused on rebellious youth such as *Rebel Without a Cause* (1955), with James Dean and Sal Mineo, and *Blackboard Jungle* (1955), with Sidney Poitier, signaled the arrival of a new consciousness among young people of all races. By 1957, the nation had become aware of teenage rebelliousness in the form of juvenile delinquency and the craze for rock-and-roll music. The enormous popularity of white singer Elvis Presley and black performers such as Fats Domino and Little Richard demonstrated that the nation's youth had left behind the musical tastes of their parents. During the fall of 1957, as Little Richard reached the top of the music charts with "Lucille" and "Long Tall Sally" and many television viewers turned to American Bandstand, a group of black high school students in Little Rock prepared to begin a new era of the civil rights struggle.

THE LITTLE ROCK NINE

"I think that the first day was probably the most afraid I ever was," fifteen-year-old Minniejean Brown observed as she recalled her arrival at Little Rock's previously all-white Central High School for the initial day of the fall term of 1957. Brown was one of the nine black students to take part in the desegregation effort initiated by Daisy Bates, head of the NAACP's local branch. Selected on the basis of their academic excellence and willingness to become racial pioneers, the nine students worked closely with Bates to prepare themselves for the hostilities they expected to face. The evening before the first day of the fall term, Arkansas Governor Orval Faubus announced he was sending National Guardsmen to deal with the anticipated violence. When the nine black students arrived on the morning of September 4, they quickly realized that the Guardsmen were positioned to block them from entering the school, not to protect them from a jeering mob of white segregationists. "I

As result of the incident, Brown was suspended. A few months later, after a second suspension for "verbal retaliation after provocation," she was expelled. With Bates's help, Brown was able to continue her schooling at New York's New Lincoln High School, living with Mamie and Kenneth Clark, whose research had contributed to the *Brown* decision. The remaining eight students completed the school year in Little Rock, and in June 1958 Ernest Green became the first black student to graduate from Central High. Although Green recalled that there was no applause when he received his diploma, he was satisfied to have finally "cracked the wall."

Though federal power prevailed, Faubus won a third term as governor—and three more after that. Still defiant, he closed all public schools in Little Rock the following year rather than proceed with desegregation. White students attended private schools or schools outside the city, while most African Americans had no school to attend. Finally, following another Supreme Court ruling in 1959, the Little Rock school board reopened Central and resumed the process of desegregating the city's schools. The Little Rock Nine emerged from their harrowing experiences as heroes and role models for many discontented black youths. The NAACP honored them in 1958 with its highest honor, the Spingarn Medal, previously won by Thurgood Marshall and Martin Luther King Jr.

■ Little Rock Nine member Minniejean Brown transferred to a private, desegregated school in New York City in 1958, following a suspension for defending herself against white attacks at Central High School.

Stirrings of Grassroots Revolt

As the Little Rock Nine approached the end of their first semester at Central High, Ella Baker arrived in Atlanta to take on the task of running the SCLC's headquarters. She recalled being disappointed that little had been done to prepare for her arrival. More important, she faced the task of revitalizing an organization that had accomplished little in the year since its founding. Baker was aware that King and other SCLC leaders had made some gains at the local level, but they were ministers who had less history of involvement in the civil rights movement than she did. The fifty-four-year-old Baker had organized consumer cooperatives in New York City during the depression years before joining the NAACP staff in 1940. As the NAACP's director of branches, she traveled extensively, and her contacts with grassroots leaders convinced her that Walter White's bureaucratic leadership often stifled local initiative. Discouraged, she resigned in 1946. During the early 1950s, she headed the NAACP's New York branch and led an effort to end the *de facto*—as opposed to *de jure*, or legally imposed—segregation of New York's school system. After Rosa Parks launched the Montgomery bus boycott, Baker joined with Rustin and leftist white lawyer Stanley Levison to form In Friendship to raise funds for southern civil rights activities. It was Rustin and Levison who convinced King that Baker was the right person to organize the SCLC's headquarters. Although she was disturbed that the decision was made without consulting her—"I don't like anyone to commit me"—she put her hurt feelings aside and agreed to leave New York for Atlanta.

As Baker did her best to invigorate the SCLC, a few local movements, often involving young people, were developing without much guidance from regional or national groups. In 1958, members of NAACP Youth Councils in Wichita, Kansas, and Oklahoma City began using the "sit-down" tactic to desegregate segregated lunch counters. When teenagers in St. Petersburg, Florida, tried to use a public swimming pool, officials responded by closing the pool. In October 1958, over 10,000 students joined baseball star Jackie Robinson and actor Harry Belafonte in a Youth March for Integrated Schools in Washington, DC. (King was scheduled to speak at this event but was bedridden, having barely survived a stabbing by a deranged black woman as he autographed copies of his new book, *Stride Toward Freedom: The Montgomery Story,* at a New York department store.)

During 1959, there were other indications of growing impatience among African Americans with the pace of civil

Melba Pattillo on Being a Racial Pioneer

Melba Patillo was one of the Little Rock Nine. In 1958, after her first year at Central High School, Arkansas Governor Orval Faubus closed all public high schools in the city rather than allow desegregation. White students could go to private academies, but black students had no schools at all to attend. In the excerpt below, Patillo recounts a phone call she received from a friend, Marsha, who had stayed at all-black Horace Mann High rather than transfer to Central High.

"What's gonna happen to us now? Who do you think you are?" she snapped at me from the other end of the line. Sniffing and spewing anger at me, she was barely able to catch her breath. "I'm not gonna get to be a senior this year, and it's all your fault."

"But . . . ," I protested. She cut me off.

"This means we won't have a senior day, senior picnic or a senior prom," she growled. "How can we have anything with our schools closed?" Her voice was angry, her words rude and loud enough to hurt my ears. . . .

I knew they were weary of trying to survive all of the penalties segregationists had dished out to them for supporting us. They blamed those of us who had integrated Central High for all their hardship and now school closed. That meant more hardship, more disappointment, more inconveniences.

When Mother Lois came home after school, I was still distraught over the wrath that was directed at me from my own people. I understood their anger, because they were losing so much. But why didn't they see that our going to Central High would help our people in the long run? Why was their blame so harsh?

"You can't allow anger to stop your doing what you know is right," Mother Lois said, setting her briefcase down on the dining-room table. "Like Grandmother India says, you're opening a door at Central for Marsha and all other Negroes."

Mother Lois sat down as she continued, "When I'd get discouraged about my schoolwork Grandma India would say to me, 'I work hard for my dollar, scrubbing, sweating. I know there's a better life and no one else is going to be a dollar-a-day maid in this family.'"

—from White Is a State of Mind *by Melba Pattillo Beals, copyright © 1999 by Melba Beals. Used by permission of G.P. Putnam's Sons, a division of Penguin Group (USA) Inc.*

To view a longer version of this document, please go to www.ablongman.com/carson/documents.

rights reform. This shift in attitude was reflected in *Raisin in the Sun,* Lorraine Hansberry's highly acclaimed play that opened on Broadway that year. In her story of the Younger family's effort to build a better life for themselves in Chicago, the twenty-eight-year-old Hansberry touched on many of the concerns that fueled black militancy during the 1960s, especially racial discrimination in housing and employment, generational differences between African Americans, and increasing identification with Africa. A still stronger indication of changing attitudes was the television documentary *The Hate That Hate Produced,* which drew attention to the racial separatist doctrines of the Nation of Islam and Malcolm X.

National civil rights leaders could ignore the Nation of Islam, given its small following, but they took more seriously a challenge from Robert F. Williams, head of the NAACP's branch in Monroe, North Carolina. Williams had attracted controversy in 1957 when—abandoning the NAACP's tradition of nonviolence—he suggested that members of the local branch arm themselves against Klan attacks. Two years later, his views became more extreme when he suggested retaliation against an all-white jury that had acquitted a white man of raping a black woman. The NAACP's national office suspended him from his post, but Williams, a military veteran, continued to argue his position forcefully. As an NAACP member and the nation's best-known advocate of nonviolence, King felt compelled to respond by speaking out against Williams at the NAACP annual convention. He published a more extended rebuttal that blamed black impatience on "half-hearted and inadequate" federal enforcement of the *Brown* decision. King noted that even Gandhi accepted armed self-defense "for those unable to master pure nonviolence," but he insisted that calls for "retaliatory violence" would "mislead Negroes into the belief that this is the only path." Instead, he argued that forceful nonviolent tactics were more effective than "a few acts of organized violence." He conceded, however, that nonviolence required "dedicated people, because it is a backbreaking task to arouse, to organize, and to educate tens of thousands for disciplined, sustained action."

In 1956, King had called for greater militancy in his address to the NAACP convention, but just three years later the controversy concerning Williams served as a reminder that King's own organization, the SCLC, had done little to stimulate nonviolent protest movements in the South. By the end of 1959, Ella Baker was convinced that the SCLC should focus its attention on the development of "potential leaders" for "a vital movement of nonviolent direct mass action" throughout the South. Increasingly concerned that the SCLC was devoting its resources to "routine procedures for promoting registration and voting," she argued instead that the group should "develop and use our major weapon—mass resistance." What was needed was "the development of people who are interested not in being leaders as much as in developing leadership among other people." King himself recognized the validity of some criticisms of his leadership. He began making plans to leave Dexter church and move to Atlanta in order to devote all of his time to the SCLC. King also decided that Bayard Rustin should be hired to make the SCLC more effective. But Baker still doubted that the SCLC could become the kind of group she saw as necessary. Although King had emerged from a mass movement of the kind Baker wanted to stimulate throughout the South, would he take the risk of directly involving himself and the SCLC in local protest campaigns? Was he the kind of "creative leader" who could stir up "dynamic mass action"?

THE STUDENT SIT-IN MOVEMENT

Having grown up in Chicago and attended Howard University, Diane Nash remembered feeling "stifled and boxed in" after transferring to Nashville's Fisk University in 1959. She found it difficult to adjust to the segregation she experienced living in the South for the first time. Moreover, she saw segregation as responsible for the South's "slow progress in industrial, political and other areas" and "the weakening of American influence abroad as a result of race hatred." Nash's outlook brightened, however, when she heard about James Lawson's nonviolence workshop, which had already attracted students from several of Nashville's other black colleges.

> Segregation was responsible for "the weakening of American influence abroad."
> —*Diane Nash*

Nash was immediately impressed by Lawson, a black theology student who seemed deeply committed to using nonviolent tactics to bring about social change. During the early 1950s, he had chosen to go to prison rather than serve in the military. Paroled to the Methodist Board of Missions, Lawson spent three years as a missionary in India, where he studied Gandhian ideas. After returning to the United States, he became a field secretary of the Fellowship of Reconciliation, the pacifist group that during the 1940s had hired Bayard Rustin and James Farmer to work on race relations.

After discussing his plans with King in 1958, Lawson decided to move to Nashville, enrolling at the divinity school of predominantly white Vanderbilt University. With support from the SCLC's Nashville affiliate, Lawson began training students in the Gandhian philosophical foundations of nonviolent direct action. Most of Lawson's initial recruits were black students studying to become ministers, notably John Lewis, Bernard Lafayette, and James Bevel of American Baptist Theological Seminary. Nash, raised as a Catholic, nevertheless found she had much in common with the other participants. She began to see nonviolent tactics as "applied religion" designed "to bring about a climate in which there is appreciation of the dignity of man and in which each individual is free to grow and produce to his fullest capacity." By November 1959, Nash and other participants in Lawson's workshop had already begun "test sit-ins" at Nashville department stores. Before they could put their ideas into practice, however, four teenagers in Greensboro, North Carolina, began a new stage of the southern civil rights struggle.

Spread of the Sit-ins

"We always got together and talked about the events that were occurring across the nation and the world," David Richmond recalled of his "bull sessions" with Izell Blair, Franklin McCain, and Joseph McNeil. The four students at North Carolina A&T College had also belonged to NAACP youth groups in high school, but they decided on their own to take action as they talked about the racial discrimination confronting them off-campus. "We challenged each other," Richmond remembered. Late in the afternoon of February 1, 1960, they walked into a Woolworth's "five-and-

Students stage a sit-in at Greensboro's Woolworth's.

dime" store where black students often bought school supplies but were not allowed to eat. The black woman who worked behind the counter chastised them, "You know you are supposed to eat at the other end." The four students were uncertain about what would happen, but they remained seated until the store closed, when they promised to be back in the morning when it opened.

The word *sit-in* had not yet been coined, but the four Greensboro students discovered that other students were eager to use this simple tactic to put segregationists on the defensive. The next morning, about thirty students occupied most of Woolworth's lunch-counter seats. By the third day, student protesters formed the Students Executive Committee for Justice to coordinate protests that culminated at the end of the week in a march of several thousand students from the A&T campus to Greensboro's downtown. Meanwhile, black students at nearby black colleges began planning similar protests of their own. By the end of the first week, the sit-in movement had spread through North Carolina to all-black Hampton Institute and to other places in Virginia. In the first major arrests of the sit-in campaign, police in Raleigh, North Carolina, arrested forty-one students on February 12.

Spurred by news of these protests, Nash and other workshop participants began organizing a major protest campaign in Nashville that began on February 13 with a sit-in by 124 carefully trained and disciplined black students. On February 27, police arrested student protesters who had occupied all the seats at a downtown lunch counter, but more students quickly took the places of those taken away. In all, eighty-two demonstrators, including Diane Nash, were arrested that day, and sixty more were arrested the following week. Black residents reacted to the jailing of students by supporting a boycott of downtown businesses. On April 19, a bomb exploded at the home of Alexander Looby, a black city councilman who had served as legal counsel to the arrested students. Rather than deterring the protests, this violence prompted 2,500 demonstrators to march silently to City Hall, where Diane Nash confronted Nashville's mayor, forcing him to concede that segregation was wrong. Soon afterward, the campaign achieved its first major concessions when several businesses ended their segregation policies.

During the spring, student-led sit-ins achieved similar success in other communities. Although black colleges had experienced protests before, these had usually been about issues such as student rules or poor food in dining halls. Suddenly, students on dozens of campuses demonstrated their eagerness to risk jail in expanding the meaning of the *Brown* decision and speeding the pace of racial change. By the end of the school year, more than 3,000 students had been arrested.

A New Black Consciousness

By forcing concessions from white leaders, student activists transformed their own self-image. They became, as Nash put it, "suddenly proud to be called 'black.'" Students acting independently rather than on behalf of a civil rights group initiated the protests and grew ever-more confident in their ability to direct campaigns without adult leadership. Although many of the students were affiliated with NAACP youth groups or received support from local NAACP branches, the new movement offered an implicit challenge to the cautious strategy of the nation's oldest civil rights group. NAACP leaders, for their part, gave public support to the sit-ins but privately questioned the usefulness of student-led mass protests. Marshall only reluctantly agreed to provide legal assistance to students "who violated the sacred property rights of white folks." King's response to the sit-ins was far more favorable. He applauded the students for taking their "honored places in the world-wide struggle for freedom." He was particularly impressed by their willingness to remain nonviolent despite provocation and to go to jail to achieve change. Yet, although he sympathized with the student protestors, he remained reluctant to involve his group in a direct action campaign.

For Ella Baker, however, the sit-in movement was a welcome response to her pleas for mass militancy at the local level. Impatient with King's cautious leadership and disenchanted with the SCLC's failure to build on the momentum of the Montgomery bus boycott movement, she saw the student activists as "refreshing indeed" to those like herself "who bear the scars of battle, the frustrations and the disillusionment that come when the prophetic leader turns out to have heavy feet of clay." She admired the strong desire of student activists to remain independent of adult leadership. The local student protest groups seemed to confirm her view that the civil rights movement did not need a "strong, savior-type leader" like King. By this time, Baker also knew the male clergymen who ran the SCLC wanted to replace her with a male minister (Virginia minister Wyatt Walker was their candidate) who would be less contentious.

Aware that her time in the SCLC was limited, she proposed that the group sponsor a meeting of student sit-in leaders from across the South. Baker invited more than one hundred young people to discuss nonviolent philosophy and tactics at an Easter weekend leadership training session at North Carolina's Shaw College in Raleigh, where she had been an undergraduate in the 1920s. Nearly 300 students showed up, including a dozen southern white students. Both King and James Lawson were invited to speak. Lawson's address came close to capturing the tone of student militancy, especially when he criticized the NAACP for stressing "fund-raising and court action rather than developing our greatest resources, a people no longer the victims of racial evil who can act in a disciplined manner to implement the constitution."

Baker resisted pressure to have the students at the meeting with the SCLC or other existing civil rights groups. "I thought they had the right to direct their own affairs and even make their own mistakes," she later explained. The students decided to form the Student Nonviolent Coordinating Committee (SNCC—pronounced "snick"), selecting Fisk student Marion Barry as chairman. The statement of purpose Lawson drafted for the new group affirmed "the philosophical or religious ideal of nonviolence as the foundation of our purpose, the presupposition of our faith, and the manner of our action." Initially unable to afford its own quarters, SNCC established its office in SCLC's Atlanta headquarters, where Baker still worked. As the protest leaders who affiliated with SNCC met over the next few months, many found that Baker's ideas about organizing coincided with their own desire to keep their local sit-in groups free from the control of older and more cautious civil rights organizations and leaders. "She was much older in terms of age," Nashville activist John Lewis recalled, "but I think in terms of ideas and philosophy and commitment she was one of the youngest persons in the movement." Most of the students who affiliated with SNCC also admired King, but they increasingly saw themselves as spearheads of the southern civil rights struggle. Although King himself was barely in his thirties, there was already a generational gulf dividing student advocates of civil disobedience and the somewhat more cautious SCLC leaders.

Even when King, after moving to Atlanta, joined students in an October 1960 sit-in at a department store, he did so only at their prodding, and he later admitted that he took part "only as a follower, not a leader." His arrest, however, attracted national attention and unexpectedly played a crucial role in the 1960 presidential election. When Georgia authorities released the protesters after several days in jail, they promptly rearrested King on charges of violating conditions of his earlier parole for driving in Atlanta with his Alabama driver's license. King was then sentenced to six months at hard labor—"all over a traffic violation," he complained. King feared for his life at Georgia's Reidville State Prison; as a prominent black leader, he was sure to be the target of prison violence. Civil rights advocates mobilized to have King released on bond, and Democratic candidate John Kennedy telephoned Coretta Scott King to express concern while his brother and campaign manager Robert Kennedy worked behind the scenes to secure King's release. A Georgia judge agreed to release King. News of John Kennedy's intervention strengthened his support among black voters and contributed to his narrow victory over Republican Richard Nixon.

Although King was skeptical about Kennedy's commitment to civil rights reform and reluctant to publicly support either candidate, he was disappointed by Nixon's unwillingness to take a similar action, given the cordial relations he had established with the vice president when they met in Ghana in 1957. "I really considered him a moral coward," King later wrote. "I am convinced that he lost the election because of that."

CONCLUSION

The 1950s are often viewed as a period of complacency and conformity in the United States, but the spread of civil rights activism shows that discontent simmered in many black communities. To be sure, Cold War anticommunism had quieted the once powerful voices of W. E. B. Du Bois and Paul Robeson, but youthful political activism emerged as a major challenge to NAACP dominance at the national level. Less than two years after the organization achieved its great victory in the *Brown* case, the Montgomery bus boycott demonstrated that many black southerners were eager to challenge the Jim Crow system and speed the pace of racial reform. As a result of the success of the boycott, King emerged as a major civil rights leader whose stature, in time, surpassed that of NAACP leaders Roy Wilkins and Thurgood Marshall.

But King himself was a product of the Montgomery boycott movement rather than its initiator. Like many subsequent local protest movements of the late 1950s and afterward, the boycott was a grassroots movement that relied on the initiatives of local activists more than existing civil rights groups. In the decade following the student protest at Virginia's Moton High School, youthful leaders initiated many local protest movements and forced older, more established leaders to follow. Moreover, the Little Rock Nine managed to force the hand of the federal government by refusing to back down in the face of mob violence. When President Eisenhower reluctantly sent troops to Little Rock, young black people elsewhere learned a lesson that shaped subsequent African American politics: Local protests could break down racial barriers and capture the attention of the nation and even the world. By the early 1960s, King's prominence in the civil rights movement was well established, but the 1960 wave of sit-ins made clear that the increasingly militant African-American freedom struggle was not under the control of any one leader or organization.

FURTHER READING

Abernathy, Ralph David. *And the Walls Came Tumbling Down: An Autobiography* (New York: Harper and Row, 1989).

Beals, Melba Pattillo. *Warriors Don't Cry: A Searing Memoir of the Battle to Integrate Little Rock's Central High* (New York: Washington Square, 1994).

Branch, Taylor. *Parting the Waters: America in the King Years, 1954–1963* (New York: Simon and Schuster, 1988).

Brinkley, Douglas. *Rosa Parks* (New York: Viking Penguin, 2000).

Carson, Clayborne, et al., eds. *The Papers of Martin Luther King, Jr.*, vol. III, *Birth of a New Age, December 1955–December 1956* (Berkeley: University of California Press, 1997).

Chafe, William H. *Civilities and Civil Rights: Greensboro, North Carolina, and the Black Struggle for Freedom* (New York: Oxford University Press, 1980).

Clark, Septima. *Echo in My Soul* (New York: E. P. Dutton, 1962).

Halberstam, David. *The Children* (New York: Random House, 1998).

King, Martin Luther, Jr. *Stride Toward Freedom: The Montgomery Story* (New York: Harper and Row, 1958).

Kluger, Richard. *Simple Justice: The History of Brown v. Board of Education and Black America's Struggle for Equality* (New York: Random House, 1975).

Levine, Ellen. *Freedom's Children: Young Civil Rights Activists Tell Their Own Stories* (New York: Avon, 1993).

Moody, Anne. *Coming of Age in Mississippi* (New York: Dell, 1965).

Morris, Aldon D. *Origins of the Civil Rights Movement: Black Communities Organizing for Change* (New York: Free Press, 1984).

Ransby, Barbara. *Ella Baker and the Black Freedom Movement: A Radical Democratic Vision* (Chapel Hill: University of North Carolina Press, 2003).

Robinson, Jo Ann. *The Montgomery Bus Boycott and the Women Who Started It* (Knoxville: University of Tennessee, 1989).

Tyson, Timothy B. *Radio-Free Dixie: Robert F. Williams and the Roots of Black Power* (Chapel Hill: University of North Carolina Press, 1999).

Whitfield, Stephen J. *A Death in the Delta: The Story of Emmett Till* (New York: Free Press, 1988).

Williams, Juan. *Thurgood Marshall: American Revolutionary* (New York: Crown, 1998).

CHAPTER 18

Standing in a sea of flags, marchers wait for the signal to move into Montgomery at conclusion of the Selma-to-Montgomery voting rights march of 1965.

Marching Toward Freedom, 1960–1966

Freedom Riders Challenge Segregation

"We can't let them stop us with violence," Diane Nash told James Farmer during the freedom ride campaign of May 1961. "If we do, the movement is dead." Nash, a leader in the Nashville Student Movement and the new Student Nonviolent Coordinating Committee (SNCC), had just turned twenty-three. Farmer, age forty-one, had a lifetime of experience with civil rights activism. He had been Nash's age when he helped found the Congress of Racial Equality (CORE). This was his second freedom ride, having participated in CORE's 1947 Journey of Reconciliation, which involved sending black and white volunteers on a bus ride through the South to test local compliance with a Supreme Court ruling banning segregation in interstate transportation. In the 1961 freedom ride campaign, Farmer joined twelve other riders, seven of them white, on two buses that left Washington, DC, on a trip that was intended to culminate in New Orleans. The riders purposely disregarded signs designating waiting rooms and restrooms as "Colored Only" and "Whites Only." The activists soon found that while bus companies might be willing to comply with the antisegregation laws, white segregationists in the Deep South were not.

Farmer and the other participants encountered increasing violence as they ventured farther into the South. In Rock Hill, South Carolina, several riders were assaulted; outside Anniston, Alabama, someone in an angry mob threw a firebomb into the bus. The freedom riders escaped, but a photograph of the burning bus became front-page news across the nation. When the second bus arrived at Birmingham, Alabama, the riders were savagely beaten with pipes and baseball bats. Ignoring warnings of violence, Birmingham police were conveniently absent. In light of the attacks, Farmer decided to call off the ride. Then he got a phone call from Diane Nash.

"Would you have any objections to members of the Nashville Student Movement, which is SNCC, going in and taking up the Ride where CORE left off?" she asked.

CHAPTER OUTLINE

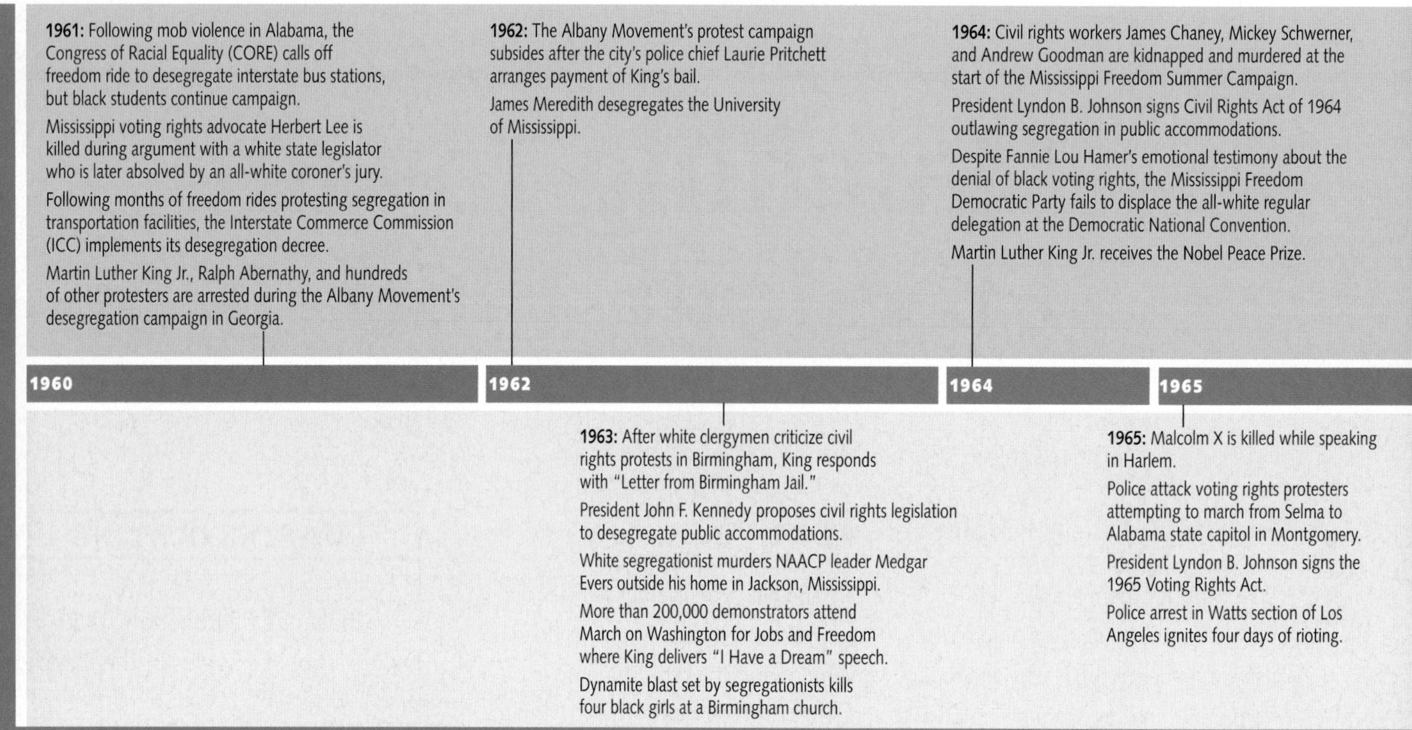

"You realize it may be suicide," Farmer warned.

"We fully realize that," replied Nash, undeterred. "Let me send in fresh nonviolent troops to carry the Ride on. Let me bring in Nashville students to pick up the baton and run with it."

Though she had only recently been an undergraduate student at Fisk, Nash was herself a movement veteran. A participant in James Lawson's workshops on nonviolence, she had been instrumental in the sit-ins that desegregated Nashville lunch counters. Earlier in 1961 she had joined an antisegregation "jail-in" in Rock Hill, South Carolina, serving a thirty-day jail sentence to make the point that nonviolent demonstrators should not accept bail money and thereby become dependent on the financial and legal assistance of others. On returning to Nashville, she dropped out of Fisk to devote herself full time to the movement, working on behalf of both SNCC and SCLC. "I'll be doing this for the rest of my life," she told a *Jet* magazine reporter.

After gaining Farmer's reluctant assent, Nash called Birmingham minister and civil rights leader Fred Shuttlesworth to inform him that students would begin arriving to continue CORE's campaign. She quickly mobilized support in Nashville, securing financial backing from black ministers in the local SCLC affiliate and recruiting student volunteers. Ten young people stepped forward. "Several made out wills," she recalled. "A few more gave me sealed letters to be mailed if they were killed. Some told me frankly that they were afraid, but they knew this was something that they must do because freedom was worth it."

The Nashville contingent left for Birmingham on May 17, the seventh anniversary of the *Brown* decision, but as they arrived, Birmingham's notoriously racist police chief, Theophilus Eugene "Bull" Conner, ordered the new freedom riders taken to the Birmingham jail. The following night, he released them at the Alabama state border. They walked in the dark to a black farmer's home, where they telephoned Nash. She immediately sent a car to return them to Birmingham, even as news reports claimed that they were back at their campuses. "The police chief wasn't going to get off that easily," Nash explained.

Within days, more freedom riders gathered at Shuttlesworth's home in Birmingham. Injecting new energy into the southern struggle, they boarded buses, undeterred by the mob assault in Birmingham or the violence they later encountered on arriving at Montgomery's bus terminal. Martin Luther King Jr., who declined Nash's initial request to join the free-

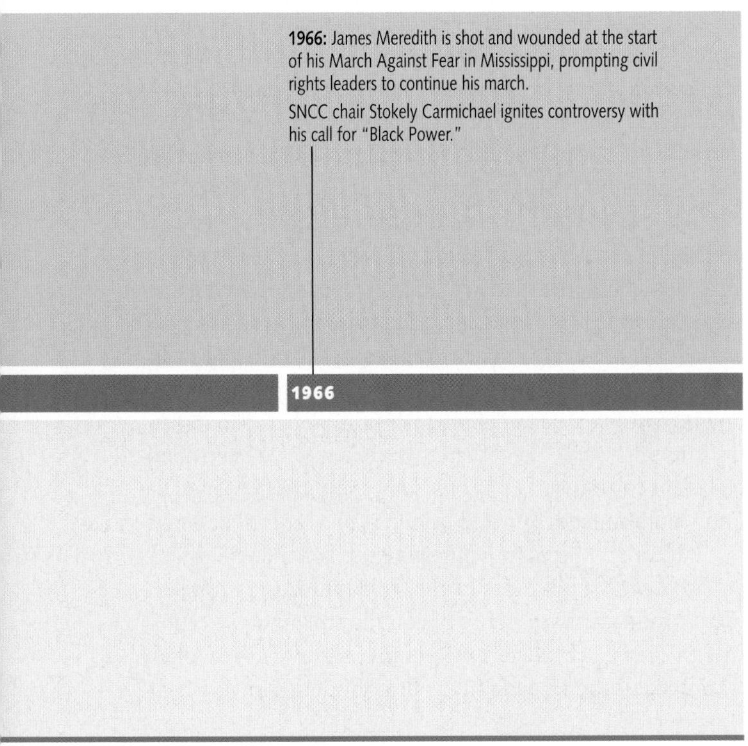

dom ride campaign, responded to the Montgomery violence by addressing an evening rally at a local black church. White rioters laid siege to the packed church, keeping occupants inside until U.S. marshals and Alabama National Guardsmen intervened to restore order.

Thus, within a week of Nash's decision to continue the freedom ride, student activists had prodded Farmer and King toward greater militancy and forced state and federal officials to intervene on their behalf. Segregationist violence had not deterred them but instead had made them more determined. The youthful freedom riders were, in Nash's words, "dead serious. We're ready to give our lives."

Diane Nash's determination to resume the freedom rides soon had major consequences for the southern civil rights movement. During May and June of 1961, the Freedom Ride Coordinating Committee she headed attracted a growing number of veterans of the sit-ins of the previous year, and this cadre of activists spearheaded a determined assault against the bastions of Jim Crow. Although the sit-in movement of 1960 had not reached the rural Deep South (there had been no sit-ins in the entire state of Mississippi), the freedom ride campaign spurred local civil rights leaders in rural Georgia, Alabama, and Mississippi to greater activism.

The freedom rides and the subsequent voting rights efforts in the Deep South posed a challenge to newly elected president John F. Kennedy. In January 1961, the forty-three-year-old Kennedy announced in his inaugural address that the torch had been passed to a new generation born in the twentieth century, but the young president could not have anticipated that during his administration still younger African Americans, many of them college students, would pick up the torch of advancing the cause of human rights. By 1961, thirty-two-year-old Martin Luther King Jr. had already become better known and more influential than older black leaders such as CORE's Farmer and the NAACP's Roy Wilkins and Thurgood Marshall. But Nash and other impatient SNCC workers were taking the initiative even from King.

Black students spearheaded the desegregation protests of the early 1960s, but African Americans of all ages and backgrounds were soon affected by the increasing militancy. Although student activists saw their direct action tactics as preferable to King's more cautious approach and the NAACP's reliance on litigation and lobbying, these alternative strategies did not necessarily conflict with one another. The increasing diversity of organizations and leaders made the civil rights struggle more difficult for anyone to control or suppress. Like Roosevelt, Truman, and Eisenhower, President Kennedy tried to avoid taking a stand on divisive and controversial civil rights issues, but he and his successor, Lyndon B. Johnson, were forced to respond to escalating demands for major civil rights reforms. Overcoming decades of southern intransigence, African Americans prodded national leaders to enact the Civil Rights Act of 1964 and the Voting Rights Act of 1965. But even these reforms did not still the festering racial discontents that became evident as southern mass protests gave way to mass insurrections in the urban North.

By the mid-1960s, the civil rights struggle had become a liberation struggle that sought not only to eliminate racial barriers but also to deal with poverty and the legacy of past injustices. Having overcome the Jim Crow system, African Americans engaged in intense debates about the future direction of the struggle. Influenced by black nationalist leaders such as Malcolm X, some activists who had once used nonviolence to bring about desegregation began to call for black power and racial separation. As the focus of the black struggle shifted from the rural South to the urban North, established black leaders such as King once again faced challenges from younger activists more willing to display greater militancy to achieve ever more ambitious goals.

GRASSROOTS STRUGGLES IN THE DEEP SOUTH

The Mississippi prison called Parchman Farm seemed a throwback to slavery. "I'd heard about Parchman in the same way I'd heard about Mississippi—in tones of horror and terms of brutality," freedom rider John Lewis recalled. A recent graduate of Nashville's American Baptist Theological Seminary, Lewis was the youngest of the original group of CORE freedom riders and had been beaten during a stop in Rock Hill, South Carolina. He left to be interviewed for a Quaker program to build homes in Africa or India, but on learning that his fellow freedom riders had been attacked by mobs in Alabama's Anniston and Birmingham, Lewis volunteered to continue the ride as one of Diane Nash's recruits. He was among those knocked unconscious when the freedom riders' bus arrived in Montgomery on May 20, 1961 and still wore head bandages from that assault when he rode another bus from Montgomery to Jackson, Mississippi.

After Lewis and dozens of other freedom riders were arrested as their buses arrived in Jackson, they were held in local jails and then sent to Parchman, where most served their sixty-day sentences. Lewis and other prisoners were forced to stand naked for two and a half hours after being strip-searched. "I could see that this was an attempt to break us down, to humiliate and dehumanize us, to rob us of our identity and self-worth," Lewis later wrote. A decade later, a federal court ruled that the prison's living conditions violated the Fourteenth Amendment and "modern standards of decency."

Although Mississippi officials expected that conditions at Parchman would deter further freedom rides, imprisonment produced a new sense of community among freedom riders. Lewis recalled exchanging ideas with Stokely Carmichael, the fast-talking, self-confident Howard Uni-

National Guard soldiers escort Freedom Riders along their ride from Montgomery, Alabama, to Jackson, Mississippi.

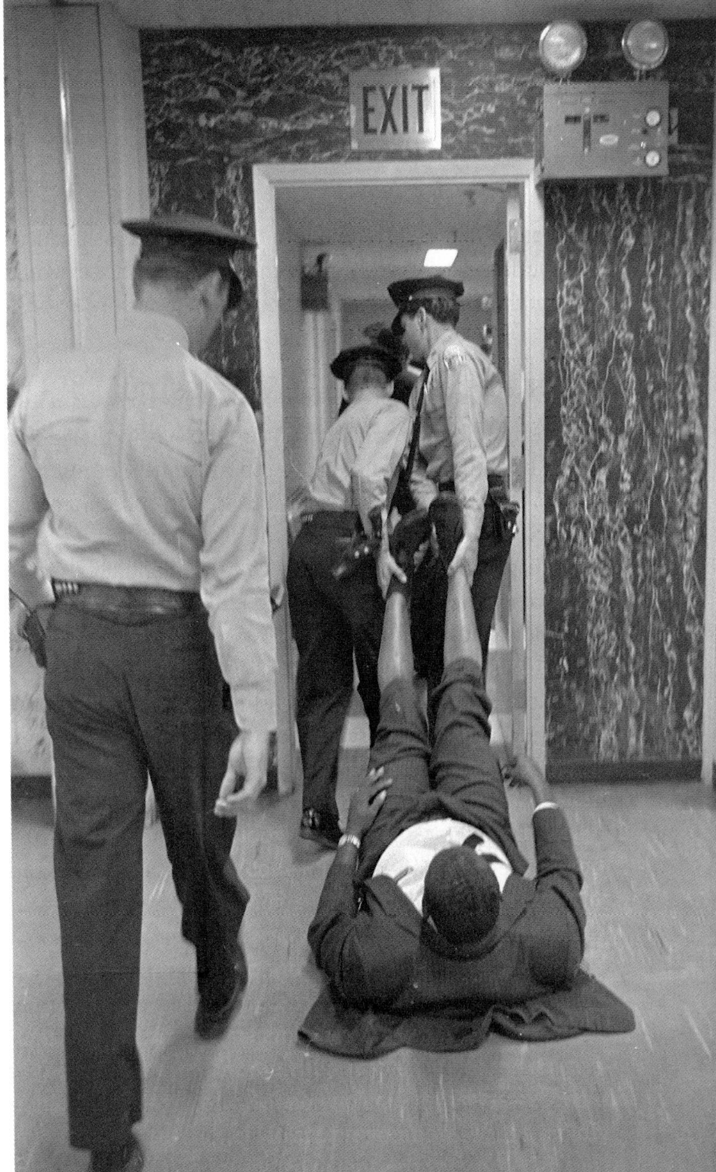

■ New Orleans police officers haul away Reverend Avery Alexander, who was participating in a sit-in protest against the city's racial policies in the City Hall cafeteria on Halloween, 1963.

versity philosophy major who sharply questioned the Christian-Gandhian principles that guided most of the Nashville student activists. "He was as different from me as night from day, both in personality and in philosophy," Lewis recalled, "but for some reason I liked him." After his release in July, Lewis boarded a train back to Nashville, but the experience had changed him. "If there was anything I learned from that long, bloody trip of 1961, it was this—that we were in for a long, bloody fight here in the American South."

The freedom riders' determination set them on a collision course with the Kennedy administration. Their slogan—"Freedom Now"—and their demand for attention to civil rights was at odds with the priority of the new president, who wanted to focus on Cold War concerns such as removing Fidel Castro's new revolutionary government in Cuba. Black voters had played a crucial role in Kennedy's election, but the administration feared it would alienate southern white Democrats if it supported civil rights reforms. In June, when Diane Nash joined a delegation that met with Attorney General Robert Kennedy, the president's brother, she doubted he would follow through on his promise that the Justice Department would seek a new ruling from the Interstate Commerce Commission to eliminate segregation at bus terminals. Nash also rejected Kennedy's plea that the freedom riders concentrate on voter registration rather than continuing more controversial direct action protests like the freedom rides. The administration went ahead with plans to arrange financial backing for efforts to register black voters. Although student activists recognized the importance of voting rights and welcomed the prospect of securing funds for full-time staff members, Nash felt the Kennedy administration merely wanted to redirect their militancy toward less controversial goals.

During the summer of 1961, the increasingly bitter conflict between those such as Nash who wanted to continue desegregation protests and those who favored a shift toward voting rights efforts threatened SNCC's future. When John Lewis heard about the dispute after he emerged from Parchman in July, he joined Nash in rejecting the administration's financial incentives for voter registration efforts. "Direct action was what had gotten us this far," Lewis explained. "SNCC had been created and built on the foundation of confrontation—disciplined, focused, aggressive, nonviolent confrontation."

Although the debate over SNCC's future at first threatened to split it apart, the group's adviser, Ella Baker, fashioned a compromise that divided the organization into a voter registration wing and a direct action wing under Diane Nash. This organizational division became unimportant, however, as SNCC field secretaries sent to Mississippi and southwest Georgia soon found that segregationist opposition to any kind of civil rights activity was far more intense in rural areas of the Deep South than in the urban areas, where most of the sit-ins had occurred. In addition to rigorously enforcing segregation laws, southern white officials restricted black political participation through literacy tests, poll taxes, intimidation, and outright violence against people who dared to challenge the status quo. Although black residents constituted almost half of Mississippi's population, less than 5 percent were registered to vote, and few of these were in the state's rural areas. "We would learn almost immediately that voter

"We would learn almost immediately that voter registration was as threatening to the white establishment in the South as sit-ins and Freedom Rides."—John Lewis

■ Arrested numerous times during his lifetime, it was in Birmingham that Martin Luther King Jr. defended his protest strategy in his eloquent "Letter from Birmingham City Jail."

Sea of injustice and find their way into the promised land of integration and freedom."

King whispered to himself, "I must go." This decision proved a crucial turning point in the Birmingham campaign. As anticipated, the police arrested him and other marchers for "parading without a permit," but King's jailing increased the campaign's national support. Singer and actor Harry Belafonte raised sufficient bail bonds to sustain the movement, and President Kennedy phoned Coretta Scott King to express concern about her husband's arrest.

While jailed, King learned that eight white city clergymen had publicly denounced the Birmingham campaign as "unwise and untimely." Recognizing the opportunity to defend his protest strategy, he began drafting a response letter. King's eloquent "Letter from Birmingham City Jail" argued that white resistance to black equality had forced blacks to move outside legal channels and create a crisis rather than wait forever for change: "When you are harried by day and haunted by night by the fact that you are a Negro, living constantly at tiptoe stance, never quite knowing what to expect next, and are plagued by inner fears and outer resentments; when you are forever fighting a degenerating sense of 'nobodiness'—then you will understand why we find it difficult to wait." Seeing himself as caught between the "force of complacency" in black communities and the "force of bitterness and hatred" represented by black racial separatists, King insisted that he offered "the more excellent way of love and nonviolent protest." If this alternative had not emerged, he wrote, "by now many streets of the South would, I am convinced, be flowing with blood."

> "When you are forever fighting a degenerating sense of 'nobodiness'—then you will understand why we find it difficult to wait."
>
> —*Martin Luther King Jr.*

After King's jailing, the Birmingham demonstrations increased in intensity, and so did the arrests. By early May, more than 3,000 had been jailed. Faced with the possibility that Birmingham officials, like those in Albany, would crush the movement through mass arrests, SCLC leaders followed the urging of former Nashville student activist James Bevel to allow children to participate in marches. It was a risky decision, but it greatly expanded participation in the demonstrations. "For the first time in the civil rights movement, we were able to put into effect the Gandhian principle: 'Fill up the jails,'" King observed. On May 7, after thousands of schoolchildren marched into Birmingham's business district, police used fire hoses and police dogs to disperse them. Worldwide news coverage of the police attacks and the chaotic conditions in Birmingham's downtown area proved decisive in Kennedy's decision to send a Justice Department official to initiate negotiations between civil rights advocates and the city's white leaders.

Concerned that continuing protests would severely damage the city's economy, some local businessmen privately indicated their readiness to negotiate a settlement. King was caught between Kennedy administration officials seeking to suspend the protests and Shuttlesworth and other local leaders who wanted to continue them until concessions were actually implemented. Although relations between King and Shuttlesworth frayed as they debated whether to call off the demonstrations, the two were finally able to agree on a settlement calling for gradual desegregation of public facilities and a modest expansion of employment opportunities for black workers. City officials also agreed to release jailed demonstrators. Having achieved his first major victory since the Montgomery bus boycott, King jubilantly proclaimed that "the walls of segregation" would crumble in Birmingham.

Just as the protests subsided, however, a bomb exploded at the home of King's brother, a Birmingham minister involved in the movement, and another unexploded bomb was discovered near the room King often used at the Gaston Motel. In response, angry demonstrators clashed with police. King feared the truce would unravel in violence, but President Kennedy mobilized federal troops to restore order. Rather than give in to segregationist intimidation, Birmingham's white leaders reaffirmed the agreement they had negotiated with protesters.

By this time, the Birmingham protests had sparked many others elsewhere in the nation. An estimated 930 protest demonstrations took place in more than one hundred cities during the spring and summer of 1963. In contrast to the earlier student-led sit-ins, some of these mass demonstrations involved large numbers of working-class blacks, and large-scale protests occurred in northern as well as southern cities. Chicago experienced major protests against public school segregation, and San Francisco police arrested hundreds of demonstrators demanding job opportunities in downtown hotels. King and other leaders of national civil rights organizations tried with only modest success to guide the escalating mass marches and demonstrations of 1963. The protests indicated that the civil rights movement had become national.

In *The Fire Next Time* (1962), James Baldwin expressed the increasingly militant mood of black Americans.

James Baldwin and the New Black Militancy

The difficulties black leaders faced were largely hidden from public view, but they did not escape the notice of the gifted black writer James Baldwin. Born in Harlem, Baldwin was deeply affected by the changing climate of American race relations during the 1950s and 1960s, even though he had left the United States in 1948 to live in Paris. "I left America because I doubted my ability to survive the fury of the color problem here," he once explained. His acclaimed early novels, *Go Tell It On the Mountain* (1953) and *Giovanni's Room* (1956), paid little attention to civil rights issues, but he found it difficult to avoid being drawn into the movement during his visits to the United States. When he took an assignment from a magazine to travel through the South to report on the struggle, the resulting perceptive articles soon made him an important and influential spokesperson for the new black militancy.

Baldwin was particularly interested in King, seeing him as increasingly "beleaguered"—caught between "his enemies in the white South" and black Americans who had become "bitter, disappointed, skeptical." When Baldwin first interviewed King in 1957, he was impressed by the Montgomery minister's singular abilities as a preacher. Himself the son of a Harlem preacher, Baldwin felt that King's "secret" lay "in his intimate knowledge of the people he is addressing, be they black or white, and in the forthrightness with which he speaks of those things which hurt and battle them." By 1961, however, Baldwin realized King faced a difficult challenge as he attempted to steer a path between militancy and moderation.

In a 1961 essay entitled "The Dangerous Road Before Martin Luther King," Baldwin predicted the problems King would face as he moved beyond the traditional accommodationist role played by black leaders such as Booker T. Washington, who had aimed "not to make the Negro a first-class citizen but to keep him content as a second-class one." King, according to Baldwin, would have to "break, at last, with the habits and attitudes, stratagems, and fears of the past" in order to remain an effective leader. Baldwin concluded that the southern civil rights struggle was the beginning of a painful process of transforming African American identity: "The Negro who will emerge out of this present struggle—whoever, indeed, this dark stranger may prove to be—will not be dependent, in any way at all, on any of the props and crutches which help form our identity now."

Baldwin's journalistic investigation of the black struggle brought him into contact with not only King and black student protesters but also followers of the Nation of Islam's Elijah Muhammad and the group's outspoken minister, Malcolm X. As a Harlem native, Baldwin understood why many disillusioned urban blacks had turned from Christianity toward the racial separatism of the Black Muslims. After interviewing Malcolm in 1961, Baldwin came to share the Muslim minister's skepticism about the use of nonviolent tactics to achieve civil rights reforms. "In the United States, violence and heroism have been made synonymous except when it comes to blacks, and the only way to defeat Malcolm's point is to concede it and to ask oneself why this is so," Baldwin remarked. He added, "There *is* no reason that black men should be expected to be more patient, more forbearing, more farseeing than whites; indeed, quite the contrary."

> "There *is* no reason that black men should be expected to be more patient, more forbearing, more farseeing than whites."
> *—James Baldwin*

Early the following year, Baldwin described the increasingly militant mood of black Americans in a best-selling book of essays, *The Fire Next Time*. He shocked many readers when he posed the question, "Do I really want to be integrated into a burning house?" Questioning whether "the four-hundred-year travail of the American Negro should result merely in his attainment of the present level of the American civilization," he concluded that the "only thing white people have that black people need, or should want, is power—and no one holds power forever." Although Baldwin's basic message was that white and black Americans could redeem themselves by accepting their common multiracial culture, he also warned that without such understanding the nation might destroy itself: "The Negroes of this country may never be able to rise to power, but they are very well placed indeed to precipitate chaos and bring down the curtain on the American dream."

In May 1963, Baldwin assembled a group of civil rights leaders and several politically active entertainers, including Harry Belafonte and Lena Horne, for a meeting at Attorney General Robert Kennedy's New York apartment. Baldwin hoped the group would convey the dissatisfaction black Americans felt in the aftermath of the Birmingham campaign. A former freedom rider angrily berated Kennedy, and several other black participants sharply questioned the Kennedy administration's failure to respond to black civil rights demands. This angry exchange reflected the changing mood of many African Americans in the North who admired the sacrifices of southern civil rights protestors yet saw few changes in their everyday lives. Black Americans recognized the need for new civil rights legislation, but they also recognized that legislation to eliminate *de jure,* or legally mandated, segregation in the South would have no effect on the widespread *de facto* segregation in the North.

After Robert Kennedy told the president of the emotions displayed at the New York meeting, the two concluded that black discontent would not be assuaged without major new civil rights legislation. King had previously seen President Kennedy as lacking emotional involvement with racial issues: "He had never really had the personal experience of knowing the deep groans and passionate yearnings of the Negro for freedom, because he just didn't know Negroes generally and he hadn't had any experience in the civil rights struggle." But this began to change after Alabama governor George Wallace challenged a Supreme Court order calling for the desegregation of the University of Alabama by barring black students.

This challenge to federal authority and the mass protests in Birmingham were clearly on President Kennedy's mind when he delivered a nationally televised address explaining the need for civil rights legislation to desegregate public accommodation. He asked white Americans to contemplate the plight of black citizens: "Who among us would be content to have the color of his skin changed and stand in his place? Who among us would be content with the counsels of patience and delay?" Kennedy declared that a "moral crisis" faced the nation and told listeners that civil rights demands could not be "quieted by token moves or talk." He pleaded, "It is time to act in the Congress, in your state and local legislative body, and above all, in all our daily lives."

March on Washington for Jobs and Freedom

The Kennedy administration proposed legislation to end racial segregation and discrimination, but its prospects for passage were by no means assured. Filibusters by southern senators had defeated or severely weakened previous civil rights bills, and no one was certain Kennedy would risk his other priorities to push the legislation through Congress. The President realized, however, that he also faced risks if the legislation did *not* pass, given the escalating black discontent. During the spring of 1963, veteran civil rights and labor leader A. Philip Randolph added to the pressure on Kennedy by calling for a march on Washington. It was the same tactic he had used to wrest concessions from President Franklin Roosevelt in 1941. Randolph hoped the proposed march would similarly push Kennedy's hand as well as give discontented black people a nonviolent outlet for their frustrations.

As he tried to build support for the march, Randolph found that black leaders were far from united, with some fearing the march might turn into a massive act of civil disobedience. Therefore, Randolph, King, and other national civil rights leaders met with President Kennedy on June 22 at the White House. While assuring the president of their support for new civil rights legislation, the delegation also made clear that substantial changes would have to come quickly to prevent black discontent from exploding into violence. When Kennedy initially objected to the march, Randolph responded, "Negroes were already in the streets. It is very likely impossible to get them off." Further, he advised Kennedy, "If they are bound to be in the streets in any case, is it not better that they be led by organizations dedicated to civil rights and disciplined by struggle rather than to leave them to other leaders who care neither about civil rights nor about nonviolence?" Kennedy decided to support the efforts of established leaders such as Randolph to remain in control of planning the event, and members of his administration helped secure funding for the major civil rights groups.

Kennedy's concerns extended beyond the possibility that the march might get out of control. Following the White House meeting with civil rights leaders, the president talked privately with King about his fear that southern politicians would exploit allegations that communists were active in the civil rights movement. The president's worries led Attorney General Robert Kennedy to give in to FBI director J. Edgar Hoover's request for secret surveillance of King. Although the resulting surveillance uncovered no evidence of communist influence on King, it eventually produced other damaging information, including indications that King was involved in extramarital sexual relationships.

Anticommunist fears also imperiled Bayard Rustin's role as march organizer after southerners in Congress called attention to Rustin's involvement with communists during the 1930s. By 1963, however, Rustin was viewed by many

It was during the 1963 March on Washington for Jobs and Freedom that Martin Luther King Jr. made his famous "I Have a Dream" speech.

civil rights supporters as a political moderate when compared to SNCC militants, and his political history was less a source of vulnerability than his homosexuality was. Randolph gave Rustin crucial support, insisting segregationists not be allowed to discredit the best qualified person to mobilize national support for the march.

The March on Washington for Jobs and Freedom, on August 28, 1963, was the largest civil rights demonstration ever held. Randolph, Rustin, and other march organizers drew support from a wide range of labor and religious groups, attracting more than 200,000 supporters to the area in front of the Lincoln Memorial. Many arrived by chartered buses sponsored by black churches and local organizations all over the country. The march brought together many of the black leaders associated with earlier racial advances. Former baseball star Jackie Robinson was there, as was CORE leader James Farmer, Urban League head Whitney Young, and U.N. diplomat Ralph Bunche. Roy Wilkins spoke on behalf of the

future direction. Some questioned SNCC's previous commitment to nonviolence and interracialism. An anonymous paper for a staff retreat indicated tensions over gender issues, noting women activists were often asked to perform mundane tasks rather than participate in decision making. Acknowledging growing doubts about SNCC's future, Moses likened SNCC to "a boat in the middle of the ocean. It has to be rebuilt in order to stay afloat. It also has to stay afloat in order to be rebuilt."

MALCOLM X AND THE FREEDOM STRUGGLE

When John Lewis and ten SNCC colleagues accepted Harry Belafonte's invitation to tour West Africa soon after the Democratic convention, they found that little news about SNCC had crossed the Atlantic. They did, however, often hear African students referring to Nation of Islam leader Malcolm X with admiration. "Back in America, we were considered radical by the mainstream elements of both the movement and society in general," Lewis observed. In Africa, however, "we were dismissed as mainstream, and it was Malcolm who was embraced." After three weeks as guests of Guinean president Sékou Touré, most SNCC leaders returned to the United States, but Lewis and Don Harris continued on to Liberia, Ghana, Ethiopia, and Kenya. There a flight delay led to a chance meeting with the African American leader who had captured the imagination of young Africans. When they encountered Malcolm X in Nairobi, they were surprised that the black nationalist leader was eager to talk. "The man who sat with us in that hotel room was enthusiastic and excited—not angry, not brooding." Having just attended a meeting in Cairo of Third World nations—those that refused to be aligned with either the United States or the Soviet Union in the Cold War—Malcolm was convinced African nations should push the United Nations to address American racial issues. "He got most enthusiastic about his idea of bringing the case of African Americans before the General Assembly of the United Nations and holding the United States in violation of the United Nations' Human Rights Charter," Lewis recalled.

Break with the Nation of Islam

After becoming the best-known spokesman of the Nation of Islam, Malcolm grew increasingly dissatisfied with the apolitical stance of Elijah Muhammad, who had led the

By the early 1960s, Malcolm X was becoming increasingly dissatisfied with the Nation of Islam. He left the group in 1964 to form the Organization of African American Unity. He was assassinated in 1965.

group since the 1930s. In 1962 he was dismayed when Muhammad advised restraint after Los Angeles police killed a Nation of Islam member during a raid. The following year, after the murder of Mississippi NAACP leader Medgar Evers and after the Birmingham church bombing that killed four children, Malcolm felt constrained by his role as Muhammad's spokesman. "I made comments—but not what should have been said about the climate of hate that the American white man was generating and nourishing." Rather than standing on the front lines of struggle, Malcolm and the Nation of Islam were being bypassed by the new militancy. "It could be heard increasingly in the Negro communities: 'Those Muslims *talk* tough, but they never *do* anything, unless somebody bothers Muslims.'"

Malcolm's loyalty to Elijah Muhammad was tested when he was ordered to refrain from public statements after he called Kennedy's assassination a case of "chickens come home to roost." Even while serving his ninety-day suspension, Malcolm refused to remain out of public view. In February 1964, he accepted boxer Cassius Clay's invitation to attend his fight against heavily favored heavyweight champion Sonny Liston in Miami. Malcolm knew the brash young challenger and Olympic gold medalist had secretly joined the Nation of Islam. Clay's self-promotion—"I am the greatest," he proclaimed—set him apart from the typically self-disciplined members of the Nation of Islam, but Malcolm appreciated Clay's charisma and potential influence in black communities. Malcolm sat at ringside when Clay stunned the sports world by defeating Liston. The following morning, Clay again shocked boxing fans by acknowledging his affiliation with the Nation of Islam. Soon afterward, he announced he was abandoning his "slave name" for a new name, Muhammad Ali.

During the spring of 1964, Malcolm's *hajji* to Mecca—the pilgrimage required of Muslims—led him to realize that some of Elijah Muhammad's religious teachings were in conflict with orthodox Islam. Upon his return, he announced he was leaving the Nation of Islam to form the Organization of African-American Unity (OAAU) in order to bring together black militant groups. "I'm not out to fight other Negro leaders or organizations," Malcolm told reporters. "As of this minute, I've forgotten everything bad that the other leaders have said about me, and I pray they can also forget the many bad things I've said about them." Most members of the Nation of Islam refused to join Malcolm's new group. Even Ali decided his loyalty to Elijah Muhammad transcended his friendship with Malcolm. Nonetheless, freed from the constraints of his Nation of Islam role, Malcolm was more able to express the festering racial discontent that was becoming evident in black urban communities. In July 1964, the shooting of a fifteen-year-old Harlem youth by an off-duty white policeman sparked three days of rioting that left one Harlem resident dead. Soon afterward, five black residents died in a riot in Rochester, New York.

The Final Months

By the time he met with SNCC activists in Nairobi, Malcolm was seeking to build ties with militant civil rights activists. Malcolm's sense of the international implications of the African American freedom struggle paralleled the views of earlier black leaders such as W. E. B. Du Bois, and SNCC members were coming to see him as a potential ally. Malcolm regretted the failure of the Nation of Islam to con-

Mourners march and sing through Jackson, Mississippi, in a funeral procession for slain civil rights leader Medgar Evers.

tribute to the southern freedom struggle, and SNCC workers wanted to expand their organizing efforts into northern inner-city black communities. Soon after Malcolm and the two SNCC workers returned to the United States, their convergence of perspectives became evident when Lewis and Harris proposed that SNCC establish "an African Bureau or Secretariat" that would expand the group's contacts in Africa and "with any other countries or groups of people in other countries who can be help to us and the Cause." For his part, Malcolm invited Fannie Lou Hamer and SNCC's Freedom Singers to participate in a Harlem rally, where he pledged support for the voting rights campaign. "I want Mrs. Hamer to know that anything we can do to help them in Mississippi, we are at their disposal."

Malcolm toned down his earlier harsh criticisms of national civil rights leaders. At a gathering arranged by Juanita Poitier, wife of actor Sidney Poitier, he tried to find common ground with A. Philip Randolph, Whitney Young of the Urban League, and Dorothy Height of the National Council of Negro Women. For several years he had tried to start a dialogue with King, writing to him on several occasions. King rebuffed Malcolm's entreaties, however, and their brief encounter in 1964 outside a Senate hearing room was limited to cordial greetings. "Now you're going to be investigated," Malcolm quipped as photographers recorded the meeting. When New Yorkers welcomed King to the city after his trip to Norway to accept the 1964 Nobel Peace Prize, Malcolm attended the event and spoke with members of King's staff who noticed him in the audience. Nevertheless, he made clear that a gulf still lay between his perspective and that of King. "I don't want the white man giving me medals," he commented afterward. "If I'm following a General . . . and the enemy tends to give him awards, I get suspicious of him. Especially if he gets a peace medal before the war is over."

> "I don't want the white man giving me medals."
> —*Malcolm X*

In early February 1965, Malcolm kept a promise he had made to Lewis and Harris and accepted SNCC's invitation to come to Alabama, where SNCC and the SCLC were involved in a major voting rights campaign. "I believe they have an absolute right to use whatever means are necessary to gain the vote," he affirmed at a rally in Selma. Shortly after his rousing speech, Malcolm assured Coretta Scott King, who was in Selma on behalf of her jailed husband, he had not come to make things more difficult for voting rights workers. "I really did come thinking that I could make it easier," Malcolm explained. "If the white people realize what the alternative is, perhaps they will be more willing to hear Dr. King."

Malcolm's speech in Selma was the most visible indication of his desire to ally himself with black veterans of the civil rights movement, but less than three weeks later, on February 21, he was dead. Members of the Nation of Islam assassinated him as he was beginning a speech at New York's Audubon Ballroom. Even while he attempted to forge strong bonds between the OAAU and other black groups, Malcolm's relations with his former associates in the Nation of Islam had deteriorated into open hostility. In *Muhammad Speaks*, his former protégé Louis X (later Farrakhan) denounced him as a traitor "worthy of death" for departing from Elijah Muhammad's teaching that white people were "a race of devils."

Facing fierce opposition from Nation of Islam loyalists and unable to attract many of his former associates to his new group, Malcolm died before he could transform the African American freedom struggle from within. Despite the gulf between Malcolm's view and his own commitment to nonviolence, John Lewis believed Malcolm "had come to articulate better than anyone else on the scene—including King—the bitterness and frustration of black Americans." After his wife reported on her meeting with Malcolm, King had hoped Malcolm had changed in positive ways. He wrote a note of condolence to Malcolm's widow: "While we did not always see eye to eye on methods to solve the race problems, I always had a deep affection for Malcolm and felt that he had the great ability to put his finger on the existence and root of the problem."

The assassination of Malcolm X did not destroy his influence in the African American freedom struggle. Many of his ideas—especially his advocacy of a positive racial identity and his pan-African perspective—coincided with the conclusions many black activists had drawn from their own political experiences. With the 1965 publication of Alex Haley's *Autobiography of Malcolm X*, Malcolm's life and thoughts reached an audience that far exceeded those who had heard him speak during his lifetime.

VOTING RIGHTS AND VIOLENCE

The day before Malcolm X's Harlem funeral, twenty-six-year-old Jimmy Lee Jackson died of a gunshot wound incurred during a voting rights demonstration in Marion, Alabama. In the weeks after Malcolm's visit to Alabama, the voting rights campaign in the surrounding areas had been marked by repeated Freedom Day marches to voter registration offices and escalating clashes between demonstrators and police. On several occasions Jackson had tried to register to vote, but Alabama officials had blocked him and others, using intimidation and violence. Fewer than one in five black Alabama residents of voting age were registered, and most of those were in the state's urban areas. On February 18, 1965, as Jackson and his family marched from a black church toward the Marion courthouse, state troopers ordered them to disperse. Jackson and his mother and grandfather took refuge in a café, but troopers followed and beat them, knocking Jackson against a cigarette machine before shooting him in the stomach. When Jackson died on February 26, civil rights workers from SNCC and SCLC pledged to step up their protests. In the next few weeks, a voting rights campaign that had been largely ignored outside Alabama captured the nation's attention and led to the passage of major civil rights legislation.

The Selma-to-Montgomery March

Reacting to Jackson's death, Diane and James Bevel proposed a protest march from Selma to Montgomery, a distance of about 50 miles, to confront Governor Wallace. The idea quickly gathered support. King and other SCLC officials saw the Selma protests of 1965 as comparable to the Birmingham campaign of 1963. Through a carefully orchestrated series of events, they would draw the nation's attention to brutal forces of repression—with sheriff Jim Clark in the Bull Connor role—and thereby prod President Johnson to introduce new voting rights legislation, just as the Birmingham protests had prompted passage of the 1964 Civil Rights Act. Late in 1964, Johnson had told King that southern congressmen, whose votes he needed to enact his Great Society social legislation, would prevent passage of new voting rights legislation, but King was not convinced. "The President said nothing could be done," King recalled. "But we started a movement."

As was the case in Albany, Georgia, SNCC workers had already established a project in Selma before King's arrival, and they saw themselves as more connected than SCLC staffers to the sentiments of local black leaders. Depicting King as an interloper who would displace local leadership, SNCC announced plans to hold a People's Conference to formulate programs for black communities in the Deep South. Other SNCC organizers sought to avoid open conflicts with the SCLC by establishing projects in Selma's surrounding rural areas, where the SCLC did not plan to operate. Resentment of King, however, became evident at planning meetings for the march to Montgomery. SNCC chair John Lewis was one of the few members of the group who favored participating in the march.

When about 2,000 demonstrators left Brown's Chapel on Sunday, March 7, to march to Montgomery, Lewis was surprised that King had left Selma to deliver a sermon at his Atlanta church. Thus, along with Hosea Williams of the SCLC, Lewis led marchers across Pettus Bridge on the outskirts of Selma, where a large contingent of state troopers and deputies waited under the command of Sheriff Clark. When the marchers were ordered to disperse, the combined police force chased the marchers back across the bridge with tear gas and billy clubs. Lewis, who suffered a fractured skull, was one of several marchers injured. News photographs and television coverage of the violence at Pettus Bridge—activists called it "Bloody Sunday"—shocked civil rights supporters throughout the nation and drew hundreds more civil rights sympathizers to Selma.

When the marchers regrouped, many directed their anger not only against Alabama officials but also against King, because of his absence during the crucial march, and against the federal government for failing to intervene. Even SNCC workers who had opposed the march now argued for its resumption in order to demonstrate that police violence would not prevail. While SCLC representatives tried unsuccessfully to convince a federal judge to order state officials to allow the march, SNCC workers insisted that a march planned for March 10, take place regardless of whether it was approved by a federal court. When the second march crossed Pettus Bridge and once again confronted a police barricade, King was among those in the lead, but he provoked more criticism when he told the marchers to turn around rather than risk further violence. That evening a group of white Selma residents killed James Reeb, a northern white minister who had joined the demonstrations.

During the next few days, SCLC officials secured a federal court order allowing a march, but by this time relations between SCLC and SNCC had seriously deteriorated. Rather than favoring further nonviolent protests to gain the sympathy of northern liberals, many SNCC organizers in

TABLE 18.2 Civil Rights Victories, 1961–1965

Following months of freedom rides protesting segregation in transportation facilities, the Interstate Commerce Commission (ICC) implemented its desegregation decree in 1961.

James Meredith desegregates the University of Mississippi in 1962.

Civil Rights Act of 1964 outlaws segregation in public accommodations.

The 1965 Voting Rights Act outlaws educational requirements for voting and empowers U.S. attorney general to assign federal registrars to enroll voters.

Alabama concluded they should focus on building independent black-controlled movements in the rural areas surrounding Selma. Nevertheless, SCLC's strategy produced its intended result. In a March 15 televised address, President Johnson announced he would propose voting rights legislation to Congress. At the end of his speech, Johnson referred to the freedom song that had become the anthem of the movement, assuring the nation "We Shall Overcome."

After several postponements, civil rights advocates finally gained court permission to proceed with the march. The march to Montgomery began again on March 21. It was the culmination of a stage of the African American freedom struggle that led to the passage of the landmark Voting Rights Act of 1965, but it was also the last major racial protest movement to receive substantial white support. When the marchers reached Montgomery, King delivered one of his most memorable speeches. As he stood on the capitol steps, within sight of Dexter Avenue Church, where he had first emerged as a boycott leader a decade before, King asked how much more sacrifice would be required to overcome segregation. "So I stand before you this afternoon with the conviction that segregation is on its deathbed in Alabama and the only thing uncertain about it is how costly the segregationists and Wallace will make the funeral." King insisted the movement not abandon its nonviolent principles. "Our aim must never be to defeat or humiliate the white man but to win his friendship and understanding," he told the crowd. "We must come to see that the end we seek is a society at peace with itself, a society that can live with its conscience."

In August, the legislation President Johnson introduced became the Voting Rights Act of 1965. It eliminated many of the obstacles that had prevented black southerners from voting. Use of literacy tests was suspended, and federal registrars were authorized in areas with a history of discrimination. But the Act's passage was only part of a sequence of governmental efforts in 1964 and 1965 intended to transform newly gained civil rights into tangible gains. "You do not take a person who, for years, had been hobbled by chains and liberate him, bring him up to the starting line of a race and then say, 'You are free to compete with all the others,'" Johnson explained in a Howard University speech in June 1965. Johnson's "war on poverty" included an Equal Opportunity Act with the goal of ending poverty and unemployment through job training programs, adult education, and loans to small businesses. The Johnson administration also secured legislation to help poor people by providing food stamps and educational programs such as Head Start for preschool children. Community action programs were instituted to encourage poor people to organize in their own communities. The Johnson administration also created a new Department of Housing and Urban Development (HUD) with responsibility for low-rent housing and urban renewal programs. Its first secretary was Robert Weaver, a former member of the unofficial Black Cabinet under President Franklin Roosevelt.

Johnson's Great Society proposals had a major impact on American society, but as with Roosevelt's New Deal, the results were uneven and did not improve the lives of all African Americans. While programs such as Medicare and student loans intended for middle-class Americans received ample funding, Johnson's war on poverty received only a small portion of government spending. In addition, by the summer of 1965, Johnson had begun to shift his attention from the Great Society programs to the escalating conflict in Vietnam, where thousands of American troops had been sent to counter communist forces. Moreover, during the year following the passage of the Voting Rights Act, it became clear that civil rights reforms had produced rising expectations among black Americans. The death of the Jim Crow system in the South did not obscure the reality that other forms of segregation and racial discrimination still existed in all parts of the nation.

The Voting Rights Act was the last major victory of the civil rights movement, but few of the activists who had struggled for it found time to celebrate. Within days of President Johnson's signing of the act, the arrest of a black man in Los Angeles led to several days of deadly violence that began in the Watts section of the city and then spread through south-central Los Angeles. More than thirty black residents were killed by police, and National Guardsmen were sent to the city. Newspapers referred to the violence as a riot, but some residents saw it as a rebellion—an expression of widespread resentment of police brutality and harassment and of white ownership of businesses located in black residential areas. With about 30,000 black people of Los Angeles participating in the violence, arson, and looting, property damage was extensive in many neighborhoods. Frightened homeowners in white suburban enclaves flooded sporting goods stores to purchase guns. Violence in Los Angeles demonstrated that civil rights laws had done little to relieve the problems of black residents in America's large cities. Visiting Los Angeles as the violence subsided, King talked with residents and struggled to understand what had happened. "At a time when the Negro's aspirations were at a peak, his actual conditions of employment, education, and housing were worsening," he commented. He predicted the Watts insurrection was "the beginning of a stirring of a deprived people . . . who had been by-passed by the progress of the previous decade."

The stirring that King predicted was actually the beginning of a major new stage of black militancy and political development. Since the 1950s, increasingly massive civil rights protests in the South had captured the nation's attention and produced major civil rights reforms. Overcoming the southern Jim Crow system had required years of sacrifice and innovative leadership, but King and other veterans of the southern struggle realized that still more would be required to deal with problems that were national rather than regional in scope.

During the march through Mississippi, Stokely Carmichael, chairman of SNCC, delivers a "black power" speech to a crowd in front of Mississippi State Capitol in March 1966.

BLACK POWER

Stokely Carmichael was skeptical about the usefulness of the Selma-to-Montgomery march; he and other SNCC organizers used it as an opportunity to contact local leaders in the rural area between the two communities. Soon afterward, he became director of a new project in Lowndes County, which had no registered black voters even though most residents were black. The Lowndes County staff believed a new approach was needed to deal with the entrenched segregationist resistance in rural Black Belt areas such as Lowndes County. They expected to demonstrate that black organizers working with local black leaders could build a new kind of militant movement. Like the Mississippi Freedom Democratic Party, the Lowndes County Freedom Organization (LCFO) was independent of Alabama's white-controlled Democratic Party. It was registered as a legitimate political group able to field candidates in elections.

The significance of the emblem chosen for the new group—a snarling black panther—was unmistakable. "The black panther is an animal that when it is pressured it moves back until it is cornered," explained LCFO leader John Hulett, "then it comes out fighting for life or death. We felt we had been pushed back long enough and that it was time for Negroes to come out and take over." Soon known as the Black Panther Party, the new political group captured the imagination of SNCC staff members who believed African Americans, in the North as well as the South, should abandon interracial alliances and nonviolent principles and instead create independent, black-controlled political institutions.

> "We felt we had been pushed back long enough and that it was time for Negroes to come out and take over." —*John Hulett*

For years, John Lewis had thought of Carmichael as a colleague, even a friend. Although the two activists argued often since they met in Mississippi's Parchman Prison during the 1961 freedom rides, they respected each other's commitment. Lewis had been arrested more than twenty times since the early 1960s, and Carmichael had acquired his own reputation for fearlessness as an SNCC project director in Mississippi and Alabama. During the summer of 1964 they became reacquainted while participating in the Summer Project. They both backed SNCC's decision to oppose the escalation of American military involvement in Vietnam, but Lewis was a conscientious objector to all wars, while Carmichael accepted Malcolm X's view that "any means necessary" should be used in the black freedom struggle. Lewis was disturbed as SNCC moved away from its earlier nonviolent ideals; in contrast, members of Carmichael's staff often carried weapons, and many voting rights meetings in Lowndes County were protected by armed guards.

When SNCC staff gathered in May 1966 for the organization's annual meeting, Lewis did not expect serious opposition to his continuing as chair even though he knew he was being criticized as out of touch with the staff and that his critics were prepared to back Carmichael as his replacement. Indeed, when the vote was taken, Lewis was overwhelmingly reelected, and Ruby Doris Robinson, a veteran of the 1961 Rock Hill jail-in, was selected to replace James Forman as executive secretary. Under normal circumstances, this would have ended the matter, but others challenged the vote. Some

Stokely Carmichael on Black Power

SNCC chair Stokely Carmichael quickly became identified with the "black power" slogan he introduced during the completion of James Meredith's "march against fear" across Mississippi. In the article from which this excerpt is taken, he explains the grassroots origins of the idea and its meaning for black people and white people in America.

The concept of "black power" is not a recent or isolated phenomenon: It has grown out of the ferment of agitation and activity by different people and organizations in many black communities over the years. Our last year of work in Alabama added a new concrete possibility. In Lowndes County, for example, black power will mean that if a Negro is elected sheriff, he can end police brutality. If a black man is elected tax assessor, he can collect and channel funds for the building of better roads and schools serving black people—thus advancing the move from political power into the economic arena. In such areas as Lowndes, where black men have a majority, they will attempt to use it to exercise control. This is why they seek control. Where Negroes lack a majority, black power means proper representation and sharing of control. It means the creation of power bases from which black people can work to change statewide or nationwide patterns of oppression through pressure from strength—instead of weakness. . . .

White America will not face the problem of color, the reality of it. The well-intentioned say: "We're all human, everybody is really decent, we must forget color." But color cannot be "forgotten" until its weight is recognized and dealt with. White America will not acknowledge that the ways in which this country sees itself are contradicted by being "black" and always have been. Whereas most of the people who settled this country came here for freedom or for economic opportunity, blacks were brought here to be slaves. When the Lowndes County Freedom Organization chose the black panther as its symbol, it was christened by the press "the Black Panther Party," but the Alabama Democratic Party, whose symbol is a rooster, has never been called the White Cock Party. No one ever talked about "white power" because power in this country *is* white. All this adds up to more than merely identifying a group phenomenon by some catchy name or adjective. The furor over that black panther reveals the problems that white America has with color and sex; the furor over "black power" reveals how deep racism runs and the great fear which is attached to it.

—from Stokely Carmichael, "What We Want," New York Review of Books, *September 22, 1966. Reprinted by permission of Mabel Carmichael.*

To view a longer version of this document, please go to *www.ablongman.com/carson/documents*.

staff members saw the anti-Lewis campaign as an opportunity to infuse the group with racial separatist ideas. "What it was about, in the end, was who was 'blackest,' and it was hard to tell where the lines were drawn," Lewis recalled.

After arguing until dawn, exhausted staff members narrowly voted to elect Carmichael SNCC's new chair. News reports of the leadership change framed it as a sign that the interracial civil rights coalition, responsible for previous reforms and new federal legislation, was weakening. Carmichael was quoted as advising white civil rights workers to begin focusing their energies on white communities. For Lewis, who resigned from SNCC a few months later, the vote marked the end of an era that extended back to the group's founding in 1960. "Wounds were opened that would never heal," he recalled. "I didn't consider it so much a repudiation of me as a repudiation of ourselves, of what we *were*, of what we stood for."

Soon after his election, Carmichael gained national attention when he became involved in a protest march that began with the shooting of James Meredith, who had deseg-

The civil rights movement focused national attention on the police brutality used against peaceful African American demonstrators.

regated the University of Mississippi in 1962. Meredith had undertaken a solitary "march against fear" across the state of Mississippi. When a sniper shot him in June 1966, Meredith was taken to a Memphis hospital, and civil rights leaders quickly gathered at his bedside and pledged to continue the march. Carmichael, King, and newly elected CORE chair Floyd McKissick then met at the church where James Lawson, once the mentor of the Nashville student group, served as pastor. They quickly agreed to issue a call for civil rights supporters to join them at the spot where Meredith had been shot.

The Mississippi march was an unexpected event that brought together many veterans of earlier civil rights campaigns. But, as marchers assembled, King quickly noticed changes. Younger activists made it clear they did not accept nonviolent principles or welcome white participation in the march. When some marchers began to sing the civil rights anthem "We Shall Overcome," a few young black marchers countered that the title should be changed to "We Shall Overrun." At the end of the first day, when march leaders gathered, King insisted the march remain committed to nonviolent principles, but he faced strong opposition from members of SNCC, CORE, and the Deacons for Defense, a group of Louisiana activists who offered to provide armed protection for the march. When Carmichael suggested that white participation in the march should be deemphasized, King realized the movement was abandoning its earlier ideals. "As I listened to Stokely, I thought about the years that we had worked together in communities all across the South, and how joyously we had then welcomed and accepted our white allies in the movement."

The next day, walking at the front of the column and heading south to the Mississippi Delta, King and Carmichael continued their dialogue. Carmichael had heard reports that black residents responded enthusiastically to the slogan "Black Power," which was a shortened version of the phrase "black power for black people" used by SNCC workers in Lowndes County. Carmichael's first opportunity to use the slogan publicly came after police in Greenwood arrested him for erecting tents at a local black school so marchers could rest for the night. After his release, Carmichael announced at a rally, "This is the twenty-seventh time I have been arrested. I ain't going to jail no more." He argued that African Americans had been demanding freedom for six years and had gotten nothing. "What we gonna start saying now is Black Power." He shouted the slogan repeatedly; each time the audience shouted back, "Black Power!" Again and again, members of the audience shouted in unison the slogan that suddenly galvanized their emotions.

The two words had been combined by others long before. Richard Wright used them as the title for his book on African politics, written in the early 1950s, and Paul Robeson had spoken of black power during those same years. Although the expression was initially just a new slogan in a movement that had produced many slogans, the two words soon came to symbolize a major shift in the self-concept of many African Americans. The civil rights legislation of the mid-1960s had opened doors of opportunity, but the struggle to achieve change had produced aspirations for even greater changes. As James Baldwin had observed in 1963, the removal of racial barriers had forced African Americans to consider whether racial integration should be the goal of the black struggle.

King recognized that the "black power" slogan expressed the widespread discontent of African Americans who remained poor and powerless despite civil rights reforms. Nevertheless, he believed the slogan "carried the wrong connotations"; press accounts had already implied it was a call for violence. In addition, it alienated potential white allies. But Carmichael disagreed: "Power is the only thing respected in this world, and we must get it at any cost. Martin, you know as well as I do that practically every other ethnic group in America has done just this. The Jews, the Irish, and the Italians did it, why can't we?"

> "Power is the only thing respected in this world, and we must get it at any cost."—*Stokely Carmichael*

"That is just the point," King countered. "No one has ever heard the Jews publicly chant a slogan of Jewish power, but they have power. We must use every constructive means to amass economic and political power."

"What we need is a new slogan with 'black' in it," Carmichael insisted. When King responded that the slogan would confuse white allies and isolate African Americans, Carmichael admitted, "Martin, I deliberately decided to raise this issue on the march in order to give it a national forum, and force you to take a stand for Black Power."

King laughed with resignation: "I have been used before. One more time won't hurt."

CONCLUSION

Carmichael's call for black power articulated the simple fact that previous civil rights reforms had not brought about racial equality. The southern civil rights protests of the early 1960s and the voting rights campaign in the Deep South had torn down the Jim Crow system of legally enforced segregation. The gains had been important—few black Americans wanted to return to the harsh racial oppression of the years before the *Brown* decision. But the costs of civil rights gains had been high. Deadly racist violence had produced many martyrs, and the slow pace of change had produced festering resentment. Rather than bringing large numbers of black and white students together in public schools, the *Brown* decision—and subsequent years of litigation and social conflict—enabled a small number of black students to attend overwhelmingly white schools. Ten years after the *Brown* decision, almost 98 percent of southern black students still attended predominantly black schools. More generally, most black Americans still lived in predominantly black communities and still experienced living conditions inferior to those of most white people. James Baldwin had asked in *The Fire Next Time* whether racial integration was a worthwhile goal, and Malcolm X had raised the same question in even more caustic terms. The "black power" slogan expressed the determination of black Americans to achieve "freedom now," but the vagueness of the phrase also indicated the uncertainty many felt about their identity as African Americans and as American citizens.

During the late 1960s and early 1970s, African Americans continued to seek the power to change their lives for the better. Many civil rights veterans turned their attention to the complex problems of the volatile urban black ghettos. King's nonviolent principles were tested in Chicago and in a Poor People's Campaign. SNCC also established organizing efforts in northern cities. But for many civil rights veterans, their experiences in the South were scant preparation for the difficult challenges they faced in urban black communities. They discovered that black power and black unity were elusive goals.

FURTHER READING

Branch, Taylor. *Parting the Waters: America in the King Years, 1954–1963* (New York: Simon and Schuster, 1988).

———. *Pillar of Fire: America in the King Years, 1963–1965* (New York: Simon and Schuster, 1998).

Carmichael, Stokely, with Ekwueme Michael Tehlwell. *Ready for Revolution: The Life and Struggles of Stokely Carmichael [Kwame Ture]* (New York: Scribner, 2003).

Carson, Clayborne. *In Struggle: SNCC and the Black Awakening of the 1960s* (Cambridge: Harvard University Press, 1981).

———, *The Autobiography of Martin Luther King, Jr.* (New York: Warner, 1998).

———, et al., eds. *Eyes on the Prize Civil Rights Reader* (New York: Penguin, 1987).

Dittmer, John. *Local People: The Struggle for Civil Rights in Mississippi* (Urbana: University of Illinois Press, 1995).

Fleming, Cynthia Griggs. *Soon We Will Not Cry: The Liberation of Ruby Doris Robinson* (Lanham, Md.: Rowman & Littlefield, 1998).

Garrow, David. *Bearing the Cross: Martin Luther King, Jr., and the Southern Christian Leadership Conference* (New York: William Morrow, 1986).

Haley, Alex, ed. *The Autobiography of Malcolm X* (New York: Grove, 1965).

Horne, Gerald. *Fire This Time: The Watts Uprising and the 1960s* (Charlottesville: University Press of Virginia, 1995).

King, Coretta Scott. *My Life with Martin Luther King, Jr.* (New York: Holt, Rinehart, and Winston, 1969).

Lawson, Steven F. *Running for Freedom: Civil Rights and Black Politics in America, Since 1941* (New York: McGraw-Hill, 1997).

Lee, Chana Kai. *For Freedom's Sake: The Life of Fannie Lou Hamer* (Urbana: University of Illinois Press, 1999).

Lewis, John, with Michael D'Orso. *Walking with the Wind: A Memoir of the Movement* (New York: Simon and Schuster, 1998).

Manis, Andrew M. *A Fire You Can't Put Out: The Civil Rights Life of Birmingham's Reverend Fred Shuttlesworth* (Tuscaloosa: University of Alabama Press, 1999).

McWhorter, Diane. *Carry Me Home: Birmingham, Alabama: The Climatic Battle of the Civil Rights Revolution* (New York: Simon and Schuster, 2001).

Morrison, Toni, ed. *James Baldwin: Collective Essays* (New York: Library of America, 1998).

Payne, Charles M. *I've Got the Light of Freedom: The Organizing Tradition and the Mississippi Freedom Struggle* (Berkeley: University of California Press, 1995).

Raines, Howell. *My Soul Is Rested: The Story of the Civil Rights Movement in the Deep South* (New York: Penguin, 1977).

Ralph, James R., Jr. *Northern Protest: Martin Luther King, Jr., Chicago, and the Civil Rights Movement* (Cambridge: Harvard University Press, 1993).

Robnett, Belinda. *How Long? How Long? African American Women in the Civil Rights Movement* (New York: Oxford University Press, 1997).

Theoharis, Jeanne, and Komozi Woodards, eds. *Groundwork: Local Black Freedom Struggles in America* (New York: New York University, 2004).

CHAPTER 19

Romare Bearden, *The Block*, 1971. Bearden paid tribute to Harlem, presenting aspects of black neighborhood life.

Resistance, Repression, and Retrenchment, 1967–1978

Hubert "Rap" Brown Proclaims Black Power

"Violence is as American as apple pie," Hubert G. "Rap" Brown proclaimed on July 24, 1967, as he stood on a car trunk before a cheering crowd of hundreds of supporters in Cambridge, Maryland. The previous month, Brown had been elected as the new chair of the Student Nonviolent Coordinating Committee (SNCC). Though just twenty-three, he was a civil rights veteran: a participant in the 1964 Mississippi Summer Project, a leader in Howard University's SNCC-affiliated Nonviolent Action Group, and overall director of SNCC's projects in Alabama. Now he had returned to Cambridge, where in 1963 he had worked with local leader Gloria Richardson in a protest campaign that drew broad support from black workers as well as students. Known within the SNCC as an advocate of armed self-defense, Brown sounded the themes of racial pride and militancy that had characterized the speeches of his predecessor, Stokely Carmichael. But Brown went further, bluntly warning, "If America don't come around, we're going to burn it down." Rejecting Martin Luther King's ideal of a "beloved community," Brown advised against loving the "honky" (a derisive term for white people). "Shoot him to death, brother," he announced, "because that's what he is out to do to you."

No violence occurred during Brown's speech, but later in the evening he was slightly wounded when caught in an exchange of gunfire between police and

CHAPTER OUTLINE

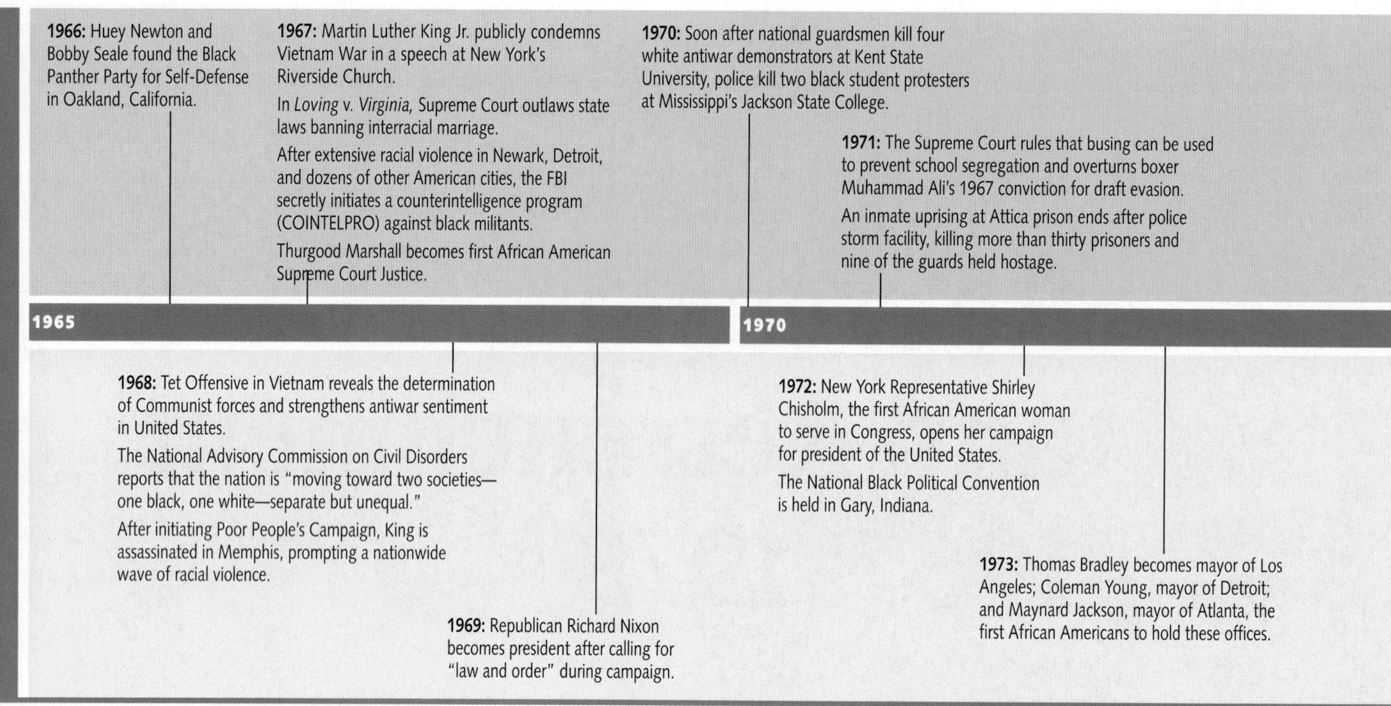

black residents. He left Cambridge before early morning fires engulfed a black elementary school and several businesses. The next day Spiro T. Agnew, Maryland's recently elected Republican governor, arrived to inspect the damage. Announcing that state officials would "immediately arrest any person inciting to riot," Agnew said of Brown, "I hope they pick him up soon, put him away, and throw away the key." The governor refused to meet with local black leaders unless they first agreed to shun "lawlessness" and denounce Brown as well as other black power advocates.

Despite lack of evidence that Brown was responsible for the Cambridge violence, Maryland officials charged him with arson and arrested him. But Brown remained defiant. "We are on the eve of a Black revolution," he predicted from jail. "The rebellions are but dress rehearsal for real revolution." Brown was released on bond, but in September he was rearrested for carrying a weapon across state lines while under indictment. Although again released on bond, he was prohibited from traveling. "Whatever they do to me is not going to stop the revolution," Brown insisted. "Whether I was out there or not, I knew that the brothers were going to take care of business."

The Cambridge violence was neither the most deadly nor the most destructive racial outbreak of the "long, hot summer" of 1967, but it signaled a new era in American politics by focusing national attention on Brown and Agnew, as well as the opposing forces they represented. Expressing the nation's volatile racial emotions in their inflammatory rhetoric, the two men suddenly rose from obscurity to national prominence and came to symbolize the growing divide between "black power" militants and white "law and order" politicians.

Some supporters of Agnew and Brown considered them moderates rather than extremists. Agnew had been elected governor with considerable black and liberal support, running against a conservative Democrat known for his opposition to open housing laws. Brown had not been expected to draw as much public attention as had the more flamboyant Carmichael during his tumultuous year as SNCC chair. In more peaceful times, Brown and Agnew might have avoided controversy, but both were soon caught up in the turbulent racial climate of the late 1960s. By threatening armed rebellion against the nation's established political order, Brown

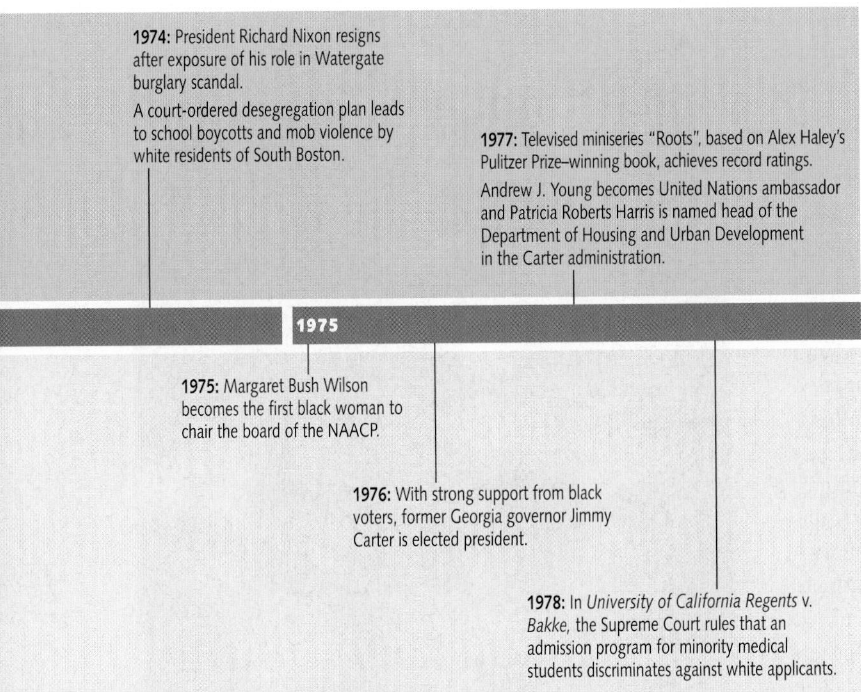

expressed the anger felt by many African Americans. But his fiery speeches also inadvertently strengthened white support for police suppression of black militancy. While Congress considered whether to pass antiriot legislation (labeled the "H. Rap Brown law" by some reporters), FBI director J. Edgar Hoover condemned not only Brown and Carmichael but also King as "vociferous firebrands." Agnew's acerbic criticisms of black militants soon made the governor a popular figure in national Republican circles.

During the years following the summer of 1967, American society remained divided over racial issues. The interracial coalition that had made possible the passage of major civil rights legislation in the mid-1960s splintered later in the decade due to bitter disputes over the Vietnam War and over policies developed to implement civil rights reforms. Two especially controversial policies were busing to achieve school desegregation and affirmative action efforts intended to reverse historical patterns of racial exclusion. The assassination of King and the white backlash against black militancy were major setbacks to those seeking civil rights reforms through nonviolence and interracial cooperation. But the black power movement faltered as well due to external repression and internal divisions. Although black power militancy encouraged racial pride and expressed resentment of longstanding racial injustices, racial unity and power proved to be elusive goals. As black militant groups struggled to survive during the 1970s, black scholars, writers, and artists gave substance to black power rhetoric through their perceptive depictions of African American life and history. The revolutionary objectives sought by Brown and other black power advocates were not achieved, but a new generation of black elected officials were able to protect previous civil rights gains and work with increasing effectiveness within the American political system.

A NEW RACIAL CONSCIOUSNESS

During 1967, the year of H. Rap Brown's rise to notoriety, twenty-three-year-old Angela Yvonne Davis returned to the United States after two years of graduate study in Germany. Although she had been abroad as black power militancy captured the nation's attention, Davis was, like many black students of the period, receptive to the new trend in African American politics. She remembered the dynamite attacks against the homes of black families, such as hers, that attempted to move into formerly all-white neighborhoods of Birmingham, Alabama. She was also aware that her mother, a teacher, had a long involvement in civil rights causes extending back to the Scottsboro campaign of the 1930s. As a teenager, her parents sent her to attend a private high school in New York that was known for its leftist-oriented curriculum. Davis was drawn to Marxist ideas, which offered her a way of making sense of the racism she had experienced in the South. "What had seemed a personal hatred of me, an inexplicable refusal of Southern whites to confront their own emotions, and a stubborn willingness of blacks to acquiesce became the inevitable consequences of a ruthless system which kept itself alive and well by encouraging spite, competition and oppression of one group by another," she remembered. "Profit was the word: the cold and constant motive for the behavior, the contempt, and the despair I had seen." She enrolled at Brandeis University, majoring in French literature. Davis was spending her junior year in Paris in the college's overseas program when she learned that acquaintances of hers were among the four children killed in the 1963 bombing of Birmingham's Sixteenth Street Baptist Church. After graduating with honors, she spent two years studying philosophy in Frankfurt, Germany, before coming to the University of California, San Diego to resume her graduate studies with noted philosopher Herbert Marcuse. There, as she prepared herself for an academic career, Davis quickly became caught up in the swift currents of black political militancy.

> "A personal hatred of me, an inexplicable refusal of Southern whites to confront their own emotions, and a stubborn willingness of blacks to acquiesce became the inevitable consequences of a ruthless system."
> —*Angela Davis*

The political climate that greeted Davis upon her return to the United States was notable not only for Brown's call for revolution but also for a much broader transformation of African American attitudes and American race relations. Years of civil rights activism, Malcolm X's militant ideas, and racial insurgences in major cities had affected the views of large numbers of young people, especially black college students. Campus visits by speakers such as Carmichael and Brown often stimulated the formation of black student organizations. During the spring, a campus visit by Carmichael sparked sustained protests against racial injustice by black students at Fisk University and Tennessee A&M. Adam Clayton Powell, the still flamboyant and controversial Harlem congressman, also stirred campus audiences as he campaigned to reverse his unseating by his House colleagues after he refused to pay a libel judgment against him. Escalating protests against the war in Vietnam and the military draft added to the climate of racial militancy and confrontations with authority. Heavyweight champion Muhammad Ali's decision to refuse military induction—"No Vietcong ever called me Nigger," the boxer remarked—was but the most publicized of many convergences of black militancy and antiwar dissent. "Become a member of the world's highest paid black mercenary army!" a SNCC poster read.

> "No Vietcong ever called me Nigger."—*Muhammad Ali*

Heavyweight boxing champion Muhammad Ali refused military induction during the Vietnam War, citing his status as a minister of the Nation of Islam.

Davis's initial contacts with SNCC activists in southern California strengthened her leftist orientation, but the new black consciousness was at least as much a cultural phenomenon as it was political radicalism. While Brown's provocative speeches expressed the anger felt by many African Americans, black power militancy often assumed less combative forms. Many black students began to set themselves apart from other students by abandoning hair-straightening products and adopting "natural" or "Afro" hair styles or, less commonly, wearing African-style clothing. At UCLA, for example, black students formed Harambee—"come together" in Kiswahili—to study African American history and culture. Nina Simone's forceful renditions of "Mississippi Goddamn" and other politically aware songs made her especially popular among black student activists of the period. Even the more mainstream hits produced by Motown singers, such as the Supremes or Marvin Gaye and Tammi Terrell, seemed to convey a new sense of racial distinctiveness and urgency. Some proponents of black cultural nationalism pointedly rejected the tradition of black leftist politics, arguing that black politics should be rooted in distinctively African or African American values. Harold Cruse's *The Crisis of the Negro Intellectual* (1967) persuaded many readers that black leftists of the 1930s and 1940s had been misled by the white—often Jewish—leaders of the Communist Party. Cruse, who had once been a Communist himself, lamented the failure of African Americans to develop a political strategy that emphasized the role of black cultural institutions.

Davis rejected Cruse's argument and joined the Communist Party's Che Lumumba Club during 1968, but the black cultural transformation of the late 1960s would exert a more pervasive and more enduring influence among African Americans than would the political militancy of the period. Neither Davis's leftist views nor Cruse's advocacy of cultural nationalism encompassed the complex mixture of trends affecting African Americans in the years following the passage of historic civil rights legislation. Black radicalism and separatism coexisted uneasily with other racial trends that brought African Americans closer to the mainstream, even as racial conflicts became more visible. Thus, the year of Brown's rise to notoriety was also the year that Thurgood Marshall was named the first black Supreme Court justice, that Edward Brooke of Massachusetts took office as the first black U.S. senator since Reconstruction, that the Supreme Court in *Loving* v. *Virginia* outlawed state laws banning interracial marriage, and that Carl Stokes of Cleveland, Ohio, and Richard Hatcher of Gary, Indiana, became the first black mayors of major cities.

It was also the year that black actor Sidney Poitier became Hollywood's most successful male actor by playing movie roles that suggested that racial divisions could be bridged. An immigrant from the Bahamas, Poitier had sympathized with leftist causes during the 1940s while he was a struggling actor, but as his movie career blossomed during the 1950s he avoided political controversy while quietly supporting civil rights groups. Although an actor of considerable range, who won acclaim for his portrayal of an embittered black man in the stage and film versions of Lorraine Hansberry's *A Raisin in the Sun,* Poitier usually played characters able to suppress anger and win the respect of white Americans. In 1964, he became the first African American to win a best actor Academy Award for his performance in *Lilies of the Field*. During 1967, he starred in three of the year's hit films: in *To Sir with Love,* playing a teacher who wins the love and respect of his students; in *Guess Who's Coming to Dinner,* playing a highly successful doctor who charms the parents of his white fiancée; and, in the police drama *In the Heat of the Night,* playing a police detective who gains the grudging respect of a southern white sheriff. Such roles brought Poitier to the pinnacle of Hollywood success, but he was also constrained by stereotyped roles that contrasted with the nation's racial hostilities. Stung by black criticisms of his integrationist screen image, Poitier reassessed his career. Rejecting the kind of roles that had made him a star, he turned instead to film directing and more challenging roles in independent films.

KING AND THE WARS AGAINST COMMUNISM AND POVERTY

Martin Luther King was also reassessing his future in light of black power controversies and the upsurge in racial violence. Troubled by the increasing discontent in black communities, he did his best to steer a middle course between agitators like Brown and Carmichael and more moderate civil rights leaders, such as NAACP leader Roy Wilkins or Whitney Young of the Urban League. He regretted that his differences with SNCC's new leaders had become embittered and public. "This debate might well have been little more than a healthy internal difference of opinion," he later wrote, "but the press loves the sensational and it would not allow the issue to remain within the private domain of the movement." He also would have preferred to avoid becoming ensnarled in the increasingly intense national debate about the war in Vietnam. He did speak out when Georgia legislators objected to SNCC's antiwar stance by refusing to seat former SNCC staff member and newly elected state representative Julian Bond. But otherwise King limited himself to calling for a negotiated settlement of the conflict while encouraging his wife, Coretta, to continue her long-standing peace activism.

Nonetheless, he felt guilty that his cautious calls for negotiations had done little or nothing to slow the escalation of the Vietnam conflict. "At best, I was a loud speaker but a quiet actor, while a charade was being performed," he admitted later. Like other civil rights advocates, King saw the African American freedom struggle as stalled—unable to transform legal rights into better living conditions for many poor black people. The political coalition that had achieved major civil rights reforms seemed in danger of disintegrating due to white resentment of black militancy and disputes over the war. As American bombing and troop levels increased and antiwar demonstrations intensified, images of burned and wounded children pushed him closer to a decisive stand on

■ Leading the march against the Vietnam War are Dr. Benjamin Spock, the famed pediatrician who wrote an enormously popular advice book for parents, and Dr. Martin Luther King Jr. in a parade on Chicago's State Street, March 25, 1967.

the war issue. Then, in January 1967, he was glancing through an issue of the leftist magazine *Ramparts* when an illustrated story, "The Children of Vietnam," caught his attention. He was disturbed by a photograph showing a Vietnamese mother holding her dead baby, killed in an American air attack. King had previously hesitated to speak out against President Lyndon Johnson's war policies, worried that publicly criticizing the war would prevent any future access to the White House and alienate many SCLC donors. But after seeing the photographs, he decided he must take a stand. "Never again," he vowed to himself, "will I be silent on an issue that is destroying the soul of our nation and destroying thousands and thousands of little children in Vietnam."

Three months later, on April 4, King made public his views on the war in an address to an overflow audience at New York City's Riverside Church. Challenging those who said that he should stick to racial issues, he charged that the war consumed funds that might otherwise be used to fight poverty in black communities. He also noted that black casualties in the war were disproportionately high. "We were taking the black young men who had been crippled by our society," he charged, "and sending them eight thousand miles away to guarantee liberties in Southeast Asia which they had not found in southwest Georgia and East Harlem." King explained that it was difficult to persuade African Americans to use nonviolent tactics while his nation used "massive doses of violence" to achieve its goals in Vietnam: "I knew that I could never again raise my voice against the violence of the oppressed in the ghettos without having first spoken clearly to the greatest purveyor of violence in the world today: my own government." He warned, "A nation that continues year after year to spend more money on military defense than on programs of social uplift is approaching spiritual death."

Former SNCC chair John Lewis, in the audience at Riverside Church that day, recalled the speech as King's "greatest," and Stokely Carmichael was pleased when he heard King deliver his antiwar message again at Atlanta's Ebenezer Baptist Church. Many white antiwar activists also applauded King's stand, but the NAACP's Wilkins was sharply critical due to his concern that the war issue would split the civil rights movement. President Johnson's solicitor general, Thurgood Marshall, advised King against diverting his energy from civil rights reform. FBI director Hoover sent Johnson an ominous private note depicting King as "an instrument in the hands of subversive forces seeking to undermine our nation."

Despite intense criticism, King refused to back down. "The ultimate measure of a man is not where he stands in moments of convenience, but where he stands in moments of challenge, moments of great crisis and controversy," King told the SCLC staff. King also believed it was necessary to move beyond civil rights legislation to eliminate economic inequities in the North as well as the South. He found that the problems facing the Chicago Freedom Movement, SCLC's first northern venture, were in some respects even more difficult to confront than southern legalized segregation. When he had confronted southern racists in Birmingham and Selma, northern white liberals and Democratic politicians at least offered verbal support, but white mobs in the Chicago suburb of Cicero responded to his "open housing" marches with bricks and bottles as well as with racist epithets. "I can say that I had never seen, even in Mississippi, mobs as hostile and hate-filled as in Chicago," King remarked.

> "The ultimate measure of a man is not where he stands in moments of convenience, but where he stands in moments of challenge, moments of great crisis and controversy."
> —*Martin Luther King Jr.*

Moreover, the Democratic machine of Mayor Richard Daley outmaneuvered him by publicly supporting his goals while refusing to offer substantial concessions. Although SCLC's Operation Breadbasket, directed by former North Carolina A&T student activist Jesse Jackson, was somewhat successful in increasing employment and franchise ownership opportunities for African Americans, the Chicago campaign produced few tangible gains. By the spring of 1967, King had become disgusted with the failure of Chicago officials to implement an open housing agreement and other commitments. "The city's inaction," King warned, was "another hot coal on the smoldering fires of discontent and despair that are rampant in our black communities."

Racial Violence and White Repression

"If every Negro in the United States turns to violence," King remarked in 1967, "I will choose to be that one lone voice preaching that this is the wrong way." During that summer, King's determination was tested as the racial violence spread through dozens of the nation's urban black communities. An especially deadly insurgency erupted in Newark on July 13 after a crowd objecting to the arrest of a black taxi driver began throwing rocks at police. The following six days of civil disorder resulted in twenty-three deaths, more than 1,000 injuries, and widespread property damage. Soon afterward, still more deadly violence occurred in Detroit following a police raid on an illegal bar in a black neighborhood. Police were unable to regain control until National Guardsmen and army paratroopers arrived. The death count in Detroit reached forty-three, and arrests exceeded 7,000.

King feared that such racial violence would strengthen the influence of black power leaders who challenged his nonviolent strategy. He lamented the growing popularity of books such as Frantz Fanon's *The Wretched of the Earth* (1961), which promoted violence as a "psychologically healthy and tactically sound method for the oppressed," and *Black Power: The Politics of Liberation in America* (1967), written by Stokely Carmichael and black political scientist Charles Hamilton, which depicted African Americans as a colonized group. The latter book argued that black power represented "the last reasonable opportunity" for the United States "to work out its racial problems short of prolonged destructive guerilla warfare." King himself saw outbreaks of violence as inevitable, given the nation's neglect of the deeply rooted social inequities affecting African Americans. "The nation waited until the black man was explosive with fury before stirring itself even to partial concern," he observed.

Despite King's determination to offer effective alternatives to violence, he found it increasingly difficult to counter the rising influence of black power proponents such as Carmichael and Brown. Insisting that the black power slogan had negative connotations, King declined to attend the National Conference on Black Power held in Newark in July 1967 soon after the rioting there had ended. Although Carmichael himself was traveling abroad and could not attend, the conference attracted 1,000 delegates and revealed the growing popularity of black power ideas. Several SNCC workers, including Brown, spoke, and all the major civil rights organizations, including King's SCLC, were represented, although NAACP and Urban League leaders continued to denounce the black power slogan. The most influential figures at the conference, however, were not

A state policeman searches a youth on Detroit's 12th Street on July 24, 1967, while his companions lean against the wall waiting their turn.

the veterans of the southern civil rights struggle but black nationalists from northern cities who sought to speak for discontented ghetto residents.

Newark poet and dramatist Amiri Baraka set the tone for the meeting when he appeared wearing bandages from a police beating and spoke approvingly of his city's recent "rebellion of black people for self-determination." Once part of the community of Beat poets that included Allen Ginsberg, Baraka, then known as Leroi Jones, had become politically active after touring Cuba in 1960 as part of a delegation of writers. His increasing militancy was evident in his controversial 1964 play *The Dutchman,* which featured a deadly encounter on a New York subway between Clay, a young middle-class black man who has survived by suppressing his racial anger, and Lulu, a seductive yet sadistic white woman who brings Clay's anger to the surface. Following the assassination of Malcolm X in 1965, Baraka became an outspoken black nationalist, leaving his white wife and moving to Harlem, where he organized the Black Arts Repertory Theater School. His 1965 poem "Black Art" offered an agenda for militant black writers: "we want poems that kill." Baraka's writings inspired the Black Arts Movement of the late 1960s. Shortly before the Newark conference, Baraka adopted the cultural nationalist perspective of Maulana Karenga, a former UCLA graduate student who served as "master teacher" of US—the group's slogan: "Wherever we are, US is."

While black power proponents saw themselves as expressing black urban discontent, their speeches were less a cause than an outgrowth of the continuing urban violence, which was usually ignited by resentment of police instead of black power rhetoric. Nonetheless, white critics of black militancy, such as Maryland governor Agnew and FBI director Hoover, insisted that black power speeches caused violence. After the extensive racial violence of the summer of 1967, Hoover convinced Johnson to unleash a secret counterintelligence program (COINTELPRO) "to expose, disrupt, misdirect, discredit, or otherwise neutralize the activities of black nationalist, hate-type organizations and groupings, their leadership, spokesmen, membership, and supporters and to counter their propensity for violence and civil disorder." Among the groups selected for "intensified attention" in COINTELPRO were the SNCC, CORE, the Louisiana-based Deacons for Defense and Justice, and the Nation of Islam. Even the SCLC was on Hoover's list, despite King's well-known opposition to black nationalist ideas.

At about the same time Johnson approved the FBI's COINTELPRO against black organizations, he also established a National Advisory Commission on Civil Disorders to determine the root causes of the urban violence. Its report, issued in 1968, concluded that military force alone could not suppress urban racial violence and predicted that the nation was "moving toward two societies, one white, one black—separate and unequal." Still, Johnson did little to respond to its call for "a greatly enlarged" national commitment to action.

Although King's antiwar stance angered Johnson, both men were dismayed by the destructive impact of racial violence and antiwar dissent on the interracial coalition that had made possible Johnson's landslide victory in 1964. The Democratic Party's support among northern white workers declined as calls for black power contributed to the "white backlash." The deterioration in relations between African Americans and Jews also weakened the party, since these two groups had traditionally supported Democratic liberalism. King viewed black anti-Semitism as "immoral and self-destructive," but he could do little to stem black resentment of Jewish store owners in black communities. Black-Jewish conflicts were exacerbated following the outbreak of war in the Middle East during June 1967. Jews who had previously supported the civil rights struggle were angered when black activists in the SNCC and other groups voiced support for the Palestinian struggle against Israel.

■ **TABLE 19.1 Political and Civil Rights Organizations**

Black Panther Party: Formed in 1966 in Oakland by Huey Newton and Bobby Seale, the party initially emphasized armed self-defense but also developed "survival programs" for black communities.

Congressional Black Caucus: Founded in 1971 by black representatives to develop legislative strategies to deal with the concerns of African Americans.

National Black Feminist Organization (NBFO): A loosely organized group formed in 1973 to promote the interests of black women.

National Black Political Assembly: Formed to carry on the effort begun at the 1972 black convention in Gary, Indiana, to build an independent national black political force.

People United to Serve Humanity (PUSH): Led by Jesse Jackson, PUSH used the threat of boycotts to prod major corporations to make economic concessions.

The Poor People's Campaign and Memphis

By the fall of 1967, King concluded that dramatic steps had to be taken to reverse the cycle of declining white support for racial reform and escalating racial violence. When he addressed SCLC's annual meeting, he called for "restructuring the whole of American society," insisting that "the problem of racism, the problem of economic exploitation, and the problem of war are all tied together." Later in the year he announced that SCLC would "dramatize the whole economic problem of the poor" through a Poor People's Campaign that would bring the poor of all races to Washington in order to, in King's words, "place the problems of the poor at the seat of government of the wealthiest nation in the history of mankind."

Convinced that "the time has come for a return to mass nonviolent protest," King realized that the Poor People's Campaign would face even more opposition than his stand on Vietnam. Nonetheless, he believed that dramatic protests were needed to emphasize the urgency of the poverty issue. "We have, through massive nonviolent action, an opportunity to avoid a national disaster and create a new spirit of class and racial harmony," he asserted. By early 1968 the Poor People's Campaign had attracted support from Mexican Americans, Native Americans, and other activists, as King sought to bridge racial and ethnic boundaries, but most black power proponents saw little promise in King's efforts. Carmichael, for example, agreed merely to refrain from opposing the Poor People's Campaign while indicating his preference for an all-black united front.

As King traveled extensively, trying to build support for the campaign, Johnson remained preoccupied with repelling the Communist offensive launched during a Vietnamese Tet holiday at the end of January 1968. Moreover, the war had absorbed the budget surplus that Johnson had expected to fund his administration's antipoverty efforts and other Great Society programs. Disturbed that "not a single basic cause of riots has been corrected," King began to complain in speeches that the "dream" he had described at the March on Washington in 1963 had turned into a "nightmare."

In March 1968, King accepted an invitation to join a march in Memphis, where black sanitation workers had gone on strike. He hoped that a successful resolution of this dispute would give momentum to his broader effort on behalf of black people. King was disheartened, however, when a few demonstrators disrupted the march by breaking windows in downtown stores. Facing press criticism of his failure to control marchers, he felt compelled to return to the city to show that nonviolent tactics could still be effective. On April 3, he stayed at the black-owned Loraine Motel, while his staff tried to obtain a march permit and convince young gang members not to disrupt this protest.

When King spoke at a mass rally that evening, he was exhausted by the demands placed on him but encouraged by the enthusiasm of the audience. He assured the sanitation workers that he was pleased to have joined their struggle and was convinced that justice would ultimately prevail. "I just want to do God's will, and He's allowed me to go up to the mountain," he told the cheering audience. "And I've looked over, and I've seen the Promised Land. I may not get there with you, but I want you to know tonight that we, as a people, will get to the Promised Land!"

The following day, April 14, as King stood on the balcony outside his motel room, an assassin killed him with a single rifle shot. A white escaped convict, James Earl Ray, later confessed to the killing, although he claimed that he was a "patsy" acting for others—a claim made more credible by later revelations of the FBI's COINTELPRO activities against King.

News of King's death prompted deadly outbursts of racial violence in more than one hundred communities. As buildings burned within a mile of the White House, President Johnson proclaimed April 7 a day of national mourning. He also sent 20,000 troops, many of them trained for service in Vietnam, to quell the uprisings, which took forty-six lives. Carmichael warned that further violence would follow the death of "the one man of our race that this country's older generations, the militants and the revolutionaries and the masses of black people would still listen to." But John Lewis, who was working on behalf of recently announced presidential candidate Robert Kennedy when he learned of King's death, expressed dismay at the suggestion that violence was the only adequate black response: "What way was this to respond to the death of one of the most peaceful leaders of our time?"

King's funeral in Atlanta's Ebenezer Church was officiated by longtime friend Ralph Abernathy, who succeeded him as SCLC president. Among the tens of thousands of mourners were black leaders, including Roy Wilkins, Thurgood Marshall, and Jackie Robinson, who had criticized King's antiwar stand. Both Carmichael and Lewis represented SNCC. Presidential candidate Kennedy, Vice President Hubert Humphrey, and former vice president Richard Nixon were also there in a brief moment of national unity. But the shared grief did not bridge the deep political divisions that had hampered King's work during his final years. Although the Poor People's Campaign continued under Abernathy, by early summer it was disbanded without gaining significant concessions. Without King's leadership, SCLC declined in effectiveness.

BLACK SOLDIERS IN VIETNAM

For Army Major Colin Powell, King's death had been an "abrupt reminder" that "racism still bedeviled America." During his training at Fort Benning's Ranger school in Georgia, Powell, the son of Jamaican immigrants, said he felt "plunged back into the Old South every time I left the post." His wife was familiar with racism as well, having lived in Birmingham during the 1963 civil rights demonstrations. Powell recalled that as he served as a military advisor in Vietnam, his father-in-law had "sat up nights, a shotgun across his lap, ready to defend his home against fellow Americans of a different color." But Powell also recalled that he and other black military officers rejected the subsequent trend toward black power militancy. "We heard the radical black voices—Stokely Carmichael, Eldridge Cleaver, and H. Rap Brown with his 'Burn, baby, burn!'—with uneasiness," Powell recalled. "We were not eager to see the country burned down. We were doing well in it." Yet he understood the sources of the growing racial anger. "Each of us had experienced enough racial indignities to understand the riots unleashed in black ghettoes in the wake of the King assassination."

"We were not eager to see the country burned down. We were doing well in it."—*Colin Powell*

Like previous major wars, Vietnam profoundly affected the lives of many African Americans. For black soldiers who served in Vietnam, the war offered an opportunity to demonstrate once again that they were prepared to fight for freedom on many fronts. However, controversies in the United States over civil rights and black power reverberated in Vietnam, while at the same time disagreements concerning American intervention in Vietnam affected the civil rights and black power movements. On both the home front and the battlefields, the backdrop of violence shaped the way racial issues were viewed and discussed. Daily newscasts brought the war to the television sets of civilians; some called it the "living room war." The brief tours of duty—no more than a year in Vietnam for most soldiers—reduced the isolation of soldiers. Moreover, as King pointed out in his antiwar speech at Riverside Church, the war

Wallace Terry's 1984 book describes the Vietnam War from the black soldier's perspective.

■ Black U.S. Marines greet each other with the black power salute in Vietnam in 1968.

affected domestic racial policies by diverting federal funds that might otherwise be spent on the war on poverty and other Great Society social programs.

Back in 1962, when Powell first arrived as a military advisor in Vietnam, few Americans paid much attention to the ongoing civil war of the Vietnamese. The conflict had its roots in the American ambivalence during the 1940s about supporting movements against European colonialism, especially if those movements were seen as Communist inspired. In 1954, after Vietnamese nationalists had defeated France, the United States opposed the reunification of previously French-controlled South Vietnam with North Vietnam, led by Communist nationalist Ho Chi Minh. Powell was among the more than 16,000 American advisors sent by President John F. Kennedy to prop up a pro-American South Vietnamese regime that had little popular support. Powell was wounded in combat, but he remained convinced that it was "right to draw the line against communism anywhere in the world." He began to doubt, however, whether the war could be won without a major escalation of American involvement.

By the time Powell returned for his second tour in Vietnam in 1968, more than a half million American troops were there. In August 1964 President Johnson had used the pretext of a North Vietnamese attack against American naval forces in the Gulf of Tonkin to secure a Congressional resolution authorizing military force to resist Communist aggression. Despite sending more and more troops to Vietnam, however, Johnson found that victory was elusive against a determined guerilla army backed by North Vietnamese regular troops. Unlike the military advisors of the earlier period, the American combat soldiers Powell saw when he returned were often draftees rather than volunteers. African-Americans made up about 11 percent of the nation's population; yet more than 16 percent of military inductees during 1967 were black, and the proportion of black soldiers was often even higher in combat units. Young black men were less likely than their white counterparts to escape the military draft by going to college or by volunteering for National Guard service.

Like the rest of the nation, the American troops in Vietnam were divided along racial lines. "Young blacks, particularly draftees, saw the war, not surprisingly, as even less their fight than the whites did," Powell observed. "They had less to go home to. This generation was more likely to be reached by the fireworks of H. Rap Brown than the reasonableness of the late Martin Luther King." Many black draftees resented those in authority, including Powell and other officers. "I was living in a large tent and I moved my cot every night," Powell remembered, "partly to thwart Viet Cong informants who might be tracking me, but also because I did not rule out attacks on authority from within the battalion itself."

After finishing his tour in 1969, Powell had become disillusioned with the conduct of the war. He rejected "the one-size-fits-all rationale of anticommunism" that had led to American involvement in a war rooted "in nationalism, anticolonialism, and civil strife beyond the East-West conflict." He was also disturbed that "poorer, less educated, less privileged" young men had been victims of "raw class discrimination," while "sons of the powerful and well placed" avoided combat service. Although the war in Vietnam marked the culmination of the desegregation of the armed forces, it also served as a reminder that the military was not isolated from the racial problems that affected American society as a whole. "We understood the bitterness of black GIs who, if they were lucky enough to get home from Vietnam in one piece, still faced poor job prospects and fresh indignities," Powell remembered.

THE RISE AND FALL OF THE BLACK POWER MILITANCY

While Colin Powell served as a military officer in Vietnam, the Black Panther Party for Self-Defense was urging black men not to "fight and kill other people of color in the world" who were "being victimized by the white racist government of America." Bobby Seale and Huey Newton, who had become friends while attending a junior college in Oakland, California, formed the party in October 1966. Dissatisfied with existing black political groups, they believed that a more militant organization was needed. Seale, the party's chairman, and Newton, its minister of defense, drafted a ten-point platform that included far-reaching demands, but the party's initial popularity was due largely to its call for an immediate end to police brutality against black people. Insisting that the Second Amendment of the U.S. Constitution gave them the right to carry weapons, armed Black Panthers began "patrolling the pigs" (their derogatory term for police) to observe and report police misconduct. The new group gained national press coverage in the spring of 1967 when a contingent of Black Panthers, most of them wearing the group's distinctive black leather jackets and black berets, carried their weapons to California's capitol to protest a gun control law the legislature was considering. In October of the same year, police charged Newton with killing an Oakland policeman who had stopped a car containing Newton and another party member. The Black Panther Party's subsequent "Free Huey" campaign soon made the group the best-known and most controversial black militant group of the late 1960s.

■ Black Panthers march in New York to protest the murder trial of cofounder Huey P. Newton in Oakland, California, on July 22, 1968.

Black Panther Party Platform

In October 1966, Huey Newton and Bobby Seale drew up the Ten-Point Program of their newly-founded Black Panther Party for Self-Defense. Although the Black Panthers underwent numerous changes during the following decade as a result of leadership changes and external repression, this document remained the group's guiding statement of purpose.

1. We want freedom. We want the power to determine the destiny of our Black community.
2. We want full employment for our people.
3. We want an end to the robbery by the white man of our Black community. We believe that this racist government has robbed us and now we are demanding the overdue debt of forty acres and two mules.
4. We want decent housing, fit for shelter of human beings.
5. We want education for our people that exposes the true nature of this decadent American society. We want education that teaches us our true history and our role in present-day society.
6. We want all Black men to be exempt from military service.
7. We want an immediate end to POLICE BRUTALITY and MURDER of Black people.
8. We want freedom for all Black men held in federal, state, county and city prisons and jail.
9. We want all Black people when brought to trial to be tried in court by a jury of their peer group or people from their Black communities, as defined by the Constitution of the United States. We believe that the courts should follow the United States Constitution so that Black people will receive fair trials.
10. We want land, bread, housing, education, clothing, justice, and peace. And as our major political objective, a United Nations-supervised plebiscite to be held throughout the Black colony in which only Black colonial subjects will be allowed to participate, for the purpose of determining the will of Black people as to their national destiny. When, in the course of human events, it becomes necessary for one people to dissolve the political bonds which have connected them with another, and to assume, among the powers of the earth, the separate and equal station to which the laws of nature and nature's God entitle them, a decent respect to the opinions of mankind requires that they should declare the causes which impel them to separation.

We hold these truths to be self-evident, that all men are created equal; that they are endowed by their Creator with certain inalienable rights; that among these are life, liberty, and the pursuit of happiness. That, to secure these rights, governments are instituted among men, deriving their just power from the consent of the governed; that, whenever any form of government becomes destructive of these ends, it is the right of the people to alter or to abolish it, and to institute a new government, laying its foundation on such principles, and organizing powers in such form, as to them shall seem most likely to effect their safety and happiness.

—from Clayborne Carson, et al., eds., The Eyes on the Prize Civil Rights Reader, *(Penguin: New York, 1991).*

To view a longer version of this document, please go to *www.ablongman.com/carson/documents*.

The Emergence of Eldridge Cleaver

The effort to mobilize support for Newton soon brought together black militants from many different backgrounds and with varied political perspectives. Eldridge Cleaver, who became the party's Minister of Information shortly before Newton's arrest, quickly emerged as the key figure in this effort to build support. A gang member in Los Angeles during his youth, Cleaver's political evolution had begun as he was serving a prison term for rape. Raping white women, he initially thought, was "insurrectionary," a way of "trampling upon the white man's laws" by "defiling his women."

But then he decided that he had "gone astray—astray not so much from the white man's law as from being human, civilized." Like Malcolm X, Cleaver educated himself in prison. He wrote insightful essays, later collected in the best-selling book *Soul on Ice* (1967), that brought him to the attention of white sympathizers who gained his release from prison. In his writings, Cleaver set himself apart from James Baldwin, whose book *The Fire Next Time* (1963) had expressed the black militancy of the early 1960s. He dismissed Baldwin as a victim of self-hatred and homosexuality, calling instead for a bold black heterosexual masculinity: "We shall have our manhood. We shall have it or the earth will be leveled by our attempts to gain it." Cleaver's decision to join the Black Panthers came after he observed a standoff between Oakland police and an armed guard of Black Panthers escorting Malcolm X's widow, Betty Shabazz. He was amazed that the Panthers refused to disarm and withdrew from the scene still holding their guns.

Cleaver's prominence as a writer and his forceful presence as a speaker contributed to the rapid growth of the campaign to free Newton. During the fall of 1967 he gained the backing of California's newly organized Peace and Freedom Party, comprised mainly of antiwar activists. Other leftist groups also offered support, appreciating that Black Panthers rejected racial separatism. In his effort to build black support, Cleaver saw Stokely Carmichael as a key figure. Not only had Carmichael gained national prominence as a black power advocate, he had also attracted international attention as a result of his travels during the summer and fall of 1967. Cuba's Fidel Castro had greeted him, and there had been extensive press coverage of his statements in Havana calling the summer's black urban rebellions the beginning of a revolution. Then Carmichael had flown to North Vietnam, prompting angry calls in Congress for the confiscation of his passport upon his return. Carmichael met in Hanoi with Vietnamese leader Ho Chi Minh, who recalled his brief stay in Harlem as a young man and related his memories of hearing Marcus Garvey deliver a speech. By the time Carmichael returned after additional stops in several African nations, his status as the nation's foremost black militant had been confirmed. Cleaver and Seale met with Carmichael, persuaded him to speak at "Free Huey" rallies planned for February 1968, and invited him to become the Black Panther Party's prime minister.

> "We shall have our manhood. We shall have it or the earth will be leveled by our attempts to gain it."
> —*Eldridge Cleaver*

Seale and Cleaver hoped Carmichael's support would lead to an alliance with SNCC. They contacted other SNCC leaders, including H. Rap Brown, to invite them to help build the party. The well-attended rallies at the Los Angeles Sports Arena and the Oakland Auditorium attracted a wide array of black leaders, ranging from Los Angeles black nationalist Maulana Karenga to Berkeley city councilman Ronald Dellums. These rallies marked a period of rapid expansion for the Black Panthers, with dozens of chapters forming in cities throughout the nation. The party's recruits included college students, but many of the rank-and-file members were "street brothers" like Cleaver. Black women also filled the party's ranks, although armed black males shaped its public image. The Black Panthers attracted substantial white support as well. The Peace and Freedom Party raised funds for Newton's defense and agreed to make Cleaver its presidential candidate in the 1968 presidential election. Once hardly known outside the San Francisco Bay area, the Black Panthers were sufficiently confident to present a petition at the United Nations calling on African nations and Cuba to support Newton and stop the "genocide" against African Americans. When Newton's trial began in July 1968, thousands of Black Panthers and sympathizers mobilized outside the Oakland courthouse to demand his release.

High Tide of Black Rebellion

The growth of support for the Black Panthers was only one aspect of the upsurge in racial militancy during 1968. The explosion of racial anger that followed King's assassination in April signaled that the nation was indeed close to chaos, if not revolution. Discontent continued to grow on college campuses as well as urban ghettoes. Although black colleges had been relatively quiet in the years since the 1960 sit-ins, student activism was widespread during the late 1960s. Clashes between police and students at Mississippi's Jackson State and at Houston's Texas Southern left two students dead at Jackson and one at Texas Southern. Early in 1968, an assault by police and National Guardsmen on unarmed student demonstrators at South Carolina State College resulted in the deaths of three students and the wounding of several dozen more. Black students at predominant black Bowie State College in Maryland, Tuskegee Institute in Alabama, and Howard University protested white governance and the lack of black studies programs by seizing buildings and calling strikes. Students at numerous predominantly white colleges and universities demanded black studies programs and increased admission of black students. An extended student strike at San Francisco State University that began in 1967 led to the creation of the

First Person: Pauli Murray on Black Separatism

When Pauli Murray was a law student at Howard University during the 1940s, she had urged NAACP lawyers to attack the Plessy v. Ferguson separate-but-equal doctrine. Although there were limited opportunities for women lawyers such as Murray, she became a successful writer, publishing Proud Shoes *in 1956. She also became a pioneer in the women's rights movement, serving on a study committee for President John F. Kennedy's Commission on the Status of Women in 1961–1963 and helping to found the National Organization for Women in 1966. Two years later, she accepted a teaching post at Brandeis University and unexpectedly found herself on the defensive as black student activists challenged her ideas. She recorded her thoughts about the experience in her autobiography,* Song in a Weary Throat.

From the moment I arrived on campus, I was thrown into fundamental philosophical and moral conflict with the advocates of a black ideology as alien to my nature and as difficult for me to accept as white ethnocentrism. The emerging racial rhetoric smacked of an ethnic "party line" and made absolutely no sense to me; in turn, some of my most deeply held values about universal human dignity were considered obsolete by young black radicals. . . .

Little in my recent academic experiences had equipped me to cope with a sudden sea change in racial attitudes on the part of those who were enjoying privileges my generation of civil rights fighters had never known. . . . While Dr. King's assassination in the intervening period understandably stirred up passions of a sorely tried people, it seemed to me that the excessively churlish, racially inspired rhetoric of the more radical black students was misplaced in the comparatively sympathetic atmosphere of Brandeis University. . . .

A new phase of the struggle emerged, variously called Black Power, Black Liberation, and in its most extreme form, Revolutionary Black Nationalism, profoundly affecting the outlook of thousands upon thousands of people of color who embraced the new movement as a means of survival and self-respect. Emphasis shifted from interracial cooperation to self-determination and a strong identification with the rising African nations and other nonwhite third world peoples. "Black and white together, we shall overcome"—the song of the old civil rights movement—was discarded by many, who now shouted "Black is beautiful," Black Consciousness," or "Black Nationhood."

A generation of Negro students, in their infancy when the historic 1954 desegregation decision was handed down by the Supreme Court and whose entire lives were shaped by continuous, overt racial strife, were now entering college, bringing with them a legacy of nearly two decades of unrelieved turbulence. . . . For a time, I was living in a world turned upside down; in a complete reversal of goals that had fired my own student activism, some of the young militants were now demanding separate dormitories and cultural centers, from which whites were to be excluded, as well as Afro-American/Black Studies departments controlled by blacks, taught by black professors, and attended exclusively by black students.

—from Song in a Weary Throat *by Pauli Murray (New York: HarperCollins).*

To view a longer version of this document, please go to *www.ablongman.com/carson/documents*.

willingness of white authorities to crush black militancy with superior power. When police and state troopers retook the prison, they shot to death forty-three people, including ten of the guards being held hostage.

Although there was criticism of the tactics used to storm Attica prison, there was considerable popular support for law-and-order policies. Similarly, even though the FBI's COINTELPRO against the Black Panthers and other black militants included illegal and even deadly activities, they were nonetheless effective. By the time of the Attica revolt, the influence of the Black Panthers and other black radicals had declined dramatically from the group's heyday in 1968. Although Cleaver continued to advocate revolution from Algeria, Newton had expelled him and many of his supporters. The inflammatory speeches of Cleaver and other Black Panthers not only led to repression but also damaged the party's black support. Rather than attributing the decline of the Black Panthers entirely to the police and FBI repression, Newton acknowledged his group had contributed to its own decline. The title of an essay he published during 1971 offered an explanation of the party's rapid rise and fall: "On the Defection of Eldridge Cleaver from the Black Panther Party and On the Defection of the Black Panther Party from the People."

By the early 1970s, black power militancy was no longer a significant political force. Instead of Black Panthers with guns, popular films were beginning to offer another version of black militancy as a source of popular entertainment. In 1969 Sidney Poitier starred in *The Lost Man*, a low-budget film made in Paris in which he played a black militant leader who turns to robbery to finance revolutionary struggle. Although Poitier's departure from his previous screen persona appealed to only a small audience, independent black filmmaker Melvin van Peebles reached far more viewers with *Sweet Sweetback's Baadasssss Song*, released two years later. Starring in his own film, van Peebles played a pimp who retaliates for the beating of a black boy by assaulting two police officers. Although the flimsy plot consisted mainly of an extended chase, the film earned many times its cost of production. Its leading character was violent and sexually aggressive in ways that Poitier was never allowed to be in the 1950s and 1960s. Audiences in black communities cheered as the film ended with the message "A BAADASSSSS NIGGER IS COMING BACK TO COLLECT SOME DUES."

The surprise success of van Peebles convinced Hollywood studios that there was a large black audience ready for films featuring violence-prone black male heroes. During the next few years, more than a dozen black action films were released by Hollywood studios. *Super Fly* (1972) starred Ron O'Neal as a Harlem cocaine dealer, while several *Shaft* films starred Richard Roundtree as a super-confident black detective. Some critics used the term "blaxploitation" to describe such films that gave black audiences a chance to cheer black male heroes. Rather than the political messages associated with the Black Panther Party, the new heroes were loners, either criminals outside the law or detectives working on the margins of the criminal justice system. The blaxploitation films popularized new racial stereotypes, but they did provide starring roles for black male actors, including athletes-turned-actors such as football stars Jim Brown and O. J. Simpson.

DIVERGING DIRECTIONS OF BLACK POLITICS

While some black filmmakers tried to remake the rebelliousness of the 1960s into the popular culture of the 1970s, Jesse Jackson also transformed the militancy he had displayed in southern civil rights demonstrations into a political style that would work as electoral politics supplanted black radicalism. Jackson had first attracted attention as one of the youngest members of SCLC's staff, but he became still more prominent even as SCLC declined after King's assassination. Some of his former colleagues resented Jackson's ambitiousness, claiming he had once misled reporters by suggesting that King had died in his arms. But no one questioned his dedication. "He was willing to commit himself to the struggle with few if any reservations," SCLC administrator Andrew Young remembered.

Jackson's drive had been evident during his formative years in Greenville, South Carolina, where as the son of an unwed mother he had overcome class as well as racial barriers. He excelled as a student and athlete in high school and became student body president at North Carolina A&T, where he became a protest leader during the early 1960s. In 1965, he left his studies at Chicago Theological Seminary to take part in the Selma to Montgomery March, impressing SCLC officials with his fiery speeches. When King became involved the following year in the Chicago campaign, he recruited Jackson to run SCLC's Operation Breadbasket, created to achieve economic gains for black residents. Following King's death, he decided to leave SCLC and transform Operation Breadbasket into an independent group called Operation People United to Save (later changed to Serve) Humanity (PUSH). By the early 1970s, Jackson's PUSH associates sensed he would become a major national leader. "I

National Black Political Agenda, 1972

The following excerpt is from the fifty-five page document addressed to African Americans, prepared at the end of the National Black Political Convention held in Gary, Indiana, in May 1972. The Black Agenda was intended to serve as a set of ideals and assumptions around which black Americans could unify.

White Realities, Black Choice

For more than a century we have followed the path of political dependence on white men and their systems. From the Liberty Party in the decades before the Civil War to the Republican Party of Abraham Lincoln, we trusted in white men and white politics as our deliverers. Sixty years ago, W. E. B. Du Bois said he would give the Democrats their "last chance" to prove their commitment to equality for Black people—and he was given riots and official segregation in peace and in war.

Nevertheless, some twenty years later we became Democrats in the name of Franklin Roosevelt, then supported his successor Harry Truman, and even tried a "non-partisan" Republican General of the Army named Eisenhower. We were wooed like many others by the superficial liberalism of John F. Kennedy and the make-believe populism of Lyndon Johnson. Let there be no more of that. . . .

The Politics of Social Transformation

So, we come to Gary confronted with a choice. But it is not the old conventional question of which candidate shall we support, the pointless question of who is to preside over a decaying and unsalvageable system. No, if we come to Gary out of the realities of the Black communities of this land, then the only real choice for us is whether or not we will live by the truth we know [and] whether we will move to organize independently, move to struggle for fundamental transformation, for the creation of new directions, toward a concern for the life and the meaning of Man. Social transformation or social destruction, those are our only real choices.

If we have come to Gary on behalf of our people in America, in the rest of this hemisphere, and in the Homeland—if we have come for our own best ambitions—then a new Black Politics must come to birth. If we are serious, the Black Politics of Gary must accept major responsibility for creating both the atmosphere and the program for fundamental, far-ranging change in America. Such responsibility is ours because it is our people who are most deeply hurt and ravaged by the present systems of society. That responsibility for leading the change is ours because we live in a society where few other men really believe in the responsibility of a truly humane society anywhere.

—from The National Black Political Agenda, Gary, Indiana, 1972 *(Washington, DC: National Black Political Convention, 1972), pp. 2, 3.*

To view a longer version of this document, please go to *www.ablongman.com/carson/documents.*

thought he was perhaps the most intense person that I had ever met," recalled Jackson advisor Richard Hatcher, who had become the first black mayor of Gary, Indiana, in 1967. Weekly PUSH rallies attracted large, enthusiastic crowds. "Black, whites, lots of college students would come and fill that auditorium every Saturday morning, because they knew there would be an opportunity to hear him speak," Hatcher remembered.

The National Black Political Convention

The 3,000 delegates and 5,000 observers who came to Gary, Indiana, in March 1972 for the National Black Political Convention reflected the political diversity within black communities. Planners of the gathering included not only Hatcher and Michigan congressman Charles C. Diggs but southern politician could support civil rights. When as governor of Georgia, Carter announced that he would run for president in the 1976 election, few observers gave him much chance. But Carter was able to campaign as a pro-civil rights southerner, attracting black support without alienating white Democrats. He won endorsements from congressman Andrew Young and Martin Luther King Sr. Running against President Gerald Ford, a Michigan Republican weakened by his decision to pardon Nixon for his Watergate crimes, Carter won with overwhelming support from black voters.

As president, Carter appointed a number of prominent African Americans to high positions in his administration. Andrew Young became ambassador to the United Nations, while Patricia Roberts Harris, former dean of Howard University's law school, became secretary of the Department of Housing and Urban Development and the first black woman to serve as a cabinet member. Eleanor Holmes Norton, a former SNCC worker and one of the founders of the National Black Feminist Organization, became chair of the Equal Employment Opportunity Commission, the agency charged with enforcing civil rights policies. Former SNCC chair John Lewis also joined the Carter administration as associate director of Action, the federal volunteer agency. Lewis had spent the early 1970s directing the Voter Education Project, and the slogan of that organization suggested a theme of the decade following voting rights reforms: "Hands That Pick Cotton Now Can Pick Our Elected Officials."

Actors Cicely Tyson (left) and Maya Angelou look lovingly at Kunta Kinte in a scene from the 1977 television miniseries "Roots."

The "Roots" Phenomenon

During the first year of Carter's presidency, the phenomenal success of the "Roots" television series increased popular awareness of African American history, while at the same time drawing attention to the brutalities of past racial oppression. In some respects, *Roots* served as a corrective to earlier violence-filled blaxploitation films. Such films had provided roles for black actors, mostly as action heroes, but they were rarely well crafted and did not offer positive depictions of African American women. Roles for black women were usually limited to portrayals of prostitutes or as love interests of male stars, although Pam Greer achieved some success as a female action hero.

Among the few black women who achieved a measure of success during this period was Cicely Tyson, who resisted taking roles she found demeaning. The daughter of strictly religious Caribbean immigrants in New York, Tyson had turned to modeling and then acting after first working as a secretary for the American Red Cross. "I know God did not put me on the face of this earth to bang on a typewriter for the rest of my life," she later explained. Devoting herself to becoming a serious actor, she struggled financially while building her reputation in small stage productions. During the 1960s, she had a continuing role on television in the short-lived series "East Side, West Side," and then gained critical acclaim in Jean Genet's avant-garde play *The Blacks*, which also starred James Earl Jones, Maya Angelou, and Roscoe Jones. Afterwards, Tyson continued to seek roles that "had to do with educating as well as entertaining." Her performance as a Louisiana sharecropper in the 1972 film *Sounder* boosted her career. Playing the wife of a man imprisoned for stealing food for his family, she displayed quiet strength and dignity as her character confronts racist local white people and endures the absence of her husband and later her son, who sets off alone to find his father. The performance earned her an Academy Award nomination and prompted one leading film critic to proclaim her "the first great black heroine on the screen." Soon after the success of *Sounder*, Tyson was chosen for the starring role in *The Autobiography of Miss Jane Pittman* (1974), an adaptation of Ernest Gaines's novel about a black woman who survives from the Civil War to the era of civil rights protests. Tyson convincingly depicted the travails of the ex-slave who survives hard times during Reconstruction to become a 110-year-old civil rights protester who courageously uses a whites-only drinking fountain. *Jane Pittman* attracted high ratings, won Tyson a best actress Emmy, and encouraged Hollywood to produce "Roots" (1977), a major historical television miniseries based on Alex Haley's Pulitzer Prize–winning family saga.

In "Roots," Tyson played the mother of an African youth, Kunta Kinte, who is enslaved and brought to America. Although she had only a supporting role in the first episode of the series, she again received acclaim for her contribution to what became a historic event. *Roots* became television's most widely viewed drama, attracting some 130 million viewers. For many Americans of all races, the series became a source of education as well as entertainment. Its depiction of the capture and enslavement of Kunta Kinte (played by LeVar Burton) allowed viewers to gain a sense of the horrors of the middle passage on slave ships and the cruelty of the slave system. For African Americans, Haley's somewhat fictionalized account of his family history, based on twelve years of research, became a substitute for unknown aspects of their own history. By debunking the myth that it was impossible for black people to trace their family roots, Haley encouraged an explosion of genealogical research. *Roots: The Saga of an American Family* sold more than 8 million copies, and Haley's lectures, which recounted the story of his research, drew large crowds. Although black writer Margaret Walker Alexander charged that Haley had copied elements of her own historical epic *Jubilee* (1966), Haley gained the enviable reputation of having produced two of the era's most influential books: *Roots* and *The Autobiography of Malcolm X*.

"Roots" demonstrated the large potential audience for well-made films that illuminated African American history; yet for the most part, the black presence on television and in American films continued to serve the purpose of entertainment rather than enlightenment.

CONCLUSION

In the decade after H. Rap Brown attracted national attention as a black power proponent, there had been many changes in African American political life. The nation's racial divisions became visible as never before as black militants confronted white authorities in cities, on college campuses, and even in prisons. The violence of urban racial conflict and of warfare in Vietnam fueled calls for racial separatism and revolution. Although black power militancy encouraged racial pride and expressed resentment of long-standing racial injustices, racial unity and power remained elusive goals. The revolutionary objectives sought by Brown and other black power advocates were not achieved, but a new generation of black elected officials was able to protect previous civil rights gains and work with increasing effectiveness within the American political system. The era's most enduring gains came from the emergence of black elected officials who rejected black power rhetoric in favor of black political influence. Many African Americans found much to hope for in the election of Democrat Jimmy Carter in 1976, and their votes helped put him in office. But the racial gains were balanced against setbacks, as white resistance to affirmative action and school busing remained widespread. Thus, at the end of the 1970s, African American politics faced new challenges within an increasingly conservative political climate.

FURTHER READING

Brown, Elaine. *A Taste of Power: A Black Woman's Story* (New York: Random House, 1994).

Cleaver, Kathleen, and George Katsiaficas. *Liberation, Imagination, and the Black Panther Party* (New York: Rutledge, 2001).

Collier-Thomas, Bettye and V. P. Franklin, ed. *African American Women in the Civil Rights-Black Power Movement* (New York: NYU, 2001).

Hampton, Henry, and Steve Fayer. *Voices of Freedom: An Oral History of the Civil Rights Movement* (New York: Bantam, 1990).

Jones, Charles. *The Black Panther Party Reconsidered* (Black Classic Press, 1998).

Lawson, Steven F. *In Pursuit of Power: Southern Blacks and Electoral Politics, 1965–1982* (New York: Oxford University Press, 1985).

Marable, Manning. *Race, Reform, and Rebellion: The Second Reconstruction in Black America, 1945–1990* (Jackson: University Press of Mississippi, 1984, 1991).

McKnight, Gerald. *Last Crusade: Martin Luther King, Jr., the FBI, and the Poor People's Campaign* (Boulder, CO: Westview Press, 1998).

Nelson, William E., Jr., and Philip J. Meranto. *Electing Black Mayors: Political Action in the Black Community* (Columbus: Ohio State University Press, 1977).

O'Reilly, Kenneth. *"Racial Matters": The FBI's Secret File on Black America, 1960–1972* (New York: Free Press, 1989).

Van Deburg, William. *New Day in Babylon: The Black Power Movement and American Culture* (Chicago: University of Chicago Press, 1992).

Westheider, James E. *Fighting on Two Fronts: African Americans and the Vietnam War* (New York: New York University Press, 1997).

Woodard, Komozi. *A Nation within a Nation: Amiri Baraka (LeRoi Jones) and Black Power Politics* (Chapel Hill: University of North Carolina Press, 1999).

CHAPTER 20

■ **Faith Ringgold, *For the Woman's House* (1971). Best known for her painted quilts, this oil-canvas painting captures the many roles and faces of black women.**

Source: Faith Ringgold, Work: For the Woman's House, 1971, oil on canvas mounted on wood panel, 96 x 96 inches.

The Search for New Directions During a Conservative Era, 1979–1991

Michele Wallace on the Discontents of Black Women

"I went from obscurity to celebrity to notoriety overnight," said Michele Wallace as she recalled the response to her controversial 1979 book *Black Macho and the Myth of the Superwoman*. "At twenty-six I had written the book from hell and my life would change forever."

Although surprised by the intensity of the attacks against her, Wallace knew *Black Macho* would spark controversy. Even though still a teenager during the heyday of the black power movement, she had formed strong opinions about black militant leaders, and now she was ready to express her views publicly. A self-described "black American princess" who grew up in Harlem and attended the private New Lincoln School, she had sympathized with the civil rights movement and initially admired Stokely Carmichael and other black power advocates. However, by the time she entered Howard University in the late 1960s, her attitudes had been transformed by the emerging women's liberation movement. She soon left Howard—"between the fraternities and the Black Power antics, misogyny ran amuck on a daily basis down there"—to enroll at New York's City College. Along with her artist mother, Faith Ringgold, she joined a small group of black women, many of them civil rights and antiwar activists, who identified with the new women's liberation movement.

CHAPTER OUTLINE

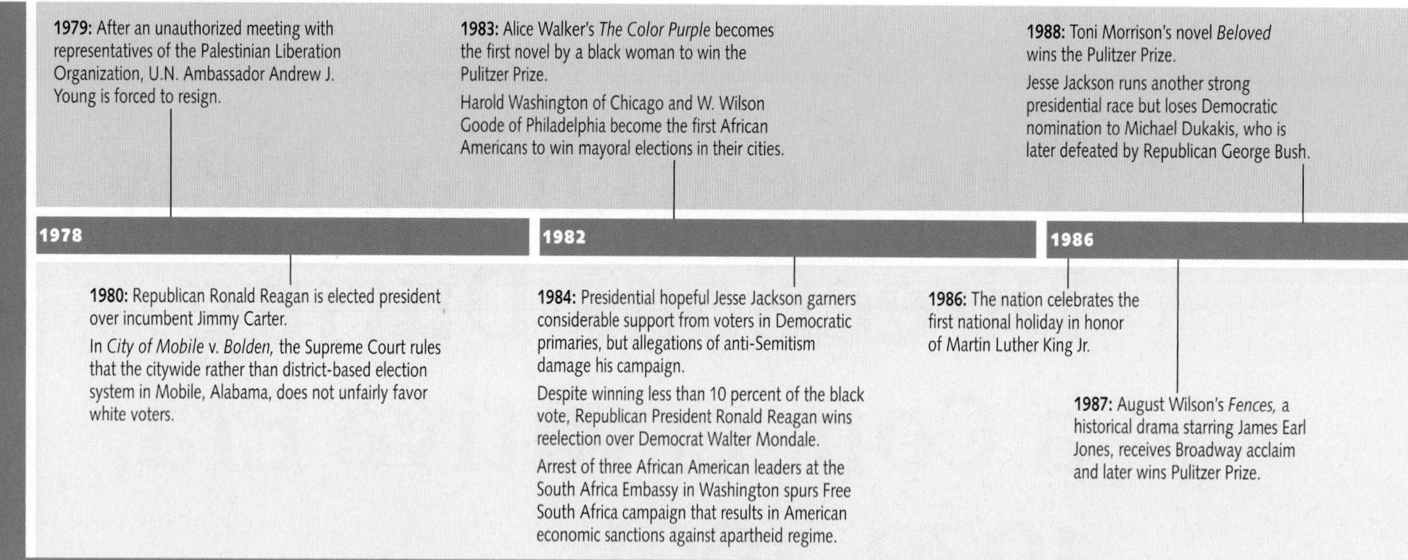

No longer content with the agenda of the National Organization for Women (NOW), founded in 1966 to campaign to enforce the sex discrimination provisions of the 1964 Civil Rights Act, Wallace and other black feminists of the early 1970s favored greater militancy for women's rights. They also believed both black power leaders and white feminists gave insufficient attention to the concerns of black women. Wallace felt there was "a basic communication gap" between black women and white women on some issues: "When the middle-class white woman said 'I want to work,' in her head was a desk in the executive suite, while the black woman saw a bin of dirty clothes, someone else's dirty clothes." In 1973, believing black women should entrust their liberation neither to black men nor white women, Wallace became one of the founders of the National Black Feminist Organization (NBFO).

During the 1970s, only a small minority of black women identified themselves as feminists, but Wallace was convinced her views reflected the submerged discontents of many black women. In *Black Macho,* she insisted that black power leaders had not only failed to achieve racial unity but had instead fostered increasing tensions between black men and black women. Black power militancy had been tragic rather than heroic—an opportunity missed due to the "growing distrust, even hatred, between black men and black women." Wallace blamed the "narcissistic macho" of black male militants "blinded by their resentment of black women, their envy of white men, and their irresistible urge to bring white women down a peg."

Wallace argued that Richard Wright's 1940 book *Native Son* had been "the starting point of the black writer's love affair with Black Macho," since the Bigger Thomas character "could only come to life in the act of punishing the white man." During the 1960s, the black macho theme was vividly expressed, according to Wallace, in Eldridge Cleaver's *Soul on Ice,* in which the Black Panther leader admitted "practicing" on black women before raping white women as "an insurrectionary act" of revenge against white men. She claimed Cleaver and other black power spokesmen equated black liberation with the violent assertion of black manhood. "Black Power meant wooly heads, big black fists, and stern black faces, gargantuan omnipotent black male organs, big black rifles and foot-long combat boots . . . black men looting and rioting in the streets, taking over the country by brute force, arrogant lawlessness and an unquestionable sexual authority granted them as the victims of four hundred years of racism and abuse." But the hyper-heterosexuality of black male militants, she concluded, had not overcome white racism.

Although white feminists, such as *Ms.* magazine founder Gloria Steinem, applauded Wallace as a major black voice, some black activists saw her as a tool of white feminists or even a racial traitor who exaggerated the sexism of black power figures. Wallace's public appearances attracted hecklers. She opened herself to criticism from other feminists by alleging that black women activists wanted "to be models of fragile Victorian womanhood" and "were not allowed to do

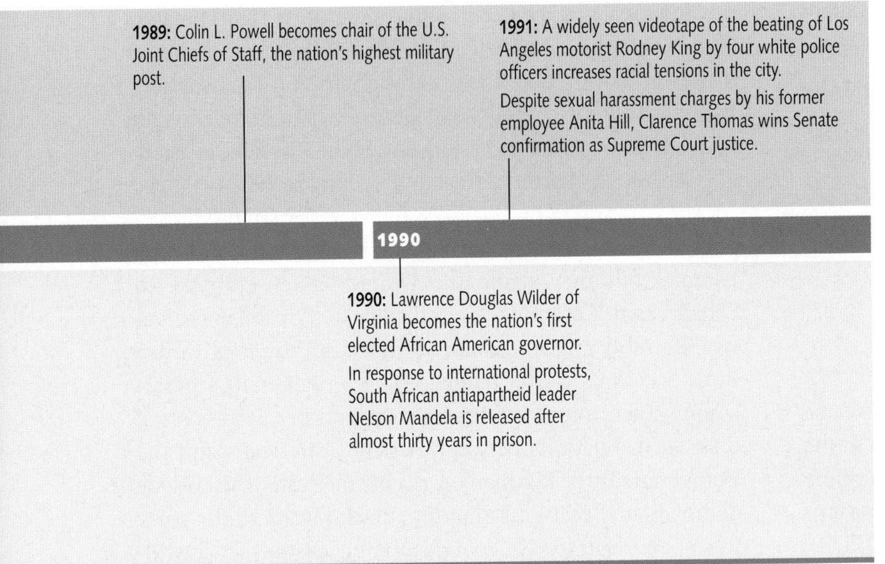

anything important in the Black Movement." This certainly did not apply to women such as Ella Baker, Diane Nash Bevel, and Ruby Doris Robinson of SNCC or Kathleen Cleaver, Erika Huggins, and Elaine Brown of the Black Panther Party.

Former civil rights worker and writer Alice Walker offered a qualified defense of *Black Macho* for providing "many good things that (though not as original as she thinks) can be very helpful to us, if we will *hear* them." But she criticized Wallace's assertion that black women accepted stereotypical roles as unfeminine "Mother Earth" types or as "superwomen." Walker insisted, "I've been hacking away at that stereotype for years, and so have a good many other black writers." Wallace herself later conceded that her incendiary polemic was "destined to be misread and misunderstood in its own time."

The controversy over *Black Macho* exposed the simmering conflicts among African Americans that erupted as the ambitious hopes and expectations of the 1960s gave way to new racial realities. Black feminist writers did not have much immediate impact on black politics, but during the 1980s they reached a growing audience of receptive readers. A new generation of articulate, college-educated black women—many of them beneficiaries of Title VII of the 1964 Civil Rights Act, which outlawed employment discrimination based on race, color, religion, sex, and national origin—began to assert themselves and express their frustrations with male leaders who ignored their special concerns as women. Black women also began to play more prominent roles in African American intellectual life. An outpouring of innovative visual art, music, dance, drama, and literature by black women illuminated their distinctive experiences while challenging the emphasis on the assertion of black manhood that had pervaded the Black Arts movement. Maya Angelou, Toni Morrison, Alice Walker, and many others produced insightful, sometimes caustic, portrayals of male-female relationships among black people. During a decade in which depictions of African Americans in the nation's mass media were still often distorted and demeaning, black women artists and intellectuals in many fields contributed in new and important ways to the continuing struggle of African Americans to create positive and realistic self-images.

The emergence of black feminism coincided with the growing prominence of black elected officials, including a considerable number of women, who rejected black power militancy in favor of more conventional leadership styles. These officials focused their attention on achieving reform rather than revolution and on protecting rather than extending previous civil rights gains. Under the Republican administrations of Ronald Reagan and his successor, George Bush, no new civil rights legislation was enacted, but the NAACP and the Congressional Black Caucus fought effective defensive battles to preserve affirmative action programs. In addition, African Americans mobilized successful campaigns for a holiday celebrating Martin Luther King Jr.'s birthday and for economic sanctions against the South African government's apartheid policies.

Yet little was achieved during this period to address the problems of economically hard-pressed black Americans who had not benefited from previous civil rights reforms. Despite increasingly visible black affluence, poverty remained endemic in black communities, especially among growing numbers of single women raising children by themselves. Indications of black progress contrasted sharply with highly visible signs of social deterioration, especially urban drug abuse and violent crime. The tensions dividing African Americans were suggested by the simultaneous popularity in the late 1980s of male-dominated gansta rap and of black feminist writings. During the early 1990s, class, gender, and ideological conflicts among African Americans captured the nation's attention as black lawyer Anita Hill made sexual harassment accusations against her former boss, Clarence Thomas, the black federal appeals judge nominated to replace retiring Supreme Court Justice Thurgood Marshall.

FINDING A PLACE IN THE POLITICAL SYSTEM

During the summer of 1979, Andrew Young suddenly became involved in a controversy that threatened his position as the U.S. ambassador to the United Nations. When reporters learned of his informal meeting with the United Nations representative of the Palestinian Liberation Organization (PLO), Jewish-American leaders voiced strong objections. The highest-ranking black appointee in President Jimmy Carter's administration, Young had placed his job in jeopardy by contacting a group that his own government labeled as terrorist. Ironically, Young's rapid rise in politics had resulted from his ability to display not only the cautiousness needed to thrive in electoral politics but also the commitment required to win respect in the civil rights movement.

An ordained minister of the United Church of Christ, Young had worked with the National Council of Churches before accepting Martin Luther King Jr.'s invitation to become executive director of the Southern Christian Leadership Conference (SCLC). Rather than engaging in civil disobedience, he became a self-described "organizational man, the nonimage staff person" within SCLC. In the aftermath of King's assassination, he won a congressional seat representing a predominantly white district in Atlanta. Along with Barbara Jordan of Texas, he was among the first African Americans since Reconstruction to represent a southern state in Congress. In 1976, he was one of the first black elected officials to support the presidential campaign of Georgia governor Jimmy Carter. After Young's efforts to rally black voters helped elect Carter, he was rewarded with the UN post.

Despite Young's remarkable success in electoral politics, his civil rights experiences shaped his perspective in ways that sometimes put him at odds with his own government's foreign policies. He saw his stance in favor of Israeli-Palestinian coexistence as consistent with the views of the progressive Israelis he met on a 1966 trip to Israel. "Unfortunately, the Jewish community in America tended to identify with the right-wing element in Israeli politics," Young lamented in explaining his underestimation of the response to the PLO meeting. As the controversy over Young's action quickly escalated, he decided to resign rather than threaten Carter's chances for reelection. He continued to believe, however, that he had done nothing wrong. "It's absolutely necessary for the United States of America to be able to talk with anybody, on any occasion, anywhere," he later insisted.

Although Carter defused the controversy over the "Andrew Young affair," he failed in his reelection bid. Beleaguered by his inability to free Americans held hostage by Islamic militants inside the United States embassy in Tehran, Iran, Carter was soundly defeated by the conservative Republican candidate, former California governor Ronald Reagan. Carter retained his overwhelming support among black voters, but Young's resignation sowed seeds of distrust in relations between African Americans and the Democratic Party. For many African Americans, the episode demonstrated that long-standing black loyalty to the party was not enough to save Young's job. Carter was seen as willing to offend many black supporters in order to avoid offending Jewish supporters. It mattered little that Carter appointed a black diplomat to replace Young. Carter's defeat, however, meant the White House was now occupied by an even less responsive president.

A New Conservative Era

When Reagan announced early in his presidency that the "era of big government" was over, black civil rights leaders feared his targets included the agencies established to enforce civil rights legislation as well as the remaining remnants of Lyndon Johnson's antipoverty programs. While Reagan made clear his antigovernment stance did not extend to programs such as Social Security and Medicare that benefited middle-class Americans, he exploited widespread antitax sentiment and white resentment of black "welfare mothers."

Unlike former vice president Spiro Agnew and former Alabama governor George Wallace, who had linked conservatism with explicit attacks against black militants, Reagan rarely commented on racial issues, but he indicated his insensitivity to black concerns when he began his campaign by appearing with former Dixiecrat leader Strom Thurmond at a states' rights rally held in Philadelphia, Mississippi, the site of the 1964 murders of three civil rights workers. With the Supreme Court divided over the constitutionality of school busing and affirmative action programs intended to combat racial discrimination, the new president's future appointments to the Court were matters of great concern to African Americans. As Reagan's first term began in 1981, black leaders were forced to find ways to influence a conservative president who had gained office with little black support.

Reaganism and the Debate Over Affirmative Action

A Black Alternatives Conference held in San Francisco soon after the 1980 presidential election revealed that not all African Americans opposed Reagan's conservative views. Although the participants represented a variety of viewpoints, most of those who attended agreed the time had come for a departure from the Democratic liberalism that had shaped black electoral politics since the New Deal era. Many described themselves as neoconservatives to indicate they had been drawn to conservatism only after becoming disillusioned with governmental programs such as affirmative action that had been developed to implement civil rights reforms. The participants departed from the black political mainstream, but some saw themselves as linked to the tradition of black self-help efforts of Marcus Garvey and Booker T. Washington. Tony Brown, the host of a popular television talk show, was the best known of the black participants. Less known at the time was Clarence Thomas, a Yale-educated lawyer who soon joined the Reagan administration. Perhaps the most influential of the participants was one of the conference's organizers, economist Thomas Sowell, whose writings had already had an impact on other black conservatives. For Sowell, the gathering in San Francisco marked a new stage in African American intellectual development: "It brought together blacks who debated their differing viewpoints in an atmosphere wholly free of rancor, of attempts to be blacker-than-thou, and without any charges of 'selling out' or the like."

> "Blacks . . . debated their differing viewpoints in an atmosphere wholly free of rancor, of attempts to be blacker-than-thou, and without any charges of 'selling out.'"—*Thomas Sowell*

Sowell had not always been a conservative. During the mid-1950s, when he was an undergraduate first at Howard and then at Harvard University, he had been drawn to Marxian economics, the topic of his senior honors thesis. As a graduate student in economics at the University of Chicago, however, Sowell rejected Marxism, preferring instead the libertarian views of his advisor, Milton Friedman, an economist who advocated minimal government involvement in the economy. As he observed the rise of civil rights activism in the early 1960s, he "welcomed the dismantling of the old Jim Crow laws" but questioned whether removing racial barriers would bring economic gains for African Americans.

Economist Thomas Sowell was one of many black conservatives who opposed affirmative action and black militancy.

Sowell, a professor at Cornell University during the late 1960s, was dismayed when armed black student militants seized a campus building there. He began to speak out against the "academic paternalism" of college administrators who gave in to black militant demands and criticized Cornell's affirmative action policies. Disagreeing with those who insisted affirmative action was necessary to redress the consequences of past discrimination, Sowell argued that civil rights policies should be limited to removing current racial barriers to individual advancement. In general, he insisted that governmental efforts to achieve equality were likely to be less effective than simply allowing market forces to work, as employers would eventually hire qualified black workers in order to compete effectively. Sowell's 1975 book *Race and Economics* was one of many publications of the period that popularized the notion that it was counterproductive to combat discrimination through government action. Like other black conservatives, Sowell resented implications that his own career success had resulted from racial preferences. He later wrote that the respect he once received from students was no longer evident in the 1970s when he taught at UCLA: "What happened in between was 'affirmative action' hiring of minority faculty."

The conservative views of Sowell and others provided an interpretive framework for explaining studies showing that not all African Americans benefited from civil rights reforms. As black sociologist William Julius Wilson observed in his influential book *The Declining Significance of Race* (1978), the problems of the black poor had not been greatly affected by civil rights laws or affirmative action programs, which he claimed resulted in a gulf between the black middle class, which *had* benefited from reforms, and the black "underclass," which was "in a hopeless state of stagnation, falling further and further behind the rest of society." Although Wilson supported governmental programs focused on economic rather than racial problems, conservative analysts insisted governmental welfare programs had produced a debilitating "culture of poverty" passed down through generations of welfare recipients. While liberals decried the funding cuts that had undermined Johnson's War on Poverty, conservatives called for still further cutbacks in the remnants of the antipoverty efforts. Moreover, some conservatives called for harsher policies forcing welfare recipients to work and punishing the criminal behavior they associated with the black underclass. Scholars continued to question whether the underclass concept accurately described the black poor, but Sowell's writings marked the beginning of a broad shift away from the liberal assumptions underlying the social policies of Franklin Delano Roosevelt and Lyndon Johnson.

From the time he took office in 1981, Reagan indicated his administration would be less responsive than Carter's to the concerns of civil rights leaders. Reagan's early appointees to the federal courts and the Justice Department were often conservatives who questioned the need for school busing and affirmative action to remedy past discrimination. Sowell himself was widely mentioned as a possible member of Reagan's administration, but he instead accepted a non-teaching senior fellow post at the Hoover Institution, a think tank located on the Stanford University campus, which gave him time and resources to spend writing articles and books that continued to influence the conservative movement. Clarence Thomas's decision to become Assistant Secretary for Civil Rights in the Department of Education, however, was a clear indication of the Reagan administration's new direction.

Like Sowell, Thomas came late to conservatism. At Holy Cross during the late 1960s, he had identified with Bigger Thomas's anger and admired Malcolm X. As a Yale law student, he voted in the 1972 presidential election for Democratic liberal George McGovern. But he was deeply affected when he read Sowell's *Race and Economics* and later met the author at a book signing. By the time Thomas joined the Reagan administration as the person in charge of enforcing school desegregation policies, he was known as a critic of busing and affirmative action. Reagan soon promoted Thomas to an even more visible position as head the Equal Employment Opportunity Commission (EEOC). Thomas replaced Eleanor Holmes Norton, a Yale law graduate who had participated in SNCC's Mississippi voting rights campaign during the 1960s. Replacing the first woman to become chair of the EEOC, Thomas quickly angered civil rights leaders by abandoning requirements that employers meet timetables and numerical goals in hiring minority workers. The EEOC's budget and staff declined during Thomas's tenure, reducing its ability to investigate discrimination complaints from minorities and women. The time required for the Commission to process complaints grew to ten months as 40,000 cases awaited action.

Reagan's appointees to the Justice Department's Civil Rights Division were similarly critical of government efforts to implement civil rights legislation. Justice Department officials suggested the racial policies of private all-white educational institutions, such as South Carolina's Bob Jones University, might not violate federal law. Furthermore, the department gave only qualified support for legislation to renew the Voting Rights Act of 1965. In this case, however, Reagan was not able to overcome voting rights supporters who mobilized in 1982 to pass a strengthened bill with enough votes to ensure that a presidential veto would be overridden.

The Civil Rights Commission—the agency established to investigate civil rights violations—became a battleground due to a well-publicized clash between Reagan and one of the Carter appointees he hoped to replace: historian and former civil rights activist Mary Frances Berry. Berry's sharp criticisms of Reagan's civil rights policies made her vulnerable, but she was able to overturn her firing by challenging it in court. Nevertheless, Reagan appointees came to dominate the Commission during the 1980s.

In addition to initiating these shifts in civil rights policies, the Reagan administration reduced funding for domestic welfare programs. Consistent with the philosophy that American society was overgoverned but also responding to the white backlash that put him in the White House, Reagan gained passage for tax cuts that disproportionately benefited wealthy individuals. Although he argued that the benefits of reduced taxes for the wealthy would eventually "trickle down" to those less fortunate, Reagan's critics were unconvinced. Black unemployment increased from 11 percent in 1982 to 16 percent in 1984, while the Reagan administration cut back on programs benefiting those in the lower tiers of society: food stamps, job training, aid to low-income students, federal grants for the redevelopment of inner cities, and health services. At the end of Reagan's first term, 36 percent of African American families had an annual income below the federal government's stated poverty line.

Although civil rights proponents faced many setbacks during Reagan's first term, the successful campaign for a national holiday honoring Martin Luther King provided cause for rejoicing. The initial proposal for the holiday had been put forth by Michigan congressional representative John Conyers soon after King's assassination, and the Congressional Black Caucus continued to back the idea through the 1970s. The idea did not garner much political support, however, until the 1980s, when Coretta Scott King spearheaded a renewed effort to pass legislation authorizing the holiday. King's widow had emerged as a national leader in her own right in the years since her husband's assassination and had established the King Center in Atlanta to carry on the legacy of nonviolent struggle. Skillfully attracting the endorsement of political figures as well as singer Stevie Wonder, who wrote a popular "Happy Birthday" song honoring King, she was able to build support for the holiday legislation. In 1983 Congress approved the bill, and Reagan, despite voicing reservations, signed the legislation calling for annual observance of the holiday beginning in 1985.

JESSE JACKSON'S 1984 PRESIDENTIAL CAMPAIGN

"Mr. Reagan cuts energy assistance to the poor, cuts job training, cuts breakfast and lunch programs for children—and then says to an empty table, 'Let us pray.'" Jesse Jackson's sardonic remark aroused black audiences during 1983, especially when he added, "Apparently Mr. Reagan is not familiar with the structure of prayer. You thank the Lord for the food you are about to *receive*, not the food that has just *left*. I think we should pray, but not pray for the food that's left. Pray for the man that took the food . . . to leave." Jackson's forceful criticisms of Reagan contributed to his emergence as the nation's most influential black political figure. But he was also a critic of Democratic leaders such as Jimmy Carter, whom he saw as insufficiently responsive to black concerns. Jackson had reacted bitterly to Andrew Young's forced resignation, describing it as a "capitulation" to pressures from Jewish leaders. His skepticism about both major political parties derived from his background as a civil rights activist in the 1960s. Whereas both Jackson and Young had adjusted to the new political realities of the 1970s and 1980s, the former displayed elements of the rhetorical style associated with the black power era.

Jackson had been Young's colleague on the SCLC staff during the 1960s, but the two men displayed quite different leadership skills in the years after King's death. Young had grown up in New Orleans, raised in middle-class comfort by college-educated parents. Jackson was born in Greenville, South Carolina, to an unwed mother and spent his formative years seeking to overcome class as well as racial barriers. While Young served as SCLC's chief administrator, Jackson had been one of its brash, outspoken young firebrands, his oratorical skills honed as he spearheaded civil rights demonstrations while attending North Carolina A&T College in Greensboro. As Young became a Democratic Party insider during the 1970s, Jackson remained an outsider, at times giving verbal support to the idea that African Americans should form an independent political party. He transformed SCLC's Operation Breadbasket in Chicago into an independent group called Operation People United to Serve Humanity (PUSH), which used boycotts to expand black economic opportunities. While Young returned to Atlanta after his resignation from the UN post and eventually became mayor, Jackson built on the anger caused by Young's forced resignation in 1979.

Jackson attracted considerable publicity by quickly arranging a trip to the Middle East. It was a bold gambit meant to demonstrate that black leaders no longer feared castigation for questioning the nation's foreign policies, as Du Bois and Robeson had been in the early Cold War years or King during the Vietnam War. Although Jackson indicated he wanted to hear from both Israelis and Palestinians, his visit intensified Jewish fears that black leaders were backing the Palestinian side. Black-Jewish relations took a further turn for the worse when subsequent newspaper photographs showed Jackson visiting a Palestinian refugee camp and hugging Palestinian leader Yasser Arafat. SCLC head Joseph Lowery also headed a black delegation to the Middle East, but Jackson's mission, which included meetings with Syrian and Egyptian leaders, drew far more attention. Although he held no political office, Jackson demonstrated that leaders of other nations saw him as worthy of respect. After his Middle East tour, the news media increasingly depicted Jackson as the nation's preeminent black leader.

In the United States, Jackson developed extensive contacts throughout the nation not only through Operation

TABLE 20.1 Political and Civil Rights Organizations

Congressional Black Caucus: Formed in 1971 by black representatives to develop legislative strategies to deal with the concerns of African Americans.

Free South Africa Movement: This offshoot of Randall Robinson's lobbying group TransAfrica spearheaded the protest campaign to enact U.S. sanctions against South Africa's apartheid regime.

Nation of Islam: Following the death of Elijah Muhammad in 1975, Louis Farrakhan reconstituted this religious group under his leadership.

National Rainbow Coalition: Formed in 1985, the Rainbow Coalition carried on the political effort begun the previous year in Jesse Jackson's initial presidential campaign.

PUSH activities but also through his prominent role in the 1972 Gary Convention and his subsequent efforts to register black voters. While black political leaders generally saw Reagan's landslide victory in 1980 as a major setback, Jackson saw signs of hope. In the early 1970s, he had backed the idea of building a new political party to compete with the Republicans and Democrats. Even after abandoning this idea in favor of the strategy of increasing black influence within the Democratic Party, Jackson believed mobilizing black voters was the key to black political success. He knew the number of black registered voters had almost doubled since the passage of the 1965 Voting Rights Act. But 7 million black adults—a number larger than Reagan's margin of victory—were still not registered in 1980. If these potential voters were registered, he believed, black voters could change the outcome of national as well as local elections. They could also force future Democratic presidents to be more responsive to their concerns.

The Harold Washington Campaign

Jackson had a chance to test his strategy when Harold Washington announced his 1983 run to become Chicago's first black mayor. Washington began his political career as a loyalist to the Democratic machine that dominated Chicago politics. As King had discovered in 1966 when he took on Chicago mayor Richard J. Daley, the Democratic Party machine was a powerful force able to retain the loyalty of many black residents through its control of city patronage. Black congressman William Dawson had long played a major role in the machine by reliably delivering black votes to Democratic candidates. Washington himself had launched his political career by succeeding his father as a Democratic precinct captain. But during the 1970s, his dismay over issues such as police brutality caused him to break with the Democratic machine. When Daley died in 1977, Washington ran unsuccessfully to replace him.

By the time of the next mayoral election, however, Washington had reason to believe he had a better chance to win. First, there were two major white candidates, incumbent mayor Jane Byrne and the former mayor's son, Richard M. Daley. Second, the efforts of Jackson and others to register black voters during the 1980 election had dramatically increased the potential power of Chicago's black residents, who constituted about 40 percent of the city's population.

Although Washington was not personally close to Jackson, he realized Jackson's ability to arouse black audiences would make him an indispensable ally. Jackson, for his part, recognized that helping elect Washington would demonstrate his own political clout in the nation's second-largest city. The election gained national significance when well-known Democratic leaders quickly mobilized on behalf of Byrne and Daley. While Senator Edward Kennedy supported Byrne in return for her support in the 1980 presidential campaign, Walter Mondale, who was leading the field of Democratic candidates for the 1984 presidential election, supported Daley. The intervention of these two national Democratic leaders enraged Jackson and other Washington supporters, who saw Kennedy and Mondale as abandoning Washington, just as Carter had abandoned Young. While Washington ran a skillful campaign, handling himself well in debates with the other candidates, Jackson mobilized black voters. He even succeeded in overcoming the apolitical stance of the Nation of Islam, convincing the group's leader, Louis Farrakhan, to encourage his followers to register.

Washington won a closely fought primary election. Most of his support came from black voters, as he received only about 6 percent of the white vote and about 13 percent of the Latino vote. Although the mayor's race in Chicago was usually decided in the Democratic primary, Washington's election was still in question until he managed to prevail over his Republican opponent in the general election. He was able to increase his white support to about 19 percent while retaining his overwhelming support in black neighborhoods.

Washington's victory in Chicago provided considerable encouragement for black leaders seeking ways to respond to Reagan's election. Within weeks of the election, some black activists suggested that the effectiveness of the Chicago voter registration campaign could be replicated elsewhere in the nation. Jackson was among the first to suggest that a black presidential candidate would stimulate a nationwide effort to register black voters. Even if the black candidate did not win, newly registered black voters might succeed in electing black candidates to Congress or to local offices. Few people who knew Jackson

■ Jesse Jackson was more succesful than any previous black presidential candidate in attracting white support and identifying with the plight of poor people of all races.

doubted he would offer himself as the best available black presidential candidate.

Run, Jesse, Run

In June 1983, when Jackson called for a meeting of black leaders to discuss the possibility of a black presidential candidacy, not all of those invited thought it a good idea. Most of them strongly opposed Reagan, but some prominent civil rights leaders, including Coretta Scott King and Andrew Young, argued privately that Jackson would damage the prospects of a liberal white candidate with a better chance to defeat Reagan. Leading black mayors, including Detroit's Coleman Young, Birmingham's Richard Arrington, and Los Angeles's Tom Bradley, were hesitant to support a person who had never before run for political office. Despite these misgivings, however, Jackson received sufficient encouragement to continue mobilizing support for a presidential campaign. By 1983, an ABC television network poll of black opinion found that Jackson was seen as the most important black leader by a wide margin over runner-up Andrew Young.

Jackson's supporters insisted his candidacy would enable African Americans to gain the balance of power within the Democratic Party and thereby force the party to support more progressive policies. With the departure of southern whites for the Republican Party, black voters had become an increasingly important element of the Democratic coalition, although they had little say about the party's direction. Political scientist Ronald Walters, one of Jackson's strategists, argued, "The major candidates and the party apparatus have believed that the Black vote is a captured vote, unable to mount credible strategies of leverage, so the tendency increasingly has been to ignore the importance of the vote and the policy interests it represents."

Jackson formally announced his candidacy late in 1983 and proved an effective campaigner, surprising his critics and even many of his supporters. Most reporters who covered his campaign did not believe he had a chance of winning, but he distinguished himself from other candidates by expressing strong support for civil rights, labor unions, women's rights, and environmental causes. Acknowledging that his presidential campaign grew out of the "black perspective," Jackson nonetheless insisted, "This candidacy is not for blacks only." He asserted that he empathized with the plight of poor white people in Appalachia "because I have known poverty. I know the pain of anti-Semitism because I have felt the humiliation of discrimination. I know firsthand the shame of bread lines and the horror of hopelessness and despair because my life has been dedicated to empowering the world's rejected to become respected." Addressing increasingly enthusiastic crowds, he often referred to his background as a way of expressing empathy: "I *do* understand. I was born out of wedlock to a teen-age mother, who was born to a teen-age mother. How do I understand? I never slept in the house with my natural father one night in my life. I *understand*."

> "I know firsthand the shame of bread lines and the horror of hopelessness and despair because my life has been dedicated to empowering the world's rejected to become respected." —*Jesse Jackson*

In January 1984, Jackson's campaign received an unexpected boost when he flew to Syria to secure the release of a black Navy pilot, Lieutenant Robert O. Goodman Jr., whose plane had been shot down over Syrian positions in eastern Lebanon. Although State Department officials had been unable to gain Goodman's freedom, Jackson was able to capitalize on his contacts from his 1979 trip to Syria. By bringing home Goodman, he achieved an important goal that had eluded State

Jesse Jackson Addresses the 1984 Democratic National Convention

Founder of the People United to Serve Humanity (PUSH), Jesse Jackson was a candidate for the Democratic presidential nomination in 1984 and 1988. Below is an excerpt from his impassioned address before the 1984 Democratic National Convention in San Francisco, California.

Tonight we come together bound by our faith in a mighty God, with genuine respect and love for our country, and inheriting the legacy of a great party, the Democratic Party, which is the best hope for redirecting our nation on a more humane, just and peaceful course. This is not a perfect party. We are not a perfect people. Yet, we are called to a perfect mission: our mission to feed the hungry; to clothe the naked; to house the homeless; to teach the illiterate; to provide jobs for the jobless; and to choose the human race over the nuclear race. . . .

My constituency is the desperate, the damned, the disinherited, the disrespected, and the despised. They are restless and seek relief. They've voted in record numbers. They have invested faith, hope and trust that they have in us. The Democratic Party must send them a signal that we care. I pledge my best to not let them down. . . .

Our flag is red, white and blue, but our nation is a rainbow—red, yellow, brown, black and white—and we're all precious in God's sight.

—*from Rev. Jesse L. Jackson, Sr. Address Before the Democratic National Convention, San Francisco, CA, July 18, 1984.*

To view a longer version of this document, please go to *www.ablongman.com/carson/documents*.

Department officials. Jackson's unexpected diplomatic success prompted many voters to take him more seriously as a presidential candidate. Early in 1984, he won several state Democratic primaries and ran close races in others. Suddenly journalists covering the campaign began to consider the possibility that Jackson might actually win the nomination.

But Jackson's campaign experienced a major setback when a black reporter quoted him referring to New York City as "Hymie-town," a slang reference to its large Jewish population. Nation of Islam leader Louis Farrakhan, who had urged his followers to support Jackson and provided the candidate with a security force, made things worse for Jackson by urging the black community to ostracize the reporter, adding that one day "traitors" like him would be killed. Farrakhan later remarked to a reporter that Hitler was "wickedly great." Jewish leaders, already critical of Jackson for his embrace of PLO leader Yasser Arafat, saw his ties to Farrakhan as confirmation of an underlying anti-Semitism. Although Jackson denied he was anti-Semitic and denounced Farrakhan's comments, his campaign lost momentum as he struggled to defend himself. On the defensive for the rest of the primaries, Jackson still received about 3.5 million votes overall and arrived at the Democratic National Convention in San Francisco with 300 delegates committed to him.

By this time Jackson realized he could not win the nomination, but he had won far more support than Shirley Chisholm had attracted twelve years earlier. He had demonstrated that a black candidate could not only mobilize black voters but a substantial minority of all Democratic voters. Although Walter Mondale became the Democratic nominee, Jackson's moving speech to the convention stirred the delegates. He acknowledged his flaws: "If, in my low moments, in word, deed or attitude, through some error of temper, taste, or tone, I have caused anyone discomfort, created pain, or revived someone's fears, that was not my truest self." Describing himself as "not a perfect servant," he asked for patience: "God is not through with me yet." He presented his vision of a "rainbow" nation capable of overcoming its differences:

> America is not like a blanket—one piece of unbroken cloth, the same color, the same texture, the same size. America is more like a quilt: many patches, many pieces, many colors, many sizes, all woven and held together by a common thread. The white, the Hispanic, the black, the Arab, the Jew, the woman, the native American, the small farmer, the businessperson, the environmentalist, the peace activist, the young, the old, the lesbian, the gay, and the disabled make up the American quilt.
>
> Even in our fractured state, all of us count and fit somewhere.

> "America is not like a blanket—one piece of unbroken cloth, the same color, the same texture, the same size. America is more like a quilt: many patches, many pieces, many colors, many sizes, all woven and held together by a common thread."—*Jesse Jackson*

Jackson showed he was far from finished as a major political figure. Despite Ronald Reagan's landslide victory over Mondale in the 1984 election, Jackson was able to keep his Rainbow Coalition together in the years afterward. His effectiveness as a campaigner had surprised many observers, and in 1988 his second run for the presidency proved even more successful.

The Free South Africa Campaign

"The Reagan policy of 'constructive engagement' amounts to little more than letting the South African government go and do what it feels like doing," Eleanor Holmes Norton told reporters outside the South African embassy in Washington, DC, just weeks after the 1984 election. She announced that, along with two other black leaders, she intended to remain inside the embassy until the South African government released its political prisoners, including African National Congress leader Nelson Mandela, and ended its apartheid policies, which denied basic civil rights to black residents.

There had been growing dissatisfaction among African Americans regarding the Reagan administration's reluctance to enforce UN economic sanctions against South Africa. The Congressional Black Caucus had repeatedly called for sanctions, but the president refused to budge from his stance of constructive engagement, which rejected the idea of forcing a Cold War ally to change its racial policies. "We felt we had to do something," Norton explained.

A law professor at Georgetown University, Norton had attracted attention when Reagan fired her as head of the EEOC due to her sharp attacks on his civil rights policies. She was accompanied to the South African embassy by Mary Frances Berry, who despite Reagan's opposition had held on to her position on the Civil Rights Commission, and Walter Fauntroy, a leader of SCLC before becoming the congressional representative of Washington, DC. The embassy protest was organized by Randall Robinson, head of the antiapartheid lobby group Trans-Africa, who had been working for several years to mobilize American support for the South African freedom movement. When the three leaders inside the embassy announced their intentions, the South African ambassador abruptly left, while his aide pleaded, "Is there anything we can do to work this out?" Berry replied bluntly, "You can comply with the demands."

The three protesters were arrested and taken to a nearby police station, where they were charged with a misdemeanor for unlawful entry of an embassy. Quickly released on bail, they held a press conference to announce the founding of the Free South Africa Movement. Over the following year, daily protests, including civil disobedience, were staged at the embassy as other black leaders and civil rights proponents joined the movement. Rosa Parks, Stevie Wonder, and Coretta Scott King, as well as several of her children, were among the many prominent figures who came to be arrested. More than 6,000 protesters were eventually arrested at the embassy and at South African consulates around the country. South African Episcopal Bishop Desmond Tutu, winner of the 1984 Nobel Peace Prize, strengthened the campaign by delivering a number of antiapartheid speeches in the United States. Student protests on a scale not seen since the early 1970s resulted in universities such as Columbia and Stanford adopting policies against investing endowment funds in companies that did business in South Africa. Many cities, states, and pension funds took similar action, pressuring large corporations to withdraw their South African investments.

This campaign marked the first time since the 1960s that African Americans had spearheaded a national campaign of nonviolent direct action. Extensive news coverage of the black uprisings that occurred throughout South Africa in 1985 added impetus to the American protests. The immediate goal of the Free South Africa Movement was to prod Congress to pass legislation mandating economic sanctions in order to pressure the South African government to change its racial policies. When California congressman Ronald Dellums introduced the Comprehensive Anti-Apartheid Act of 1986, most political observers gave the bill little chance of passage. Similar bills had previously failed. But the spreading protests convinced many political leaders, including some Republicans, to back sanctions. Both the House and the Senate passed the bill, but Reagan vetoed it, forcing sanctions supporters to seek the support of two-thirds of the members of both houses in order to override the veto.

In September 1986, the Democrat-controlled House voted against the president. The following month, Randall Robinson sat in the Senate chamber between Coretta Scott King and Jesse

■ The Free South Africa movement marked the first time since the 1960s that black Americans launched a national campaign of nonviolent direct action.

Jackson as the Senate also overrode the veto. "We had won. We had turned the course of the most powerful country on earth," Robinson jubilantly recalled. During the next few years, worldwide enforcement of economic sanctions as well as continued protests within South Africa weakened the apartheid system, finally leading to the dismantling of apartheid laws and the release of Mandela from prison in 1990.

THE POPULARIZATION OF MODERN BLACK FEMINISM

Alice Walker was among several black writers who participated in the Free South Africa Movement, but she attracted far more attention due to the controversy sparked by her best-selling Pulitzer Prize–winning novel, *The Color Purple* (1982), and by the film based on the book. While African Americans were largely in agreement regarding the issue of economic sanctions against South Africa, there were sharp differences of opinion regarding Walker's views of relations between black men and black women. As Michele Wallace had endured fierce criticism after publishing *Black Macho and the Myth of the Superwoman,* so too did Walker become the target of attacks after her book appeared. Yet, while the influence of Wallace's book had been felt mainly within the small community of black feminists, Walker's best-selling novel reached a vast audience, and the film was one of the decade's most popular Hollywood dramas. "The attacks, many of them personal and painful, continued for many years, right alongside the praise, the prizes, the Oscar award nominations," Walker recalled.

The Color Purple Controversy

The Color Purple was a work of fiction rather than a political statement, but it expressed views that were becoming

A Radical Black Feminist Statement

To address racism in the larger women's movement and sexism in the black community, radical black feminists formed the Combahee River Collective during the mid 1970s. Below is an excerpt of their statement of feminist principles written in the late 1970s.

We are a collective of black feminists who have been meeting together since 1974. During that time we have been involved in the process of defining and clarifying our politics, while at the same time doing political work within our own group and in coalition with other progressive organizations and movements. The most general statement of our policies at the present time would be that we are actively committed to struggling against racial, sexual, heterosexual, and class oppression and see as our particular task the development of integral analysis and practice based upon the fact that the major systems of oppression are interlocking. The synthesis of these oppressions creates the conditions of our lives. As black women we see black feminism as the logical political movement to combat the manifold and simultaneous oppressions that all women of color face. ...

Black women's extremely negative relationship to the American political system (a system of white male rule) has always been determined by our membership in two oppressed racial and sexual castes. ...There have always been black women activists—some known, like Sojourner Truth, Harriet Tubman, Frances E. W. Harper, Ida B. Wells Barnett, and Mary Church Terrell, and thousands upon thousands unknown—who had a shared awareness of how their sexual identity combined with their racial identity to make their whole life situation and the focus of their political struggles unique. Contemporary black feminism is the outgrowth of countless generations of personal sacrifice, militancy, and work by our mothers and sisters.

A black feminist presence has evolved most obviously in connection with the second wave of the American women's movement beginning in the late 1960s. Black, other Third World, and working women have been involved in the feminist movement from its start, but both outside reactionary forces and racism and elitism within the movement itself have served to obscure our participation. In 1973 black feminists, primarily located in New York, felt the necessity of forming a separate black feminist group. This became the National Black Feminist Organization (NBFO).

Black feminist politics also have an obvious connection to movements for black liberation, particularly those of the 1960s and 1970s. Many of us were active in those movements (civil rights, black nationalism, the Black Panthers), and all of our lives were greatly affected and changed by their ideology, their goals, and the tactics used to achieve their goals. It was our experience and disillusionment within these liberation movements, as well as experience on the periphery of the white male left, that led to the need to develop a politics that was antiracist, unlike those of white women, and antisexist, unlike those of black and white men. ...

Our politics initially sprang from the shared belief that black women are inherently valuable, that our liberation is a necessity not as an adjunct to somebody else's but because of our need as human persons for autonomy. This may seem so obvious as to sound simplistic, but it is apparent that no other ostensibly progressive movement has ever considered our specific oppression a priority or worked seriously for the ending of that oppression. Merely naming the pejorative stereotypes attributed to black women (e.g., mammy, matriarch, Sapphire, whore, bulldagger), let alone cataloguing the cruel, often murderous, treatment we receive, indicates how little value has been placed upon our lives during four centuries of bondage in the Western hemisphere. We realize that the only people who care enough about us to work consistently for our liberation is us. Our politics evolve from a healthy love for ourselves, our sisters, and our community which allows us to continue our struggle and work.

—from Combahee River Collective, "A Black Feminist Statement" in Capitalist Patriarchy and the Case for Socialist Feminism, *ed. Zillah Eisenstein, pp. 362-372.*

To view a longer version of this document, please go to www.ablongman.com/carson/documents.

increasingly popular among black women. Walker was a founder of the National Black Feminist Organization during the 1970s, but she preferred to use the term *womanist* to describe the qualities—"outrageous, audacious, courageous, or *willful* behavior"— she thought should unite black women. Walker's attitudes had been shaped by her formative experiences as a black girl growing up in a sharecropper family in rural Georgia. As a child, she had withdrawn into the world of books after being temporarily blinded and scarred by a pellet from her brother's BB gun. After surgery removed the scar, Walker excelled in school, becoming valedictorian of her class. While a student at Spelman College in the early 1960s, she participated in civil rights protests, ignoring rebukes from college officials who saw this as inappropriate for students of the women's college. After transferring to New York's Sarah Lawrence College and graduating in 1965, she went to Mississippi to register black voters.

Late in the 1960s, Walker decided to pursue a career as a writer. While teaching at Jackson State University, she was inspired by fellow instructor Margaret Walker, author of the poetry collection *For My People* (1942) and the epic slave narrative *Jubilee* (1966). Walker learned about her older colleague's difficult relationship with Richard Wright, author of *Native Son* (1940). Most importantly, she learned of the writings of Zora Neale Hurston, who had broken new ground during the 1930s in her depictions of black women. As Walker pursued her own writing career, she revived interest in Hurston's work by publishing *I Love Myself When I Am Laughing . . . And Then Again When I Am Looking Mean and Impressive: A Zora Neal Hurston Reader* (1979). Walker later remarked that "a people [should] not throw away their geniuses. . . . [I]t is our duty as artists and as witnesses for the future to collect them."

As Zora Neale Hurston had, Walker created female characters that focused readers' attention on relationships within black families and black communities rather than on external black-white relations. In *The Color Purple,* her narrator, an uneducated southern black woman named Celie, is oppressed less by white racists than by her stepfather, who rapes her and takes away her children, and by her abusive husband, whom she calls Mister (thus Celie's husband lacks a personal name but gains a title that southern whites rarely applied to African Americans). Celie internalizes the scorn inflicted on her by men but nonetheless finds solace in a succession of nurturing relationships with black women. Her sister Nettie is sexually accosted by Mister and then sent away to find a new life as a missionary in Africa. Her sister-in-law Sophia sets an example by refusing to be dominated by her husband. Shug, Mister's free-spirited girlfriend, introduces her to the pleasures of sex. *The Color Purple* reveals the brutality of gender oppression and the indomitable spirit of a woman who endures and ultimately prevails. "If and when Celie rises to her rightful, earned place in society across the planet, the world will be a different place," Walker asserted after the publication of her novel.

Alice Walker, author of the Pulitzer Prize-winning novel *The Color Purple* (1983). Many criticized Walker for portraying black men too harshly.

Whoopi Goldberg and Danny Glover in a scene from the movie *The Color Purple*. The film was nominated for ten Academy Awards, including Best Picture.

Walker's career was built on a foundation established by earlier black women writers, especially Hurston. During the 1970s, she benefited from the growing interest among publishers for books written by African Americans. Although new black studies programs initially stimulated sales of books expressing black power militancy, the entry of black women scholars into the field and the emergence of women's studies programs stimulated interest in black feminist writings. Maya Angelou's bestselling memoir *I Know Why the Caged Bird Sings* (1970), the story of her struggle to find her voice (she became mute upon being raped as a child) was widely studied as a metaphor for the oppression experienced by many women. While Toni Morrison worked as an editor at Random House, she encouraged black activists such as Angela Davis and Muhammad Ali to write accounts of their lives. Morrison then launched her own distinguished literary career with the publication of her first novel, *The Bluest Eye* (1970), the poignant story of a black girl who seeks love and acceptance through a desire to be blond and blue-eyed. Morrison later produced other critically applauded and widely read works, including *Song of Solomon* (1975) and her masterpiece, *Beloved* (1987), a historical novel about a black woman who kills her children rather than allow them to be returned to slavery. Gloria Naylor's *The Women of Brewster Place* (1982) depicted the experiences of seven diverse black women living in decaying rented houses on a walled-off street of an urban neighborhood. Ntozake Shange introduced black feminist ideas to Broadway audiences in her hit play *For Colored Girls Who Have Considered Suicide When the Rainbow is Enuf* (1975), which was later performed by many drama groups. Poets Audre Lorde, Sonia Sanchez, and June Jordan were other influential feminist writers who blended militant feminist advocacy and intimate revelation of black women's perspectives on male-female relations.

Like Walker, many of these black women writers had been participants in the black struggles of the 1960s. Angelou accepted Martin Luther King Jr.'s invitation to become northern coordinator of SCLC after establishing herself as a successful writer and actor. Lorde taught at Mississippi's Tougaloo College during the black power era. Sanchez's early works, such as *We a BaddDDD People* (1970), reflected the influence of Malcolm X and the Black Arts movement. Despite their activist backgrounds, however, their criticisms of the sexism of black males made them vulnerable to charges of racial disloyalty. Moreover, in the late 1970s some black feminists adopted a more radical perspective, as expressed in the Combahee River Collective Statement issued by black lesbian feminists: "We realize that the liberation of all oppressed peoples necessitates the destruction of the political-economic systems of capitalism and imperialism as well as patriarchy."

During the 1980s, Walker bore the brunt of antifeminist attacks due to her prominence as an author and political activist. Black critic Darryl Pinckney argued that Walker had depicted black men "at a distance—that is, entirely from the point of view of the women—as naifs incapable of reflection, tyrants filled with impotent, or as totemic do-gooders." The Los Angeles NAACP branch protested the depiction of black males in the film of *The Color Purple*. Moreover, Walker's decision to allow Steven Spielberg, a white director, to bring her book to the screen prevented some critics from acknowledging the film as a major Hollywood breakthrough in the depiction of African Americans. Since the early 1970s, opportunities for black actors had been largely limited to blaxploitation films such as *Sweet Sweetback's Baadasssss Song* (1971), *Shaft* (1971), and *Superfly* (1972)—black male action figures acting out revenge fantasies—or stereotype-filled comedies. In contrast, the black actors in *The Color Purple* were able to display a fuller range of talents. Former stand-up comic Whoopi Goldberg won an Academy Award nomination in the lead role, as did Margaret Avery (Shug) and Oprah Winfrey (Sophia). Danny Glover was praised for his portrayal of Mister.

Some critics claimed Spielberg had exaggerated the anti-male aspects of Walker's book, turning male characters into caricatures or failing to show how social conditions had shaped the behavior of black men. Despite receiving eleven Academy Award nominations—a record for a picture with a mainly black cast—*The Color Purple* won no Academy Awards.

Race and Popular Culture

To a considerable extent, Walker attracted controversy because she was washing dirty linen in public—that is, making white people aware of conflicts among African Americans. She faced a dilemma similar to that of earlier generations of black writers: how to depict African Americans accurately but also positively so as to refute rather than inflame white racial prejudices. Langston Hughes, Zora Neale Hurston, Richard Wright, and James Baldwin had each addressed this dilemma as they shed new light on previously ignored facets of black life.

The Color Purple reached a large multiracial audience, but it offered only one perspective of African Americans in the mass media and popular culture. Walker's feminist or womanist views gained increasing acceptance during the 1980s; however, they were not evident in many of the decade's popular television shows and films.

Despite the film's success at the box office and the earlier enormous popularity of the television series "Roots," white producers in Hollywood remained reluctant to invest in black historical (or even contemporary) dramas, preferring instead comedies. They assumed white Americans were willing to see black actors on television or in films, but only if they were cast along with white actors in prominent roles. Racial issues could only be treated lightly, with humor, if at all. On television, "The Jeffersons," a spinoff of the earlier hit "All in the Family," established a model for situation comedies, or sitcoms, that explored the comic possibilities of placing black people in a white-dominated racial environment. Variations of this genre included "Diff'rent Strokes" and "Webster" (black orphans adopted by white families), "Benson" (black butler of a white family), and "White Shadow" (black basketball players and their white coach). "The Cosby Show," the television hit starring and produced by Bill Cosby, departed somewhat from this trend toward isolating African American comic figures from a black cultural context. It featured a black family, though the upper middle-class milieu of the Huxtables was enjoyed by only a tiny proportion of African Americans (and only a somewhat larger proportion of white people).

Hollywood films similarly featured formulaic black characters who lacked ties to realistic black communities and adjusted uneasily (and often comically) to life among white people. After winning acclaim for her performance in *The Color Purple,* Whoopi Goldberg went on to a successful film career playing black characters in largely white settings, winning a supporting actor Oscar for her role in *Ghost* (1990). In a variation of this theme, veteran actor Morgan Freeman's career received a dramatic boost when he played a longtime chauffeur who becomes friends with the rich white woman he drives around. *Driving Miss Daisy* (1989) won the Oscar for best picture, and Freeman, honored for the year's best supporting performance by a male actor, was able to move from supporting to major roles in which he costarred with white actors.

By far the most popular black film star of the 1980s was comic Eddie Murphy, who capitalized on the black-white cultural clash formula in *Trading Places* (1983) and two enormously profitable *Beverly Hills Cop* (1984, 1987) films. In these action-comedy films, Murphy played a stereotypically hip black man interacting with and gradually winning the friendship of unhip white characters. Like other black actors who achieved stardom in this period, Murphy demonstrated that a black film star could appeal to white audiences while also remaining distinctively black, so long as he remained humorous rather than threatening. "I'm not angry," Murphy told a reporter. "I never have been much of a fighter. If somebody white called me 'nigger' on the street, I just laughed." The rapid rise to stardom of Murphy gave rise to other successful buddy films pairing black actors with white counterparts to produce comic sparks. After his *Color Purple* role, Danny Glover achieved stardom

> "I never have been much of a fighter. If somebody white called me 'nigger' on the street, I just laughed."
> —*Eddie Murphy*

■ A scene from "The Cosby Show" which depicted life of an upper-middle class black family. While the program had popular appeal, many critics complained it did not accurately represent most black families.

in a series of highly popular *Lethal Weapon* movies featuring white actor Mel Gibson.

Although many hit movies of the 1980s used racial culture clash themes, a few films made serious attempts to illuminate African American life and history. These were typically made on smaller budgets than action films and benefited from the eagerness of black actors to take relatively low-paying roles in meaningful projects. These included *A Soldier's Story* (1984), based on Charles Fuller's Pulitzer Prize–winning World War II drama; *Cry Freedom* (1987), based on the life of South African freedom fighter Steve Bantu Biko; and *Glory* (1989), depicting the heroic black soldiers who took part in the Civil War battle at Fort Wagner. Denzel Washington, who appeared in each of these films and won an Academy Award for his supporting role in *Glory*, emerged as the highest-paid black film star since Sidney Poitier's heyday in the 1960s. Like Poitier, Washington appealed to white as well as black filmgoers, usually playing roles that required him to keep tight rein on anger and sexuality while achieving goals through diplomacy and discipline.

While most black actors in the film industry made do with the limited range of roles offered by Hollywood films, film director Spike Lee demonstrated the possibilities for making significant African American films outside the studio system. Lee's *She's Got to Have It* (1986) was one of the few films of the decade that dealt with feminist ideas—even though its female leading character is seen from the perspective of her male pursuers, who ultimately find her inexplicable. Because Lee's small-budget film made a substantial profit, he was able to obtain Hollywood financing for subsequent films while maintaining artistic control. Lee confronted important issues in his early feature films: color prejudices among African Americans in *School Daze* (1988), urban racial violence in *Do the Right Thing* (1989), the declining popularity of jazz in *Mo' Better Blues* (1990), and interracial marriage in *Jungle Fever* (1991). When Lee directed an epic film biography of Malcolm X during the early 1990s, he overcame the reluctance of Hollywood producers to provide an adequate budget by successfully appealing to wealthy black entertainers such as Bill Cosby, Oprah Winfrey, Tracy Chapman, and Janet Jackson as

but some of these leaders believed any concession to Jackson would weaken the party's efforts to attract white support. They concluded after the election that Dukakis's defeat had resulted from his liberal reputation; thus, future Democratic candidates should veer away from the Lyndon Johnson tradition of civil rights reform. At the same time, Farrakhan and others were not only criticizing party leaders for disrespecting Jackson but also criticizing Jackson for his continued party loyalty. After the Democratic Party suffered its third consecutive presidential setback, many African Americans were beginning to look seriously for alternative ways to achieve racial goals.

Black neoconservatives of the 1980s argued that affirmative action and other racial preference programs were no longer necessary, but there were many indications that the nation was still plagued by racial problems. Black Americans continued to enter the middle class in larger numbers. Whereas in 1940 hardly more than one in twenty black men and women held middle-class occupations, by 1990 nearly one in three black men and nearly three of every five black women worked in white-collar jobs. But poverty remained the lot of many undereducated African Americans, the percentage of black children with unmarried mothers jumped significantly, and the chance of a black child to be raised in a household without a father was three times as great as in white families. The conservative politics of the Reagan and Bush administrations did little to address these problems, and the dismantling of the Great Society programs continued.

But even as conservative policies chipped away at antipoverty programs, individual African Americans continued to excel. Lawrence Douglas Wilder of Virginia became the nation's first elected African American governor. Only months after Nelson Mandela's release from prison, President Bush appointed Colin Powell head of the Joint Chiefs of Staff, the first African American to occupy the highest military office in the armed services. Powell began to attract attention in Republican circles as a valuable military aide, leading to an appointment as Ronald Reagan's national security advisor. Eighteen months after becoming chair of the Joint Chiefs of Staff, he played a pivotal role in overseeing Operation Desert Storm, the Persian Gulf War precipitated by the Iraqi invasion of Kuwait. Seeing this as a threat to half of the world's oil supply by Iraq's dictator, Saddam Hussein, Bush sent in half a million American troops, nearly one-quarter of them African Americans, in a five-week tank and rocket war that pulverized the Iraqi forces. Even though Jesse Jackson traveled to Iraq and met with Hussein to negotiate the release of hundreds of hostages, it was Colin Powell, seen nightly on television, who emerged from the Gulf War as the preeminent African American political figure to reckon with.

Anita Hill Versus Clarence Thomas

"For years I had spent considerable time and effort convincing myself that what happened to me no longer mattered," Anita Hill remembered thinking when she heard in 1991 that President George Bush had nominated her former boss, Clarence Thomas, to a seat on the Supreme Court. Thomas's nomination to the seat once held by Justice Thurgood Marshall had already drawn criticism from many civil rights and feminist groups, who strongly disagreed with the nominee's conservative views on affirmative action. But Hill, a law professor at Oral Roberts University, had more personal reasons for questioning Thomas's suitability to serve on the Supreme Court. Having worked for Thomas a decade earlier when both served in the Reagan administration, she had been disturbed by Thomas's behavior. She recalled that Thomas had overcome her initial skepticism about Reagan's policies—"The idea that benefits would 'trickle down' to the poor if the rich were assisted by tax breaks and the like struck me as foolish," she recalled. Nonetheless, she had been persuaded when Thomas insisted he was committed to civil rights. The relationship between the two deteriorated, however, as Hill became disturbed by her employer's sexual banter, which included, according to later testimony, vivid descriptions of pornography. Hill never lodged a sexual harassment complaint against Thomas during the three years she worked with him; as she noted, "I do not believe that in the early 1980s I lived and worked in a society, either in Washington or in Tulsa, that would have supported my right to raise a claim of harassment against the head of the EEOC." As she thought of the prospect of Thomas serving on the Supreme Court, however, Hill decided she should speak up. "For the first time I was forced to consider that it *did* matter—that the behavior was not only an offense to me but unfitting for someone who would sit on the Supreme Court," she later wrote.

"For the first time I was forced to consider that it *did* matter—that the behavior was not only an offense to me but unfitting for someone who would sit on the Supreme Court."—*Anita Hill*

Hill's decision to testify against Thomas set off a contentious national debate that touched on issues of gender and race. For several weeks in the fall of 1991, the nation-

Anita Hill Testifies before the Senate Judiciary Committee

Anita Hill worked for Clarence Thomas at the Department of Education and the Equal Employment Opportunity Commission (EEOC). In 1991, when President George H. W. Bush nominated Thomas to the Supreme Court, Hill testified before the Senate that Thomas had sexually harassed her while under his supervision. An excerpt from her testimony:

For my first months at the EEOC, where I continued to be an assistant to Judge Thomas, there were no sexual overtures. However, during the fall and winter of 1982, these began again. The comments were random, and ranged from pressing me about why I didn't go out with him, to remarks about my personal appearance. I remember him saying that some day I would have to tell him the real reason that I wouldn't go out with him.

He began to show displeasure in his tone and voice and his demeanor in his continued pressure for an explanation. He commented on what I was wearing in terms of whether it made me more or less sexually attractive. The incidents occurred in his inner office at the EEOC. . . .

I began to feel severe stress on the job. I began to be concerned that Clarence Thomas might take out his anger with me by degrading me or not giving me important assignments. I also thought that he might find an excuse for dismissing me.

—*Testimony of Anita F. Hill before the Committee on the Judiciary, United States Senate, October 11, 1991.*

To view a longer version of this document, please go to www.ablongman.com/carson/documents.

ally televised Thomas confirmation hearings captured the nation's attention. At the start of the hearings, many African Americans understood that a Republican administration would be unlikely to propose a Marshall-type nominee and took comfort in the thought that Thomas's successful nomination would at least result in a black justice on the court. If he were defeated, they feared President Bush would simply nominate a white man with similar views. Hill's claim of sexual harassment forced African Americans to take sides in a dispute between a black man and a black woman, with a seat on the Supreme Court at stake. Hill did not consider herself a black feminist, but her testimony directed the glare of publicity on issues that had long concerned feminists, such as inequality and sexual harassment in the workplace. When the modern women's liberation movement had gained momentum two decades earlier, few Americans saw sexual harassment in the workplace as a major social problem, particularly for professional women such as Hill. Even the term *sexual harassment* did not enter common usage until the 1980s. When she began her law career as Thomas's assistant, women were expected to be satisfied to have entered previously all-male domains. Thomas's Senate confirmation seemed certain, and Hill realized that testifying against Thomas would make her a target of harsh criticism, even from African Americans who saw her as damaging the reputation of a successful black man. When reporters revealed Hill's stunning sexual harassment charges, feminists and others rallied to her defense, but she faced a storm of controversy. Thomas's Republican supporters suggested she was a black militant or perhaps a feminist. Hill was dismayed that no member of the Senate Judiciary Committee who heard her testimony was willing to publicly support her. Thomas denied her charges and insisted instead that he was a victim of a "high-tech lynching." He was confirmed by a vote of 52–48.

The Hill-Thomas hearings marked the convergence of cultural and political trends in the early 1990s. Two decades earlier, black feminism had been a small-scale movement with little political impact that spread its ideas largely through the writings of black women authors such as Alice Walker and Michele Wallace. Black male leaders such as Andrew Young and Jesse Jackson still dominated African American politics during the 1970s and 1980s, although the emergence of female political leaders like Shirley Chisholm and Barbara Jordan revealed an accelerating trend. By the early 1990s, however, formerly

Anita Hill's testimony did not prevent Clarence Thomas's appointment to the U.S. Supreme Court, but it did spark an increase in political activity among women.

unconventional feminist ideas such as responding to sexual harassment in the workplace had become increasingly accepted and even commonplace, although the controversy over *The Color Purple* and the Hill-Thomas hearing demonstrated the volatility of male-female relations among African Americans.

Though Anita Hill's testimony did not prevent Thomas's appointment to the Supreme Court, it did stimulate broader awareness of the problem of sexual harassment. It also helped mobilize women activists on behalf of political candidates who responded to feminist concerns. Eleanor Holmes Norton, a pioneering black feminist who was the District of Columbia's nonvoting representative in Congress, later argued that Hill, though not a politician, had "affected the political process." Norton credited Hill for the upsurge in political activity among women that helped make 1992 a year when a record number of women were elected to national office. As Hill addressed a gathering of women political leaders shortly after her testimony, she recalled that her audience "shouted and whistled and stood on their chairs to applaud." They "foretold an era of renewed involvement as they summoned into being the political 'year of the woman,' election year 1992."

CONCLUSION

The transition from the activism of the 1960s to the conservatism of the Reagan-Bush era was challenging for many African Americans. The culmination of the long effort to pass civil rights legislation had been followed by a period of debate over the future direction of African American politics. Black neoconservatives argued that these reforms offered a sufficient basis for African American individual advancement, but Jesse Jackson succeeded in mobilizing widespread support for his 1984 and 1988 presidential campaigns by insisting that more government action was needed to ensure that equal opportunity became a reality rather than remaining an ideal. Although Reagan's conservatism prevailed in national politics during the 1980s, African Americans who disagreed with this trend were able to protect previous civil rights gains and even achieve significant victories. The King birthday legislation recognized the historical importance of the civil rights leader as the principal symbol of the modern African American freedom struggle. The Free South Africa Campaign marked the culmination of long-standing efforts by African Americans and Africans to aid one another's freedom struggles. The emergence of a strong black feminist (or womanist) movement helped black women gain the full benefit of previous civil rights struggles.

To be sure, even as some African Americans achieved breakthroughs in the 1980s, many others experienced new hardships as a result of widespread poverty and the deterioration of urban centers—problems that became the focus of subsequent black struggles. At the beginning of the 1990s, young black Americans born after the era of civil rights reforms took responsibility for ensuring that an earlier generation's racial advances were protected and perhaps even extended in new directions.

FURTHER READING

Bogle, Donald. *Prime Time Blues: African Americans on Network Television* (New York: Farrar, Straus, and Giroux, 2001).

Collins, Patricia Hill. *Black Feminist Thought: Knowledge, Consciousness, and the Politics of Empowerment* (Boston: Unwin Hyman, 1990).

Dawson, Michael C. *Behind the Mule: Race and Class in African American Politics* (Princeton, NJ: Princeton University, 1994).

Dyson, Michael Eric. *Between God and Gangsta Rap: Bearing Witness to Black Culture* (New York: Oxford Press, 1996)

Frady, Marshall. *Jesse: The Life and Pilgrimage of Jesse Jackson* (New York: Random House, 1996).

Guy-Sheftall, Beverly, ed. *Words of Fire: An Anthology of African-American Feminist Thought* (New York: New Press, 1995).

Hill, Anita. *Speaking Truth to Power* (New York: Doubleday, 1997).

hooks, bell. *Talking Back: Thinking Feminist, Thinking Black* (Boston: South End, 1989).

Marable, Manning. *Race, Reform, and Rebellion: The Second Reconstruction in Black America, 1945–1990* (Jackson: University Press of Mississippi, 1991).

Morrison, Toni, ed. *Race-ing, Justice, En-gendering Power: Essays on Anita Hill, Clarence Thomas, and the Construction of Social Reality* (New York: Pantheon, 1992).

Reed, Adolph. *The Jesse Jackson Phenomenon: The Crisis of Purpose in Afro-American Politics* (New Haven, CT: Yale, 1986).

Rivlin, Gary. *Fire on the Prairie: Chicago's Harold Washington and the Politics of Race* (New York: Henry Holt, 1992).

Robinson, Randall. *Defending the Spirit: A Black Life in America* (New York: Penguin, 1998).

Walker, Alice. *The Same River Twice: Honoring the Difficult* (New York: Scribner, 1996).

Wallace, Michele. *Black Macho and the Myth of the Superwoman* (New York: Dial Press, 1978).

Wilson, William J. *The Declining Significance of Race: Blacks and Changing American Institutions* (Chicago: University of Chicago Press, 1980).

CHAPTER 21

■ Ben Jones, *Stars II*, 1983. Jones is known for ethnic imagery and collages.

Continuing Struggles over Rights and Identity, 1992–Present

CHAPTER OUTLINE

Oprah Winfrey and Social Healing

On May 4, 1992, just days after a major Los Angeles riot following the acquittal of the policemen who had beaten black motorist Rodney King, Oprah Winfrey added to her reputation as the most influential entertainer of her time. Winfrey decided to devote that day's edition of the "Oprah Winfrey Show," the nation's most popular afternoon television program, to a discussion of the riot and its causes. Although her nationally syndicated show was normally produced in Chicago, she arranged to go to Los Angeles to bring her audience close to the scene of the violence that took more than fifty lives and resulted in more than $1 billion in property damage. "Over the last week I have, just like many of you, felt a sense of shock . . . of outrage and some tears, as people died," she explained to the Los Angeles residents invited to participate in the first of two telecasts. "What will be written into history books for our children and our grandchildren to read, the beating of Rodney King, came into our living rooms and smacked us in the face, and now we must, we *must,* listen to each other."

News coverage of the Los Angeles riot was extensive, but Winfrey's decision to address the issue reflected her confidence that she would be taken seriously and have a social impact. During her career in television, she had often been underestimated—seen simply as an engaging television personality able to connect emotionally with audiences and interviewees. A former teen beauty pageant winner, Winfrey had graduated from Tennessee State University with a major in

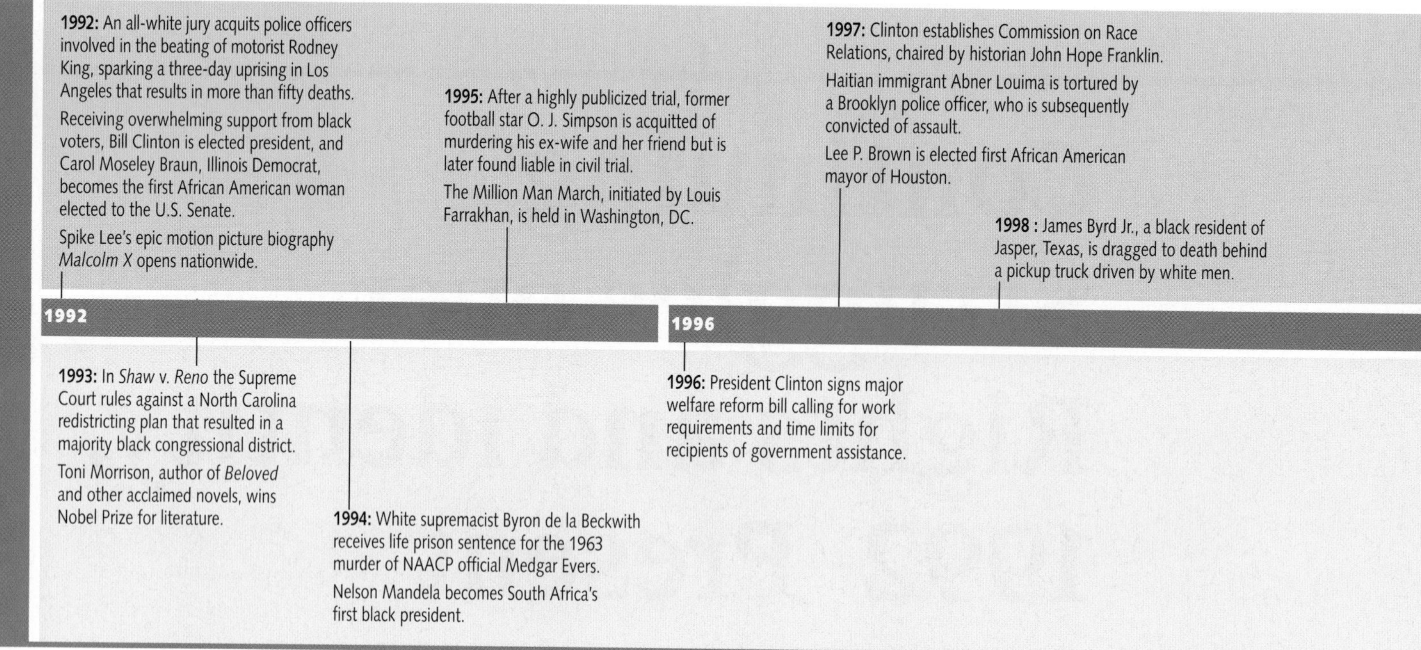

speech and drama. When she entered the field of broadcast news in the mid-1970s, there were few African American television reporters. She became Nashville's first black anchor and then moved to Chicago in 1984 to host a struggling morning show. Soon she gained high ratings and within a few years she had attracted a national audience to her talk show. She won many awards, including multiple Emmys, and became the youngest person ever selected as Broadcaster of the Year by the International Radio and Television Society.

Winfrey became an enormously wealthy and powerful figure in the entertainment industry after establishing the highly profitable Harpo Productions and becoming executive producer of her own show. She expanded her audience through involvement in serious films and television dramas. As an actress, she was nominated for an Oscar for her supporting role in the movie *The Color Purple* (1985), based on Alice Walker's novel. Her role in a film version of Richard Wright's *Native Son* won more critical acclaim. She also produced and starred in a television miniseries, *The Women of Brewster Place* (1989), based on Gloria Naylor's novel, and late in the 1990s she produced and starred in the feature film *Beloved,* based on Toni Morrison's prize-winning novel.

But even these accomplishments did not begin to suggest the extent of Winfrey's influence. Although she avoided partisan involvement with political parties or candidates, viewers of her show learned to expect enlightenment about social issues as well as entertainment. Known to millions simply as Oprah, she set herself apart from other talk show hosts by moving beyond banter about weight loss and hair fashions to deeper discussions about major social problems, including racial conflict and child abuse. When civil rights advocates staged marches into Georgia's all-white Forsythe County in the 1980s, Winfrey took her show there to interview residents as well as protesters. Her moving congressional testimony on behalf of the National Child Protection Act of 1993—she herself was a victim of child abuse—led some to call it "the Oprah bill." Her readiness to risk her own money and reputation on controversial African American films such as *Beloved* won her wide respect, as did her willingness to devote a portion of her wealth to philanthropic causes. By the end of the 1990s, her influence expanded even more as a result of the phenomenally successful Oprah's Book Club, a feature of her television program that transformed her literary selections into immediate best-sellers.

Winfrey's two television shows discussing the Los Angeles riot reflected her long-standing desire to use her exceptional success as an entertainer and producer to achieve broader goals. She conceded that a television program could not solve racial problems but insisted that conversation was a crucial step toward social healing: "People who had never talked to each

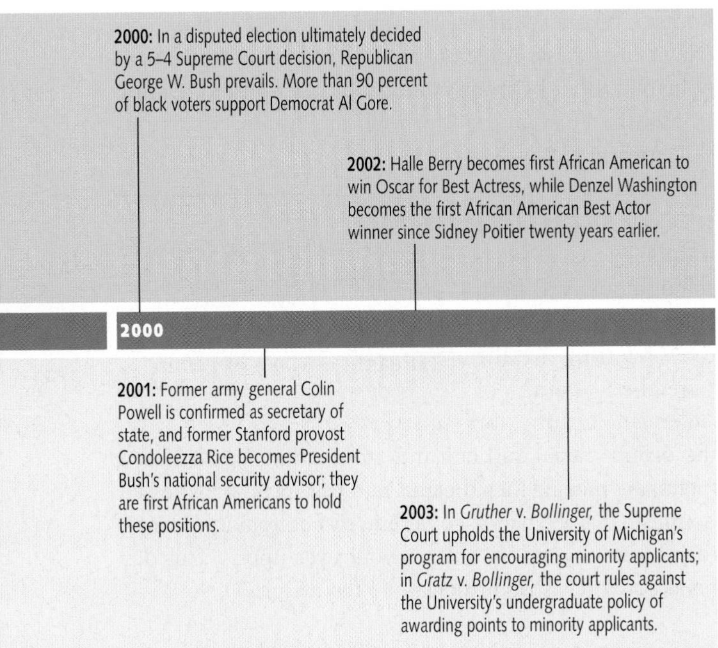

other for years came together . . . and did what should have been done a long time ago. They listened to each other." In less sure hands, the Los Angeles broadcasts might have exacerbated resentment, but Winfrey's interviewing skills encouraged residents to understand the perspectives of others. After one audience member explained how pent-up resentment led him to join in looting, a black business owner pointed out that he had to lay off employees of his looted restaurant. Winfrey was able to draw attention to long-standing grievances, such as the killing of a fifteen-year-old black youngster by a Korean shop owner and the subsequent decision of a judge to release the convicted killer on probation. But she also encouraged a Korean immigrant to explain the dangers of operating a business in a poor black neighborhood. A black Vietnam veteran described being shot by another black person while trying to stop looting of a Korean-owned store.

Through it all, Winfrey managed to keep the discussion civil without suppressing emotions. She empathized with audience members without taking sides. "I don't pretend to know a whole lot about the world," she reflected at the end of the discussion. "I do know that 'ye shall know the truth and the truth shall set you free.' And I'm hoping that everything that's been said here today . . . we will take into our hearts and be willing in our own selves to make a difference." Afterward, she was convinced she had made a difference. "It was what television should do," Winfrey said. "It was utilizing the power of media for the good. You can't do better than that, I think."

Oprah Winfrey's enormous wealth and influence made her exceptional among black Americans at the end of the twentieth century. Her example nonetheless reveals the growing diversity of African American life following the civil rights struggles of the 1960s and the rise of black feminism in the 1970s and 1980s. That Winfrey could achieve a degree of success that made her the envy of people of all races was indicative of the new opportunities that had become available by the 1990s to African Americans. The Los Angeles riot was a chastening reminder that serious racial and economic problems remained unsolved. The gulf between Winfrey and the Los Angeles rioters, some of whom were Latino rather than black, was brought home during the telecast. "Listen, Oprah, when you leave your show, you go to a lavish home," an audience member told her. "We go home to empty refrigerators, you know, crying kids, no diapers, no jobs." Black icons of success such as Winfrey, basketball superstar and product endorser Michael Jordan, and military leader and future Secretary of State Colin Powell provided highly visible indications that long-standing racial barriers had been overcome. But other highly publicized black icons—police brutality victim Rodney King, Nation of Islam leader Louis Farrakhan, rap artist and actor Tupac Shakur—symbolized class divisions among African Americans and the persistence of racial antagonism.

African American voters elected ever-increasing numbers of black public officials, including Carol Moseley Braun as the first African American woman elected to the U.S. Senate, and continued to favor Democratic candidates, providing Bill Clinton's margin of victory in the 1992 presidential race. But the widespread support for Farrakhan's call for a Million Man March in 1995 revealed considerable disenchantment with conventional electoral politics and established civil rights leaders. Centuries of collective struggle against slavery and racial discrimination had produced distinctive African American institutions, forged a common racial identity, and provided inspiration for other freedom struggles throughout the world. But the gains of struggle were unevenly shared, and racial resentment remained evident in many black communities.

Having united to overcome slavery and the Jim Crow system, African Americans faced the challenge of determining whether they had a common destiny in the era following the major civil rights reforms of the 1960s. By the 1990s, earlier African American freedom struggles were consigned to history—implanted in memories, recorded in history books, studied in college classes, celebrated in memorials and documentaries. To be sure, some black Americans still protested against racial injustices and on behalf of civil rights, but the issues were no longer as clearly framed as in the days when racism was openly expressed and backed by the brutal force of police dogs and fire hoses. African Americans still faced "glass ceilings" limiting occupational opportunities and "driving-while-black" encounters with police, but these indications of the continuing significance of race also reflected the growing importance of class, gender, and ethnicity as determinants of American racial relations. As civil rights progress produced new racial dilemmas, African Americans used their new freedoms and opportunities to discuss with one another enduring questions: How do we define ourselves? What experiences and history do we share? What is our place in a changing nation and world?

A NEW DAY FOR AFRICAN AMERICANS?

On the morning of January 20, 1993, Maya Angelou reached a new stage in her extraordinary career when she read a poem she had written at the inauguration ceremony of President William Jefferson Clinton. Angelou had already achieved much in the sixty-four years since she was born in the black ghetto of St. Louis. Her first book, *I Know Why the Caged Bird Sings* (1970), told of her struggle to overcome the trauma of being raped at age seven by her mother's boyfriend. She became mute after learning that her uncle had killed the rapist. The book ends with the birth of Angelou's son when she was sixteen. As a single parent, she worked at a series of low-paying jobs, including streetcar conductor in San Francisco, before eventually achieving success as a singer, dancer, actor, and writer. In the late 1950s, she accepted Martin Luther King Jr.'s invitation to head SCLC's northern fundraising operations, then left to become a journalist in Egypt and Ghana. After returning to the United States, her multifaceted career continued to blossom. In addition to publishing many books of poetry, she gained renown as a teacher (named to a lifetime appointment at Wake Forest University) and actor (she appeared in the *Roots* television series). Angelou became a mentor and source of inspiration for Oprah Winfrey. But her spirited reading of "On the Pulse of the Morning" at Clinton's inauguration greatly expanded her fame and influence. Her poem, later published as a best-selling book, was both patriotic and provocative, referring to the "wretched pain" of American history for the diverse racial and cultural groups that "arrived on a nightmare praying for a dream." But Angelou also expressed optimism that the nation could bravely confront its past and then move beyond it: "Lift up your eyes upon / This day break for you / Give birth again to the dream."

> "Lift up your eyes upon / This day break for you / Give birth again to the dream."—*Maya Angelou*

Racial Dilemmas of the Clinton Presidency

Clinton's decision to invite a black poet to speak at his inauguration was unprecedented and a reflection of his desire to reach out to African Americans. He was the first Democrat to hold the office since Jimmy Carter. Like Carter, his margin of victory was due to the overwhelming support of black voters. Yet, like Carter and other Democratic presidents since Roosevelt, Clinton struggled to balance his need to appeal for black support and his reluctance to risk losing white support. As a youngster in Arkansas during the 1950s, he had watched in dismay as the state's image in the nation and the world was damaged by the rioting against black students seeking to attend Little Rock's Central High School (as president, Clinton would present the Little Rock Nine with Congressional Gold Medals). He had opposed the Vietnam War and, after attending Yale Law School, campaigned for liberal Democrat George McGovern in 1972. When launching his own political career, however, he moderated his views and was sufficiently pragmatic to be elected to six terms as governor of Arkansas. By the early 1990s, he became the favored presidential candidate of Democratic Party leaders who believed the party had to break with the liberalism of Lyndon Johnson to defeat George Bush in 1992. Campaigning for the presidency as a New Democrat, Clinton drew attention to his close ties to black leaders such as former Urban League head Vernon Jordan, but he was careful to avoid being seen as beholden to black "interest groups." He made a point of speaking at the annual gathering of the Jesse Jackson Rainbow Coalition, but he used the occasion to publicly chastise

Maya Angelou read "On the Pulse of the Morning" during Bill Clinton's presidential inauguration.

rap singer Sista Souljah for suggesting that "blacks take a week and kill white people" in retaliation for racist attacks by whites. Although Clinton promised his administration would "look like America," he refused to support racial quotas. In a pre-inaugural speech at Howard University, he proclaimed Martin Luther King Jr. as "the most eloquent voice for freedom and justice of his lifetime."

Thus, from the start of his presidency, Clinton was sympathetic to black concerns yet reluctant to take controversial stands on racial issues. News reporters noted the behind-the-scenes influence of Jordan, who declined offers to join the administration but nonetheless advised the new president regarding his appointments. During his two terms in office, Clinton became the first president to appoint African Americans as secretary of commerce (Ron Brown), agriculture (Mike Espy), energy (Hazel O'Leary), veterans' affairs (Jesse Brown), labor (Alexis Herman), and transportation (Rodney Slater). He also appointed black endocrinologist Jocelyn Elders surgeon general and chose historian Mary Frances Berry to resume her role as chair of the Civil Rights Commission. Overall, Clinton appointed more African Americans to high-level posts than any other president. Of symbolic importance, he signed the 1994 King Holiday and Service Act, legislation cosponsored by Atlanta congressional representative John Lewis designed to make the King Holiday a national day for public service. On a personal level, he appeared comfortable in predominantly black settings such as black churches. Clinton also scored points when he played saxophone on a popular late-night television show hosted by black entertainer Arsenio Hall. Novelist Toni Morrison later jested that Clinton was the nation's first black president. He seemed to reflect a prevailing national consensus that black-white relations were no longer as contentious as they had been.

Yet, if the civil rights *movement* seemed to be part of history, civil rights *issues* had not gone away. For every indication of racial progress, a contrasting sign showed that racism remained a strong force. The Rodney King beating and the Los Angeles riot of 1992 were recent memories when Clinton took office. Affirmative action programs remained controversial, a continuing source of division in American politics. Many African Americans remained uncertain that civil rights gains were secure. During Clinton's first year, racial discrimination lawsuits were filed against Denny's restaurants by black customers who said they had been mistreated and denied service. Subsequent revelations that the restaurant chain actively tried to limit the number of black customers was a disturbing reminder of supposedly antiquated Jim Crow practices, although civil rights laws on the books enabled the plaintiffs to win a $45.7 million settlement. Even relatively affluent African Americans felt insecure. *The Rage of a Privileged Class* (1993) by black journalist Ellis Cose revealed that middle-class African Americans often found that expanding job opportunities brought new kinds of frustrations and racial resentments. Similarly, Cornel West's bestselling book of essays, *Race Matters* (1993), bemoaned "the widespread mistreatment of black people, especially black men, by law enforcement agencies." West recalled that his "blood began to boil" when, despite his status as an Ivy League professor, he stood on a New York street while taxis ignored him, even as he watched one stop for a "female fellow citizen of European descent." He acknowledged that the racial slights that middle-class blacks faced were "dwarfed by those like Rodney King's beating or the abuse of black targets of the FBI's COINTELPRO efforts in the 1960s and 1970s," but nonetheless, "the memories cut like a merciless knife at my soul as I waited on that godforsaken corner."

As African Americans anxiously looked for indications of Clinton's racial policies, they also sought answers to broader questions: What did African Americans want from Clinton and the federal government? Beyond protecting previous civil rights goals, what was the black agenda at the end of the twentieth century? To what extent did race still matter in American society?

The Lani Guinier Affair

Clinton's failure to name someone with strong civil rights credentials as attorney general prompted criticism by civil rights leaders, but the first major racial controversy of his administration resulted from his selection of his Yale law school classmate Lani Guinier to head the Justice Department's Civil Rights Division. A black University of Pennsylvania law professor, Guinier was a noted scholar and activist in the field of civil rights law. As a child, her Jamaican-born father, Ewart Guinier, had often told her about the racial barriers he faced in the 1930s as a Harvard student excluded from on-campus housing and socially ostracized by white students. The elder Guinier overcame these obstacles to earn advanced degrees at Columbia and New York University and was the first director of Harvard's Afro-American studies department when his daughter graduated from Radcliffe College in 1974. Her father's example and that of NAACP lawyer Constance Baker Motley inspired Lani Guinier to study at Yale Law School and then become a civil rights litigator in the Justice Department during the Carter administration. In the 1980s, she headed the voting rights program of the NAACP's Legal Defense and Education Fund. After becoming a law professor, she wrote articles suggesting that democratic ideals were often subverted by winner-take-all election systems that allowed majorities to exclude the views of minorities.

As an academic with practical experience in the field of voting rights, Guinier seemed poised to become the first black woman to head the civil rights division. But conservatives immediately mobilized to defeat her nomination by labeling her a "quota queen." Her critics claimed she favored allotting political representation according to race, ignoring her actual intention, which was to stimulate debate about the best way to achieve the ideal of representative government. As Guinier realized, throughout American history there had been many political innovations designed to guarantee minority representation—most notably the Senate, which gave each state two seats, whether it was rural and sparsely populated or urban and densely populated. Guinier urged Clinton to give her a chance to explain her views in Senate confirmation hearings, but instead he refused to go forward with the nomination, fearing a major Senate fight early in his administration.

Many African Americans criticized Clinton's capitulation, which contrasted with former President Bush's staunch support for controversial Supreme Court nominee Clarence Thomas. As pro-Guinier demonstrators marched outside the White House, Maryland representative Kweisi Mfume, chair of the Congressional Black Caucus, predicted that Clinton's action would cost him black support for other administration proposals. Clinton's failure to defend Guinier revealed that he, like previous Democratic presidents, was reluctant to take political risks to reward black voters' support. Guinier saw Clinton's capitulation not only as a personal setback but as "an unfortunate metaphor for the way race and racism are viewed in this society. We are being defined, we are being characterized, are being misrepresented by other people."

> "We are being defined, we are being characterized, are being misrepresented by other people."—*Lani Guinier*

The importance of the issues Guinier raised became apparent soon after her nomination was withdrawn when the Supreme Court announced an important ruling affecting black representation in Congress. In *Shaw* v. *Reno,* the Court invalidated an effort by North Carolina's Democratic-controlled legislature to redraw congressional district lines so one district would have a majority of black voters. In other states, redrawing of congressional districts after the 1990 census had resulted in the election of thirty-nine black congressional representatives as compared to only twenty-four two years earlier. Proponents of the redistricting argued that American political parties often redrew districts for partisan purposes following the census. But, in a 5–4 decision, the Supreme Court ruled in 1993 that the North Carolina plan was unconstitutional because it was guided by racial considerations and ordered the state legislature to redraw district lines. This decision was soon followed by similar challenges to districts with black or Latino majorities.

Contention over this issue continued during the 1990s and was only partly resolved when the Supreme Court revisited redistricting in 2001. Then, a 5–4 majority ruled in *Easley* v. *Cromartie* that race could be considered in districting as long as it was not the "dominant and controlling" consideration.

The continuing controversy over redistricting revealed the complexity of questions facing African Americans as they exercised their hard-won civil rights. Were they better off when black voters were concentrated in congressional districts rather than dispersed in predominantly white districts? Most civil rights leaders and black elected officials believed black-majority districts were necessary as long as most white voters were reluctant to vote for black candidates or even for white candidates with substantial black support. As former SNCC leader and Georgia congressional representative John Lewis noted, the civil rights movement's goal was "to move beyond race," but he added, "We are not there yet." In the years between the *Shaw* and *Easley* decisions, however, black politicians had shown they *could* successfully appeal to white voters to win mayoral races in Denver, Houston, and Seattle, suggesting that race divisions could be overcome. Thus, the Supreme Court's decisions left unsettled the basic issue raised by Lani Guinier: What political arrangement is the best means of achieving democratic ideals in a nation often divided along racial lines?

Ending Welfare and Continuing Poverty

"We should be ashamed we haven't made more progress in this economy," complained Marion Wright Edelman, head of the Children's Defense Fund. "It is totally unacceptable that with this much prosperity we have millions of uninsured children." The persistence of widespread poverty among African Americans led many people to ask why the civil rights reforms of the 1960s benefited some African Americans but not others. A Census Bureau report showed that the poverty rate for African Americans was 33 percent in 1993. Early in the Clinton administration, the issue of welfare reform revived old debates about whether black poverty resulted from enduring racial inequalities—especially insufficient educational and employment opportunities—or from deficiencies in the values and attitudes of poor people. By the early 1990s, the Democratic Party under Clinton was no longer committed to Lyndon Johnson's ambitious war on poverty. Even among African Americans there was little concern about poverty, an issue that had once spurred Martin Luther King Jr.'s Poor People's Campaign. Amid the rapid economic growth of the 1980s and 1990s, Edelman, the former Atlanta sit-in protester and civil rights lawyer who established the Children's Defense Fund, was among the few leaders to draw attention to the increasing numbers of black children being raised in poverty.

> "It is totally unacceptable that with this much prosperity we have millions of uninsured children."
> —*Marion Wright Edelman*

During his first term as president, after failing to gain passage of legislation to provide health care coverage for all Americans, Clinton concentrated on ending deficit spending by the federal government rather than launching new reform programs to deal with issues such as poverty. Trying to reverse conservative gains in the 1994 midterm elections that left Republicans in control of both houses of Congress, Clinton's strategy was to show that Democrats were actually more fiscally responsible than Republicans. Clinton also tried to follow through on his campaign promise to "end welfare as we know it." For many years, Republican politicians had exploited widespread resentment of "welfare mothers," often depicted as irresponsible, unwed black women raising their children at the expense of taxpayers. After vetoing Republican welfare legislation that included drastic cutbacks in welfare spending, Clinton succeeded during 1996 in gaining passage for a compromise welfare proposal. The Personal Responsibility and Work Opportunity Reconciliation Act required states to revise their programs so that adult welfare recipients would have to find work within two years and to end their reliance of government assistance within five years, even if they were unable to find employment. Critics pointed out that the reform did not include adequate funding to train recipients for employment or to provide adequate child care for those seeking work. Edelman complained that this legislation, combined with the rejection of Clinton's health care proposal, would have devastating consequences for many poor people. But Clinton benefited from the fact that Republicans could no longer use the issue of welfare spending against him.

In the short term, the consequences of Clinton's welfare reform were neither as dire as critics predicted nor as positive as proponents hoped. Many former welfare recipients were able to find work because the job market expanded during the late 1990s. During Clinton's presidency, the economy grew significantly; unemployment dropped from 7.2 percent to 5.5 percent; American businesses established 10 million new jobs; a 1993 tax increase in conjunction with a reduction in federal spending cut the annual deficit by 50 percent. In addition, during his second term Clinton was able to mitigate some of the harsher aspects of his legislation by revising provisions that denied disability benefits to legal immigrants and provided health care coverage for children of poor people. Clinton also established an earned income tax credit program that provided wage supplements to many low-wage workers.

A Census Bureau report showed that the poverty rate for African Americans had fallen by 2000 to an all-time low of 24 percent, from 33 percent in 1993. The poverty rate for black children, however, was higher than for African Americans as a whole, and the overall poverty rate for all children in the United States was above that of other wealthy nations (14.8 percent versus 2.9 percent for France and 1.3 percent for Sweden). Even those who found work often joined the ranks of the working poor—those who earned too little to escape poverty or near-poverty. In March 1999, the Secretary of Health and Human Services warned that though many welfare recipients had found work, their earnings typically remained below the poverty line and "most families exiting welfare continue to be poor."

Despite receiving criticism from black leaders for his Guinier retreat and for his support for legislation reducing welfare assistance, Clinton maintained the support of most African Americans. His approval rating among white Americans fell to less than 50 percent during his first year in office, while about 75 percent of black Americans approved his performance in office. Although the president did not advocate new racial reforms, he also did not reverse the civil rights progress that had been made. He welcomed the transition to black-majority rule in South Africa, supporting the decision by the white government to hold free elections in 1994. His acceptance of the prospect that Nelson Mandela would be elected president of South Africa marked a clear reversal from Reagan's policy of "constructive engagement" with the apartheid regime. Clinton received the support of more than 90 percent of black voters when he won reelection in 1996.

RACE AND THE CRIMINAL JUSTICE SYSTEM

Although Rodney King never saw himself as a racial spokesperson, he inadvertently became one. His videotaped beating by police in 1991 soon came to represent much more than merely an unfortunate encounter between a drunken black motorist and overzealous police. Instead, it became a symbol of the troubled relationship between African Americans, especially those living in the nation's inner cities, and predominantly white police forces. Filmmaker Spike Lee included footage of the beating in the opening titles of his film *Malcolm X* (1992) and invited King to attend a premier screening. But Lee's linkage of Rodney King with Malcolm's political legacy obscured the complex new realities of the problems affecting urban black communities in the years since Malcolm's death. Although King was clearly a victim of police brutality, he had self-destructively contributed to the legal problems that marked his life. Twenty-five years old at the time of the beating, he had been arrested for assaulting his estranged wife and had served a prison term for robbery. Excessive drinking contributed to his occasional quick temper and obstinacy, and his run-ins with police and the legal system would continue in subsequent years. Still, the outrage among African Americans following King's assaulting was strengthened by the belief that it reflected a pattern of racial bias on the part of police and the criminal justice system in general. A jury later awarded King $3.8 million in compensatory damages for his injuries, but the same jury acknowledged King's failings when it declined to award the punitive damages his lawyers sought.

The O. J. Simpson Case

Because of his reputation for winning legal cases against police accused of misconduct, Johnnie Cochran was one of the lawyers contacted by Rodney King's family during the days after his beating. Due to a mixup in Cochran's office, however, he did not learn of the call before King had retained another lawyer. Nonetheless, Cochran soon played a prominent role in several legal cases that greatly increased public interest in issues involving race and the criminal justice system. He represented Reginald Denny, who in 1992 became King's white counterpart when black rioters viciously beat him while a helicopter-borne television camera recorded the event. Then, in 1994, he became the leader of the defense team in the most widely publicized trial of the century: the murder trial of former football star Orenthal James (widely known as O. J. or "the Juice") Simpson.

Even before Cochran agreed to represent Simpson, the case had attracted enormous public interest. Charged with murdering his ex-wife and her male friend, both of them white, Simpson had been a celebrity before becoming the nation's most famous criminal defendant. He had won the Heisman Trophy as the best college football player while attending the University of Southern California (USC) and set numerous records as a star running back in the National Football League. He had also pursued a moderately successful acting career; in the 1974 film *The*

The beating of motorist Rodney King by Los Angeles police and the subsequent acquittal of several officers sparked riots across the city.

Klansmen he had played a man framed for murder by the police, and he also had a small role in the television series *Roots*. He had acquired still more wealth making television commercials, working as a sports announcer, and serving as spokesman for a rental car company. More than any other black athlete of his generation, he became a familiar, friendly face to Americans of all races. Because he had protected his public image by avoiding racial issues, Simpson's arrest was a shocking turn in a career that seemed to symbolize the ability of some African Americans to transcend racial barriers. Reporters from around the world covered the trial, and American television viewers saw live coverage of almost nine months of testimony—Simpson's was the longest criminal trial in California history.

Yet it was not Simpson's fame, nor even his guilt or innocence, that accounted for the historical importance of his trial. Instead, Cochran and other defense lawyers transformed the proceedings from a murder case involving a black celebrity into a public indictment of racism in law enforcement. Fifty-six years old when the trial began, Cochran's background had prepared him not only to provide effective legal advice but also to see the case within a broader racial context. After he began practicing law in the mid-1960s, he often expressed admiration for Thurgood Marshall and quoted Martin Luther King's statement that "injustice anywhere is a threat to justice everywhere." Cochran's target, however, was not the southern Jim Crow system but the more subtle kinds of racial prejudice that existed in the urban North. He quickly acquired a reputation as a no-holds-barred defense attorney. In 1977, he was named criminal trial lawyer of the year. After serving two years as Assistant District Attorney for Los Angeles County—the first African American to hold the position—Cochran returned to private practice. During the 1980s he took on several highly publicized cases involving police misconduct. He won a settlement for the family of a black former college football star whose death in police custody was made to look like a suicide, and won the highest jury award in the history of the city of Los Angeles when he represented a thirteen-year-old Latina who had been molested by a Los Angeles Police Department (LAPD) officer. Cochran also took on the case of former Black Panther Geronimo Pratt (also known as Janome Ji Jaga), who was eventually released from a long prison term when Cochran exposed a key prosecution witness as a paid police informant.

These and similar cases convinced many black residents of Los Angeles of a pattern of police misconduct. A 1985 investigation of police abuse had concluded that "the issue of equitable law enforcement continues to be one of the contentious and serious problems for residents of South Central Los Angeles." In 1988, an erroneous tip prompted a police raid that terrorized residents of several apartment buildings and resulted in extensive property damage. (Although the officers involved were eventually acquitted of criminal charges, the city paid out $3.7 million in civil damages.)

Increasing crime and the devastating impact of drugs, especially the widely available and highly addictive crack cocaine, had accelerated the deterioration of Los Angeles's central areas. During the late 1980s, the police department's antidrug Operation Hammer prompted incidents of brutal treatment of suspected gang members and drug dealers. The following decade saw more incidents of police brutality and major scandals involving police lawbreaking, not only in

Defense attorney Johnnie Cochran used race as the key factor in the O. J. Simpson trial.

Los Angeles but in New Orleans, Philadelphia, Oakland, New York, and many other places.

Despite this backdrop of overzealous law enforcement, Cochran faced an uphill struggle when he became Simpson's lead attorney. Although there were no witnesses to the killings, prosecutors presented testimony that Simpson's ex-wife had called police to stop him from assaulting her. Police testified that a bloody glove was found near his home in the Brentwood neighborhood of west Los Angeles. Cochran believed from experience, however, that Los Angeles police could not be relied on to conduct an unbiased investigation involving a black man. Moreover, he realized the attitudes of black jurors toward the police as well as Simpson would determine the outcome of the case. He remarked after the acquittal of the police officers accused of beating Rodney King, "If they had had blacks on that jury, it would have been a different story." Black jurors, he explained, "would have identified more with King rather than the police." Some of Cochran's critics saw him as an opportunist seeking publicity and too willing to play the race card in order to win cases. Christopher Darden, a black prosecutor in the Simpson trial, remarked, "Johnny Cochran was rarely subtle about his trial strategy, and it could be summed up in one word: race."

While the prosecution team insisted that race was irrelevant to the case, for Cochran it was the key factor. Prosecutors were satisfied to have ten women on the jury, but the defense was equally pleased that nine of the twelve jurors were black. Cochran suggested that physical evidence implicating the defendant could have been contaminated or planted by prejudiced police. He undermined the testimony of a white officer who had found the bloody glove by refuting his claim to have never made racist remarks, including use of the term "nigger." The trial's most dramatic point came when Cochran asked Simpson to try on the glove. When Simpson had difficulty fitting his hand into the glove, Cochran scored points with the jury: "If the glove don't fit, you must acquit." The defense team succeeded in planting seeds of doubts in the minds of jurors, who acquitted Simpson. Later polls revealed that most African Americans agreed with the verdict, while most white Americans saw it as a miscarriage of justice. (A subsequent civil trial brought by the families of the victims resulted in a verdict against Simpson, who was assessed large monetary damages.)

Simpson was spared the death penalty or a long prison term, but the legal proceedings did not answer the larger questions raised by the case. Why did African Americans differ from other Americans in their reaction to the testimony? Did the verdict indicate that the predominantly female jury sympathized more with the black male defendant than the white female victim? More generally, did the case really matter in the long term? The Simpson trial had less effect on African Americans than the Scottsboro cases of the 1930s, which produced important Supreme Court decisions such as *Powell* v. *Alabama* (which ruled the Scottsboro defendants were denied legal counsel) and *Norris* v. *Alabama* (which ruled that black jurors could not be systematically excluded). Indeed, the Simpson trial reflected the changes that had occurred in the years since the Scottsboro trials. Rather than illiterate hobos being saved from execution (but not from prison) by a Communist-led legal effort and protest campaign, a black millionaire had been set free due to the efforts of a highly paid defense team led by a black attorney. Had class, therefore, become more important than race in determining how an African American defendant was treated by the criminal justice system?

The Prison System of Racial Control

"Mass incarceration is not a solution to unemployment, nor is it a solution to the vast array of social problems that are hidden away in a rapidly growing network of prisons and jail," Angela Davis insisted during the 1990s. Davis had herself been imprisoned during the 1970s, when she was tried and acquitted on charges of aiding an unsuccessful attempt to free radical inmates. After her acquittal, Davis returned to academic life (she had been a professor at UCLA before being fired for being a Communist), first at San Francisco State and then at the University of California, Santa Cruz. She never abandoned, however, her concern about the injustices of the criminal justice system. "Most people commit crimes," she once remarked. "Some people are under much greater surveillance than others." Unlike Cochran's efforts to defend individual victims of police and prosecutorial misconduct, Davis raised a broader question: Why were African Americans and poor people in general more likely to be in prison? What should be done about the large number of African Americans and Latinos already incarcerated? While law-and-order advocates saw prisons as a way of reducing crime, Davis saw mass imprisonment as a substitute for dealing with social injustices. "Colored bodies constitute the main human raw material in this vast experiment to disappear the major social problems of our time," she insisted.

> "Mass incarceration is not a solution to unemployment, nor is it a solution to the vast array of social problems that are hidden away in a rapidly growing network of prisons and jail."—*Angela Davis*

Davis's campaign against "the prison industrial complex" reflected both how much and how little had changed since the era when police routinely used force and threats to extract confessions from black suspects and when lynch mobs took black prisoners from their cells to be hanged and burned. The Scottsboro cases, NAACP litigation, and the civil rights legislation of the 1960s had strengthened the rights of defendants and the ability of the federal courts to intervene on their behalf. Davis's acquittal demonstrated that a black radical could prevail in the courtroom, even with an all-white jury. Federal indictments of the officers involved in the King beating resulted in the conviction of two of them. The Simpson case demonstrated that a wealthy black man could put police and prosecutors on the defensive, forced to defend themselves against the charge of racial discrimination in law enforcement. But most black defendants did not have the advantage of Simpson's high-priced legal team.

The extensive publicity given Simpson's trial obscured less visible indications of racial bias in the criminal justice system. Studies conducted in the 1990s indicated that more than one in four black males in their twenties were in jail, on parole, or under some form of legal supervision. In some states, felons were barred from voting for the rest of their lives. Thus, more than a century after the end of slavery, a substantial proportion of African Americans were still not truly citizens nor legally free. Moreover, since the late 1960s, law-and-order politicians had put in place policies that strengthened the hands of police, resulting in increasing arrest and conviction rates, especially in poor, predominantly black neighborhoods. While civil rights reforms gave black Americans a greater sense of freedom, crackdowns on black militancy had sent another message: black rebelliousness would be harshly punished. The persistence of black poverty and the explosion of drug usage among all Americans were underlying conditions that contributed to a rapid increase in the prison population after the 1960s.

Thus, despite civil rights gains, black Americans were still more likely than white Americans to be mistreated by police, by prosecutors, and by the entire criminal justice system. Studies in the 1980s and 1990s revealed they were more likely to be stopped by police or arrested when stopped. While defenders of police pointed to the high incidence of criminal activity in poverty-stricken black communities, the practice of racial profiling was a concern to African Americans of every background. Even affluent black suburbanites who were uninvolved in criminal activity feared being stopped for "driving while black" by overzealous police officers.

The increased police surveillance of African Americans also increased the likelihood that African Americans engaged in criminal activity would be arrested and thereafter burdened with police records. Studies indicated that African Americans charged with crimes were more likely to be convicted. A study of nearly 700,000 California criminal cases during the 1980s revealed that white defendants were more likely to have their cases dismissed and charges dropped or to receive lighter sentences than were black defendants. In part because of their police records, black defendants convicted of crimes were more likely to serve long sentences or suffer the death penalty when convicted of capital crimes. Nationwide, capital punishment, which had been used with declining frequency during the 1960s in the United States and other advanced industrial nations, regained its popularity after

Halle Berry Accepts the Academy Award

In 2002 Halle Berry won the Best Actress Academy Award for her performance in the film Monster's Ball. *She was the first African American to win such an award.*

Oh, my God. Oh, my God. I'm sorry. This moment is so much bigger than me. This moment is for Dorothy Dandridge, Lena Horne, Diahann Carroll. It's for the women that stand beside me, Jada Pinkett, Angela Bassett, Vivica Fox. And it's for every nameless, faceless woman of color that now has a chance because this door tonight has been opened. Thank you. I'm so honored. I'm so honored. And I thank the Academy for choosing me to be the vessel for which His blessing might flow. Thank you.

—*74th Academy Awards, 2002 Best Actress Acceptance Speech, March 24, 2002.*

To view a longer version of this document, please go to *www.ablongman.com/carson/documents*.

demand for payments to compensate African Americans for past racial oppression had been put forward as early as 1867, when Pennsylvania congressman Thaddeus Stevens introduced a bill to give former slaves 40 acres of land. Congress passed the measure, but President Andrew Johnson vetoed it. In the late 1960s, SNCC leader James Forman called for a reparations payment of $500,000 to every black American. In the last decades of the century, Representative John Conyers of Michigan submitted legislation that would establish a commission to investigate the need for reparations to compensate for slavery and subsequent racial discrimination.

Although the national movement for racial reparations made little headway, a number of incidents indicated Americans were becoming more aware of historical injustices. The 1980s saw a successful effort to secure compensation for the survivors of the Japanese internment during World War II. In the 1990s, black residents of the town of Rosewood, Florida, asked the Florida legislature to pay $7 million for loss of personal liberty and life after white people invaded the town in 1923 to retaliate for an alleged sexual assault. This claim was initially rejected on the grounds that the statue of limitations had passed. When the plaintiffs submitted another claim for their property losses, they obtained a $2.1 million settlement but no official apology. In 2001, a commission established by the Oklahoma legislature recommended compensation for survivors of the 1921 Tulsa race riot. Although the legislature turned down the recommendation, it approved funds for redeveloping the riot area, establishing a memorial, and creating a scholarship funded by private donations. In 1999, black farmers won a billion-dollar settlement to compensate for the discriminatory policies of the U.S. Department of Agriculture. Clinton himself hinted that perhaps a national apology for slavery was appropriate, only to retreat when his suggestion came under attack, even from some black leaders. Jesse Jackson, for example, remarked, "If you want to apologize for slavery, then why not apologize for legal segregation and then work to end present racial discrimination?"

Redefining *Black*

Black filmmaker Marlon Riggs did not testify before John Hope Franklin's advisory panel, having died of AIDS in 1994. But his films were significant contributions to the national racial dialogue of the 1990s. Although he was only thirty-seven years old at his death, Riggs had already completed several pioneering films that illuminated previously neglected aspects of African American history. His first major documentary, the Emmy award–winning *Ethnic Notions* (1987), traced the evolution of the racial stereotypes he saw as deeply implanted in the psyche of Americans. A later film, *Color Adjustment* (1991), examined the depiction of African Americans on national television, from "Amos 'n' Andy" in the 1950s to "The Cosby Show" of the 1980s. But it was Riggs's *Tongues Untied* (1989) that focused national attention on his work and made him the target of criticism. The film was a moving, highly personal documentary that provided a wide-ranging discussion of the black gay experience. Though acclaimed by critics and awarded Best Documentary at Berlin and other film festivals, some viewers saw it as obscene because of its frank depiction of homosexuals. When the film was shown on television and conservative politicians learned that Riggs had received federal funding, the filmmaker found himself embroiled in controversy. He defended himself by insisting that gay black people were also taxpaypers "entitled to some means of representation in publicly financed art."

Even as Riggs confronted death, he was determined to complete one more film that expressed his belief that the concept of blackness should be broadened to capture the full diversity of African American life. Riggs's *Black Is . . . Black Ain't* (1995), completed after his death by his associates, was a challenge to black people "to get over the notion that you can only be unified as a people as long as everybody agrees. You know we don't achieve freedom by those means." Riggs saw his last film as initiating a much-needed conversation among African Americans: "There is a cure for what ails us as a people, and that is for us to talk to each other. We have got to start talking about the ways in which we hurt each other; and the ways in which we hurt each other is also through silence."

Riggs was one of many black intellectuals and artists who sought to understand and explain the diversity and complexity of African American lives. The proliferation of universities encouraging research on African American life made possible the emergence of black public intellectuals who expressed widely varied viewpoints in recent years. Riggs's final film reflected a trend in African American thought toward greater recognition of the extent to which racial identity was not permanent but constantly changing and not a single set of characteristics but a broad range of possibilities. For much of African American history, enslavement and racial oppression imposed a black identity on the Africans brought to the New World, and that system of oppression had also given Europeans a new identity as white people. Yet, although being black was initially an identity forced on all Americans with African ancestry, that identity was later voluntarily chosen by African Americans who came to see themselves as a group that was not only oppressed but also struggling collectively against oppression. Riggs's films suggested that the African American identity was becoming increasingly varied in the era following the major civil rights reforms of the 1960s. As did the black feminist writers of the 1980s, Riggs attacked narrow definitions of blackness that either excluded many African Americans or forced them to conform to the expectations of others.

Among the themes of late twentieth-century popular culture was that of individuals crossing cultural boundaries. The increasing amount of cultural interaction throughout the United States—and indeed throughout the world—has led to ever greater transfers of cultural information. Because of the mass communications media, African American culture had been marketed throughout the world, and African Americans had consumed aspects of the cultures of other groups. White Americans and people in other nations have become more African American in their cultural outlook, while African Americans had become more like other Americans as well as more European, more Asian, more Latin, and more African.

The 2000 Census revealed that America is becoming increasingly multiracial.

At the beginning of the twentieth century, W. E. B. Du Bois had analyzed the "double-consciousness" of African Americans—"an American, a Negro; two souls, two thoughts, two unreconciled strivings"—but at the end of the century, African American identity had become even more conflicted. A steady stream of recent writings had shown that African Americans were increasingly differentiated along lines of class, color, religion, gender, sexuality, and even race. These writings revealed the variety of individual experiences that constituted the African American experience. Black identity was no longer forcefully imposed by a Jim Crow system, but African Americans could instead choose to identify themselves with their rich history of struggles against racial barriers.

2000 Census Documents a Multiracial Nation

Increasing awareness among Americans that racial identity is socially determined rather than based on biological or

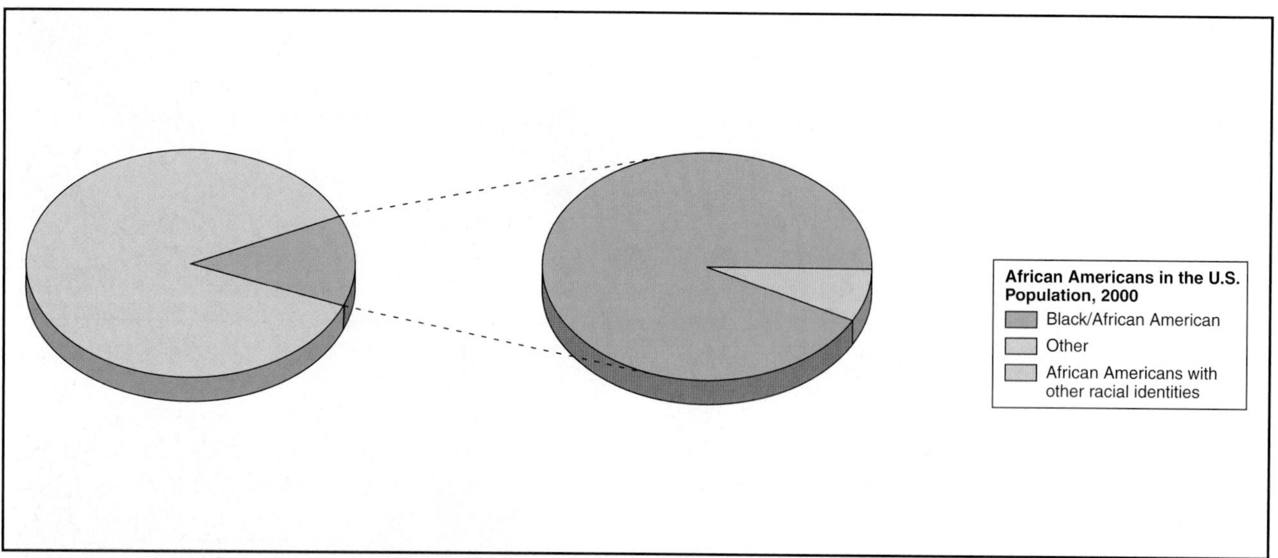

FIGURE 21.1 African Americans in the U.S. Population, 2000
Taking advantage of new census policies, millions of Americans identified themselves as multiracial in the 2000 United States Census. Racial identity is increasingly recognized as being socially determined rather than biologically determined.

genetic factors led to disputes regarding how to conduct the 2000 Census. Given that Americans are required to participate in the census count, which is conducted every ten years to allocate seats in Congress and distribute federal expenditures, it is hardly surprising that the policies and procedures of the Census Bureau have often been the subject of controversy. Throughout most of American history, African Americans had little control over how they were designated by census takers, who often assigned racial categories simply by observing skin color and other appearance factors. After 1960, however, individuals were able to identify themselves racially, although mixed-race people were still forced to choose only one category. With respect to African Americans, this policy reinforced the so-called one-drop rule, as anyone with recognizable African ancestry tended to identify as black or Negro. By the 2000 Census, increased criticism caused government officials to greatly expand the list of racial categories and to create a new category called Hispanic Origin. For the first time, multiracial and multiethnic people were able to choose more than one category to identify their ancestry.

As a result of these changes, the 2000 Census showed that the nation had not only changed rapidly over the preceding decade but also reshaped how many Americans saw their own nation. White Americans recognized that they were still a majority group, but, whereas in 1960 white people comprised 89 percent of the total population, by 2000 only 75 percent of Americans described themselves as white (another 2 percent described themselves as partly white). The 2000 Census revealed that African Americans had increased in numbers at a faster rate than white Americans, but that other minority groups had grown at an even faster rate. The number of Latinos (some of whom were African American) was now equal to the number of African Americans (some of whom were Latinos), and the former group was growing more rapidly than the latter. The number of Americans who identified themselves as having Asian ancestry had similarly increased at a faster rate than did those identified as black. Pacific Islanders were also rapidly expanding their numbers. The 2000 Census also revealed that many Americans of African ancestry took advantage of the new census policies by identifying themselves as multiracial (see Figure 21.1). The black-white divide that had been such an important factor in American history had evolved into a more complex multiracial society.

But the controversy over racial categories in the 2000 Census touched on deeper issues. If racial identity was becoming a matter of voluntary choice rather than determined by genes, imposed by white domination, or forged in collective freedom struggles, would African Americans eventually lose their sense of common identity? Such a possibility would have seemed unlikely at the beginning of the twentieth century, when race was generally assumed to be a biological category, when white supremacy was evident throughout the world, and when black freedom struggles required a strong sense of solidarity. At the beginning of the twenty-first century, the meaning of race was widely debated, colonialism and Jim Crow had been overthrown, and the struggles to overcome these systems had become part of history. Perhaps for this reason, African American historical memory had become more and more essential to the maintenance of African American identity. Rather than being rooted in African ancestry or in the experience of resisting racial oppression, African American identity was increasingly rooted in understanding African American history.

DEMOCRACY AND THE LEGACY OF RACE

Martin Luther King III understood the importance of historical understanding when he reacted to the disputed presidential election of 2000. Although Republican George W. Bush ultimately prevailed over the Democratic candidate, Vice President Al Gore, King was one of those who charged that the election was a distortion of democracy. Speaking as president of the Southern Christian Leadership Conference, the group once led by his father, he noted that the election had highlighted the ways in which, more than three decades after the passage of the Voting Rights Act of 1965, African Americans continued to be disadvantaged in the American political system. He drew particular attention to the removal of more than 94,000 Florida residents from the voter registration rolls in the months before the election. Although Florida officials, including Governor Jeb Bush, the new president's brother, claimed this was necessary to remove convicted felons from the rolls, King argued that "the overwhelming majority were innocent of any crime. He pointed out that a computerized purge of the rolls had removed many voters "whose name, birth date and gender loosely matched that of a felon anywhere in America." He added, "the legacy of slavery—commonalities of black names—aided the racial bias of the 'scrub list.'" Noting his father had led demonstrations against racial barriers to the vote, he lamented that the struggle had taken a new form. "Four decades ago, the opposition to the civil rights to vote was easy to identify—night riders wearing white sheets and burning crosses," he remarked. "Today, the threat comes from partisan politicians wearing pinstripe suits and clutching laptops."

The Disputed 2000 Election

King's complaint about the erroneous disqualification of voters was only one aspect of the ways in which the 2000 presidential election served as a reminder of the complex and continuing relationship between African American history and American democracy. The nation's founders not only created a nation in which African Americans were oppressed but also an undemocratic political system that in most places restricted voting rights to white male property owners. Two hundred years of African American civil rights struggles had moved the nation closer to democratic ideals but had not achieved universal adult suffrage. Many voters of all races and a disproportionate number of black voters faced barriers to participation in the 2000 election. Because of extended residency requirements, disfranchisement of felons, the practice of holding elections on workdays, and unnecessarily burdensome registration procedures, residents of many states found it easier to register cars than to vote. Furthermore, the nation's founders created the Electoral College, which gives states a vote for each member of the House and Senate from that state. This was intended to serve as a check on majority rule and to reassure southern states they would not be dominated by more heavily populated northern states. In most elections, the fact that large numbers of Americans do not vote is little noticed, and the Electoral College generally reflects the popular vote. But the 2000 election dramatically revealed the undemocratic aspects of the American political system.

Gore not only won the support of 90 percent of African American voters but also received about a half-million more votes than Bush. Bush's support, however, was concentrated in less populated states that carried the same weight in the Electoral College as the more densely populated states won by Gore. Thus, Bush's victories in the six sparsely populated western states of Alaska, North and South Dakota, Wyoming, Idaho, and Montana, with a combined population of less than 5 million, gave him 16 electoral votes, while Gore won several urbanized states with a combined population of more than 8 million that produced only 15 electoral votes. Despite this disparity, Bush still did not have a majority in the Electoral College without the disputed Florida vote.

Thus, the election demonstrated the importance of the issue raised by King as well as Lani Guinier—that is, the need to establish an electoral system that accurately reflects the votes of all adult citizens. Voters who supported Bush could dismiss challenges as sour grapes, but African American history provides ample evidence of the importance of enabling ever larger numbers of citizens to be represented and heard in the political system.

African Americans in an Interdependent World

President George W. Bush was elected with minimal black support, but he demonstrated his willingness to appoint African Americans to high posts in his administration by naming former military leader Colin Powell as his secretary of state and Condoleeza Rice as White House national security advisor, the first African Americans to hold these positions. Thus, an African American man born in 1937 in the South Bronx, became the nation's secretary of state, a post once held by Thomas Jefferson. An African American woman born in Birmingham, Alabama, just six months after the 1954 *Brown v. Board of Education* decision, became, a half-century later, the national security advisor to the president of the United States. Both officials had been shaped by their experiences as African Americans, even while both embraced their new roles as government leaders shaping the future of the nation and indeed the world. When Powell testified at his Senate confirmation hearings soon after President Bush nominated him, he affirmed Jefferson's dream of "popular government," but also noted that Martin Luther King Jr. "helped to answer Jefferson's prayers for black Americans, whose forbearers at that time were considered to be property, slaves, even in Jefferson's own custody." Powell acknowledged that "there is still so much that needs to be done here at home and around the world to bring that universal Jeffersonian dream to the whole world." He pledged that the guiding principle of American foreign policy would be "to help any country that wishes to join the democratic world—any country that puts the rule of law in place and begins to live by that rule, any country that seeks peace and prosperity and a place in the sun. In that light, there is no country on earth that is not touched by America, for we have become the motive force for freedom and democracy in the world."

The terrorist attacks on September 11, 2001 against New York's World Trade Center and the Pentagon focused considerable attention on the roles played by Rice and Powell in guiding the nation's foreign policy. But their prominence in the Bush administration also served as a reminder of the increasing diversity of African American experiences and attitudes in the twenty-first century. On the one hand, thousands of black soldiers had volunteered to serve in the U.S. military forces that responded to the terrorist attacks by invading Afghanistan and Iraq. Yet many African Americans opposed the war to overthrow Iraqi leader Saddam Hussein. Powell could look to his background as confirmation of his decision to join a Republican administration and to support the controversial war in Iraq. But Representative Barbara Lee, the California Democrat whose entry into politics had been inspired by Shirley Chisholm's presidential campaign, could also look to her background to justify her decision to cast the only vote in Congress against giving President Bush a free hand to wage war against terrorists.

While African American participation in the war effort continued a long tradition of fighting in all the nation's wars, Lee's action also continued a tradition of black antiwar dissent traceable to King during the Vietnam War or A. Philip Randolph during World War I or Frederick Douglass during the Mexican-American War. Although there was no single African American position on the nation's foreign policies, an April 2003 Gallup Poll revealed that only 29 percent of black respondents supported the Bush administration's decision to invade Iraq, compared to 78 percent of white respondents. This split in attitude was also evident in the critical stand taken by members of the Congressional Black Caucus. Even before the outbreak of war in March 2003, the Caucus objected to "the unilateral first strike action by the United States without a clearly demonstrated and imminent threat of attack on the United States" and warned that "any post-strike plan for maintaining stability in the region would be costly and would require a long-term commitment." Earlier black critics of American foreign policy such as W. E. B. Du Bois and Martin Luther King Jr. had

National Security Advisor Condoleeza Rice with President George W. Bush and followed by White House Chief of Staff Andrew Card. Rice is one of Bush's most influential advisors and often has the president's ear on foreign policy issues.

WM. PACA
THOS. STONE
CHARLES CARROLL OF CARROLLTON
GEORGE WYTHE
RICHARD HENRY LEE
TH. JEFFERSON
BENJA. HARRISON
THS. NELSON, JR.

GEO. ROSS
CAESAR RODNEY
GEO. READ
THO. MÍKEAN
WM. FLOYD
PHIL. LIVINGSTON
FRANS. LEWIS
LEWIS MORRIS

WILLIAM ELLERY
ROGER SHERMAN
SAMÍEL. HUNTINGTON
WM. WILLIAMS
OLIVER WOLCOTT
MATHEW THORNTON
RICHD. STOCKTON

THE CONSTITUTION OF THE UNITED STATES OF AMERICA*

Preamble

We the People of the United States, in Order to form a more perfect Union, establish Justice, insure domestic Tranquility, provide for the common defence, promote the general Welfare, and secure the Blessings of Liberty to ourselves and our Posterity, do ordain and establish this Constitution for the United States of America.

Article I.

Section 1 All legislative Powers herein granted shall be vested in a Congress of the United States, which shall consist of a Senate and House of Representatives.

Section 2 The House of Representatives shall be composed of Members chosen every second Year by the People of the several States, and the Electors in each State shall have the Qualifications requisite for Electors of the most numerous Branch of the State Legislature.

No Person shall be a Representative who shall not have attained to the Age of twenty five Years, and been seven Years a Citizen of the United States, and who shall not, when elected, be an Inhabitant of that State in which he shall be chosen.

Representatives and direct Taxes shall be apportioned among the several States which may be included within this Union, according to their respective Numbers, *which shall be determined by adding to the whole Number of free Persons, including those bound to Service for a Term of Years, and excluding Indians not taxed, three fifths of all other Persons*. The actual Enumeration shall be made within three Years after the first Meeting of the Congress of the United States, and within every subsequent Term of ten Years, in such Manner as they shall by Law direct. The Number of Representatives shall not exceed one for every thirty Thousand, but each State shall have at Least one Representative; *and until such enumeration shall be made, the State of New Hampshire shall be entitled to chuse three, Massachusetts eight, Rhode-Island and Providence Plantations one, Connecticut five, New-York six, New Jersey four, Pennsylvania eight, Delaware one, Maryland six, Virginia ten, North Carolina five, South Carolina five, and Georgia three.*

When vacancies happen in the Representation from any State, the Executive Authority thereof shall issue Writs of Election to fill such Vacancies.

The House of Representatives shall chuse their Speaker and other Officers; and shall have the sole Power of Impeachment.

Section 3 The Senate of the United States shall be composed of two Senators from each State, chosen by the Legislature thereof, for six Years; and each Senator shall have one Vote.

Immediately after they shall be assembled in Consequence of the first Election, they shall be divided as equally as may be into three Classes. The Seats of the Senators of the first Class shall be vacated at the Expiration of the second Year, of the second Class at the Expiration of the fourth Year, and of the third Class at the Expiration of the sixth Year, so that one third may be chosen every second Year; and if Vacancies happen by Resignation, or otherwise, during the Recess of the Legislature of any State, the Executive thereof may make temporary Appointments until the next Meeting of the Legislature, which shall then fill such Vacancies.

No Person shall be a Senator who shall not have attained to the Age of thirty Years, and been nine Years a Citizen of the United States, and who shall not, when elected, be an Inhabitant of that State for which he shall be chosen.

The Vice President of the United States shall be President of the Senate, but shall have no Vote, unless they be equally divided.

The Senate shall choose their other Officers, and also a President *pro tempore*, in the Absence of the Vice President, or when he shall exercise the Office of President of the United States.

**The constitution became effective March 4, 1789. Any portion of the text that has been amended is printed in italics.*

The Senate shall have the sole Power to try all Impeachments. When sitting for that Purpose, they shall be on Oath or Affirmation. When the President of the United States is tried the Chief Justice shall preside: And no Person shall be convicted without the Concurrence of two thirds of the Members present.

Judgment in Cases of Impeachment shall not extend further than to removal from Office, and disqualification to hold and enjoy any Office of honor, Trust or Profit under the United States: but the Party convicted shall nevertheless be liable and subject to Indictment, Trial, Judgment and Punishment, according to Law.

Section 4 The Times, Places and Manner of holding Elections for Senators and Representatives, shall be prescribed in each State by the Legislature thereof; but the Congress may at any time by Law make or alter such Regulations, except as to the Places of chusing Senators.

The Congress shall assemble at least once in every Year, and such Meeting *shall be on the first Monday in December, unless they shall by Law appoint a different Day*.

Section 5 Each House shall be the Judge of the Elections, Returns and Qualifications of its own Members, and a Majority of each shall constitute a Quorum to do Business; but a smaller Number may adjourn from day to day, and may be authorized to compel the Attendance of absent Members, in such Manner, and under such Penalties as each House may provide.

Each House may determine the Rules of its Proceedings, punish its Members for disorderly Behaviour, and, with the Concurrence of two thirds, expel a Member.

Each House shall keep a Journal of its Proceedings, and from time to time publish the same, excepting such Parts as may in their Judgment require Secrecy; and the Yeas and Nays of the Members of either House on any question shall, at the Desire of one fifth of those Present, be entered on the Journal.

Neither House, during the Session of Congress, shall, without the Consent of the other, adjourn for more than three days, nor to any other Place than that in which the two Houses shall be sitting.

Section 6 The Senators and Representatives shall receive a Compensation for their Services, to be ascertained by Law, and paid out of the Treasury of the United States. They shall in all Cases, except Treason, Felony and Breach of the Peace, be privileged from Arrest during their Attendance at the Session of their respective Houses, and in going to and returning from the same; and for any Speech or Debate in either House, they shall not be questioned in any other Place.

No Senator or Representative shall, during the Time for which he was elected, be appointed to any civil Office under the Authority of the United States, which shall have been created, or the Emoluments whereof shall have been encreased during such time; and no Person holding any Office under the United States, shall be a Member of either House during his Continuance in Office.

Section 7 All Bills for raising Revenue shall originate in the House of Representatives; but the Senate may propose or concur with Amendments as on other Bills.

Every Bill which shall have passed the House of Representatives and the Senate, shall, before it become a Law, be presented to the President of the United States; If he approve he shall sign it, but if not he shall return it, with his Objections to that House in which it shall have originated, who shall enter the Objections at large on their Journal, and proceed to reconsider it. If after such Reconsideration two thirds of that House shall agree to pass the Bill, it shall be sent, together with the Objections, to the other House, by which it shall likewise be reconsidered, and if approved by two thirds of that House, it shall become a Law. But in all such Cases the Votes of both Houses shall be determined by yeas and Nays, and the Names of the Persons voting for and against the Bill shall be entered on the Journal of each House respectively. If any Bill shall not be returned by the President within ten Days (Sundays excepted) after it shall have been presented to him, the Same shall be a Law, in like Manner as if he had signed it, unless the Congress by their Adjournment prevent its Return, in which Case it shall not be a Law.

Every Order, Resolution, or Vote to which the Concurrence of the Senate and House of Representatives may be necessary (except on a question of Adjournment) shall be presented to the President of the United States; and before the Same shall take Effect, shall be approved by him, or being disapproved by him, shall be repassed by two thirds of the Senate and House of Representatives, according to the Rules and Limitations prescribed in the Case of a Bill.

Section 8 The Congress shall have Power:

To lay and collect Taxes, Duties, Imposts and Excises, to pay the Debts and provide for the common Defence and general Welfare of the United States; but all Duties, Imposts and Excises shall be uniform throughout the United States;

To borrow Money on the credit of the United States;

To regulate Commerce with foreign Nations, and among the several States, and with the Indian Tribes;

To establish an uniform Rule of Naturalization, and uniform Laws on the subject of Bankruptcies throughout the United States;

To coin Money, regulate the Value thereof, and of foreign Coin, and fix the Standard of Weights and Measures;

To provide for the Punishment of counterfeiting the Securities and current Coin of the United States;

To establish Post Offices and post Roads;

In the opinion of the court, the legislation and histories of the times, and the language used in the declaration of independence, show, that neither the class of persons who had been imported as slaves, nor their descendants, whether they had become free or not, were then acknowledged as a part of the people, nor intended to be included in the general words used in that memorable instrument. . . .

It is too clear for dispute, that the enslaved African race were not intended to be included, and formed no part of the people who framed and adopted this declaration; for if the language, as understood in that day, would embrace them, the conduct of the distinguished men who framed the declaration of independence would have been utterly and flagrantly inconsistent with the principles they asserted; and instead of the sympathy of mankind, to which they so confidently appealed, they would have deserved and received universal rebuke and reprobation. . . .

But there are two clauses in the constitution which point directly and specifically to the negro race as a separate class of persons, and show clearly that they were not regarded as a portion of the people or citizens of the government then formed.

One of these clauses reserves to each of the thirteen States the right to import slaves until the year 1808, if it thinks proper. . . . And by the other provision the States pledge themselves to each other to maintain the right of property of the master, by delivering up to him any slave who may have escaped from his service, and be found within their respective territories. . . .

The only two provisions which point to them and include them, treat them as property, and make it the duty of the government to protect it; no other power, in relation to this race, is to be found in the constitution; and as it is a government of special, delegated powers, no authority beyond these two provisions can be constitutionally exercised. The government of the United States had no right to interfere for any other purpose but that of protecting the rights of the owner, leaving it altogether with the several States to deal with this race, whether emancipated or not, as each State may think justice, humanity, and the interests and safety of society, require. The States evidently intended to reserve this power exclusively to themselves. . . .

Upon a full and careful consideration of the subject, the court is of opinion, that, upon the facts stated . . . Dred Scott was not a citizen of Missouri within the meaning of the constitution of the United States, and not entitled as such to sue in its courts; and, consequently, that the circuit court had no jurisdiction of the case, and that the judgment on the plea in abatement is erroneous. . . .

We proceed . . . to inquire whether the facts relied on by the plaintiff entitled him to his freedom. . . .

The act of Congress, upon which the plaintiff relies, declares that slavery and involuntary servitude, except as a punishment for crime, shall be forever prohibited in all that part of the territory ceded by France, under the name of Louisiana, which lies north of thirty-six degrees thirty minutes north latitude and not included within the limits of Missouri. And the difficulty which meets us at the threshold of this part of the inquiry is whether Congress was authorized to pass this law under any of the powers granted to it by the Constitution; for, if the authority is not given by that instrument, it is the duty of this Court to declare it void and inoperative and incapable of conferring freedom upon anyone who is held as a slave under the laws of any one of the states.

The counsel for the plaintiff has laid much stress upon that article in the Constitution which confers on Congress the power "to dispose of and make all needful rules and regulations respecting the territory or other property belonging to the United States"; but, in the judgment of the Court, that provision has no bearing on the present controversy, and the power there given, whatever it may be, is confined, and was intended to be confined, to the territory which at that time belonged to, or was claimed by, the United States and was within their boundaries as settled by the treaty with Great Britain and can have no influence upon a territory afterward acquired from a foreign government. It was a special provision for a known and particular territory, and to meet a present emergency, and nothing more. . . .

We do not mean, however, to question the power of Congress in this respect. The power to expand the territory of the United States by the admission of new states is plainly given; and in the construction of this power by all the departments of the government, it has been held to authorize the acquisition of territory, not fit for admission at the time, but to be admitted as soon as its population and situation would entitle it to admission. . . .

It may be safely assumed that citizens of the United States who migrate to a territory belonging to the people of the United States cannot be ruled as mere colonists, dependent upon the will of the general government, and to be governed by any laws it may think proper to impose. The principle upon which our governments rest, and upon which alone they continue to exist, is the union of states, sovereign and independent within their own limits in their internal and domestic concerns, and bound together as one people by a general government, possessing certain enumerated and restricted powers, delegated to it by the people of the several states, and exercising supreme authority within the scope of the powers granted to it, throughout the dominion of the United States. A power, therefore, in the general government to obtain and hold colonies and dependent territories, over which they might legislate without restriction, would be inconsistent with its own existence in its present form. Whatever it acquires, it acquires for the benefit of the people of the several states who created it. It is their trustee acting for them and charged with the duty of promoting the interests of the whole people of the Union in the exercise of the powers specifically granted. . . .

But the power of Congress over the person or property of a citizen can never be a mere discretionary power under our Constitution and form of government. The powers of the government and the rights and privileges of the citizen are regulated and plainly defined by the Constitution itself. And, when the territory becomes a part of the United States, the federal government enters into possession in the character impressed upon it by those who created it. It enters upon it with its powers over the citizen strictly defined and limited by the Constitution, from which it derives its own existence, and by virtue of which alone it continues to exist and act as a government and sovereignty. It has no power of any kind beyond it; and it cannot, when it enters a territory of the United States, put off its character and assume discretionary or despotic powers which the Constitution has denied to it. It cannot create for itself a new character separated from the citizens of the United States and the duties it owes them under the provisions of the Constitution. The territory, being a part of the United States, the government and the citizen both enter it under the authority of the Constitution, with their respective rights defined and marked out; and the federal government can exercise no power over his person or property, beyond what that instrument confers, nor lawfully deny any right which it has reserved. . . .

These powers, and others, in relation to rights of person, which it is not necessary here to enumerate, are, in express and positive terms, denied to the general government; and the rights of private property have been guarded with equal care. Thus the rights of property are united with the rights of person and placed on the same ground by the Fifth Amendment to the Constitution, which provides that no person shall be deprived of life, liberty, and property without due process of law. And an act of Congress which deprives a citizen of the United States of his liberty or property, without due process of law, merely because he came himself or brought his property into a particular territory of the United States, and who had committed no offense against the laws, could hardly be dignified with the name of due process of law. . . .

It seems, however, to be supposed that there is a difference between property in a slave and other property and that different rules may be applied to it in expounding the Constitution of the United States. And the laws and usages of nations, and the writings of eminent jurists upon the relation of master and slave and their mutual rights and duties, and the powers which governments may exercise over it, have been dwelt upon in the argument.

But, in considering the question before us, it must be borne in mind that there is no law of nations standing between the people of the United States and their government and interfering with their relation to each other. The powers of the government and the rights of the citizen under it are positive and practical regulations plainly written down. The people of the United States have delegated to it certain enumerated powers and forbidden it to exercise others. It has no power over the person or property of a citizen but what the citizens of the United States have granted. And no laws or usages of other nations, or reasoning of statesmen or jurists upon the relations of master and slave, can enlarge the powers of the government or take from the citizens the rights they have reserved. And if the Constitution recognizes the right of property of the master in a slave, and makes no distinction between that description of property and other property owned by a citizen, no tribunal, acting under the authority of the United States, whether it be legislative, executive, or judicial, has a right to draw such a distinction or deny to it the benefit of the provisions and guaranties which have been provided for the protection of private property against the encroachments of the government.

Now, as we have already said in an earlier part of this opinion, upon a different point, the right of property in a slave is distinctly and expressly affirmed in the Constitution. The right to traffic in it, like an ordinary article of merchandise and property, was guaranteed to the citizens of the United States, in every state that might desire it, for twenty years. And the government in express terms is pledged to protect it in all future time if the slave escapes from his owner. That is done in plain words—too plain to be misunderstood. And no word can be found in the Constitution which gives Congress a greater power over slave property or which entitles property of that kind to less protection than property of any other description. The only power conferred is the power coupled with the duty of guarding and protecting the owner in his rights.

Upon these considerations it is the opinion of the Court that the act of Congress which prohibited a citizen from holding and owning property of this kind in the territory of the United States north of the line therein mentioned is not warranted by the Constitution and is therefore void; and that neither Dred Scott himself, nor any of his family, were made free by being carried into this territory; even if they had been carried there by the owner with the intention of becoming a permanent resident.

THE EMANCIPATION PROCLAMATION

By the President of the United States of America:

On January 1, 1863, when President Abraham Lincoln decreed that slaves within Confederate states would be free, black communities across the country gathered to read aloud the proclamation.

Whereas, on the twenty-second day of September, in the year of our Lord one thousand eight hundred and sixty-two, a proclamation was issued by the President of the United States, containing, among other things, the following, to wit:

> That on the first day of January, in the year of our Lord one thousand eight hundred and sixty-three, all persons held as slaves within any State or designated part of a State, the people whereof shall then be in rebellion against the United States, shall be then, thenceforward, and forever free; and the Executive Government of the United States, including the military and naval authority thereof, will recognize and maintain the freedom of such persons, and will do no act or acts to repress such persons, or any of them, in any efforts they may make for their actual freedom.
>
> That the Executive will, on the first day of January aforesaid, by proclamation, designate the States and parts of States, if any, in which the people thereof, respectively, shall then be in rebellion against the United States; and the fact that any State, or the people thereof, shall on that day be, in good faith, represented in the Congress of the United States by members chosen thereto at elections wherein a majority of the qualified voters of such State shall have participated, shall, in the absence of strong countervailing testimony, be deemed conclusive evidence that such State, and the people thereof, are not then in rebellion against the United States.

Now, therefore I, Abraham Lincoln, President of the United States, by virtue of the power in me vested as Commander-in-Chief, of the Army and Navy of the United States in time of actual armed rebellion against the authority and government of the United States, and as a fit and necessary war measure for suppressing said rebellion, do, on this first day of January, in the year of our Lord one thousand eight hundred and sixty-three, and in accordance with my purpose so to do publicly proclaimed for the full period of one hundred days, from the day first above mentioned, order and designate as the States and parts of States wherein the people thereof respectively, are this day in rebellion against the United States, the following, to wit:

Arkansas, Texas, Louisiana, (except the Parishes of St. Bernard, Plaquemines, Jefferson, St. John, St. Charles, St. James Ascension, Assumption, Terrebonne, Lafourche, St. Mary, St. Martin, and Orleans, including the City of New Orleans), Mississippi, Alabama, Florida, Georgia, South Carolina, North Carolina, and Virginia, (except the forty-eight counties designated as West Virginia, and also the counties of Berkley, Accomac, Northampton, Elizabeth City, York, Princess Ann, and Norfolk, including the cities of Norfolk and Portsmouth), and which excepted parts, are for the present, left precisely as if this proclamation were not issued.

And by virtue of the power, and for the purpose aforesaid, I do order and declare that all persons held as slaves within said designated States, and parts of States, are, and henceforward shall be free; and that the Executive government of the United States, including the military and naval authorities thereof, will recognize and maintain the freedom of said persons.

And I hereby enjoin upon the people so declared to be free to abstain from all violence, unless in necessary self-defense; and I recommend to them that, in all cases when allowed, they labor faithfully for reasonable wages.

And I further declare and make known, that such persons of suitable condition, will be received into the armed service of the United States to garrison forts, positions, stations, and other places, and to man vessels of all sorts in said service.

And upon this act, sincerely believed to be an act of justice, warranted by the Constitution, upon military necessity, I invoke the considerate judgment of mankind, and the gracious favor of Almighty God.

In witness whereof, I have hereunto set my hand and caused the seal of the United States to be affixed. Done at the City of Washington, this first day of January, in the year of our Lord one thousand eight hundred and sixty-three, and of the Independence of the United States of America the eighty-seventh.

By the President: Abraham Lincoln
William H. Seward, Secretary of State.

THE CIVIL RIGHTS CASES OF 1883

Over the course of several years, after Congress passed the Civil Rights Act of 1875, five separate test cases emerged from African Americans who were denied equal access to public facilities. These cases, as a group, were argued before the Supreme Court in March, 1883. After more than six months of deliberation, the Court concluded that the federal government had no authority to enforce the Civil Rights Act. Justice Harlan wrote a dissenting opinion, saying that the majority opinion had stripped the "soul" from the law.

Mr. Justice Bradley delivered the opinion of the court. After stating the facts . . . he continued:

The first section of the Fourteenth Amendment (which is the one relied on), after declaring who shall be citizens of the United States, and of the several States, is prohibitory in its character, and prohibitory upon the States. . . .

It is State action of a particular character that is prohibited. Individual invasion of individual rights is not the subject-matter of the amendment. It has a deeper and broader scope. It nullifies and makes void all State legislation, and State action of every kind, which impairs the privileges and immunities of citizens of the United States, or which injures them in life, liberty or property without due process of law, or which denies to any of them the equal protection of the laws. . . .

On the whole we are of opinion, that no countenance of authority for the passage of the law in question can be found in either the Thirteenth of Fourteenth Amendment of the Constitution; and no other ground of authority for its passage being suggested, it must necessarily be declared void, at least so far as its operation in the several States is concerned. . . . *And it is so ordered.*

Mr. Justice Harlan dissenting.

The opinion in these cases proceeds, it seems to me, upon grounds entirely too narrow and artificial. I cannot resist the conclusion that the substance and spirit of the recent amendments of the Constitution have been sacrificed by a subtle and ingenious verbal criticism. . . .

I am of the opinion that such discrimination practised by corporations and individuals in the exercise of their public or quasi-public functions is a badge of servitude the imposition of which Congress may prevent under its power, by appropriate legislation, to enforce the Thirteenth Amendment; and, consequently, without reference to its enlarged power under the Fourteenth Amendment, the act of March 1, 1875, is not, in my judgment, repugnant to the Constitution.

. . . To-day, it is the colored race which is denied, by corporations and individuals wielding public authority, rights fundamental in their freedom and citizenship. At some future time, it may be that some other race will fall under the ban of race discrimination. . . .

For the reasons stated I feel constrained to withhold my assent to the opinion of the court.

PLESSY V. *FERGUSON* (1896)

When Homer Plessy led a challenge to Louisiana's segregated trains, he started a series of events that led the Supreme Court, in 1896, to conclude that the races may be separated, as long as public facilities—such as trains and schools—were "equal."

Mr. Justice Brown, after stating the case, delivered the opinion of the court.

This case turns upon the constitutionality of an act of the General Assembly of the State of Louisiana passed in 1890, providing for separate railway carriages for the white and colored races. Acts 1890, No. 111, p. 152. . . .

The constitutionality of this act is attacked upon the ground that it conflicts both with the Thirteenth Amendment of the Constitution, abolishing slavery, and the Fourteenth Amendment, which prohibits certain restrictive legislation on the part of the States. . . .

A statute which implies merely a legal distinction between the white and colored races—a distinction which is founded in the color of the two races, and which must always exist so long as white men are distinguished from the other race by color—has no tendency to destroy the legal equality of the two races, or re-establish a state of involuntary servitude. Indeed, we do not understand that the Thirteenth Amendment is strenuously relied upon by the plaintiff in error in this connection. . . .

The object of the [Fourteenth] amendment was undoubtedly to enforce the absolute equality of the two races before the law, but in the nature of things it could not have been intended to abolish distinctions based upon color, or to enforce social, as distinguished from political equality, or a commingling of the two races upon terms unsatisfactory to either. Laws permitting, and even requiring, their separation in places where they are liable to be brought into contact do not necessarily imply the inferiority of either race to the other, and have been generally, if not universally, recognized as within the competency of the state legislatures in the exercise of their police power. The most common instance of this is connected with the establishment of separate schools for white and colored children, which has been held to be a valid exercise of the legislative power even by courts of States where the political rights of the colored race have been longest and most earnestly enforced. . . .

. . . Legislation is powerless to eradicate racial instincts or to abolish distinctions based upon physical differences, and the attempt to do so can only result in accentuating the difficulties of the present situation. If the civil and political rights of both races be equal one cannot be inferior to the other civilly or politically. If one race be inferior to the other socially, the Constitution of the United States cannot put them upon the same plane. . . .

Affirmed.

Mr. Justice Harlan dissenting.

. . . However apparent the injustice of such legislation may be, we have only to consider whether it is consistent with the Constitution of the United States. . . .

I am of opinion that the statute of Louisiana is inconsistent with the personal liberty of citizens, white and black, in that State, and hostile to both the spirit and letter of the Constitution of the United States. If laws of like character should be enacted in the several States of the Union, the effect would be in the highest degree mischievous. Slavery, as an institution tolerated by law would, it is true, have disappeared from our country, but there would remain a power in the States, by sinister legislation, to interfere with the full enjoyment of the blessings of freedom; to regulate civil rights, common to all citizens, upon the basis of race; and to place in a condition of legal inferiority a large body of American citizens, now constituting a part of the political community called the People of the United States, for whom, and by whom through representatives, our government is administered. Such a system is inconsistent with the guarantee given by the Constitution to each State of a republican form of government, and may be stricken down by Congressional action, or by the courts in the discharge of their solemn duty to maintain the supreme law of the land, anything in the constitution or laws of any State to the contrary notwithstanding.

For the reasons stated, I am constrained to withhold my assent from the opinion and judgment of the majority.

BROWN V. *BOARD OF EDUCATION OF TOPEKA* (1954)

Brown *comprised five different lawsuits aimed at school desegregation. Thurgood Marshall and other NAACP attorneys argued that segregation in public schools was psychologically harmful. In May, 1954, the Supreme Court unanimously overturned the* Plessy *decision and ruled that educational facilities were "inherently unequal" and thus unconstitutional under the Fourteenth Amendment.*

Mr. Chief Justice Warren delivered the opinion of the Court.

These cases come to us from the States of Kansas, South Carolina, Virginia, and Delaware. They are premised on different facts and different local conditions, but a common legal question justifies their consideration together in this consolidated opinion. . . .

Today, education is perhaps the most important function of state and local governments. Compulsory school attendance laws and the great expenditures for education both demonstrate our recognition of the importance of education to our democratic society. It is required in the performance of our most basic public responsibilities, even service in the armed forces. It is the very foundation of good citizenship. Today it is a principal instrument in awakening the child to cultural values, in preparing him for later professional training, and in helping him to adjust normally to his environment. In these days, it is doubtful that any child may reasonably be expected to succeed in life if he is denied the opportunity of an education. Such an opportunity, where the state has undertaken to provide it, is a right which must be made available to all on equal terms.

We come then to the question presented: Does segregation of children in public schools solely on the basis of race, even though the physical facilities and other "tangible" factors may be equal, deprive the children of the minority group of equal education opportunities? We believe that it does. . . .

We conclude that in the field of public education the doctrine of "separate but equal" has no place. Separate educational facilities are inherently unequal. Therefore, we hold that the plaintiffs and others similarly situated for whom the actions have been brought are, by reason of the segregation complained of, deprived of the equal protection of the laws guaranteed by the Fourteenth Amendment. . . .

KEY PROVISIONS OF THE CIVIL RIGHTS ACT OF 1964

The Civil Rights Act of 1964 outlawed racial discrimination in schools, restaurants, theaters, and other public places where Jim Crow laws had long reigned. The Act also prohibited large employers from discriminating against racial and religious minorities as well as women.

An Act

To enforce the constitutional right to vote, to confer jurisdiction upon the district courts of the United States to provide injunctive relief against discrimination in public accommodations, to authorize the Attorney General to institute suits to protect constitutional rights in public facilities and public education, to extend the Commission on Civil Rights, to prevent discrimination in federally assisted programs, to establish a Commission on Equal Employment Opportunity, and for other purposes.

Be it enacted by the Senate and House of Representatives of the United States of America in Congress assembled, that this Act may be cited as the "Civil Rights Act of 1964."

Title I—Voting Rights

Section 101. . . .(2) No person acting under color of law shall—

(A) In determining whether any individual is qualified under State law or laws to vote in any Federal election, apply any standard, practice, or procedure different from the standards, practices, or procedures applied under such law or laws to other individuals within the same county, parish, or similar political subdivision who have been found by State officials to be qualified to vote;

(B) deny the right of any individual to vote in any Federal election because of an error or omission on any record or paper relating to any application, registration, or other act requisite to voting, if such error or omission is not material in determining whether such individual is qualified under State law to vote in such election;

(C) employ any literacy test as a qualification for voting in any Federal election unless (i) such test is administered to each individual and is conducted wholly in writing, and (ii) a certified copy of the test and of the answers given by the individual is furnished to him within twenty-five days of the submission of his request made within the period of time during which records and papers are required to be retained and preserved pursuant to title III of the Civil Rights Act of 1960 (42 U.S.C. 1974–74e; 74 Stat. 88): Provided, however, That the Attorney General may enter into agreements with appropriate State or local authorities that preparation, conduct, and maintenance of such tests in accordance with the provisions of applicable State or local law, including such special provisions as are necessary in the preparation, conduct, and maintenance of such tests for persons who are blind or otherwise physically handicapped, meet the purposes of this subparagraph and constitute compliance therewith.

Title II—Injunctive Relief Against Discrimination in Places of Public Accommodation

Section 201. (a) All persons shall be entitled to the full and equal enjoyment of the goods, services, facilities, and privileges, advantages and accommodations of any place of public accommodation, as defined in this section, without discrimination or segregation on the ground of race, color, religion, or national origin. (b) Each of the following establishments which serves the public is a place of public accommodation within the meaning of this title if its operations effect commerce, or if discrimination or segregation by it is supported by State action:

(1) any inn, hotel, motel, or other establishment which provides lodging to transient guests, other than an establishment located within a building which contains not more than five rooms for rent or hire and which is actually occupied by the proprietor of such establishment as his residence;

(2) any restaurant, cafeteria, lunchroom, lunch counter, soda fountain, or other facility principally engaged in selling food for consumption on the premises, including, but not limited to, any such facility located on the premises of any retail establishment; or any gasoline station;

(3) any motion picture house, theater, concert hall, sports arena, stadium or other place of exhibition or entertainment;

(4) any establishment (A) (i) which is physically located within the premises of any establishment otherwise covered by this subsection, or (ii) within the premises of which is physically located any such covered establishment, and (B) which holds itself out as serving patrons of such covered establishment. . . .

(d) Discrimination or segregation by an establishment is supported by State action within the meaning of this title if such discrimination or segregation

(1) is carried on under color of any law, statute, ordinance, or regulation; or

(2) is carried on under color of any custom or usage required or enforced by officials of the State or political subdivision thereof; or

(3) is required by action of the State or political subdivision thereof. . . .

Section 202. All persons shall be entitled to be free, at any establishment or place, from discrimination or segregation of any kind on the ground of race, color, religion, or national origin, if such discrimination or segregation is or purports to be required by any law, statute, ordinance, regulation, rule, or order of a State or any agency or political subdivision thereof.

Section 203. No person shall (a) withhold, deny, or attempt to withhold or deny, or deprive or attempt to deprive, any person of any right or privilege secured by section 201 or 202, or (b) intimidate, threaten, or coerce, or attempt to intimidate, threaten, or coerce any person with the purpose of interfering with any right or privilege secured by section 201 or 202, or (c) punish or attempt to punish any person for exercising or attempting to exercise any right or privilege secured by section 201 or 202.

Section 204. (a) Whenever any person has engaged or there are reasonable grounds to believe that any person is about to engage in any act or practice prohibited by section 203, a civil action for preventive relief, including an application for a permanent or temporary injunction, restraining order, or other order, may be instituted by the person aggrieved and, upon timely application, the court may, in its discretion, permit the Attorney General to intervene in such civil action if he certifies that the case is of general public importance. Upon application by the complainant and in such circumstances as the court may deem just, the court may appoint an attorney for such complainant and may authorize the commencement of the civil action without the payment of fees, costs, or security. . . .

Section 206. (a) Whenever the Attorney General has reasonable cause to believe that any person or group of persons is engaged in a pattern or practice of resistance to the full enjoyment of any of the rights secured by the title, and that the pattern or practice is of such a nature and is intended to deny the full exercise of the rights herein described, the Attorney General may bring a civil action in the appropriate district court of the United States by filing with it a complaint

(1) signed by him (or in his absence the Acting Attorney General),

(2) setting forth facts pertaining to such pattern or practice, and

(3) requesting such preventive relief, including an application for a permanent or temporary injunction, restraining order or other order against the person or persons responsible for such pattern or practice, as he deems necessary to insure the full enjoyment of the rights herein described. . . .

Title III—Desegregation of Public Facilities

Section 301. (a) Whenever the Attorney General receives a complaint in writing signed by an individual to the effect that he is being deprived of or threatened with the loss of his right to the equal protection of the laws, on account of his race, color, religion, or national origin, by being denied equal utilization of any public facility which is owned, operated, or managed by or on behalf of any State or subdivision thereof, other than a public school or public college as defined in section 401 of title IV hereof, and the Attorney General believes the complaint is meritorious and certifies that the signer or signers of such complaint are unable, in his judgment, to initiate and maintain appropriate legal proceedings for relief and that the institution of an action will materially further the orderly progress of desegregation in public facilities, the Attorney General is authorized to institute for or in the name of the United States a civil action in any appropriate district court of the United States against such parties and for such relief as may be appropriate. And such court shall have and shall exercise jurisdiction of proceedings instituted pursuant to this section. The Attorney General may implead as defendants such additional parties as are or become necessary to the grant of effective relief hereunder. . . .

Title IV—Desegregation of Public Education

Definitions

Section 401. As used in this title—. . . .

(b) "Desegregation" means the assignment of students to public schools and within such schools without regard to their race, color, religion, or national origin, but "desegregation" shall not mean the assignment of students to public schools in order to overcome racial imbalance. . . .

Survey and Report of Educational Opportunities

Section 402. The Commissioner shall conduct a survey and make a report to the President and the Congress, within two years of the enactment of this title, concerning the lack of availability of equal educational opportunities for individuals by reason of race, color, religion, or national origin in public educational institutions at all levels in the United States, its territories and possessions, and the District of Columbia. . . .

Title V—Commission on Civil Rights . . .

Duties of the Commission

Section 104. (a) The Commission shall—

(1) investigate allegations in writing under oath or affirmation that certain citizens of the United States are being deprived of their right to vote and have that vote counted by reason of their color, race, religion, or national origin; which writing, under oath or affirmation, shall set forth the facts upon which such belief or beliefs are based;

(2) study and collect information concerning legal developments constituting a denial of equal protection of the laws under the Constitution because of race, color, religion, or national origin or in the administration of justice;

(3) appraise the laws and policies of the Federal Government with respect to denials of equal protection of the laws under the Constitution because of race, color, religion, or national origin or in the administration of justice;

(4) serve as a national clearinghouse for information in respect to denials of equal protection of the laws because of race, color, religion, or national origin, including but not limited to the fields of voting, education, housing, employment, the use of public facilities, and transportation, or in the administration of justice;

(5) investigate allegations, made in writing and under oath or affirmation, that citizens of the United States are unlawfully being accorded or denied the right to vote, or to have their votes properly counted, in any election of presidential electors, Members of the United States Senate, or of the House of Representatives, as a result of any patterns or practice of fraud or discrimination in the conduct of such election. . . .

Title VI—Nondiscrimination in Federally Assisted Programs

Section 601. No person in the United States shall, on the ground of race, color, religion, or national origin, be excluded from participation in, be denied the benefits of, or be subjected to discrimination under any program or activity receiving Federal financial assistance.

Section 602. Each Federal department and agency which is empowered to extend Federal financial assistance to any program or activity, by way of grant, loan, or contract other than a contract of insurance or guaranty, is authorized and directed to effectuate the provisions of section 601 with respect to such program or activity by issuing rules, regulations, or orders of general applicability which shall be consistent with achievement of the objectives of the statue authorizing the financial assistance in connection with which the action is taken. No such rule, regulation, or order shall become effective unless and until approved by the President. Compliance with any requirement adopted pursuant to this section may be effected

(1) by the termination of or refusal to grant or to continue assistance under such program or activity to any recipient as to whom there has been an express finding on the record, after opportunity for hearing, of a failure to comply with such requirement, but such termination or refusal shall be limited to the particular political entity, or part thereof, or other recipient as to whom such a finding has been made and, shall be limited in its effect to the particular program, or part thereof, in which such non-compliance has been so found, or

(2) by any other means authorized by law:

Provided, however, that no such action shall be taken until the department or agency concerned has advised the appropriate person or persons of the failure to comply with the requirement and has determined that compliance cannot be secured by voluntary means. In the case of any action terminating, or refusing to grant or continue, assistance because of failure to comply with a requirement imposed pursuant to this section, the head of the federal department or agency shall file with the committees of the House and Senate having legislative jurisdiction over the program or activity involved a full written report of the circumstances and the grounds for such action. No such action shall become effective until thirty days have elapsed after the filing of such report. . . .

Title VII—Equal Employment Opportunity . . .

Discrimination Because of Race, Color, Religion, Sex, or National Origin

Section 703. (a) It shall be an unlawful employment practice for an employer—

(1) to fail or refuse to hire or to discharge any individual, or otherwise to discriminate against any individual with respect to his compensation, terms, conditions, or privileges of employment, because of such individual's race, color, religion, sex, or national origin; or

(2) to limit, segregate, or classify his employees in any way which would deprive or tend to deprive any individual of employment opportunities or otherwise adversely affect his status as an employee, because of such individual's race, color, religion, sex, or national origin.

(b) It shall be an unlawful employment practice for an employment agency to fail or refuse to refer for employment, or otherwise to discriminate against, any individual because of his race, color, religion, sex, or national origin, or to classify or refer for employment any individual on the basis of his race, color, religion, sex, or national origin.

(c) It shall be an unlawful employment practice for a labor organization—

(1) to exclude or to expel from its membership, or otherwise to discriminate against, any individual because of his race, color, religion, sex, or national origin;

(2) to limit, segregate, or classify its membership, or to classify or fail or refuse to refer for employment any individual, in any way which would deprive or tend to deprive any individual of employment opportunities, or would limit such employment opportunities or otherwise adversely affect his status as an employee or as an applicant for employment, because of such individual's race, color, religion, sex, or national origin; or

(3) to cause or attempt to cause an employer to discriminate against an individual in violation of this section.

(d) It shall be an unlawful employment practice for any employer, labor organization, or joint labor-management committee controlling apprenticeship or other training or retraining, including on-the-job training programs, to discriminate against any individual because of his race, color, religion, sex, or national origin in admission to, or employment in, any program established to provide apprenticeship or other training. . . .

Other Unlawful Employment Practices

Section 704. (a) It shall be an unlawful employment practice for an employer to discriminate against any of his employees or applicants for employment, for an employment agency to discriminate against any individual, or for a labor organization to discriminate against any member thereof or applicant for membership, because he has opposed any practice made an unlawful employment practice by this title, or because he has made a charge, testified, assisted, or participated in any manner in an investigation, proceeding, or hearing under this title.

(b) It shall be an unlawful employment practice for an employer, labor organization, or employment agency to print or publish or cause to be printed or published any notice or advertisement relating to employment by such an employer or membership in or any classification or referral for employment by such a labor organization, or relating to any classification or referral for employment by such an employment agency, indicating any preference, limitation, specification, or discrimination, based on race, color, religion, sex, or national origin, except that such a notice or advertisement may indicate a preference, limitation, specification, or discrimination based on religion, sex, or national origin when religion, sex, or national origin is a bona fide occupational qualification for employment.

Equal Employment Opportunity Commission

Section 705. (a) There is hereby created a Commission to be known as the Equal Employment Opportunity Commission, which shall be composed of five members, not more than three of whom shall be members of the same political party, who shall be appointed by the President by and with the advice and consent of the Senate. One of the original members shall be appointed for a term of one year, one for a term of two years, one for a term of three years, one for a term of four years, and one for a term of five years, beginning from the date of enactment of this title, but their successors shall be appointed for terms of five years each, except that any individual chosen to fill a vacancy shall be appointed only for the unexpired term of the member whom he shall succeed. The President shall designate one member to serve as Chairman of the Commission, and one member to serve as Vice Chairman. The Chairman shall be responsible on behalf of the Commission for the administrative operations of the Commission, and shall appoint, in accordance with the civil service laws, such officers, agents, attorneys, and employees as it deems necessary to assist it in the performance of its functions and to fix their compensation in accordance with Classification Act of 1949, as amended. . . .

Title VIII—Registration and Voting Statistics

Section 801. The Secretary of Commerce shall promptly conduct a survey to compile registration and voting statistics in such geographic areas as may be recommended by the Commission on Civil Rights. Such a survey and compilation shall, to the extent recommended by the Commission on Civil Rights, only include a count of persons of voting age by race, color, and national origin, and determination of the extent to which such persons are registered to vote, and have voted in any statewide primary or general election in which the Members of the United States House of Representatives are nominated or elected, since January 1, 1960. Such information shall also be collected and compiled in connection with the Nineteenth Decennial Census, and at such other times as the Congress may prescribe. The provisions of section 9 and chapter 7 of title 13, United States Code, shall apply to any survey, collection, or compilation of registration and voting statistics carried out under this title: Provided, however, that no person shall be compelled to disclose his race, color, national origin, or questioned about his political party affiliation, how he voted, or the reasons therefore, nor shall any penalty be imposed for his failure or refusal to make such disclosure. Every person interrogated orally, by written survey or questionnaire or by any other means with respect to such information shall be fully advised with respect to his right to fail or refuse to furnish such information.

KEY PROVISIONS OF THE VOTING RIGHTS ACT OF 1965

The Voting Rights Act of 1965 forced the South to give up literacy tests, poll taxes, and other methods used to prevent black people from voting. It also empowered federal officials to register voters in areas with a history of denying black voter rights.

An Act

To enforce the fifteenth amendment to the Constitution of the United States, and for other purposes.

Be it enacted by the Senate and House of Representatives of the United States of America in Congress assembled, That this Act shall be known as the "Voting Rights Act of 1965."

Section 2. No voting qualification or prerequisite to voting, or standard, practice, or procedure shall be imposed or applied by any State or political subdivision to deny or abridge the right of any citizen of the United States to vote on account of race or color.

Section 3. (a) Whenever the Attorney General institutes a proceeding under any statute to enforce the guarantees of the fifteenth amendment in any State or political subdivision the court shall authorize the appointment of Federal examiners by the United States Civil Service Commission in accordance with section 6 to serve for such period of time and for such political subdivisions as the court shall determine is appropriate to enforce the guarantees of the fifteenth amendment (1) as part of any interlocutory order if the court determines that the appointment of such examiners is necessary to enforce such guarantees or (2) as part of any final judgment if the court finds that violations of the fifteenth amendment justifying equitable relief have occurred in such State or subdivision: Provided, That the court need not authorize the appointment of examiners if any incidents of denial or abridgment of the right to vote on account of race or color (1) have been few in number and have been promptly and effectively corrected by State or local action, (2) the continuing effect of such incidents has been eliminated, and (3) there is no reasonable probability of their recurrence in the future.

(b) If in a proceeding instituted by the Attorney General under any statute to enforce the guarantees of the fifteenth amendment in any State or political subdivision the court finds that a test or device has been used for the purpose or with the effect of denying or abridging the right of any citizen of the United States to vote on account of race or color, it shall suspend the use of tests and devices in such State or political subdivisions as the court shall determine is appropriate and for such period as it deems necessary. . . .

Section 4. (a) To assure that the right of citizens of the United States to vote is not denied or abridged on account of race or color, no citizen shall be denied the right to vote in any Federal, State, or local election because of his failure to comply with any test or device in any State with respect to which the determinations have been made under subsection (b). . . .

(b) The provisions of subsection (a) shall apply in any State or in any political subdivision of a state which (1) the Attorney General determines maintained on November 1, 1964, any test or device, and with respect to which (2) the Director of the Census determines that less than 50 per centum of the persons of voting age residing therein were registered on November 1, 1964, or that less than 50 per centum of such persons voted in the presidential election of November 1964. . . .

(c) The phrase "test or device" shall mean any requirement that a person as a prerequisite for voting or registration of voting (1) demonstrate the ability to read, write, understand, or interpret any matter, (2) demonstrate any educational achievement or his knowledge of any particular subject, (3) possess good moral character, or (4) prove his qualifications by the voucher of registered voters or members of any other class. . . .

Section 6. Whenever (a) a court has authorized the appointment of examiners pursuant to the provisions of section 3 (a), or (b) unless a declaratory judgment has been rendered under section 4 (a), the Attorney General certifies with respect to any political subdivision named in, or included within the scope of, determinations made under section 4 (b) that (1) he has received complaints in writing from twenty or more residents of such political subdivision alleging that they have been denied the right to vote under color of law on account of race or color, and that he believes such complaints to be meritorious, or (2) that in his judgment (considering, among other factors, whether the ratio of nonwhite persons to white persons registered to vote within such subdivision appears to him to be reasonably attributable to violations of the fifteenth amendment or whether substantial evidence exists that bona fide efforts are being made within such subdivision to comply with the fifteenth amendment), the appointment of examiners is otherwise necessary to enforce the guarantees of the fifteenth amendment, the Civil Service Commission shall appoint as many examiners for such subdivision as it may deem appropriate to prepare and maintain lists of persons eligible to vote in Federal, State, and local elections. . . . Examiners and hearing officers shall have the power to administer oaths. . . .

Section 10. (a) The Congress finds that the requirement of the payment of a poll tax as a precondition to voting (i) precludes persons of limited means from voting or imposes unreasonable financial hardship upon such persons as a precondition to their exercise of the franchise, (ii) does not bear a reasonable relationship to any legitimate State interest in the conduct of elections, and (iii) in some areas has the purpose or effect of denying persons the right to vote because of race or color. Upon the basis of these findings, Congress declares that the constitutional right of citizens to vote is denied or abridged in some areas by the requirement of the payment of a poll tax as a precondition to voting.

(b) In the exercise of the powers of Congress under section 5 of the fourteenth amendment and section 2 of the fifteenth amendment, the Attorney General is authorized and directed to institute forthwith in the name of the United States such actions, including actions against States or political subdivisions, for declaratory judgment or injunctive relief against the enforcement of any requirement of the payment of a poll tax as a precondition to voting, or substitute thereof enacted after November 1, 1964, as will be necessary to implement the declaration of subsection (a) and the purposes of this section. . . .

Section 11. (a) No person acting under color of law shall fail or refuse to permit any person to vote who is entitled to vote under any provision of this Act or is otherwise qualified to vote, or willfully fail or refuse to tabulate, count, and report such person's vote.

(b) No person, whether acting under color of law or otherwise, shall intimidate, threaten, or coerce, or attempt to intimidate, threaten, or coerce any person for voting or attempting to vote, or intimidate, threaten, or coerce, or attempt to intimidate, threaten, or coerce any person for urging or aiding any person to vote or attempt to vote, or intimidate, threaten, or coerce any person for exercising any powers or duties under section 3 (a), 6, 8, 9, 10, or 12 (e).

Photo Credits

Chapter 11

Chapter Opener 268 The Granger Collection, New York; 272 Schomburg, Photos & Prints Division; 274 Getty Images; 276 Library of Congress; 279 Getty Images; 280 Antique Textile Resource; 282 Ohio State Historical Society; 286 National Archives of Canada/C-02997; 287 The Granger Collection, New York; 288 Library of Congress; 289 Corbis.

Chapter 12

Chapter Opener 292 Courtesy Frederic Remington Art Museum, Ogdensburg, New York; 298 Private Collection; 299 Library of Congress; 300 Bildarchiv Preussicher Kulturbesitz/Art Resource, NY; 303 Corbis; 307 Hampton University Museum, Hampton, Virginia; 308L Churchill Downs, Inc./Kinetic Corporation; 308R Library of Congress; 311 Illinois Labor History Society; 313 Ursuline Convent Archives, Toledo, OH; 314 Courtesy The Flint Institute of Arts, Mrs. Charles S. Mott Collection; 317 Library of Congress.

Chapter 13

Chapter Opener 320 Schomburg Center for Research in Black Culture, The New York Public Library, Astor, Lenox and Tilden Foundations; 324 Corbis; 325 Ohio Historical Society; 326 National Afro-American Museum & Cultural Center; 329 The New-York Historical Society; 332 Courtesy, Janice L. and David Frent; 335L Schomburg, General Research Division/Schomburg Center for Research in Black Culture, The New York Public Library, Astor, Lenox and Tilden Foundations; 335R A'Lelia Bundles/Walker Family Collection/madamcjwalker.com; 336 Library of Congress; 337 Saskatchewan National Archives; 338 Urban Archives, Temple University; 339 Urban Archives, Temple University.

Chapter 14

Chapter Opener 346 Courtesy Louisiana State Museum; 350 Courtesy, Military Antiques & Museum, Petaluma, CA; 350BL Emmett Scott's Official History of the American Negro in World War, 1919; 350BR Emmett Scott's Official History of the American Negro in World War, 1919; 350TL Emmett Scott's Official History of the American Negro in World War, 1919; 350TR Emmett Scott's Official History of the American Negro in World War, 1919; 351 Private Collection; 353 Library of Congress; 354L Private Collection; 354R Private Collection; 359 James VanDerZee/©Donna Mussenden VanDerZee; 363 Urban Archives, Temple University; 367 James VanDerZee/©Donna Mussenden VanDerZee; 370 Richard Samuel Roberts/Bruccoli Clark Layman, Inc.; 371 Getty Images.

Chapter 15

Chapter Opener 374 Photograph Courtesy of Gwendolyn Knight Lawrence/Art Resource, NY/© 2004 Jacob and Gwendolyn Lawrence Foundation/Artists' Rights Society (ARS), New York; 380 Corbis; 384 Corbis; 386 Corbis; 388 Courtesy of the Franklin D. Roosevelt Presidential Library/National Archives (NLR-PHOCO-A-67107[1]); 389 Corbis; 393 Library of Congress; 394 Joanna T. Steichen Collection/Carousel Research/The National Portrait Gallery, Smithsonian Institution/Art Resource, NY; 395 Duke University, Rare Books, Manuscripts & Special Collections Library (Plate no. 8887-4); 396 Corbis; 397 Getty Images; 398 AP/Wide World Photos.

Chapter 16

Chapter Opener 400 Private Collection Courtesy of Michael Rosenfeld Gallery, LLC, New York, NY. Permission Courtesy of the Aaron and Alta Sawyer Douglas Foundation; 404 Library of Congress; 405 Library of Congress; 407 Walter Neagle, Bayard Rustin Estate; 408 Great Lakes Division, Chicago/National Archives; 409 Getty Images; 410 Library of Congress; 416 United Nations Photo; 416 United Nations Photo; 417 Corbis; 422 Sogolon Archives; 423 Getty Images; 424 Time Life Pictures/Getty Images.

Chapter 17

Chapter Opener 426 The Theater Collection, Museum of the City of New York; 430 Comstock Royalty Free Division; 433 Corbis; 435 AP/Wide World Photos; 437 Corbis; 439L Highlander Research Center Archives; 439R AP/Wide World Photos; 441 AP/Wide World Photos; 443 Library of Congress; 444L Corbis; 444R Corbis; 446 AP/Wide World Photos; 449 Bruce Roberts/Photo Researchers, Inc.; 450 The White House Photo Office.

Chapter 18

Chapter Opener 452 Matt Herron/Take Stock; 456 Bruce Davidson; 457 AP/Wide World Photos; 458 Pearson Education/PH College; 460 AP/Wide World Photos; 462 Corbis; 463 James Baldwin, "The Fire Next Time," New York: The Modern Library Edition, 1995; 465 AP/Wide World Photos; 466 Fair Street Pictures; 468 AP/Wide World Photos; 470 Corbis; 471 Corbis; 475 Matt Herron/Take Stock; 475 Getty Images; 477 AP/Wide World Photos.

Chapter 19

Chapter Opener 482 ©Gordon Parks; 486 AP/Wide World Photos; 488 AP/Wide World Photos; 490 Random House, Inc.,

D

E

J

K

L

M

N

O

P

Q

R

S

Y

Z

Notable Figures in African American History

James Forten
(1766–1842)

Jarena Lee
(1783–unknown)

Prince Hall
(1735–1807)

Thomas Peters
(1738–1792)

Crispus Attucks
(c. 1723–1770)

Absalom Jones
(1746–1818)

Paul Cuffe
(1759–1817)

David Walker
(1785–1830)

1720 — 1740 — 1760 — 1780

Benjamin Banneker
(1731–1806)

Phillis Wheatley
(1753–1784)

Denmark Vesey
(1767–1822)

Sojourner Truth
(1798–1833)

Venture Smith
(c. 1729–1805)

Olaudah Equiano
(c. 1745–1797)

Richard Allen
(1760–1831)

Martin Delany (1812–1885)

Joseph Cinque (c. 1811–1879)

Harriet Tubman (1820–1913)

Mary Ann Shadd Cary (1823–1893)

Frances Ellen Watkins Harper (1825–1911)

Nat Turner (1800–1831)

Henry Bibb (1815–1854)

Emanuel Fortune (1832–1903)

George Washington Carver (1864–1943)

Mary Church Terrell (1863–1954)

Ida B. Wells-Barnett (1862–1931)

Madam C. J. Walker (1867–1919)

W. E. B. Du Bois (1868–1963)

1800 | 1820 | 1840 | 1860

Maria Stewart (1803–1874)

Hiram Revels (1822–1901)

Scott Joplin (1868–1917)

Henry Highland Garnet (1815–1882)

Booker T. Washington (1856–1915)

Paul Laurence Dunbar (1872–1906)

Frederick Douglass (c. 1817–1885)

Claude McKay
(1890–1948)

Rosa Parks
(c. 1913–)

A. Philip Randolph
(1889–1979)

Charles Houston
(1895–1950)

Pauli Murray
(1910–1985)

Dorie Miller
(1919–1943)

Marcus Garvey
(1887–1940)

Richard Wright
(1908–1960)

Billie Holiday
(1915–1959)

Jack Johnson
(1878–1946)

Ralph Bunche
(1903–1971)

1870 | 1880 | | 1900 | 1910

Zora Neale Hurston
(1891–1960)

Louis Armstrong
(1901–1971)

Bayard Rustin
(1912–1987)

Paul Robeson
(1898–1976)

Fannie Lou Hamer
(1917–1977)

Mary McLeod Bethune
(1875–1955)

Jackie Robinson
(1919–1972)

Thurgood Marshall
(1908–1993)

Muhammed Ali
(1942–)

Malcom X
(1925–1965)

Louis Farrakhan
(1933–)

Stokely Carmichael
(1941–1998)

Eldridge Cleaver
(1935–1998)

Shirley Chisolm
(1924–)

Alice Walker
(1944–)

Condoleeza Rice
(1954–)

1920 | 1930 | 1940 | 1950 | 1960

Harold Washington
(1922–1987)

Angela Davis
(1944–)

Oprah Winfrey
(1954–)

Hank Aaron
(1934–)

Tupac Shakur
(1971–1996)

Huey Newton
(1942–1989)

Colin Powell
(1937–)

Martin Luther King, Jr.
(1929–1968)

Spike Lee
(1957–)

Diane Nash
(1938–)

Jesse Jackson
(1941–)

Andrew Young
(1932–)

Toni Morrison
(1931–)